AWS Certified Advanced Networking - Specialty

Technology Workbook

---

www.ipspecialist.net

Document Control

Proposal Name	:	AWS Advanced Networking - Specialty
Document Version	:	Version 1
Document Release Date	:	18-March-2019
Reference	:	ANS - C00

Registered in England and Wales
Company Registration No: 10883539
Registration Office at: Office 32, 19-21 Crawford Street, London W1H 1PJ, United Kingdom
www.ipspecialist.net

Feedback:
If you have any comments regarding the quality of this book, or otherwise alter it to better suit your needs, you can contact us through email at info@ipspecialist.net
Please make sure to include the book's title and ISBN in your message.

About IPSpecialist

IPSPECIALIST LTD. IS COMMITTED TO EXCELLENCE AND DEDICATED TO YOUR SUCCESS.

Our philosophy is to treat our customers like family. We want you to succeed, and we are willing to do everything possible to help you make it happen. We have the proof to back up our claims. We strive to accelerate billions of careers with great courses, accessibility, and affordability. We believe that continuous learning and knowledge evolution are the most important things to keep re-skilling and up-skilling the world.

Planning and creating a specific goal is where IPSpecialist helps. We can create a career track that suits your visions as well as develop the competencies you need to become a professional Network Engineer. We can also assist you with the execution and evaluation of your proficiency level, based on the career track you choose, as they are customized to fit your specific goals.

We help you STAND OUT from the crowd through our detailed IP training content packages.

Course Features:

- Self-Paced learning
  - Learn at your own pace and in your own time
- Covers Complete Exam Blueprint
  - Prep-up for the exam with confidence
- Case Study Based Learning
  - Relate the content with real life scenarios
- Subscriptions that suits you
  - Get more and pay less with IPS subscriptions
- Career Advisory Services
  - Let the industry experts plan your career journey
- Virtual Labs to test your skills
  - With IPS vRacks, you can evaluate your exam preparations
- Practice Questions
  - Practice questions to measure your preparation standards
- On Request Digital Certification
  - On request digital certification from IPSpecialist LTD

About the Authors:

This book has been compiled with the help of multiple professional engineers. These engineers specialize in different fields e.g. Networking, Security, Cloud, Big Data, IoT etc. Each engineer develops content in his/her own specialized field that is compiled to form a comprehensive certification guide.

About the Technical Reviewers:

Nouman Ahmed Khan

AWS-Architect, CCDE, CCIEX5 (R&S, SP, Security, DC, Wireless), CISSP, CISA, CISM, Nouman Ahmed Khan is a Solution Architect working with a major telecommunication provider in Qatar. He works with enterprises, mega-projects, and service providers to help them select the best-fit technology solutions. He also works as a consultant to understand customer business processes and helps select an appropriate technology strategy to support business goals. He has more than 14 years of experience working in Pakistan/Middle-East & UK. He holds a Bachelor of Engineering Degree from NED University, Pakistan, and M.Sc. in Computer Networks from the UK.

Abubakar Saeed

Abubakar Saeed has more than twenty-five years of experience, managing, consulting, designing, and implementing large-scale technology projects, extensive experience heading ISP operations, solutions integration, heading Product Development, Pre-sales, and Solution Design. Emphasizing on adhering to Project timelines and delivering as per customer expectations, he always leads the project in the right direction with his innovative ideas and excellent management skills.

Areeba Tanveer

Areeba Tanveer is an AWS Certified Solution Architect – Associate working professionally as a Technical Content Developer. She holds a Bachelor's of Engineering degree in Telecommunication Engineering from NED University of Engineering and Technology. She also worked as a Project Engineer in Pakistan Telecommunication Company Limited (PTCL). She has both the technical knowledge and industry sounding information, which she utilizes effectively when needed.

Syed Hanif Wasti

Syed Hanif Wasti is a Computer Science graduate working professionally as a Technical Content Developer. He is a part of a team of professionals operating in the E-learning and digital education sector. He holds a Bachelor's Degree in Computer Sciences from PAF-KIET, Pakistan. He has completed his training of MCP and CCNA. He has both the technical knowledge and industry sounding information, which he uses efficiently in his career. He previously worked as a Database and Network administrator and obtained a good experience in software development.

Uzair Ahmed

Uzair Ahmed is a professional technical content writer holding a Bachelor's Degree in Computer Science from PAF-KIET University. He has sound knowledge and industry experience in SIEM implementation, .NET development, machine learning, Artificial intelligence, Python and other programming and development platforms like React.JS Angular JS Laravel.

Afia Afaq

Afia Afaq works as a Technical Content Developer. She holds a Bachelor of Engineering Degree in Telecommunications Engineering from NED University of Engineering and Technology. She also has worked as an intern in Pakistan Telecommunication Company Limited (PTCL) as well as in Pakistan Meteorological Department (PMD). Afia Afaq uses her technical knowledge and industry sounding information efficiently in her career.

Hira Arif

Hira Arif is an Electrical Engineer Graduate from NED University of Engineering and Technology, working professionally as a Technical Content Writer. Prior to that, she worked as a Trainee Engineer at Sunshine Corporation. She utilizes her knowledge and technical skills profoundly when required.

Free Resources:

With each workbook bought from Amazon, IPSpecialist offers free resources to our valuable customers.

Once you buy this book, you will have to contact us at support@ipspecialist.net or tweet @ipspecialistnet to get this limited time offer without any extra charges.

Free Resources Include:

Exam Practice Questions in Quiz Simulation: IP Specialists' Practice Questions have been developed keeping in mind the certification exam perspective. The collection of these questions from our technology workbooks is prepared keeping the exam blueprint in mind, covering not only important but necessary topics as well. It is an ideal document to practice and revise your certification.

Career Report: This report is a step-by-step guide for a novice who wants to develop his/her career in the field of computer networks. It answers the following queries:

- Current scenarios and future prospects.
- Is this industry moving towards saturation or are new opportunities knocking at the door?
- What will the monetary benefits be?
- Why to get certified?
- How to plan and when will I complete the certifications if I start today?
- Is there any career track that I can follow to accomplish specialization level?

Furthermore, this guide provides a comprehensive career path towards being a specialist in the field of networking and highlights the tracks needed to obtain certification.

IPS Personalized Technical Support for Customers: Good customer service means helping customers efficiently, in a friendly manner. It is essential to be able to handle issues for customers and do your best to ensure they are satisfied. Providing good service is one of the most important things that can set our business apart from the others of its kind.

Great customer service will result in attracting more customers and attain maximum customer retention.

IPS is offering personalized TECH support to its customers to provide better value for money. If you have any queries related to technology and labs, you can simply ask our technical team for assistance via Live Chat or E-mail.

Become an Author & Earn with Us

If you are interested in becoming an author and start earning passive income, IPSpecialist offers "Earn with us" program. We all consume, develop and create content during our learning process, certification exam preparations, and while searching, developing and refining our professional careers. That content, notes, guides, worksheets and flip cards among other material is normally for our own reference without any defined structure or special considerations required for formal publishing.

IPSpecialist can help you craft this 'draft' content into a fine product with the help of our global team of experts. We sell your content via different channels as:

1. Amazon – Kindle
2. eBay
3. LuLu
4. Kobo
5. Google Books
6. Udemy and many 3rd party publishers and resellers

Our Products

Technology Workbooks

IPSpecialist Technology workbooks are the ideal guides to developing the hands-on skills necessary to pass the exam. Our workbook covers official exam blueprint and explains the technology with real life case study based labs. The content covered in each workbook consists of individually focused technology topics presented in an easy-to-follow, goal-oriented, step-by-step approach. Every scenario features detailed breakdowns and thorough verifications to help you completely understand the task and associated technology.

We extensively used mind maps in our workbooks to visually explain the technology. Our workbooks have become a widely used tool to learn and remember the information effectively.

vRacks

Our highly scalable and innovative virtualized lab platforms let you practice the IP Specialist Technology Workbook at your own time and your own place as per your convenience.

Quick Reference Sheets

Our quick reference sheets are a concise bundling of condensed notes of the complete exam blueprint. It is an ideal and handy document to help you remember the most important technology concepts related to the certification exam.

Practice Questions

IP Specialists' Practice Questions are dedicatedly designed from a certification exam perspective. The collection of these questions from our technology workbooks is prepared keeping the exam blueprint in mind covering not only important but necessary topics as well. It is an ideal document to practice and revise your certification.

Content at a glance

Table of Contents

AWS Certifications

AWS Certifications are industry-recognized credentials that validate your technical cloud skills and expertise while assisting you in your career growth. These are one of the most valuable IT certifications right now since AWS has established an overwhelming lead in the public cloud market. Even with the presence of several tough competitors such as Microsoft Azure, Google Cloud Engine, and Rackspace, AWS is by far the dominant public cloud platform today, with an astounding collection of proprietary services that continues to grow.

The two key reasons as to why AWS certifications are prevailing in the current cloud-oriented job market:

- There is a dire need for skilled cloud engineers, developers, and architects – and the current shortage of experts is expected to continue into the foreseeable future.
- AWS certifications stand out for their thoroughness, rigor, consistency, and appropriateness for critical cloud engineering positions.

Value of AWS Certifications

AWS places equal emphasis on sound conceptual knowledge of its entire platform, as well as on hands-on experience with the AWS infrastructure and its many unique and complex components and services.

For Individuals

- Demonstrate your expertise in designing, deploying, and operating highly available, cost-effective, and secured applications on AWS.
- Gain recognition and visibility of your proven skills and proficiency with AWS.
- Earn tangible benefits such as access to the AWS Certified LinkedIn Community, get invited to AWS Certification Appreciation Receptions and Lounges, obtain AWS Certification Practice Exam Voucher and Digital Badge for certification validation, AWS Certified Logo usage and access to AWS Certified Store.
- Foster credibility with your employer and peers.

For Employers

- Identify skilled professionals to lead IT initiatives with AWS technologies.
- Reduce risks and costs to implement your workloads and projects on the AWS platform.

- Increase customer satisfaction.

Types of Certification

Role-based Certification

- *Foundational* - Validate overall understanding of the AWS Cloud. Pre-requisite to achieving Specialty certification or an optional start towards Associate certification.
- *Associate*- Technical role-based certifications. No pre-requisite.
- *Professional*- Highest level technical role-based certification. Relevant Associate certification required.

Specialty Certification

- Validate advanced skills in specific technical areas.
- Require one active role-based certification.

About AWS – Certified Advanced Networking - Specialty Exam

Exam Questions	Multiple choice and multiple answer
Number of Questions	---
Time to Complete	170 minutes
Available Languages	English, Japanese, Korean, and Simplified Chinese
Exam Fee	300 USD

The AWS Certified Advanced Networking – Specialty exam validates advanced technical skills and experience in designing and implementing AWS and hybrid IT network architectures at scale. This exam is intended for those individuals who perform complex networking tasks. Example concepts you should understand for this exam include:

- Design, develop, and deploy cloud-based solutions on AWS
- Implement core AWS services according to basic architecture best practices
- Design and maintain network architecture best practices
- Design and maintain network architecture for all AWS services
- Leverage tools to automate AWS networking tasks

Recommended AWS Knowledge

- One or more years of hands-on experience developing and maintaining an AWS based application
- In-depth knowledge of at least one high-level programming language
- Understanding of core AWS services, uses, and basic AWS architecture best practices
- Proficiency in developing, deploying, and debugging cloud-based applications using AWS
- Ability to use the AWS service APIs, AWS CLI, and SDKs to write applications
- Ability to identify key features of AWS services
- Understanding of the AWS shared responsibility model
- Understanding of application lifecycle management
- Ability to use a CI/CD pipeline to deploy applications on AWS
- Ability to use or interact with AWS services
- Ability to apply a basic understanding of cloud-native applications to write codes
- Ability to write codes using AWS security best practices (e.g. using IAM roles instead of using secret and access keys in the code)
- Ability to author, maintain, and debug code modules on AWS
- Proficiency writing code for server-less applications
- Understanding of the use of containers in the development process

	Domain	%
Domain 1	Design and implement hybrid IT network architectures at scale	23%
Domain 2	Design and implement AWS networks	29%
Domain 3	Automate AWS tasks	8%
Domain 4	Configure network integration with application services	15%
Domain 5	Design and implement for security and compliance	12%
Domain 6	Manage, Optimize, and Troubleshoot the Network	13%
Total		100%

Chapter 01: Introduction to Cloud Computing

What is Cloud Computing?

Cloud Computing is the practice of using a network of remote servers hosted on the internet to store, manage and process data rather than using a local server or personal computer. It is the on-demand delivery of computing resources through a cloud service platform with pay-as-you-go pricing.

Advantages of Cloud Computing

1. **Trade capital expense for variable expense**

   Pay only for the resources consumed instead of heavily investing in data centers and servers before knowing your requirements.

2. **Benefit from massive economies of scale**

   Achieve lower variable costs than you can get on your own. Cloud computing providers, such as Amazon, build their own data centers and achieve higher economies of scale that results in lower prices.

3. **Stop guessing capacity**

   Access as much or as little resources needed instead of buying too much or too little resources by guessing your needs. Scale up and down as required with no long-term contracts.

4. **Increase speed and agility**

   New IT resources are readily available so that you can scale up infinitely with demand. The result is a dramatic increase in agility for the organizations.

5. **Stop spending money on running and maintaining data centers**

   Eliminates the traditional need for spending money on running and maintaining data centers, which are managed by the cloud provider.

6. **Go global in minutes**

   Provide lower latency at minimal cost by easily deploying your application in multiple regions around the world.

Types of Cloud Computing

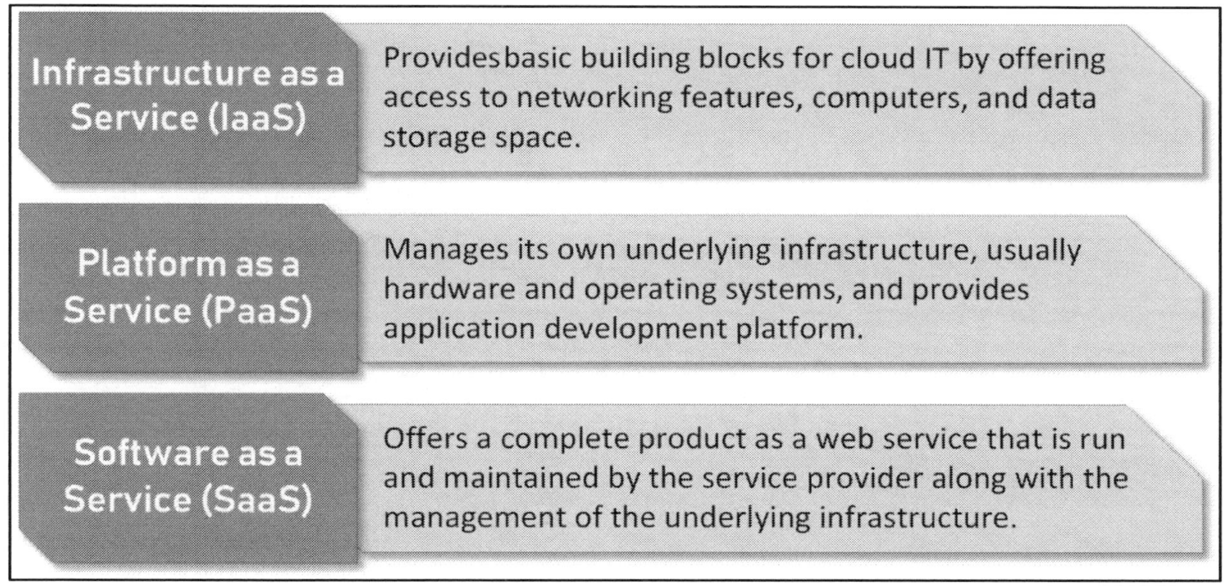

Figure 1-01: Types of Cloud Computing

Cloud Computing Deployments Models

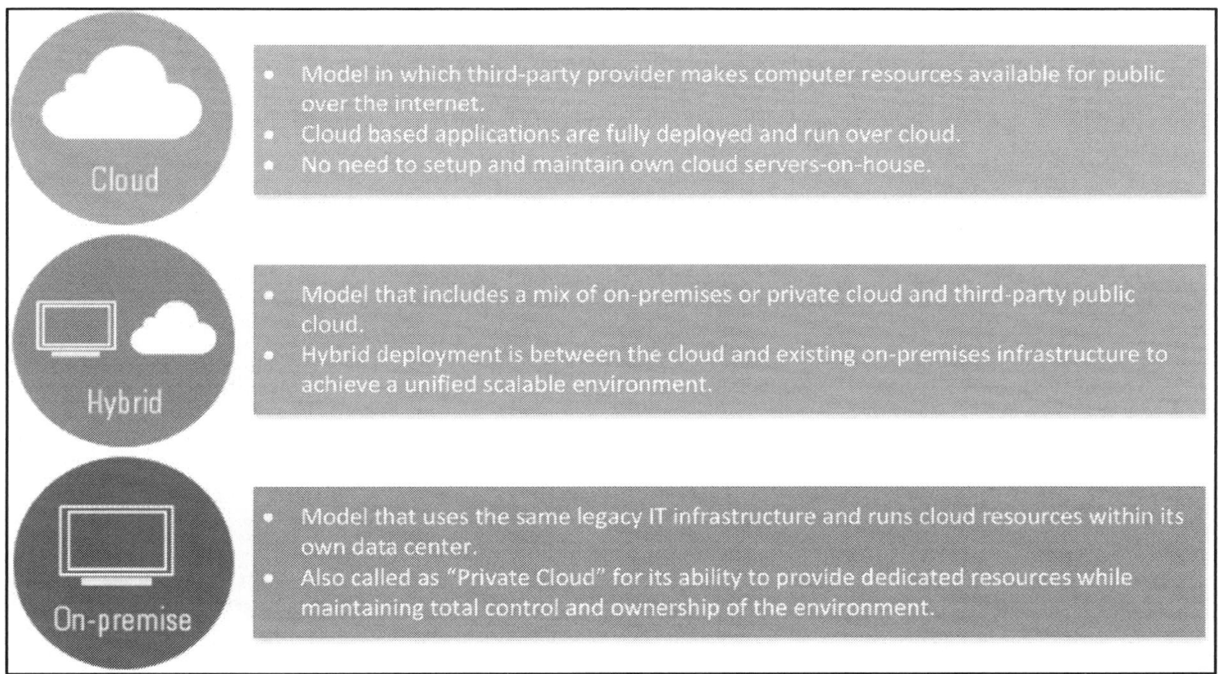

Figure 1-02: Cloud Computing Deployment Model

Amazon Web Services Cloud Platform

Amazon Web Services (AWS) is a secured cloud service platform, offering computing power, database storage, content delivery and other functionality on-demand to help businesses scale and grow. AWS cloud products and solutions can be used to build sophisticated applications with increased flexibility, scalability and reliability.

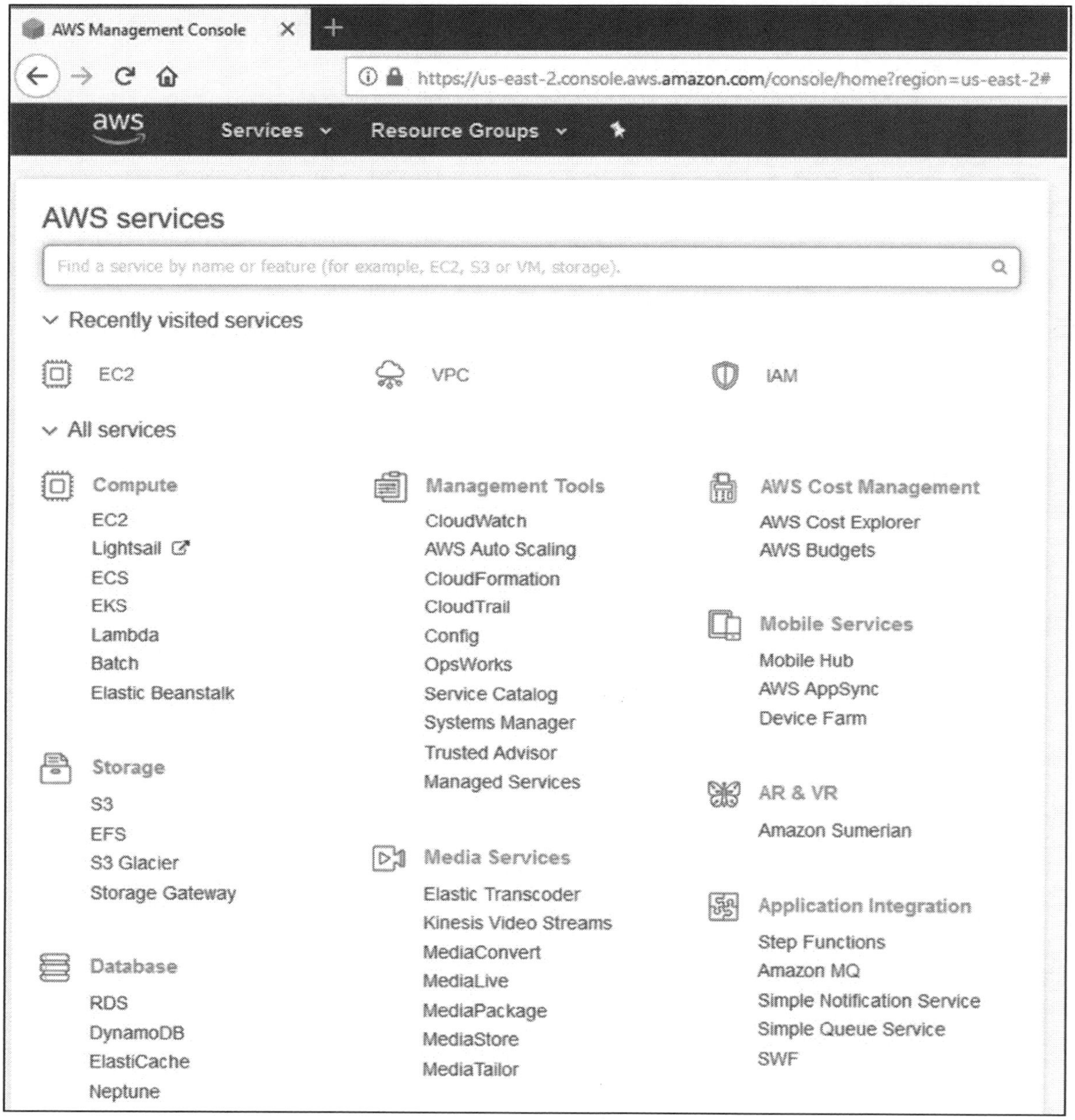

Figure 1-03: AWS Platform

The Cloud Computing Difference

This section compares cloud computing with the traditional environment; it reviews and provides the information to why these new and better practices have emerged.

IT Assets Become Programmable Resources: In a traditional environment, it would take days to weeks depending on the complexity of the environment to set up IT resources such as servers and networking hardware, etc. On AWS, servers, databases, storage, and higher-level application components can be instantiated within seconds. These instances can be used as temporary and disposable resources to meet the actual demand, while only paying for what you have used.

Global, Available, and Unlimited Capacity: With AWS cloud platform you can deploy your infrastructure into different AWS regions around the world. Virtually unlimited on-demand capacity is available to enable future expansion of your IT architecture. The global infrastructure ensures high availability and fault tolerance.

Higher Level Managed Services: Apart from computing resources in the cloud, AWS also provides other higher-level managed services such as storage, database, analytics, application, and deployment services. These services are instantly available to developers, consequently reducing dependency on in-house specialized skills.

Security Built-in: In a non-cloud environment, security auditing would be a periodic and manual process. The AWS cloud provides plenty of security and encryption features with governance capabilities that enable continuous monitoring of your IT resources. Your security policy can be embedded in the design of your infrastructure.

AWS Cloud Economics

Weighing financial aspects of a traditional environment versus the cloud infrastructure is not as simple as comparing hardware, storage, and compute costs. You have to manage other investments, such as:

- Capital expenditures
- Operational expenditures
- Staffing
- Opportunity costs
- Licensing
- Facilities overhead

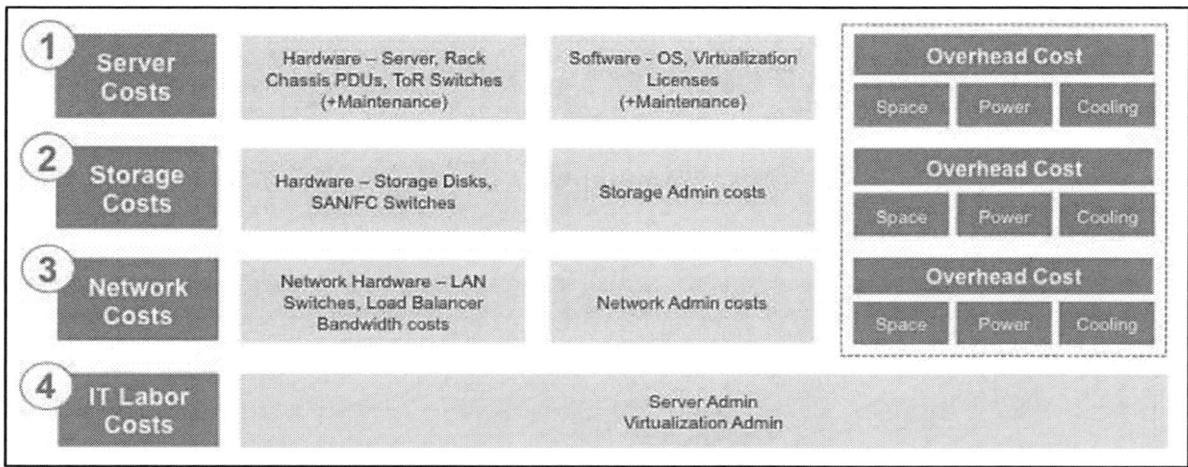

Figure 1-04: Typical Data Center Costs

On the other hand, a cloud environment provides scalable and powerful computing solutions, reliable storage, and database technologies at lower costs with reduced complexity, and increased flexibility. When you decouple from the data center, you are able to:

- **Decrease your TCO**: Eliminate the costs related to building and maintaining data centers or co-location deployment. Pay for only the resources that you have consumed.
- **Reduce complexity**: Reduce the need to manage infrastructure, investigate licensing issues, or divert resources.
- **Adjust capacity on the fly**: Scale resources up and down depending on the business needs using secure, reliable, and broadly accessible infrastructure.
- **Reduce time to market**: Design and develop new IT projects faster.
- **Deploy quickly, even worldwide**: Deploy applications across multiple geographic areas.
- **Increase efficiencies**: Use automation to reduce or eliminate IT management activities that waste time and resources.
- **Innovate more**: Try out new ideas as the cloud makes it faster and cheaper to deploy, test, and launch new products and services.
- **Spend your resources strategically**: Free your IT staff from handling operations and maintenance by switching to a DevOps model.
- **Enhance security**: Cloud providers have teams of people who focus on security, offering best practices to ensure you are compliant.

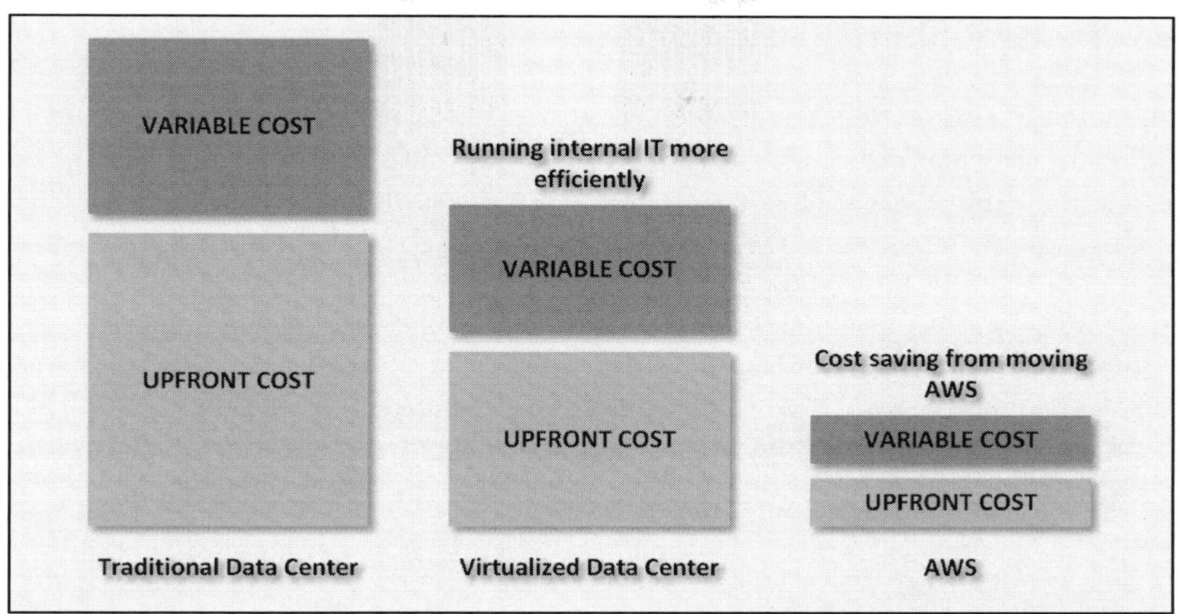

Figure 1-05: Cost Comparisons of Data Centers and AWS

AWS Virtuous Cycle

The AWS pricing philosophy is driven by a virtuous cycle. Lower prices mean more customers are taking advantage of the platform, which in turn results in driving the costs down further.

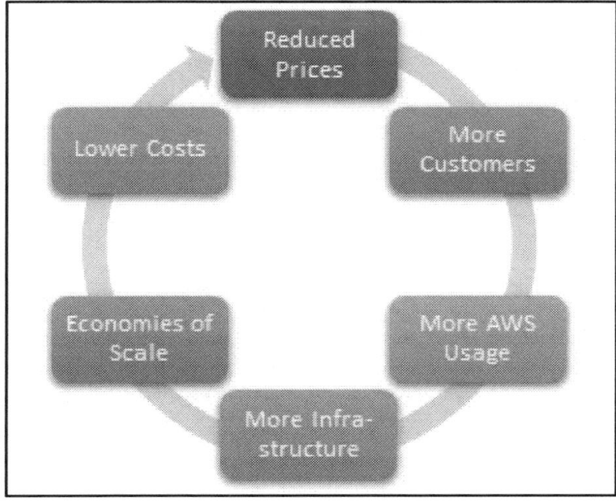

Figure 1-06: AWS Virtuous Cycle

AWS Cloud Architecture Design Principles

A good architectural design should take advantage of the inherent strengths of the AWS cloud computing platform. Below are the key design principles that need to be taken into consideration while designing.

Scalability

Systems need to be designed in such a way that they are capable of growing and expanding over time with no drop in performance. The architecture needs to be able to take advantage of the virtually unlimited on-demand capacity of the cloud platform and scale in a manner where adding extra resources results in an increase in the ability to serve additional load.

There are generally two ways to scale an IT architecture; vertically and horizontally.

Scale Vertically- Increase specifications such as RAM, CPU, IO, or networking capabilities of an individual resource.

Scale Horizontally- Increase the number of resources such as adding more hard drives to a storage array or adding more servers to support an application.

- Stateless Applications– An application that needs no knowledge of previous interactions and stores no sessions. It can be an application that when given the same input, provides the same response to an end user. A stateless application can scale horizontally since any request can be serviced by any of the available compute resources (e.g., Amazon EC2 instances, AWS Lambda functions). With no session data to be shared, you can simply add more compute resources as needed and terminate them when the capacity is no longer required.
- Stateless Components- Most applications need to maintain some kind of state information, for example, web applications need to track previous activities such as whether a user is signed in or not, etc. A portion of these architectures can be made stateless by storing state in the client's browser using cookies. This can make servers relatively stateless because the sessions are stored in the user's browser.
- Stateful Components – Some layers of the architecture are Stateful, such as the database. You need databases that can scale. Amazon RDS DB can scale up, and by adding read replicas, it can also scale out. Whereas, Amazon DynamoDB scales automatically and is a better choice. It requires the consistent addition of Read Replicas.
- Distributed Processing – Processing of a very large data requires a distributed processing approach where big data is broken down into pieces and have

computing instances work on them separately in parallel. On AWS, the core service that handles this is Amazon Elastic Map Reduce (EMR). It manages a fleet of EC2 instances that work on the fragments of data simultaneously.

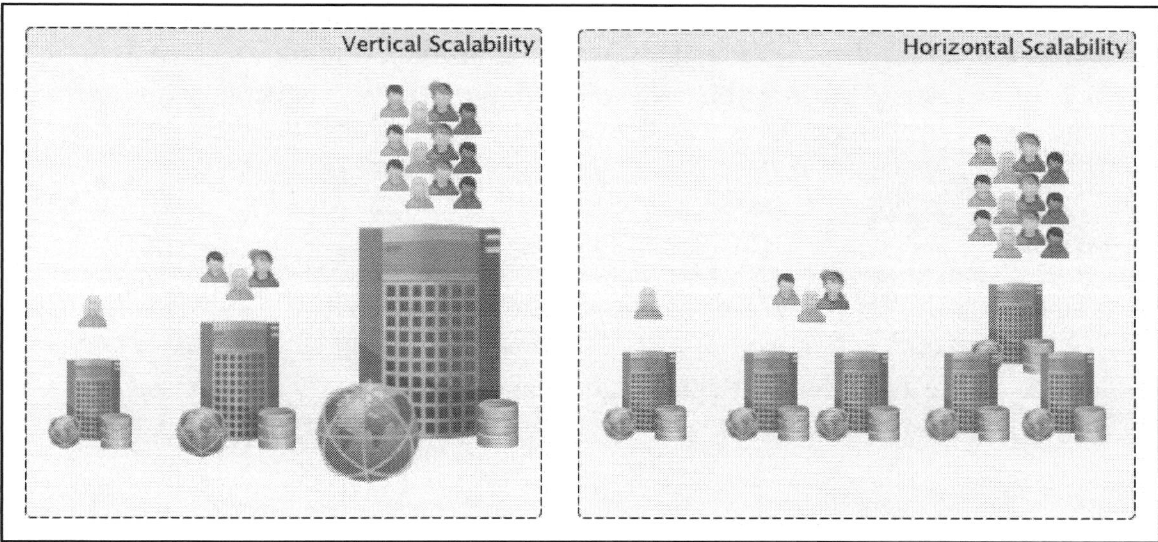

Figure 1-07: Vertical vs. Horizontal Scalability

Disposable Resources Instead of Fixed Servers

In a cloud-computing environment, you can treat your servers and other components as temporary disposable resources instead of fixed components. Launch as many as needed and use as long as you need them. If a server goes down or needs a configuration update, it can be replaced with the latest configuration server instead of updating the old one.

Instantiating Compute Resources- When deploying resources for a new environment or increasing the capacity of the existing system, it is important to keep the process of configuration and coding as an automated and repeatable process to avoid human errors and long lead times.

- Bootstrapping– Executing bootstrapping after launching a resource with the default configuration, enables you to re-use the same scripts without modifications.
- Golden Image– Certain resource types such as Amazon EC2 instances, Amazon RDS DB instances, Amazon Elastic Block Store (Amazon EBS) volumes, etc., can be launched from a golden image, which is a snapshot of a particular state of that resource. This is used in auto-scaling, for example, by creating an Amazon Machine Image (AMI) of a customized EC2 instance; you can launch as many instances as needed with the same customized configurations.

- Hybrid– Using a combination of both approaches, where some parts of the configuration are captured in a golden image, while others are configured dynamically through a bootstrapping action. AWS Elastic Beanstalk follows the hybrid model.

Infrastructures as Code– AWS assets are programmable, allowing you to treat your infrastructure as code. This lets you repeatedly deploy the infrastructure across multiple regions without the need to go and provision everything manually. AWS Cloud Formation and AWS Elastic Beanstalk are the two such provisioning resources.

Automation

One of the design's best practices is to automate whenever possible to improve the system's stability and efficiency of the organization using various AWS automation technologies. These include AWS Elastic Beanstalk, Amazon EC2 Auto recovery, Auto Scaling, Amazon Cloud Watch Alarms, Amazon Cloud Watch Events, AWS Ops Works Lifecycle events and AWS Lambda Scheduled Events.

Loose Coupling

IT systems can ideally be designed with reduced interdependency. As applications become more complex, you need to break them down into smaller loosely coupled components so that the failure of any one component does not cascade down to other parts of the application. The more loosely coupled a system is, the more resilient it is.

Well-Defined Interfaces– Using technology-specific interfaces such as RESTful APIs, components can interact with each other to reduce inter-dependability. This hides the technical implementation detail allowing teams to modify any underlying operations without affecting other components. Amazon API Gateway service makes it easier to create, publish, maintain and monitor thousands of concurrent API calls while handling all the tasks involved in accepting and processing including traffic management, authorization, and accessing control.

Service Discovery– Applications deployed as a set of smaller services require the ability to interact with each other since the services may be running across multiple resources. Implementing Service Discovery allows smaller services to be used irrespective of their network topology details through the loose coupling. In AWS platform service discovery can be achieved through Amazon's Elastic Load Balancer that uses DNS endpoints; so if your RDS instance goes down and you have Multi-AZ enabled on that RDS database, the Elastic Load Balancer will redirect the request to the copy of the database in the other Availability Zone.

Asynchronous Integration- Asynchronous Integration is a form of loose coupling where an immediate response between the services is not needed, and an acknowledgment of the request is sufficient. One component generates events while the other consumes. Both components interact through an intermediate durable storage layer, not through point-to-point interaction. An example for this is an Amazon SQS Queue. If a process fails while reading messages from the queue, messages can still be added to the queue for processing once the system recovers.

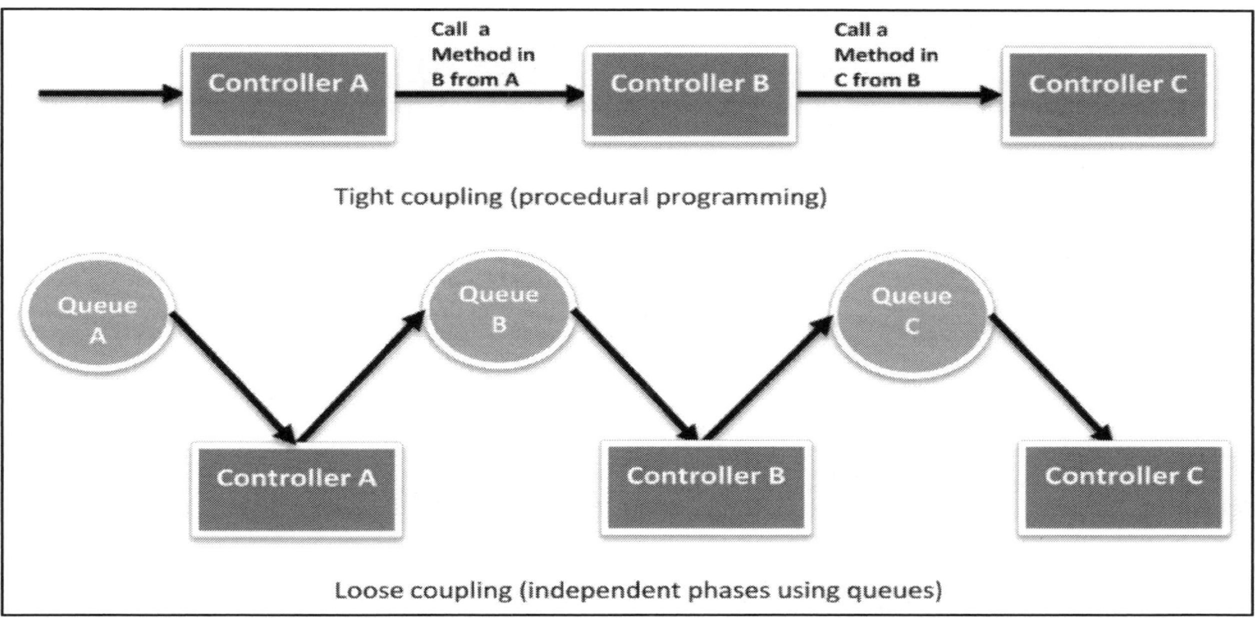

Figure 1-08: Tight and Loose Coupling

Graceful Failure- Increases loose coupling by building applications that handle component failure in a graceful manner. In the event of component failure, this helps to reduce the impact on the end users and increase the ability to progress on offline procedures.

Services, Not Servers

Developing large-scale applications requires a variety of underlying technology components. Best design practice would be to leverage the broad set of computing, storage, database, analytics, application, and deployment services of AWS to increase developer productivity and operational efficiency.

Managed Services- Always rely on services, not severs. Developers can power their applications by using AWS managed services that include databases, machine learning, analytics, queuing, search, e-mail, notifications, and many more. For example, Amazon S3

can be used to store data without having to think about capacity, hard disk configurations, replication, etc. Amazon S3 also provides a highly available static web hosting solution that can scale automatically to meet traffic demand.

EXAM TIP: Amazon S3 is great for static website hosting.

Server-less Architectures – Server-less architectures reduce the operational complexity of running applications. Event-driven and synchronous services can both be built without managing any server infrastructure. For example, your code can be uploaded to AWS Lambda compute service that runs the code on your behalf. Develop scalable synchronous APIs powered by AWS Lambda using Amazon API Gateway. Lastly combining this with Amazon S3 for serving static content, a complete web application can be produced.

EXAM TIP: For event-driven managed service/server-less architecture, use AWS Lambda. If you want to customize to your own needs, then Amazon EC2 offers flexibility and full control.

Databases

AWS managed database services remove constraints that come with licensing costs and the ability to support diverse database engines. While designing system architecture, keep these different kinds of database technologies in mind:

Relational Databases

- Often called RDBS or SQL databases.
- Consist of normalized data in well-defined tabular structures known as tables, consisting of rows and columns.
- Provide powerful query language, flexible indexing capabilities, strong integrity controls, and ability to combine data from multiple tables fast and efficiently.
- Amazon Relational Database Service (Amazon RDS) and Amazon Aurora.
- *Scalability:* Can scale vertically by upgrading to a larger Amazon RDS DB instance or adding more and faster storage. For read-heavy applications, use Amazon Aurora to horizontally scale by creating one or more Read Replicas.
- *High Availability:* using Amazon RDS Multi-AZ deployment feature creates synchronously replicated standby instance in a different Availability Zone (AZ). In

case of failure of the primary node, Amazon RDS performs an automatic failover to the standby without manual administrative intervention.

- *Anti-Patterns:* If your application does not need joins or complex transactions, consider a NoSQL database instead. Store large binary files (audio, video, and image) in Amazon S3 and only hold the metadata for the files in the database.

Non-Relational Databases

- Often called NoSQL databases
- The tradeoff query and transaction capabilities of relational databases for a more flexible data model
- Utilize a variety of data models, including graphs, key-value pairs, and JSON documents
- Amazon DynamoDB
- *Scalability:* Automatically scales horizontally by data partitioning and replication
- *High Availability:* Synchronously replicates data across three facilities in an AWS region to provide fault tolerance in case of a server failure or Availability Zone disruption
- *Anti-Patterns:* If your schema cannot be de-normalized and requires joins or complex transactions, consider a relational database instead. Store large binary files (audio, video, and image) in Amazon S3 and only hold the metadata for the files in the database

EXAM TIP: In any kind of given scenario, if you have to work on complex transactions or using JOINs, then you should use Amazon Aurora, Amazon RDS, MySQL or any other relational database. However, if you are not, then you should use a non-relational database like Amazon DynamoDB.

Data Warehouse

- A special type of relational database optimized for analysis and reporting of large amounts of data.
- Used to combine transactional data from disparate sources, making them available for analysis and decision-making.

- Running complex transactions and queries on the production database create massive overhead and require immense processing power, hence the need for data warehousing arises.
- Amazon Redshift
- *Scalability:* Amazon Redshift uses a combination of massively parallel processing (MPP), columnar data storage and targeted data compression encoding to achieve efficient storage and optimum query performance. It increases performance by increasing the number of nodes in data warehouse cluster.
- *High Availability:* By deploying production workloads in multi-node clusters, it enables the data written to a node to be automatically replicated to other nodes within the cluster. Data is also continuously backed up to Amazon S3. Amazon Redshift automatically re-replicates data from failed drives and replaces nodes when necessary.
- *Anti-Patterns:* It is not meant to be used for online transaction processing (OLTP) functions, as Amazon Redshift is a SQL-based relational database management system (RDBMS). For high concurrency workload or a production database, consider using Amazon RDS or Amazon DynamoDB instead.

Search

- Search service is used to index and search; it is in both structured and free text format.
- Sophisticated search functionality typically outgrows the capabilities of relational or NO SQL databases. Therefore a search service is required.
- AWS provides two services, Amazon CloudSearch and Amazon ElasticSearch Service (Amazon ES).
- Amazon CloudSearch is a managed search service that requires little configuration and scales automatically; whereas Amazon ES offers an open source API offering more control over the configuration details.
- *Scalability:* Both use data partitioning and replication to scale horizontally.
- *High-Availability:* Both services store data redundantly across Availability Zones.

Removing Single Points of Failure

A system needs to be highly available to withstand any failure of the individual or multiple components (e.g., hard disks, servers, network links, etc.).You should have

resiliency built across multiple services as well as multiple Availability Zones to automate recovery and reduce disruption at every layer of your architecture.

Introducing Redundancy - Have multiple resources for the same task. Redundancy can be implemented in either standby or active mode. In standby mode, functionality is recovered through secondary resource while the initial resource remains unavailable. In active mode, requests are distributed to multiple redundant compute resources when one of them fails.

Detect Failure- Detection and reaction to failure should both be automated as much as possible. Configure health checks and mask failure by routing traffic to healthy endpoints using services like ELB and Amazon Route53. Auto Scaling can be configured to replace unhealthy nodes using the Amazon EC2 auto recovery feature or services such as AWS OpsWorks and AWS Elastic Beanstalk.

Durable Data Storage– Durable data storage is vital for data availability and integrity. Data replication can be achieved by introducing redundant copies of data. The three modes of replication that can be used are: asynchronous replication, synchronous replication, and Quorum-based replication.

- Synchronous replication only acknowledges a transaction after it has been durably stored in both the primary location and its replicas.
- Asynchronous replication decouples the primary node from its replicas at the expense of introducing replication lag.
- Quorum-based replication combines synchronous and asynchronous replication to overcome the challenges of large-scale distributed database systems.

Automated Multi-Data Center Resilience–This is achieved by using the multiple Availability Zones offered by the AWS global infrastructure. Availability Zones are designed to be isolated from failures of the other Availability Zones. For example, a fleet of application servers distributed across multiple Availability Zones can be attached to the Elastic Load Balancing service (ELB). When health checks of the EC2 instances of a particular Availability Zone fail, ELB will stop sending traffic to those nodes. Amazon RDS provides automatic failover support for DB instances using Multi-AZ deployments, while Amazon S3 and Amazon DynamoDB stores data redundantly across multiple facilities.

Fault Isolation and Traditional Horizontal Scaling–Fault isolation can be attained through sharding. Sharding is a method of grouping instances into groups called shards. Each customer is assigned to a specific shard instead of spreading traffic from

all customers across every node. Shuffle sharding technique allows the client to try every endpoint in a set of shared resources until one succeeds.

Optimize for Cost

Reduce capital expenses by benefiting from the AWS economies of scale. Main principles of optimizing for cost include:

Right-Sizing- AWS offers a broad set of options for instance types. Selecting the right configurations, resource types and storage solutions that suit your workload requirements can reduce cost.

Elasticity- Implement Auto Scaling to horizontally scale up and down automatically depending upon your need to reduce cost. Automate turning off non-production workloads when not in use. Use AWS managed services wherever possible that helps in taking capacity decisions as and when needed.

Take Advantage of the Variety of Purchasing Options– AWS provides flexible purchasing options with no long-term commitments. These purchasing options can reduce cost while paying for instances. Two ways to pay for Amazon EC2 instances are:

- Reserved Capacity– Reserved instances enable you to get a significantly discounted hourly rate when reserving computing capacity as oppose to On-Demand instance pricing. Ideal for applications with predictable capacity requirements.
- Spot Instances - Available at discounted pricing compared to On-Demand pricing. Ideal for workloads that have flexible start and end times. Spot instances allow you to bid on spare computing capacity. When your bid exceeds the current Spot market price, your instance is launched. If the Spot market price increases above your bid price, your instance will be terminated automatically.

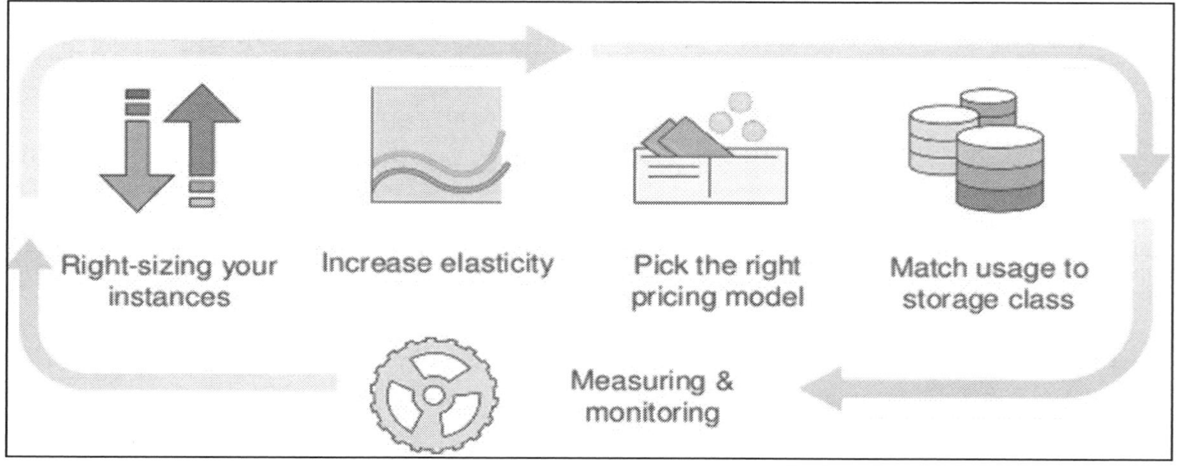

Figure 1-09. Cost Optimization Pillars

Caching

Caching is used to store previously calculated data for future use. This improves application performance and increases the cost efficiency of implementation. A good practice is to implement caching in the IT architecture whenever possible.

Application Data Caching– Application data can be stored in the cache for subsequent requests to improve latency for end users and reduce the load on back-end systems. Amazon ElastiCache makes it easy to deploy, operate, and scale an in-memory cache in the cloud.

Edge Caching– Both static and dynamic content can be cached at multiple edge locations around the world using Amazon CloudFront. This allows content to be served by infrastructure that is closer to viewers, lowering latency and providing high, sustained data transfer rates to deliver large popular objects to end users at scale.

Security

AWS allows you to improve your security in a variety of ways; it also lets the use of security tools and techniques that traditional IT infrastructures implement.

Utilize AWS Features for Defence in Depth–Isolates parts of the infrastructure by building a VPC network topology using subnets, security groups, and routing controls. Sets up web application firewall for protection using AWS WAF.

Offload Security Responsibility to AWS- Security of the underlying cloud infrastructure is managed by AWS; you are only responsible for securing the workloads you deploy in AWS.

Reduce Privileged Access– To avoid a breach of security, reduce privileged access to the programmable resources and servers. For example, defining IAM roles to restrict root level access.

Security as Code -AWS Cloud Formation scripts can be used that incorporate your security policy and reliably deploys it. Security scripts can be reused among multiple projects as part of your continuous integration pipeline.

Real-Time Auditing– AWS allows you to continuously monitor and automate controls to minimize security risk exposures. Services like AWS Config, Amazon Inspector, and AWS Trusted Advisor continually monitor IT resources for compliance and vulnerabilities. Testing and auditing in real-time are essential for keeping the environment fast and safe.

Mind Map

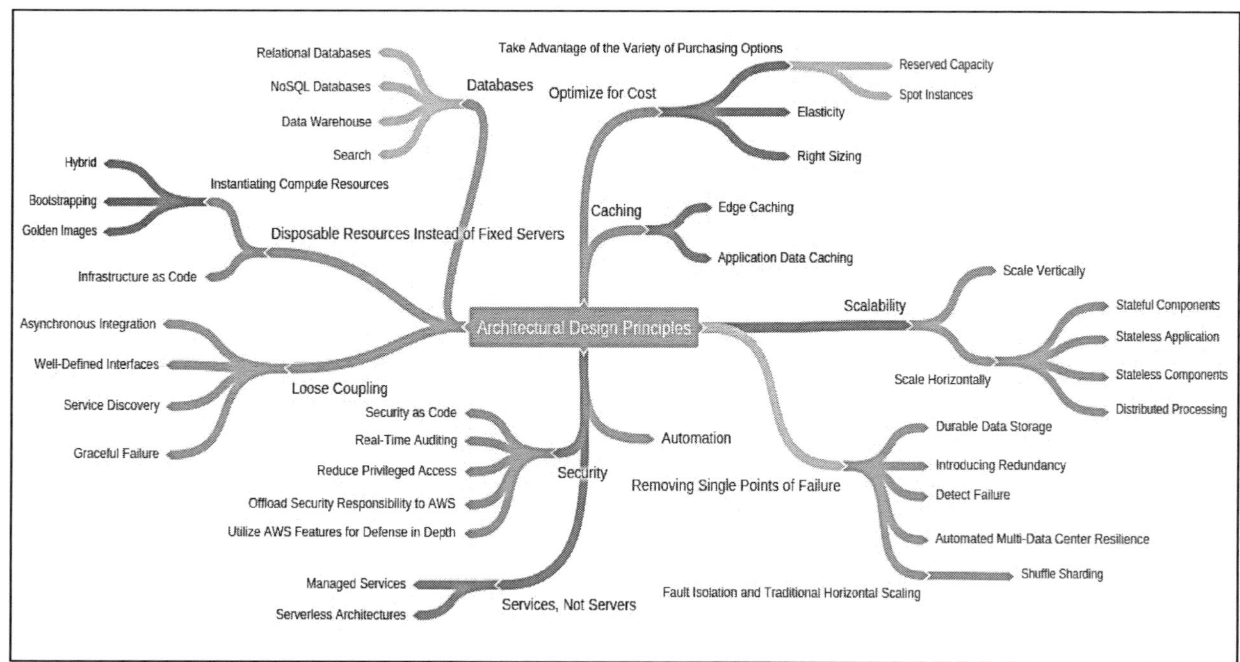

Figure 1-10. Mind Map of Architectural Design Principles

Practice Questions:

1. In AWS, which of the following maps to a separate geographic location?
   a) AWS Region
   b) AWS Datacenter
   c) AWS Edge Location
   d) AWS Availability Zone

2. Which Cloud Computing type is used to provide Basic Building Block for Cloud?
   a) IaaS
   b) SaaS
   c) PaaS
   d) FaaS

3. Which Cloud Computing Type is used as a complete product as a web service?
   a) IaaS
   b) SaaS
   c) PaaS
   d) FaaS

4. Which type of Deployment model includes mixture of on-premises, public third-party cloud and private cloud?
   a) Cloud
   b) Hybrid
   c) On-premises
   d) Cloud and Hybrid both

5. In AWS, you have ______________ and ____________ services to provide continuous monitoring service of resources.
   a) Encryption
   b) AIDA64 Extreme
   c) Rainmeter
   d) Security

6. When you use AWS instead of Traditional environment, then you get ___________ benefit. Select any 2 from the followings.

a) Decrease efficiency
b) Increase complexity
c) Deploy quickly
d) Security increases

7. Which phenomenon means “Lower prices mean more customers are taking advantage of the platform”, which in turn results in further driving down costs.
   a) Lifecycle
   b) Event cycle
   c) Virtuous cycle
   d) None of the above

8. An application that needs no knowledge of previous interactions and stores no session is termed as ____________.
   a) Stateless application
   b) Stateful component
   c) Stateful application
   d) None of the above

9. Implement Auto Scaling to horizontally scale up and down automatically depending upon your need to reduce cost is known as _____________.
   a) Caching
   b) Sizing
   c) Elasticity
   d) None of the above

10. Which type of pricing option is ideal for workloads that have flexible start and end times?
    a) Reserved
    b) On-demand
    c) Dedicated
    d) Spot

Chapter 02: Networking Refresher

Introduction

This chapter briefly contains the topics that are the building blocks of networking. It contains the 7-layers of OSI model and its working. This chapter also includes the following topics:

- The 7-Layers of OSI Model
- IPV4
- VLANs, Access Port and Trunks
- IPSec VPN
- DNS
- Border Gateway Protocol
- Multi-Exit Discriminator (MED)

The 7-Layers of the OSI Model

OSI stands for Open-System Interconnection originated by International Standards Organization (ISO), which divides the network communication into seven layers. It is a networking frame, which is used to implement protocols in different layers inside another networking frame. All the layers work collectively to transfer data from one person to another globally. It consists of seven layers.

Networking

Before discussing the 7-layers of the OSI model, a question that must be addressed is "Why networking exists?". The networking exists for one core reason, which is to allow a device or a person to communicate with another person or another device. In other words, networking allows the user running an application on machine A to communicate with another user running an application at machine B. The 7-layer model is developed to allow the communication between the devices having a difference in stacks.

7-Layer OSI Model

To understand how the 7-layer model works, let us consider that two different machines are running a different set of hardware and software and different operating systems. They both have different networking stacks and are running an application to communicate. Let us assume that they are communicating with each other through the same local network. Inside the network stack, we have seven logical components; Application, Presentation, Session, Transport, Network, Data Link, and Physical Layers.

You inject the data in the Application Layer of machine A, which is encapsulated downward to Physical Layer of machine A. Then it is accepted at the Physical Layer of machine B and goes all the way to be consumed by the Application Layer of machine B. Each layer is self-contained. Each layer is communicating with the other layer in between the stacks.

Physical Layer

The Physical Layer is only concerned with the injection of data on the physical medium. It communicates with the medium using certain electrical formats and certain stacks. It is different for different Physical Layers such as Wi-Fi, Bluetooth, etc. Physical Layer communicates to other Physical Layers using Ethernet cables. It knows how to send and receive the data. In short, machine A communicates with machine B through a wire.

Datalink Layer

Each machine has a machine address called mac address. On the Datalink Layer, we have the concept of frames, which contain different sets of information and this layer also handles sequencing and flow control.

Networking Layer

In the Networking Layer, the data is not present in the form of frames anymore. The data traverses in the form of packets from one machine to another, and each machine contains an IP address. The packets are sent from source address to destination address through routers.

Transport Layer

In this layer, the host-to-host flow control is added. The data travels in the form of segments from one machine to another. Protocols used at this layer are TCP and UDP. This layer allows sending of the segment from host A to host B or vice versa.

Session Layer

In the next layer, the session allows connecting machine A to machine B and keeps the connection open as far as the upper layer is open. Session Layer adds the concept of port, for example, TCP 80, which is for HTTP user, UDP 53 that DNS can use, etc. This allows multiple services to run on a single host.

Presentation Layer

Presentation Layer is used to present data to the Application Layer in a well-defined and standardized format. Sometimes, it is also called the Syntax Layer.

Application Layer

At layer seven, the application understands the protocols. It contains the protocols that focus on process-to-process communication across an entire IP network and provides a firm communication interface and end-user services.

Working Mechanism

Let us assume machine A wants to interact with machine B. The initial Data Layer is going to be the Application Layer, which has the knowledge of the HTTP for the web browser and knows that it is communicating with the web browser of machine B, using TCP port 80. The Application Layer with the Presentation Layer passes the data to the Session and Transport layer. The Session and Transport layer accepts the data the data is then encapsulated in the TCP header. The data is sent to the Networking Layer, which adds the destination and source IP addresses. The Network Layer sets the routing table to send the information from one hop to another hop. The packet is addressed to the Datalink Layer, which adds the mac address of the machine and passes it to the Physical Layer, which sends the information through wires where the Physical Layer of machine B is listening. The Ethernet frame is passed to the Datalink Layer of machine B. It checks the destination mac address and if it matches, it then passes the data to the Networking Layer where it checks the destination IP address. At Transport or Session layer, it is checked through which port the data is going to be intended, and then the data is de-capsulated at the Application Layer. This is a very simple and logical explanation at the machine level.

Let us assume machine A is connected to Wi-Fi and is communicating with machine B connected with ethernet. In this, the data is transmitted from the Physical Layer of machine A from Wi-Fi. It is captured wirelessly by the router, which decapsulates the information and passes it to the Ethernet gateway to transmit it to the Physical Layer of machine B. The remaining encapsulation and de-capsulation between the layers remain same.

Internet Protocol Version 4 (IPv4)

IP addressing is defined as the method of addressing and communicating between a host at regional, local and global networks. IPv4 is the Internet generation's fourth protocol. The ARPANET first used the protocols in 1983. IP is a connectionless protocol that was also discussed in OSI layers. You can transfer data from machine A to machine B by providing IP across regional, local and global networks. The device could be a pc, a mac book, a tablet, android, any IoT connected device, etc. It can be anything that sends or receives data by providing an IP. The IP address in IPv4 consists of 32 bits binary value,

which consists of 4 bytes having 2^32 available addresses. The IP address can be represented in two formats; decimal and binary.

All IP addresses are divided into portions. One part is used to identify the network (the network number), and the other part is used to identify the specific machine or host within the network or also called the host number. Subnet masks (IPv4) use the range of IP addresses that create a subnet or group of IP addresses built on the same network. For example, a subnet or a group can be used to identify all the machines in a building, department, geographic location, or on the same local area network (LAN).

IPv4 uses 32-bit addresses for Ethernet communication, which is divided into five classes: A, B, C, D and E. The Classes A, B and C have a variable bit length used for addressing the network host. While the Class D addresses are reserved for multicasting, and class E addresses are reserved for future use.

Class A has subnet mask 255.0.0.0 or /8, whereas Class B has a subnet mask, which is 255.255.0.0 or /16 and class C has a subnet mask that equals to 255.255.255.0 or /24. For example, with a /16 subnet mask, the network 192.168.0.0 may use the address range of 192.168.0.0 to 192.168.255.255. Network hosts can take any address from this range; however, address 192.168.255.255 is reserved for broadcast within the network. IPV4 can assign the maximum of 232 host addresses.

Dividing an organization's network into subnets allows it to be connected to the Internet with a single shared network address. Subnet masks and prefixes are used when a host is attempting to communicate with another system. If the system is on the same network or subnet, it will attempt to find that address on the local link. If the system is on a different network, the packet will be sent to a gateway, which will then route the packet to the correct IP address. This is called Classless-Inter Domain Routing (CIDR).

In IPv4, the subnet mask 255.255.255.0 is 32 bits and it consists of four 8-bit octets. The address 10.10.10.0 with the subnet mask 255.255.255.0 means that the subnet is a range of IP addresses from 10.10.10.0 - 10.10.10.255.

Class	Number of Network Bits	Number of Host Bits	Decimal Address Range	Subnet Mask
Class A	8 bits	24 bits	1-126	255.0.0.0
Class B	16 bits	16 bits	128-191	255.255.0.0
Class C	24 bits	8 bits	192-223	255.255.255.0
Class D	Reserved for Multicasting		224-239	N/A
Class E	Reserved for Future Use		240-255	N/A

Table 2-01: Classes with Network and Host Bits and Subnet Mask

Subnetting and Supernetting

IP Subnetting is a process of breaking a large IP network in smaller ones. During Subnetting we create multiple small networks by dividing a single large IP network. When a large network is broken into smaller ones, a subnet is created. A subnet is a single small network that is created from a large network. These small networks are known as subnets.

IP Subnets

An IP address is a 32 bits' logical address, which helps to identify a device on an IP network. This IP address can be further divided into a network portion and a host portion with the help of a subnet mask.

Address: The unique number ID assigned to one host or interface in a network.

Subnet: A portion of a network that shares a particular subnet address.

Subnet mask: A 32-bit combination used to describe which portion of an address refers to the subnet and which part refers to the host.

Let us have an example to understand Subnetting, consider you work for a large organization with a new network team. The business provides you with the /24 IP address range to use within the network. You know that /24 have enough space for 256 IP addresses ranging from 0 to 255. Let us consider the networking address provided to us is 10.0.32.0. The binary representation of this IP address is 00001010.00000000.00100000.00000000. The host portion is the last 8-bit of the IP address. If we replace all the 0's with 1's, this will provide us the last IP address of the network.

10.0.32.0 = 00001010.00000000.00100000.000000000 (First Address/ Network Address)

10.0.32.255 = 00001010.00000000.00100000.11111111 (Last Address/ Broadcast Address)

Now you have 254 useable IPs, and one IP is generally reserved for the gateway. The gateway is the path, which allows routing. If you want to devise your network by device type or by network type, you have to provide a separate different networking address based on the device or the traffic type. We can do this by performing Subnetting on the network. First, we need to check how many subnets are required in binary. When calculating the usable host per subnet, the formula 2^bits-2 is used. The subtracted two bits are reserved for network and broadcast addresses. Network address represents the network domain itself while broadcast address represents all the hosts, which belong to the network. These two addresses cannot be assigned to any individual host in the network. Each subnet represents an individual network; it also uses these two addresses.

In case of 4-subnets:

2^2=4 (2 Network Bits Are Required.)

Network Address: 10.0.32.0/26 – 10.0.32.63/26

First Usable Address: 10.0.32.64/26 – 10.0.32.127/26

Last Usable Address: 10.0.32.128/26 – 10.0.32.191/26

Broadcast Address: 10.0.32.191/26 – 10.0.32.255/26

Main Purpose of a Subnet

The primary reason for Subnetting is to use an IP address efficiently by creating sub-networks. With Subnetting, you can create multiple logical networks using a class A, B or C address. A 32-bit IP address is broken into four octets. Each octet is equal to 8 bits, which are converted into decimal separated by dots (for example, 192.168.0.100). Each octet ranges from 0 to 255 decimals.

For example, consider an IP address 192.168.0.1; its binary bit representation will be:

Decimal	192	168	0	1
Binary	11000000	10101000	00000000	00000001

Advantages of Subnetting on Private IT Systems

By setting up legitimate divisions, Subnetting causes you to keep up clean divisions inside a system.

- Enhanced system security
- Enhanced system execution
- Increasing or decreasing IP addresses per subnet

Exercise:

Consider a network 192.168.1.0/24. The requirement is to divide the network into five subnetworks where the following number host addresses are required.

- Network A requires 14 hosts
- Network B requires 28 hosts
- Network C requires two hosts
- Network D requires seven hosts
- Network E requires 28 hosts

Subnetting

Decimal	192	168	1	0
Binary	11000000	10101000	00000001	00000000
Subnet Mask	255	255	255	0

We are considering the last octet to create four subnetworks.

Decimal	192	168	1	0
Binary	11000000	10101000	00000001	00000000
Subnet Mask	255	255	255	0

Rearrange the requirement; it will be easy to divide:

- Network B requires 28 hosts
- Network E requires 28 hosts
- Network A requires 14 hosts
- Network D requires seven hosts
- Network C requires two hosts

Now, calculate the number of hosts using the following formula:

Total Number of Hosts = 2^N

Total Usable Number of Hosts = $2^N - 2$

Calculating Hosts for Network B:

Total Usable Number of Hosts = $2^N - 2$

Total Usable Number of Hosts = $2^5 - 2 = 30$

The requirement of 28 hosts can be fulfilled with this condition.

Calculating Hosts for Network E:

Total Usable Number of Hosts = $2^N - 2$

Total Usable Number of Hosts = $2^5 - 2 = 30$

The requirement of 28 hosts can be fulfilled with this condition.

Calculating Hosts for Network A:

Total Usable Number of Hosts = $2^N - 2$

Total Usable Number of Hosts = $2^4 - 2 = 14$

The requirement of 14 hosts can be fulfilled with this condition.

Calculating Hosts for Network D:

Total Usable Number of Hosts = $2^N - 2$

Total Usable Number of Hosts = $2^4 - 2 = 14$

The requirement of seven hosts can be fulfilled with this condition.

Calculating Hosts for Network C:

Total Usable Number of Hosts = $2^N - 2$

Total Usable Number of Hosts = $2^2 - 2 = 2$

The requirement of two hosts can be fulfilled with this condition.

	1st Octet	2nd Octet	3rd Octet	4th Octet							
Bits	8-bits	8-bits	8-bits	8-bits							
IP	192	168	1	0							
				128	64	32	16	8	4	2	1
Net B	11000000	10101000	00000001	0	0	0	0	0	0	0	0
	11000000	10101000	00000001	0	0	0	1	1	1	1	1
Net E	11000000	10101000	00000001	0	0	1	0	0	0	0	0
	11000000	10101000	00000001	0	0	1	1	1	1	1	1
Net A	11000000	10101000	00000001	0	1	0	0	0	0	0	0
	11000000	10101000	00000001	0	1	0	0	1	1	1	1
Net D	11000000	10101000	00000001	0	1	0	1	0	0	0	0
	11000000	10101000	00000001	0	1	0	1	1	1	1	1
Net C	11000000	10101000	00000001	0	1	1	1	0	0	0	0
	11000000	10101000	00000001	0	1	1	1	0	0	1	1

Network Bits	Host Bits

Network B: 192.168.1.0/27

Network E: 192.168.1.32/27

Network A: 192.168.1.64/28

Network D: 192.168.1.80/28

Network C: 192.168.1.96/30

Public IPV4 Addresses

Addresses which are controlled by either central global body or regional internet authority start with the Class A or /8 network. These are often referred to as a single organization. There are 126 Class A networks designated in the Class A network scheme and each network consists of over 16 million publicly routable addresses. Second is the Class B network, which lies between the range of 128 to 191 network addresses and each allows 65 thousand publicly routable addresses. Most popularly, we have Class C addresses allowing 254 public addresses per network. Class C is generally provided to ISPs to use for their public service endpoints. Next, we have Class D and Class E, which are reserved for multicasting and research purposes respectively.

Class	First Octet Range	Default Mask	Number of Networks	Hosts Per Networks
A	1-126	255.0.0.0/8	126	16,777,214
B	128-191	255.255.0.0/16	16,384	65,534
C	192-223	255.255.255.0/24	2,097,150	254
D	224-239	Reserved for Multicasting		
E	240-254	Reserved for Research		

Table 2-02: Public IPV4 Addresses

Private IPV4 Addresses

IANA defines the following IPV4 address ranges for private internets. They cannot be publicly routable in global internet. This address cannot be used for public communication.

Class	Private Networks	Subnet Mask	Address Range
A	10.0.0.0	255.0.0.0	10.0.0.0- 10.255.255.255
B	172.16.0.0- 172.31.0.0	255.240.0.0	172.16.0.0- 172.31.255.255
C	192.168.0.0	255.255.0.0	192.168.0.0- 192.168.255.255

Table 2-03: Private IPV4 Addresses

Network Address Translation

NAT is the process in which the network device or a firewall assigns a public IP address to a device or computer or group of computers inside a private network. NAT allows the single device, such as a firewall or router to act as an agent between the internet (or public network) and the local network (or private network). The main objective of NAT is to limit the number of public IP addresses an organization or company uses to provide security purposes. The NAT involves a large private network address within the private range. The private addressing schemes work better for the computers which only have to access the resources inside the network, like workstations requiring access to the file servers and printers. Routers within the private network are capable to route traffic between private addresses with no trouble. Outside the network to access the resources, like the internet, these computers must have the public address to respond to the requests.

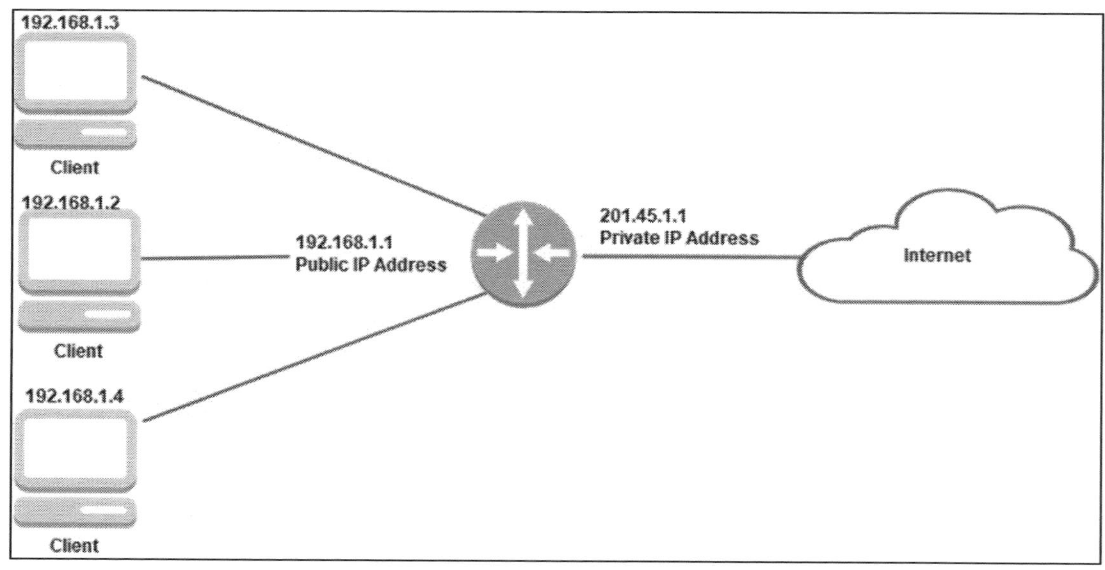

Figure 2-01: NAT Deployment

Generally, we configure a border router for NAT, i.e., the router which has one interface in the local network and another interface in the global network. When a packet is traveling outside the local (inside) network, then NAT immediately translates that local private IP address into the global public IP address. When a packet enters the local network, the global public IP address is converted into a local private IP address.

If the NAT runs out of addresses, therefore no addresses are left in the configured pool, then the packets will be dropped. An Internet Control Message Protocol (ICMP) will then send the unreachable host to the destination.

Types of NAT

There are three types of NAT:

- Static NAT
- Dynamic NAT
- Port Address Translation (PAT)

Static NAT

In this, a single Private IP address is mapped with the legally registered public address. It is a one-to-one mapping between the local and the global addresses.

Dynamic NAT

In Dynamic NAT, an unregistered IP address is translated in a registered public IP address from a pool of public IP addresses. If the IP address of the pool is not free, then the packet will be dropped, because only a fixed number of private addresses are translated into public addresses.

Port Address Translation (PAT)

In this case, many local private IP addresses are translated into a single registered IP address. PAT is also known as NAT overload. The port numbers are used to distinguish the traffic; which traffic belongs to which IP address.

VLANs, Access Port, and Trunks

VLAN

VLANs consist of a group of devices connecting through one or more LANs and are configured to communicate by being attached through the same wire. They are located on multiple LAN segments. Because VLANs are based on the logical connections instead of physical connections, they are extremely flexible. VLANs broadcast domains in a Layer 2 network. A virtual LAN is any broadcast domain that is isolated in a computer network at the Datalink Layer.

Access Port

An Access Port is used to transport the traffic by using the specified VLAN allocated to it. It will not deliver the exclusive identifying tags, unlike the Trunk Port, because the VLAN intended to it is pre-assigned.

Usually, an access port contains only a single VLAN set up on the interface, which is used to carry traffic for just a single VLAN. If the VLAN is not configured on the access port, then the interface carries the traffic using default VLAN, which is usually the VLAN1.

The access or trunk ports are unable to function at the same time, if both are configured at Ethernet Interface. An access port can only contain one VLAN, which is configured on their interface. It can carry traffic for only one VLAN.

Trunks

Trunk Port is a port, which is used to carry multiple VLANs across it. When the traffic crosses the trunk, it is tagged on entry, and it is potentially untagged on exit. A trunk port is capable of carrying untagged packets simultaneously with the 802.1Q tagged packets. When a default VLAN ID port is assigned to the trunk port, all the untagged traffic starts traveling on the default VLAN ID port for a trunk port and all the traffic is assumed to belong to the trunk port. Now this VLAN is referred to as native VLAN ID for a trunk port. The native VLAN ID is the VLAN that carries untagged traffic on trunk ports. The trunk port sends an egressing packet with a VLAN that is equal to the default port VLAN ID as untagged; the trunk port tags all the other egressing packets. If the native VLAN ID is not configured, the trunk port uses the default VLAN. A trunk port may have two or more VLANs, which are configured on their interface. They are capable of carrying traffic for several VLANs simultaneously.

IPSEC VPN

It is a technology commonly used within the on-premises environment to create hybrid on-premises environments with AWS. Now before going into details of how it works, let us first consider a scenario. You have a corporate office or datacenter using private addressing internally, and on the other hand, you have a secondary office or a data center. It can either be a cloud environment of another vendor or a data center, and you need to create a dedicated connection between them. IPSec provides a VPN tunnel connecting two public internet endpoints over which traffic is isolated and encrypted. The IPSEC VPN goes through five steps to transfer the data over VPN. The first step is introducing the interesting traffic. The interesting traffic is the data generated at the source VPN endpoint. Interesting traffic is the data, which matches with some rule set. The rule directs the router that this traffic needs to go by a reconfigured VPN tunnel. All the traffic that arrived at the source end and identified as the interesting traffic will be sent to the

next stage. The second stage is IKE phase 1. The purpose behind using the IKE phase 1 is to authenticate the IPSec peers and to build-up a secure channel between the peers to enable IKE exchanges. IKE phase 1 performs the following functions:

- Protects and authenticates the identities of the peers of IPSec.
- Negotiates a matching IKE SA (Security Association) policy between peers to protect the IKE exchange.
- Performs an authenticated Diffie-Hellman exchange with the results, which have similar shared secret keys.
- A secure tunnel is set up to negotiate IKE phase 2 parameter.

The third stage is IKE phase 2. This phase operates over the IKE phase 1. The IKE phase 2 is used to negotiate IPSec SA to set-up the IPSec tunnel. The functions performed by IKE phase 2 are as follows:

- IPSec SA parameters, which are protected by an existing IKE SA are negotiated.
- Establishes IPSec security associations.
- Re-negotiates IPSec SAs to ensure security periodically.
- An additional Diffie-Hellman exchange is performed optionally.

IKE phase 2 has one mode, called quick mode. Quick mode immediately occurs after IKE has established the secure tunnel in phase 1. The Quick mode negotiates the shared IPSec policy and derives the secretly shared keying material, which is used for the IPSec security algorithm and establishes IPSec SAs. Quick mode exchanges nonces that offer replay protection. The nonces are used to generate new shared secret key material and to prevent replay assaults from producing bogus SAs.

Quick mode is likewise used to renegotiate a new IPSec SA while the IPSec SA lifetime expires. Quick mode is used to refresh the keying material used to create the shared secret key primarily based at the keying cloth derived from the Diffie-Hellman change in phase 1. After IKE phase 2 is completed and quick mode has established IPSec SAs, information is exchanged via an IPSec tunnel in stage 4 IPsec encrypted tunnel. The specified encryption in the IPSec SA is used for encryption and decryption of packets.

The last stage is the tunnel termination stage. IPSec SAs terminate through deletion or by timing out. Time out in SA occurs when a specified number of seconds have elapsed or when a specified number of bytes have been passed through the tunnel. When the SAs terminate, the keys are also discarded. When subsequent IPSec SAs are needed for a flow, IKE performs a new phase 2 and, if necessary, a new phase 1 negotiation. A successful negotiation results in new SAs and new keys. New SAs can be established before the existing SAs expire so that a given flow can continue uninterrupted.

DNS Basics

DNS stands for Domain Name System. Domain Name System (DNS) is a name mapping system over the internet, which maps and records the names of hosts (domain names) and their mapped IP addresses. For example, there are some subdomains connected to the internet, which belong to IPSpecialist. All these systems have names within the IPSpecialist.net domain.

DNS is the platform, which is essential to the performance of the internet. At a high level, it is the look-up system responsible for changing hostname into IP address, and it also allows you to open up the hostname in the web browser to obtain an IP address. DNS is the hierarchical, which means consisting of multiple layers and fully, globally distributed system. The DNS handles different types of the domain name. The first is a generic top-level domain name such as .com, .net, .org and these are controlled by the Internet Assigned Number Authority (IANA). IANA is the global organization responsible for the management of DNS. Next, we have the country top-level domain such as .uk, .au, .se. Then, we have the subset of the global domain name named sponsored top-level domain, for example, .edu, .mil, .gov, etc.

Domain name servers are used in an Internetwork to maintain a directory of domain names with mapped IP addresses. A domain name server resolves domain names to an IP address from its database. DNS can be located anywhere in the network, and customer's internet access significantly depends upon its location and speed. DNS servers are configured as either any of the following two roles:

- **Primary DNS:** Servers which resolve domain name addresses to IP address
- **Secondary DNS:** Act as a backup server in primary DNS failure

Following are two general record types of DNS:

- **A-record:** Returns 32-bit IP address
- **AAAA-record:** Returns 128-bit IP address

DNS Hierarchy

As mentioned earlier, the DNS is hierarchical. It is like a tree structure, and just like the tree, it has a root. The DNS has the root server, the authoritative initial information source of the DNS platform. The root server consists of 300+ servers, which are geographically dispersed around the world. The 13 anycast IPs access these servers. When you attempt to connect to those IPs, you will be routed to a nearby physical route server. This helps to provide resilience and performance across the platform. Twelve operating organizations operate these 13 anycast IPs. In the root server, there is the concept of Root

Zone, which holds all the high-level gTLD information. The IANA assigns the root zones hosted by the operators of the root server.

The hierarchy starts with the root server. The operating organization hosts the root zone. The IANA manages the root zone. The root zone consists of all the top-level domains and these are both the generic one, for example, .com and the country-specific one for example .uk. The authoritative root server is a server, which contains the zone file of the domain, i.e., and it contains additional record information for that domain while the un-authoritative server is the one, which only catches the detail of that domain.

How DNS Works

Let us discuss how DNS operates from a client perspective. Consider a client, which could be a PC, Mac, tablet, etc. The device is configured with the local DNS server, which is running on the router and pointing to the local ISP. This DNS server is called the caching DNS server. Now the local DNS server checks its local cache. It also checks on the local zone file on the DNS server. The server is non-authoritative; it is just a local caching server. The DNS server picks the first configuration service to use, as the server is not configured. The DNS server performs the DNS lookup against the authoritative server for the requested domain. Now the DNS query service asks the server for the additional information of the requested domain; then it sends the request to a business DNS server to ask the record for the requested domain. The local DNS receives this response and reports them back to the client workstation. The whole process is known as the recursive DNS query; the recursive query is called recursive because the server handles everything from that point onwards.

Difference between Authoritative DNS Server and Recursive DNS Resolver

Both concepts refer to the server or DNS infrastructure, but each performs the different operation and resides at different locations inside the Pipeline of a DNS query. The recursive resolver works at the beginning of the DNS query while the authoritative server works at the end.

DNS Look-Up

The DNS is concerned with the hostname translated into the IP address. The DNS lookup has some steps:

- A user searches “ipspecialist.net” into the web browser. Query stats travel into the internet and are received by a DNS recursive resolver.
- Then the resolver queries the DNS root name server.

- The root server responds to the resolver with the top-level domain server, which holds the information for its domain. When searching for the example.com, the request is pointed towards the .com TLD.
- The resolver now requests the .com TLD.
- TLD server responds with the IP address of the domain name server.
- Recursive resolver sends the query to DNS.
- The IP address then returns to the resolver for the name server.
- The DNS resolver responds to the web browser containing the IP address of the requested domain.

Border Gateway Protocol (BGP)

BGP Fundamentals

BGP stands for Border Gateway Protocol, and it is one of the primary protocols across the internet. It is a protocol that was developed to address the de-centralized nature and massive scale of the internet. BGP operates over TCP, as TCP is the most reliable transport layer that sits on top of IP and ensures a reliable connection between hosts. By design, BGP does not provide auto-discovery system. Routers are involved in the router sharing process known as peers, manually defined and need to be mutually configured. BGP is the routing protocol, which dynamically shares the route between the peers.

The path selection in BGP is based on the route through the network. BGP makes a routing decision based on the available paths, network policies, or set of rules configured by the network administrator and is involved in making core routing decisions. In BGP, the routing takes place within the Autonomous System. An Autonomous System is a single network or an AS system is a set of networks and routers, which lie under the control of one single administrative identity. BGP Best Path Selection Algorithm works by determining the best route by selecting the shortest path to the destination. Now this differs from other routing protocols, which are either link state or distance vector routing protocol. So, BGP is known as the path vector protocol. BGP only share its best path information with its neighbor.

Autonomous System

Autonomous System is a set of routers, which lie under the single technical administration. An Autonomous System is a single network or a combination of networks and routers, which lie under the control of one single administrative identity. Networks within an Autonomous System communicate routing information to each other. An Autonomous System shares their routing information with other Autonomous System using the Border Gateway Protocol.

The Autonomous System must have an official Autonomous System Number or ASN. A unique ASN is allocated to each AS for use in BGP routing.

Peering

Two routers that have established a connection to exchange BGP information are referred to as BGP peers. The BGP peers share routing information between them through BGP sessions, which runs over TCP.

Types Of BGP

There are multiple types of BGP.

- EBGP (Exterior Border Gateway Protocol)
- IBGP (Interior Border Gateway Protocol)

Exterior Border Gateway Protocol (EBGP)

EBGP exchanges information in between the routers within a different Autonomous System.

Interior Border Gateway Protocol (IBGP)

IBGP exchanges information between the routers within the same Autonomous System.

Multi-Exit Discriminator (MED)

MED is a BGP supported matrix, which is used to influence or provide preference directive for the traffic that is entering in the network. It is used to redirect and confirm the method of route selection when providing a route to a router. The method of route selection is quite similar to BGP. BGP has the best path selection algorithm, and this algorithm is used to control the current best path to a network. This best path is used to route the traffic to the destination. BGP follows a convention of most routing protocols and the most specific prefix is always used to route the traffic to the network. If we have multiple routes for the same network and the same prefix, then one of them is chosen as the current best path, and that is known as the First Valid Path; the first route chosen as the current best path. For establishing the current best path the BGP employees the best path algorithm to evaluate the current best path against all the paths. The first attribute that is used to distinguish the routes to the same network with the same prefix is the Weight. The weight governs the outbound traffic, and it is local to the router on which it is configured. It is not advertised to any other routers within the autonomous system or to the external autonomous system. So, if the destination route is on the same network with the same prefix, then the path with the higher weight is selected as the best current path.

The second attribute is Local Preference, which is used to choose the outbound external BGP paths. The Local Preference is advertised to all internal BGP routers in the Autonomous System. Any route having default local preference that is 100, and the routes, which have a higher local preference are preferred over others. Weight and Local Preference, both are the methods by which you can influence the outbound traffic or the link or route, which you can use to direct the traffic. If you have multiple routes, which have the same local preference value and all of the proceeding checks are equal, then you should prefer the one, which has originated from the local router. That is the one that is learned using BGP command. At this point, everything else is equal, and BGP starts comparing the AS path link. AS path link is the path from the current Autonomous System to the destination and its value is updated each time when the router is re-advertised as it passes through the intermediate Autonomous System. AS Path Value can be used to influence the incoming traffic. By artificially adjusting the AS Path Value, you can influence how other Autonomous Systems pick their best path.

Next, we have the Origin Code, the origin attributes indicate the origin of the prefix, which contains three values, the prefix originated from IGP, the prefix originated from EGP, and the predecessors to BGP or the origin will be incomplete if the prefix is learned through other means. At this level, we reach Multi-exit Discriminator; a MED is a non-transitive attribute, which means it is directly used between two connected BGP pairs. MED is only used when an autonomous system has two connections to another neighboring Autonomous System. If an Autonomous System 1 has two direct connection to another autonomous system, let us say autonomous system 2; then AS 1 can hint AS 2 which link or which route should be used to reach the destination, unlike the other attributes, the lowest value of MED is preferred. In the case where during a route if everything would be same, same weight, same local preference value, same network, and same prefix, the same origination, the same destination, then an AS will pick the lowest MED value to reach the destination.

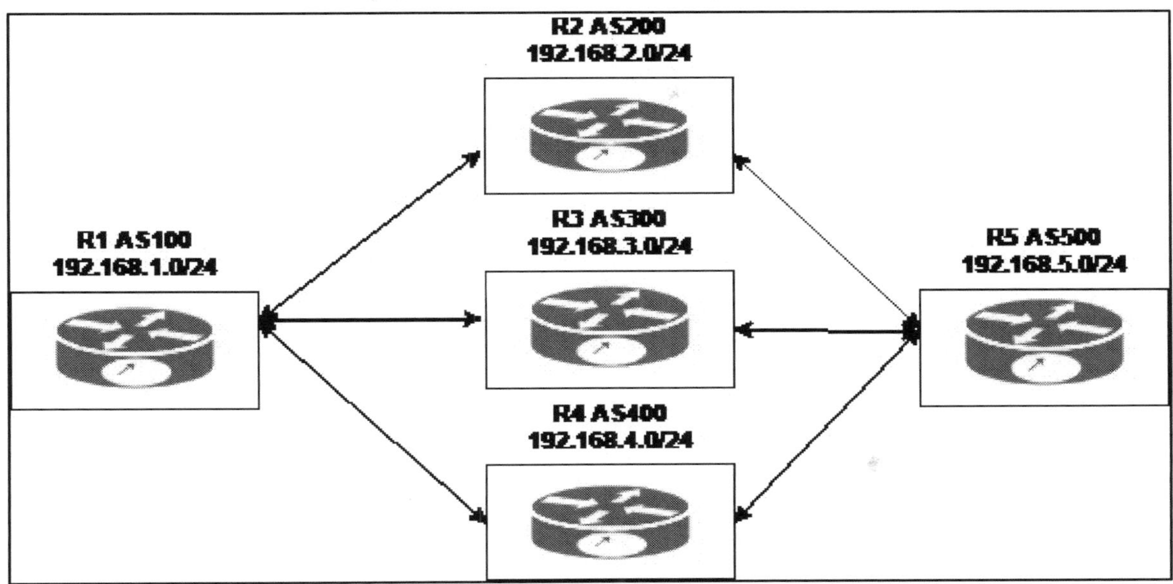

Figure 2-02: Routers Connecting in Different AS Using MED

Let us have an example in which we assign five different routers specified with different AS numbers and network addresses as shown in the figure. We are using a /24 network, which means the addresses are in Class C. The Autonomous System 100 and 200 are connected through a single link.

Similarly, R1 and R4 having AS number 100 and 400 respectively, have a single connection. In the center, we have Autonomous System 300, which are managed by R3 having two connections back to our network between Autonomous System 100 and Autonomous System 300. Lastly, we have a remote network, which uses an Autonomous System of 500, having a connection to each of the three neighboring Autonomous Systems.

In this case, all of the paths between R1 and R5 are same, and all of the subnets are of the same prefix. We also know that BGP advertises current best paths to its neighbors. In this case, we can influence the outbound traffic from R1 either by Weight or by Local Preference. BGP influencing the outbound traffic is much easier than following the inbound traffic.

Mind Map

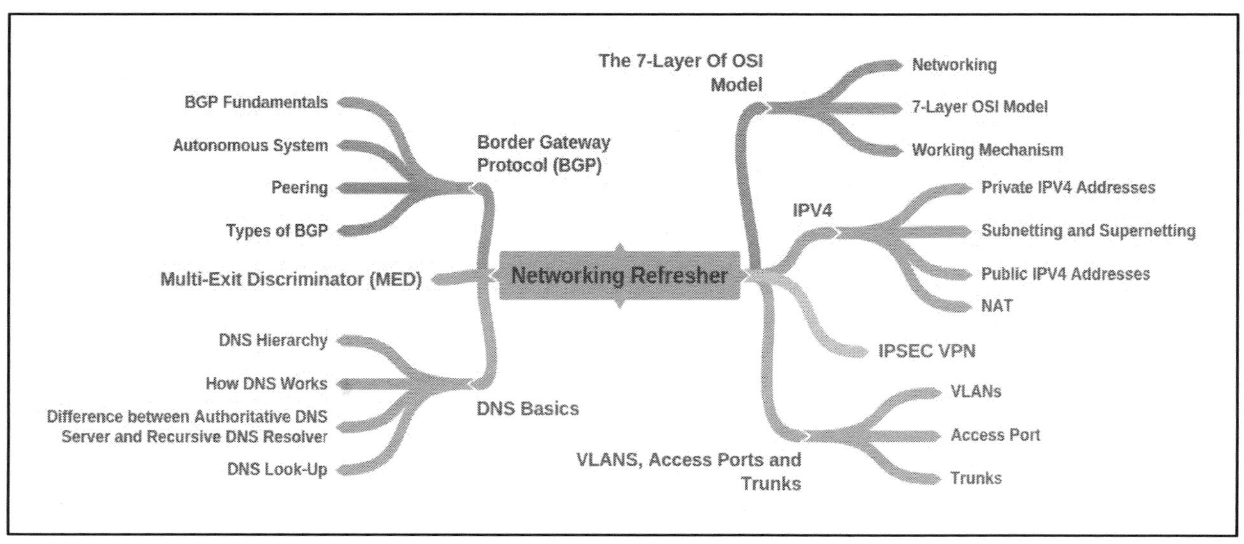

Figure 2-03: Chapter Mind Map

Practice Questions:

1. How many layers does OSI model contain?
   a) Five
   b) Three
   c) Seven
   d) Six

2. Which layer do Transmission Control Protocol (TCP) and User Datagram Protocol (UDP) work at?
   a) Transport Layer
   b) Data Link Layer
   c) Physical Layer
   d) Networking Layer

3. OSI reference model is a seven-layer reference model that is originated from the:
   a) ISO Standards
   b) ITU Standards
   c) IEEE Standards
   d) ANSI Standards

4. At which layer does Syntax Formation take place?
   a) Application
   b) Presentation
   c) Session
   d) Transport

5. Which layer provides Logical Addressing that routers use for path determination?
   a) Transport Layer
   b) Application Layer
   c) Network Layer
   d) Data Link Layer

6. Which of the following device translates hostname into IP address?
   a) DNS server
   b) Hub
   c) Firewall

d) DHCP server

7. The entire hostname has the maximum of:
   a) 31 Characters
   b) 127 Characters
   c) 63 Characters
   d) 255 Characters

8. How does the DNS server handle the request for another Domain?
   a) Directly
   b) By contacting remote DNS server
   c) The server cannot handle the request for other domains
   d) None of the above

9. How many steps does the IPSec go through to transfer the data over VPN?
   a) Five steps
   b) Four steps
   c) Six steps
   d) Three steps

10. In IPSec, the interesting traffic is generated at:
   a) At the destination VPN endpoint
   b) At the source VPN endpoint
   c) At both the VPN endpoints
   d) None of the above

11. Two routers that established connection in order to exchange BGP information are referred to as ______________.
   a) Autonomous System
   b) MED
   c) BGP Peering
   d) None of the Above

12. ______________ is BGP supported matrix used to influence or provide preference directive for the traffic that is entering in the network.
   a) IBGP
   b) EBGP

c) MED
d) IPSec

13. In BGP, preference is given to which attribute during the route by AS?
    a) High Local Preference Value
    b) Higher Weight
    c) Low MED Value
    d) Shortest AS Path Value

14. _______________ is basically a set of routers, which lie under the single technical administration.
    a) Autonomous System
    b) BGP
    c) MED
    d) IPSec VPN

15. For what reasons, the two bits are subtracted from the formula 2^bits-2? (Choose 2)
    a) Broadcast
    b) Multicast
    c) Unicast
    d) Network

16. How many hosts can be located on a network having subnet mask of 27 bits?
    a) 27
    b) 32
    c) 30
    d) 5

17. At Datalink Layer, the data is transferred in the form of:
    a) Packets
    b) Frames
    c) Segments
    d) Bits

18. The IP addresses are divided into __________ portion.
    a) Three
    b) Four
    c) Two
    d) Five

19. _______________ is a process of breaking a large IP network in smaller IP

networks.

a) Subnetting
b) Supernetting
c) NAT
d) IPSec

20. A single Private IP address is mapped with the legally registered public address in ______________.
    a) Dynamic NAT
    b) Static NAT
    c) PAT
    d) NAT

21. A ____________ is a group of devices created on one or more LANs that are configured to communicate as if they were attached to the same wire, when in fact they are located on some different LAN segments.
    a) Access Port
    b) Trunk
    c) VLAN
    d) IPSec

22. An _____________ transports traffic to and from only the specified VLAN allotted to it.
    a) Access Port
    b) Trunk
    c) VLAN
    d) IPSec

23. _______________ is a port, which carries multiple VLAN across it.
    a) Access Port
    b) Trunk
    c) VLAN
    d) IPSec

24. __________________ is used to authenticate the IPSec peers and to setup a secure channel between the peers.
    a) IKE Phase 1
    b) IKE Phase 2
    c) Interesting Traffic
    d) Tunnel Termination

25. How many hosts can be addressed on 10.0.0.0/16?
    a) 16

b) 254
c) 65536
d) 65534

Chapter 03: Design and Implement AWS Networks

Introduction

In this Chapter, we will discuss the Design and Implementation of AWS Networks. We will also discuss VPC, ENI, Elastic IP, IGW, Security Group, NACL, NAT gateway, VGW, VPC endpoint, VPC peering and Subnet architecture types in detail, which should be enough for the preparation of examination of Network Specialty.

AWS Global and Regional Infrastructure

As we know, AWS provides managed and global infrastructure. The AWS Cloud spans across 18 geographic Regions. The region is a completely independent and separate geographical area. Each region has multiple, physically separated and isolated locations known as Availability Zones. Examples of Region include London, Dublin, Sydney, etc.

Consider an example of North America region, which has 4 public regions: us-east-1 (Virginia), us-east-2 (Ohio), us-west-1 (N. California) and us-west-2 (Oregon).

What is an Availability Zone?

Availability Zone is simply a datacenter or a collection of data centers. It can be said that each AZ must have at least one data center. Each Availability Zone in a Region has separate powers, networking and connectivity to reduce the chances of two zones failing simultaneously. No two Availability Zones share a data center; however, the datacenters within a particular Availability Zone are connected over redundant low-latency, private network links. Likewise, all zones in a region are linked by highly resilient and very low latency private fiber optic connections for communication. The Availability Zones are at a certain length or distance apart from each other. Latency within AZ is 0.2 milliseconds, but AWS has targeted max 2 milliseconds for inter AZ communication. AZ is the foundation of all resilient architectures within AWS. Its architecture includes infrastructure and networking aspects. Some regions have 2, 3 or 5 AZs. In AWS, underlying structure of AZ is not publicized.

One AZ's physical location for one AWS account is different from other accounts like us-east-1a may not always have the same physical facilities that are shown to another AWS account. It means if any AZ dies, its effect on your account is different as compared to any other AWS account. Some services of AWS also have the capability of sub-AZ resilience such as EBS, which means maintaining resilience within an AZ. If a disk failure occurs,

then it does not affect the service but, if the AZ fails, then it affects the provisioning of service by EBS.

Within a region, VPC is launched as part of that region within an AWS account. VPC contains subnets, which are private and public. We have discussed in the previous chapter what private and public subnets are. Public subnets are accessible over the internet. We know in AWS one subnet is located in one AZ. You cannot expand the subnet across multiple AZ. Once AZ is selected at the creation of subnet, you cannot change it later. In AWS, some services are accessible outside the VPC as they are public. Public services include S3, DynamoDB, CloudWatch, etc. All these services can be accessed over the internet via DNS specific to their regions.

Inside the VPC, there is an Internet gateway. Using that, the VPC accesses these public resources of AWS. IGW in VPC provides internet connectivity or public access of AWS to subnets inside the VPC. Concluding that, we can say the IGW is the essential part, which provides communication between VPC resources and internet users or AWS public services.

As we know, Availability Zones are isolated from each other, and they are isolated logical constructs. Therefore, if anyone AZ goes down, it does not affect the performance of other AZ within that region.

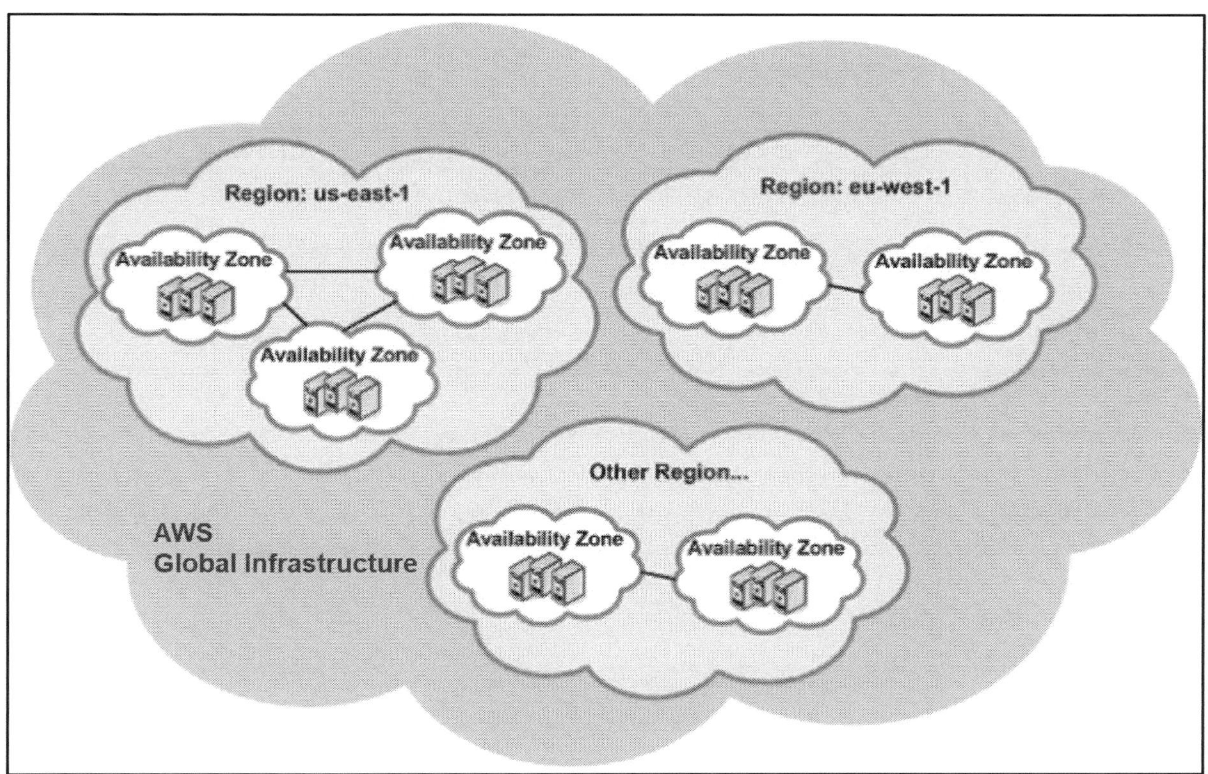

Figure 3-01: Regions and Availability Zones

What is an Edge Location?

Edge location in AWS functions like a mini data center that is used for caching. Edge Locations are AWS sites deployed in major cities and highly populated areas across the globe. There are many more Edge Locations than the Regions. Currently, there are over 102 Edge Locations. Edge Locations are used by AWS services such as AWS CloudFront to cache data and reduce latency for end-user access by using the Edge Locations as a global Content Delivery Network (CDN).

Therefore, Edge Locations are primarily used by end users who are accessing and using your services. For example, you may have your website hosted by the region in Ohio with a configured CloudFront distribution associated. When a user accesses your website from Europe, they will be re-directed to their closest Edge Location (in Europe) where cached data could be read on your website, significantly reducing latency.

VPC and Basic Networking Design

With Amazon VPC, you can provision a logically isolated portion of the AWS cloud where you can launch AWS resources in your defined virtual network. You have administrative control over your virtual networking environment, including a selection of your CIDR block, the creation of subnets, route table configuration, and network gateways.

A Virtual Private Cloud is a cloud computing model, which offers an on-demand configurable pool of shared computing resources allocated within a public cloud environment while providing a certain level of isolation from other users of the public cloud. Since the cloud (pool of resources) is only accessible to a single client in a VPC model, it, therefore, offers privacy with greater control and a secure environment where only the specified client can operate.

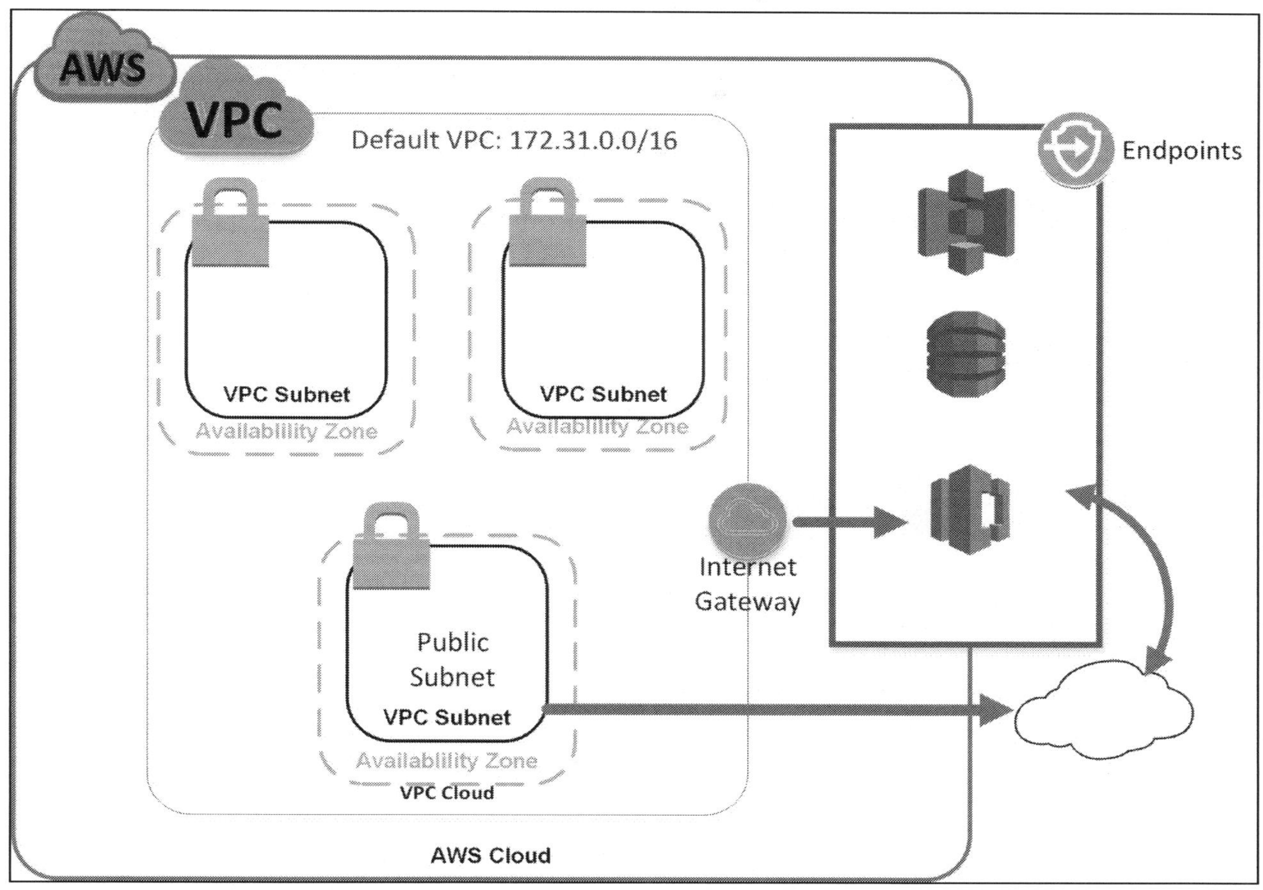

Figure 3-02: VPC Basic Network Design

VPC is a private level construct within AWS. In VPC, you define a private logical grouping of network services on which infrastructure and application services are operating. You have multiple VPC options per account or region, but you cannot span VPC across regions. You have at least one VPC per region. So AWS provides one default VPC per region, which means that each account has VPCs per region depending on the number of regions available.

As we discussed earlier, an account has a single default VPC per region, which has a set of subnets per AZ with all the required set of security groups, NACL, and route tables. Also, the communication gateway is attached. The network configuration for your Amazon VPC can be easily customized. For example, you can create a public subnet for your web servers that need to access the internet and settle your backend systems such as databases or application servers in a private subnet without internet access. You can use multiple layers of security, such as Security Groups and NACLs (Network Access Control Lists), to help in managing the access to EC2 instances in each subnet. You can also create

a hardware VPN (Virtual Private Network) connection between your corporate datacenter and your VPC, and use the AWS cloud as an extension of your corporate data center.

In AWS, you can also create your VPC quickly and easily via AWS console/ CLI/ API. You will need to provide three main things; VPC Name tag, which is unique for identifying then VPC ID is assigned to it; you can change the name tag later, CIDR block and tenancy. CIDR block and tenancy are only configurable at the creation of VPC, and these cannot be changed later.

In tenancy, there are two options available: dedicated and default. In the dedicated option, there is the use of dedicated resources on dedicated underlying hardware, which is separated from other users and AWS accounts. The price for dedicated mode is premium. If you use default mode, then you will have an option to choose a dedicated option for some resources. Therefore, always prefer to use Dedicated mode if you are sure that you want a dedicated connection.

CIDR block is a range of private IPv4 addresses, which are needed to be defined when creating a VPC. The VPC CIDR block size can be from /16 to /28. The default VPC use 172.31.0.0 /16, which means /16 subnets can be split into multiple subnets. Always try to use non-overlapping ranges of CIDR block with other VPCs or on-premises networks. Always choose CIDR block that is good for subnetting. When creating a subnet, you need to specify the CIDR block for the subnet, which is a subset of the VPC CIDR range. The allowed block size is between /28 netmask and /16 netmask. If you need more than one subnet in a VPC, make sure that the CIDR blocks of the subnets must not overlap.

Consider an example of VPC that have CIDR block 10.0.0.0/16 as shown in figure 3-04 and inside the VPC, there are 3 subnets because the region in which you create VPC has 3 AZs. Then we assign subnets IP addresses 10.0.0.0/18, 10.0.64.0/18 and 10.0.128.0/18 and still, we are left with one IP address for future use. Since we need three IP addresses, that is why we take /18 range but if we have more than 4 AZs, then we need to use /19 address range as it gives you 8 subnets address ranges.

Tiering is also important after assigning subnets in VPC. Therefore, for tiers, you need to divide your further IP address range of subnets. Tiers play an important role when you define NACL in your VPC, which has explicit deny rule on traffic. If inside AZ you want 4 tiers for the given example of VPC subnets, then you split /18 range into /20 or for extra growth inside AZ split into /21, which gives 8 portions, 2 for each tier.

For granular level of control over inbound and outbound traffic, you can use NACL with small subnets. NACL is at subnet level. Now this /21 subnet ranges provide 2048 IP addresses available for each subnet. So we can say that tier is a subnet inside a subnet. For internal VPC communication route, summarization is also an important factor. It will be

discussed later in this book. You can say that for VPC and basic Network designing, effective subnetting skill is more important than how to provide IP address ranges. If you want VPC communication with other VPC, then do not use default VPC as its CIDR block is the same 172.31.0.0/16 for all default VPC in all regions on your account or other AWS accounts. Default VPC architecture is the simplest as it has one subnet per AZ and does not provide a granular level of control. For granular level of control, you can create your customized VPC.

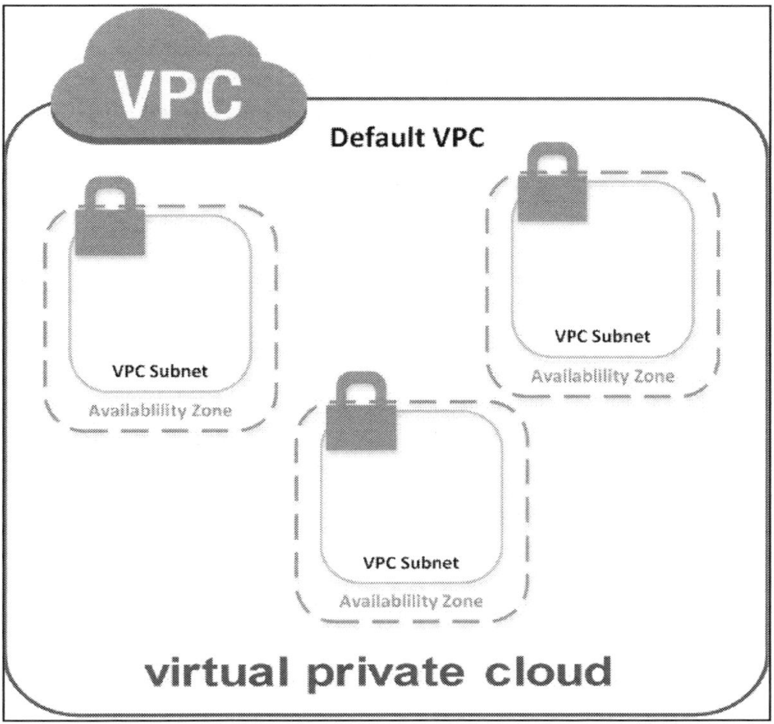

Figure 3-03: Default VPC Architecture

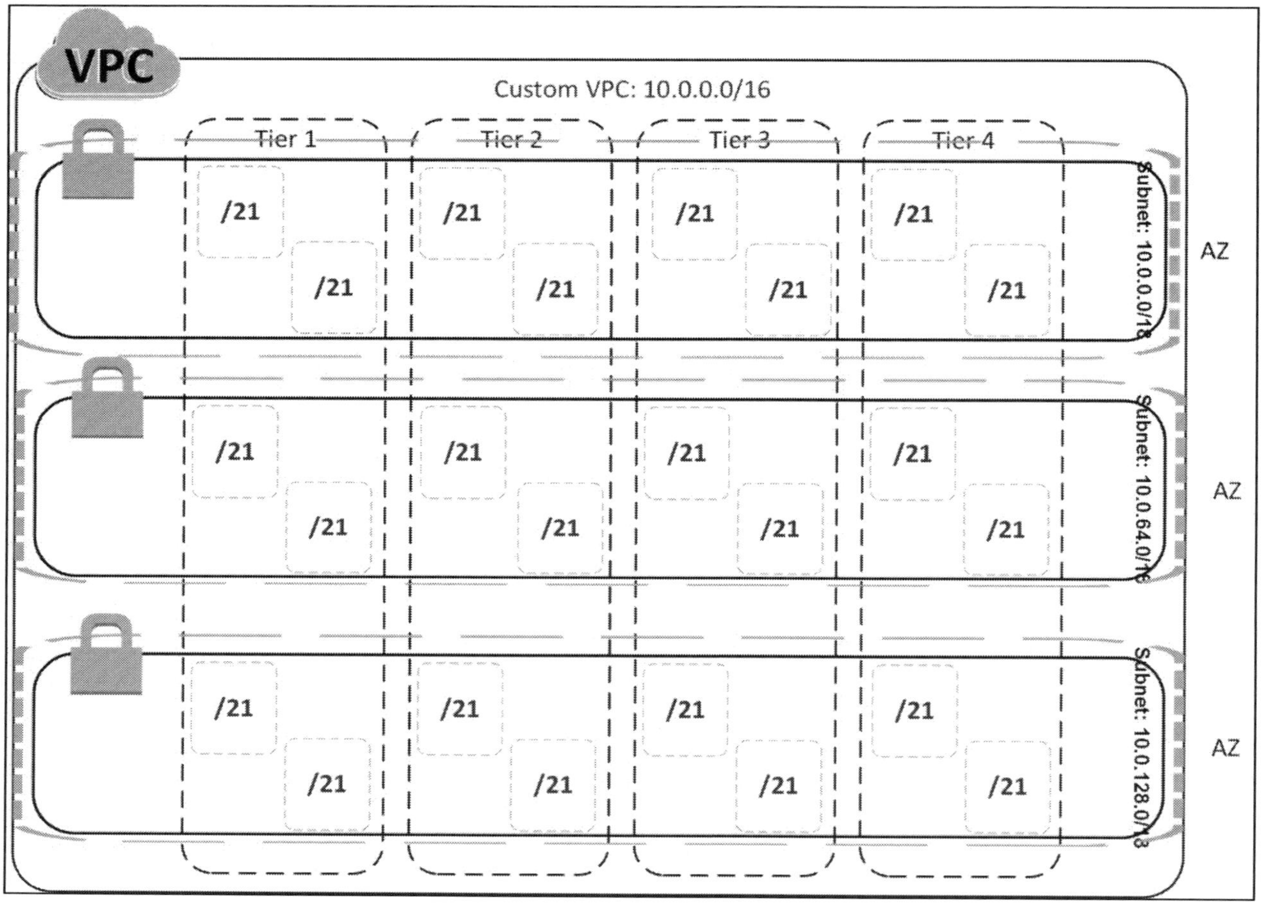

VPC

Custom VPC: 10.0.0.0/16

Tier 1 Tier 2 Tier 3 Tier 4

Subnet: 10.0.0.0/18 — AZ

Subnet: 10.0.64.0/18 — AZ

Subnet: 10.0.128.0/18 — AZ

Figure 3-04: Custom VPC Architecture

Deep Dive - VPC Router

VPC- the router is a logical component provided in VPC. For a functional VPC, it is the core component because without it, communication between local subnets is not possible. VPC routers are multiple devices that are operated at highly available situations. Each AZ or subnet has a logical device. VPC Routers interconnect all subnets and direct traffic between IGW, VGW, NAT gateways, and subnets. In each subnet CIDR block, the first four and the last one IP addresses are reserved. Meaning that these addresses are not available for you to use and these cannot be assigned to any instance. For example, in a subnet with CIDR block 10.0.0.0/20, the following five IP addresses are reserved:

- 10.0.0.0 - Network Address
- 10.0.0.1 – Reserved as the VPC router
- 10.0.0.2 – Reserved for mapping to the Amazon Provided DNS
- 10.0.0.3 – Reserved for future use

- 10.0.0.255 – It is the broadcast address. AWS does not support broadcast in a VPC. Therefore, this address is unavailable

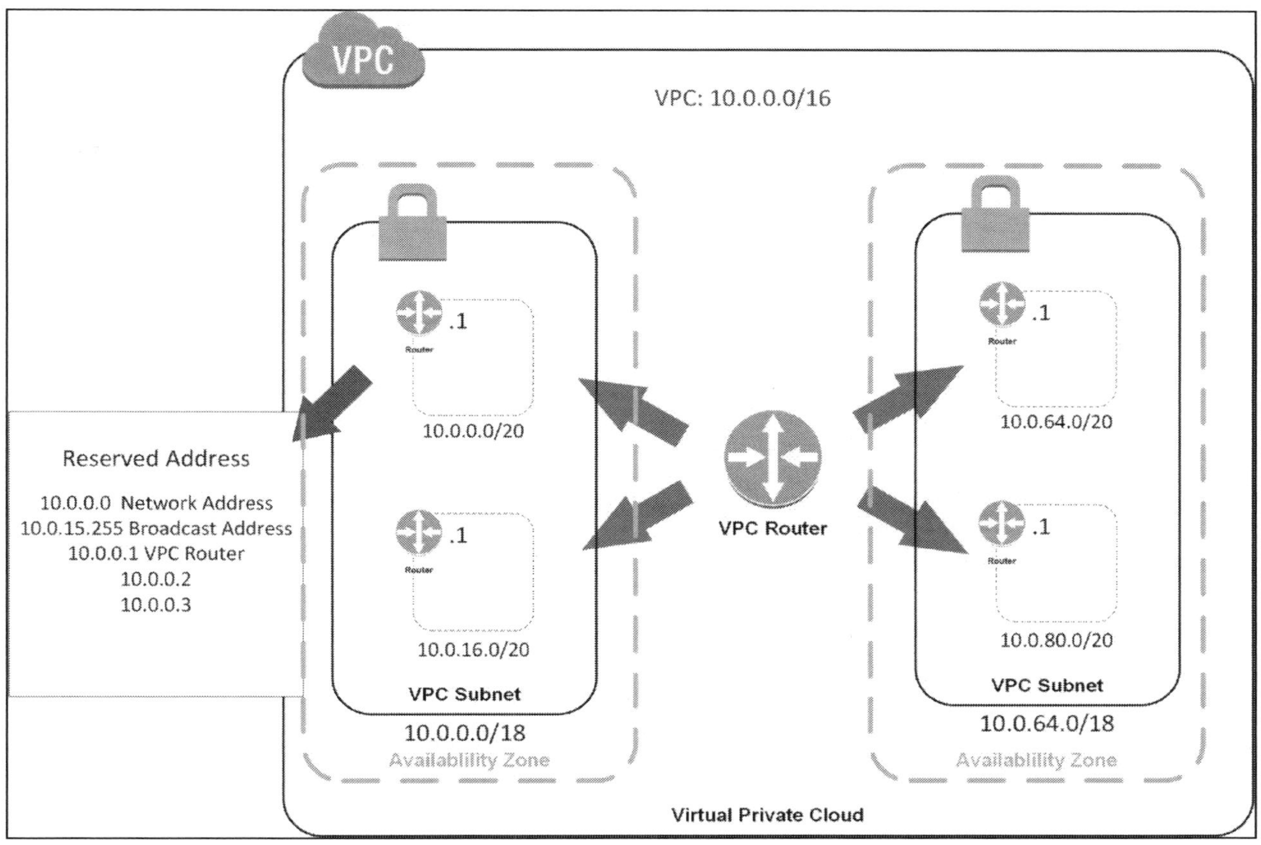

Figure 3-05: VPC Router

As you can see in the above figure (Figure: 3-05), .1 address is reserved for VPC instance or router in each subnet of VPC. This VPC needs to be available all the time or otherwise, VPC will not work as required. There are DHCP options set that are assigned to entire VPC. When an Amazon VPC is created, AWS automatically creates and associates DHCP options set with two options, Domain-Name-Servers (AmazonProvidedDNS) and Domain-Name (default domain name for the region).

DHCP service assigns internal addresses to the services within the subnet. With DHCP, Default Gateway and DNS is provided to the resources or instances. The default gateway provided in a subnet is always the VPC router. VPC router .1 interface is the first point, which hits whenever a packet is sent back and forth between subnets. VPC router is the default gateway for resources within the subnet. For understanding communication of VPC routers, you need to understand the route table.

Route table can be defined as a logical construct within a VPC that holds a set of routes called rules that are applied to the subnet. These rules determine the direction of network

traffic. A route table's rules permit EC2 instances within different subnets in a VPC to communicate with each other. You can add custom routes to the table as you are allowed to modify the route table. You can also use route tables to define which subnets are public (by directing internet traffic to the IGW) or private (by not routing the traffic to the IGW).

In each route table, there is a default route that cannot be modified or removed. It is called the local route that enables communication within the VPC. You can add additional routes to the table to direct the traffic to exit the VPC through Internet Gateway, the Virtual Private Gateway, or the NAT instance. When you do not add any specific route table to the subnet, then subnet uses the local route table. Default route table contains Destination address as VPC CIDR block and Target as local.

Destination	Target
10.0.0.0/16	Local

Table 3-01: Default Route Table

Each route in the route table particularizes a destination CIDR block and a target. The best practice is to create each subnet's specific route table. In this way, you have complete control over each subnet. For complex, hybrid, and on-premises architecture for network the route table per subnet is a better option.

Let us discuss VPC router communication with other VPC resources like VGW and IGW. VGW is used to communicate your VPC with the on-premises network by using VPN or DirectConnect while IGW is used to communicate you VPC with public AWS services or internet, it is at the edge of VPC. In the route table, we add destination 0.0.0.0/0 and target as IGW, which means that traffic that does not have any route will go towards the internet by using this route from the route table.

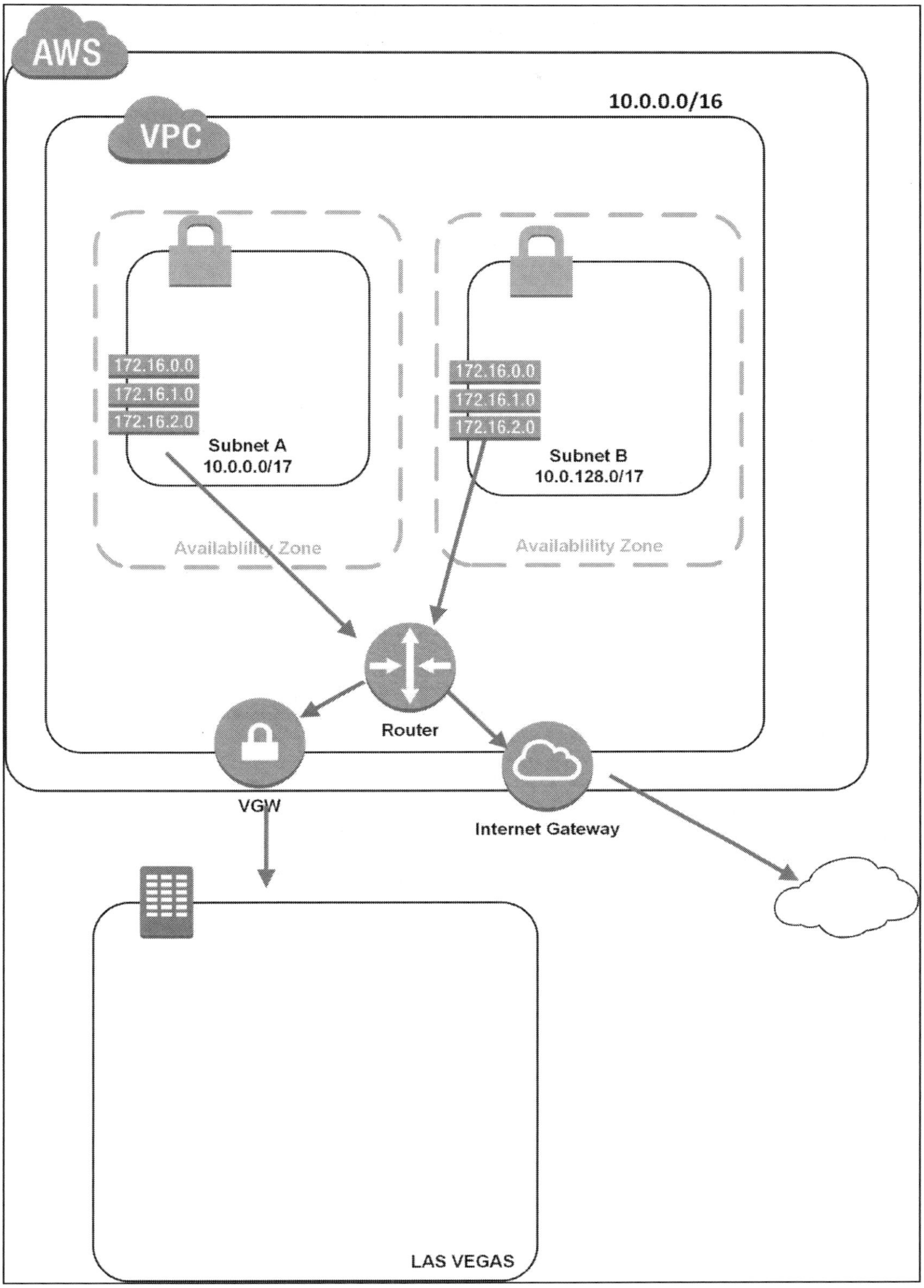

AWS
10.0.0.0/16
VPC
172.16.0.0
172.16.1.0
172.16.2.0
Subnet A
10.0.0.0/17
Availablility Zone
172.16.0.0
172.16.1.0
172.16.2.0
Subnet B
10.0.128.0/17
Availablility Zone
Router
VGW
Internet Gateway
LAS VEGAS

Figure 3-06: VPC Router Communication with other VPC Components

Deep Dive - ENI, Elastic IP and Internet Gateway (IGW)

Elastic Network Interface (ENI)

Elastic Network Interface is a virtual interface that can be attached to an instance in a VPC. ENIs are only available within a VPC and are associated with a subnet upon creation. When ENI is attached to the instance, it provides instance network connectivity. One instance has at least one ENI connected to it, but depending on the size of instance, the ENI can be more.

An ENI can include the following attributes:

- Primary private IPv4 address
- Secondary private IPv4 address(**es**)
- Elastic IP address per private IPv4 address and publically routable
- Public IPv4 address, which can be auto-assigned to the network interface for eth 0 when you launch an instance
- IPv6 address(**es**)
- Security groups
- MAC address
- Source/Destination check flag
- Description

If you assign a second network interface to an instance through an ENI, it will allow it to be dual-homed (network presence in different subnets). An ENI created independently of a specific instance exists irrespective of the lifetime of any instance to which it is attached.

ENI allows you to make a management network, use security appliances in VPC, create dual-homed instances with workloads on distinct subnets, or create a cost-effective highly available solution.

ENI attached to the instance at creation time works differently as compared to the ENI that is attached to the running instance.

When ENI is created with the instances, it is allocated with a primary ID, which cannot be changed. Secondary addresses can be allocated by explicitly specifying or auto allocating. Secondary addresses on externally created ENI can also be allocated automatically or by explicitly specifying. ENI on the instance is limited by machine type, not by ENI; that means the number of ENIs depend on the size of EC2 instances.

When an ENI is created with EC2 instance, a Dynamic, but non-elastic public IP address is also created. This address is not changeable later, and you cannot use this in externally

created ENIs. This Public IP address is allocated dynamically from AWS pool. If the instance is stopped or started, its public IP is changed.

As we know, ENIs also have the attributes of Elastic External IPs. If the Elastic External IP is attached with the primary interface of the instance, then it overwrites or replaces non-elastic public IP associated with an instance or an instance ENI.

ENI can be moved between instances within AZ, but you cannot move ENI to another AZ or subnet. ENI moved with MAC address, External IP address and internal IP address within AZ. Security Group in an ENI is attached to the network interface, not to the instance. If a Security Group is attached to the instance, it will be attached to the primary ENI of that instance.

Elastic IP Addresses (EIPs)

Elastic IP addresses are designed for dynamic cloud computing. These are static, public IPv4 addresses in the pool that AWS manages in each region. You can allocate an IP to your account from the pool (pull) or return it to the pool (release). EIPs allow you to sustain a set of IP addresses that remain embedded even if the basic system might be changed over time.

The critical points to understand EIPs for the exam are:

- First, allocate an EIP to use within a VPC and then assign it to an instance.
- EIPs are region-specific, that is, an EIP in one region cannot be assigned to an instance within a VPC in a different region.
- Network interfaces and EIPs have a one-to-one relationship.
- EIPs can be moved from one instance to another, either in the same VPC or in a different VPC within the same region.
- EIPs remain associated with your AWS account; you must explicitly remove them.

EIPs are billed when they are allocated to your account, even when they are not associated with a resource.

Internet Gateway (IGW)

Internet Gateway (IGW) is a highly available, horizontally scaled and redundant component of VPC that allows communication between the instances in VPC and the internet. An IGW performs Network Address Translation (NAT) for instances that have been assigned public IP addresses and provides a target in the route table for internet routable traffic. IGW is a region-level and highly available networking construct.

EC2 instances that are residing inside an Amazon VPC are only aware of their private IP addresses. When an instance sends traffic to the internet, the IGW translates the reply

address to the instance's Elastic IP (EIP) address and maintains the map for the instance's public and private addresses. When the instance receives traffic from the internet, the IGW translates the destination address (instance's Public IP) to the internet's private IP and routes the traffic to the Amazon VPC.

IGW aims to give an inbound VPC resource the access to the public resource that may be public internet or AWS public resources. The traffic from the instances goes to the Internet Gateway via VPC router. To direct the route, we need to modify the route table as we discussed earlier, or attach individual route table to each subnet.

Therefore, it is concluded that Internet Gateway only works if the instance has public IP and subnet or instances inside the subnet has a valid route to IGW.

To create a public subnet with internet access, you must do the followings:

- Attach an Internet Gateway to your VPC
- Create a subnet rule to route all non-local traffic to the IGW
- Configure network ACL and security groups to allow relevant traffic to and from the internet

To enable an EC2 instance to send/receive traffic from the internet:

- Assign a public IP address or Elastic IP address

You can spread the route to all destinations not specifically known to the route table, or you can span the route to a smaller range of IPs. The following diagram (Figure 3-07) shows a VPC with a subnet, route table, an internet gateway, and an EC2 instance with a private and an elastic IP address.

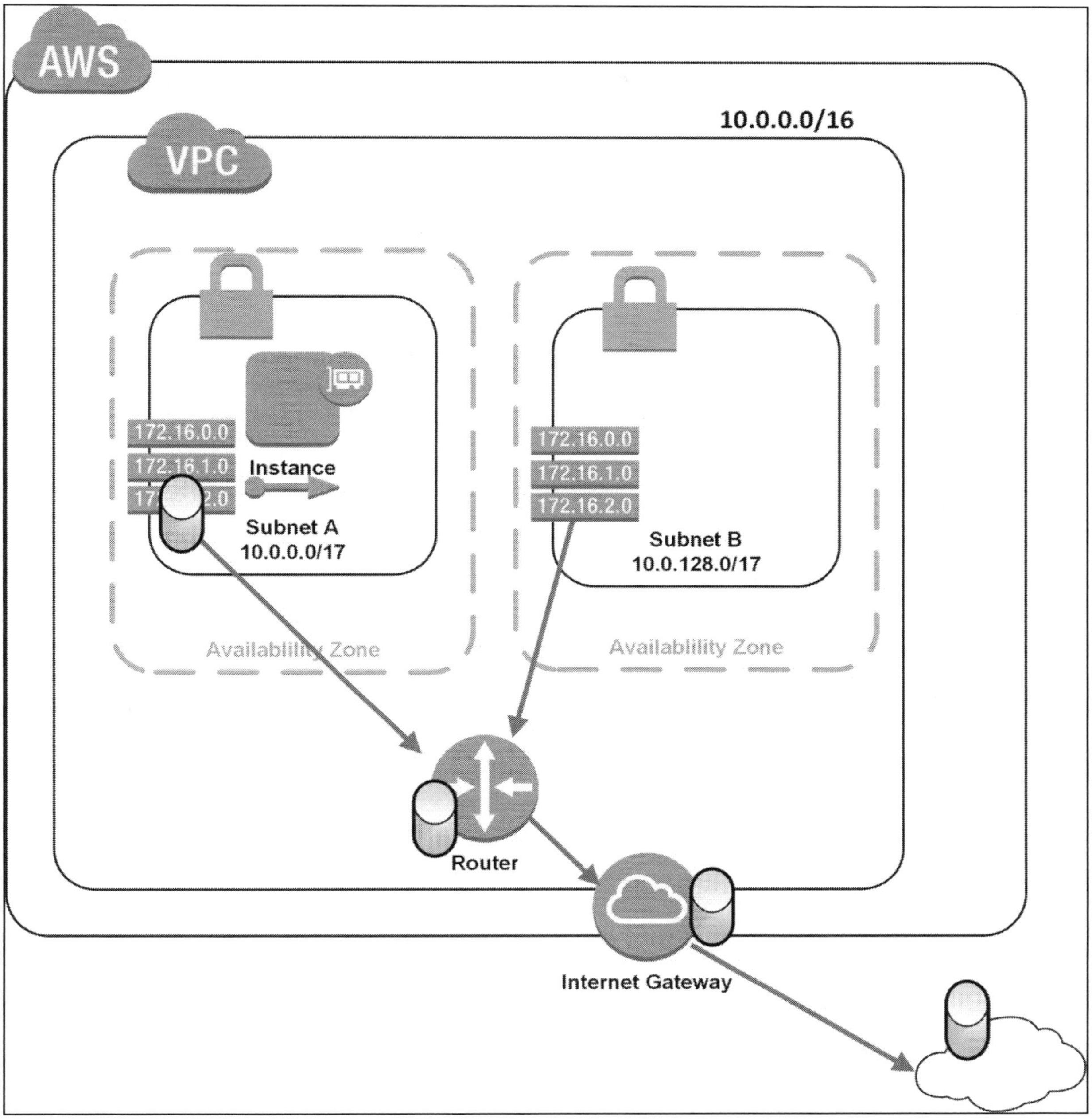

AWS
VPC
10.0.0.0/16
172.16.0.0
172.16.1.0
Instance
Subnet A
10.0.0.0/17
Availablility Zone
172.16.0.0
172.16.1.0
172.16.2.0
Subnet B
10.0.128.0/17
Availablility Zone
Router
Internet Gateway

Figure 3-07: Basic Internet Gateway Architecture

Single Design

Consider a VPC, which has two AZs, and we have two-zone architectures, which are application and management. Each zone has one subnet in each AZ. Overall we have 4 subnets. There is VPC router, which performs routing as well as connectivity towards IGW. There are two instances, one is primary and the other is back up. These instances sit in the middle of subnets because these instances are dual-homed/ multi-home instances, when you connect two ENIs to each instance. One ENI is in public and the other one is in

private subnet. A public subnet is an application, and private subnet is management. Security Groups are linked to ENI, not to the instance. Hence, we must create two Security Groups; one for management and the other for the application.

Application Security Group allows incoming traffic path on the port of application users while management security group allows only app service on port TCP 22 from a corporate address range. Now create elastic IP and attach it to the public interface of the primary instance. Now via IGW, any internet user can connect to the primary instance through this Elastic IP.

On the backend, support staff can access application backend instance via DirectConnect or VPN from on-premises. In this architecture, by using Elastic IP, we design portable endpoint for incoming traffic, as we can move Elastic IP to another instance and then traffic will shift towards that ENI.

Deep Dive - Security Group and NACL

In this portion of the chapter, we will discuss core network security constructs within AWS. Both of them are operating at different layers. In Amazon Virtual Private Cloud (VPC), there two ways to connect your VPC to a corporate network: VPG and CGW. A Virtual Private Gateway (VPG) is the Amazon VPC side of a VPN connection between the two networks. In the figure 3-08, a VPG is used as ingress and egress point for corporate datacenter, while IGW is used as communication with public endpoints. Now consider two subnets inside a VPC on each AZ and a VPC router, which routes traffic between egress points and subnets using route table. In both subnets, there are EC2 instances. A Security Group is an object-based filter (this will be discussed in detail later on).

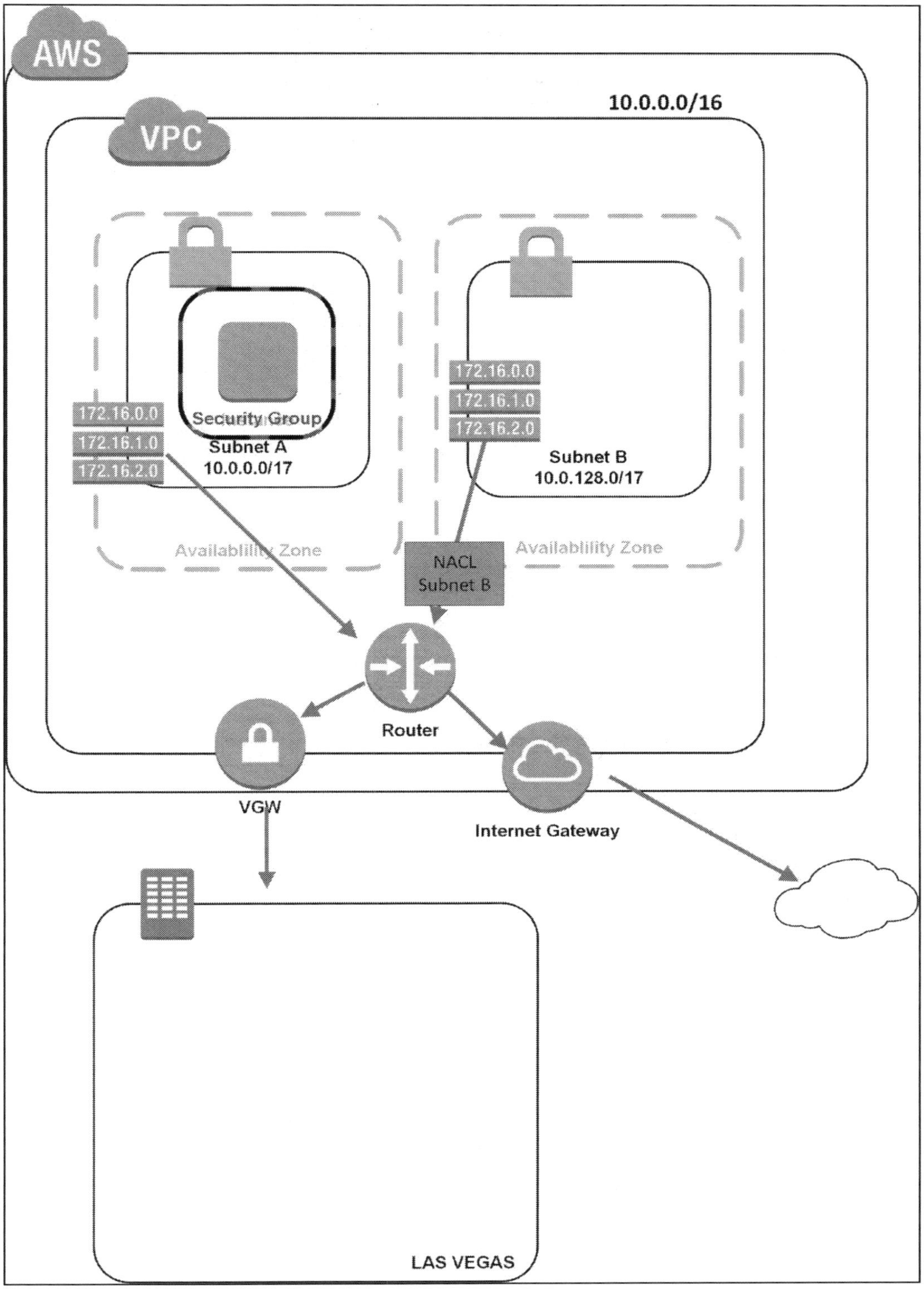

Figure 3-08: Security Group and NACL in VPC

Security Groups

A Security Group acts like a firewall that manages inbound and outbound traffic of your instances and other AWS resources. When you launch an EC2 instance in a VPC, you can assign at most five Security Groups to that instance. If an instance is launched without specifying a security group, then it will be launched into the default Security Group for Amazon VPC. The default Security Group allows all communication inside the security group and allows all outbound traffic. You can modify the default Security Group, but you cannot delete it. When you assign a Security Group, it is wrapped-up around the object on which it is applied. SG can also be added to the group of the instance to apply a set of rules to multiple things. SG is applied to ENI that is attached to an instance in VPC. As we discussed multi-home instance earlier, SG can also be applied to multi-home instances that have separate subnets.

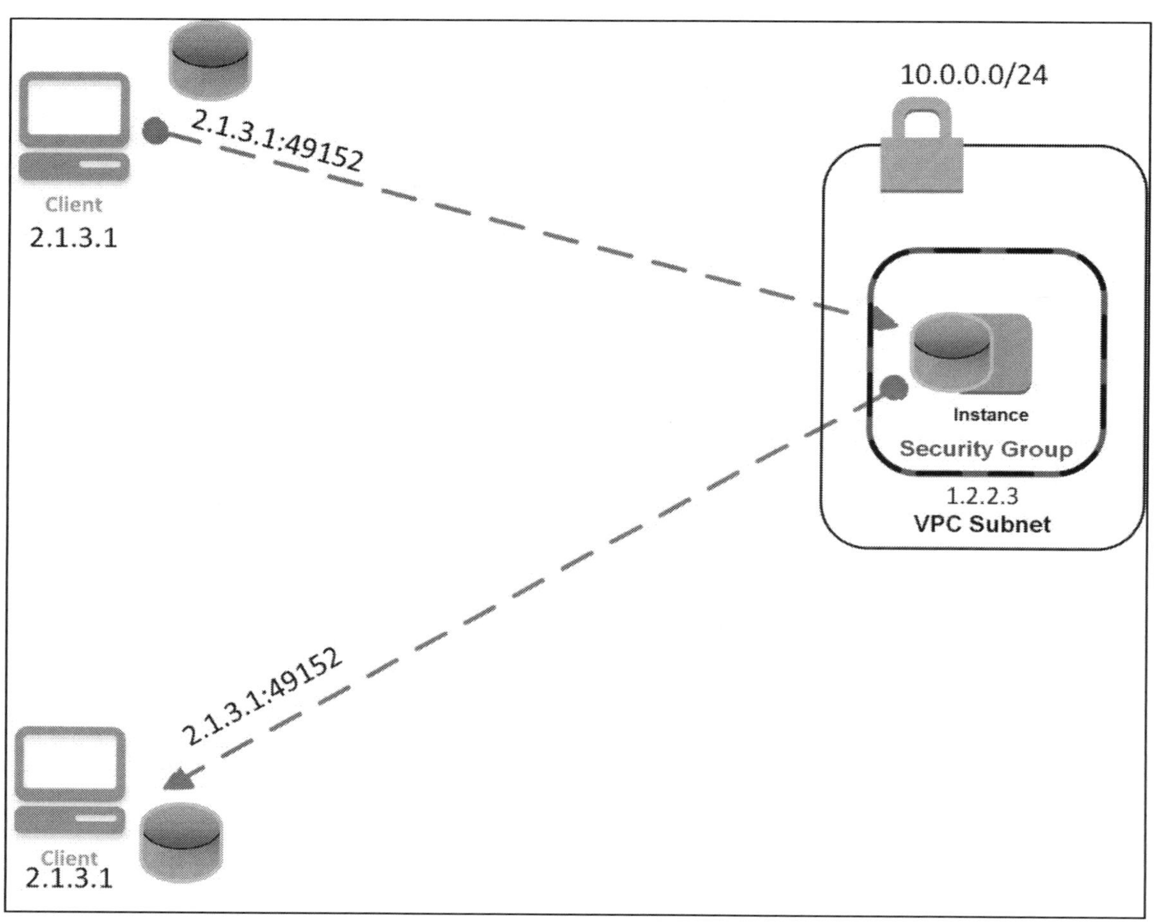

Figure 3-09: Example of Security Group Architecture

EXAM TIP: Security Groups act at the instance level, not the subnet level.

In SG, you cannot define "deny" option to specific IP addresses or CIDR ranges. It has only "allow" option, but it has implicit deny option if you do not set any allow rule then

it's by default deny. In default SG, all outbound traffic is allowed. In default SG, when you create with an object, no incoming rule is defined, so it is by default "deny" and all outgoing traffic is allowed. SG is stateful, so once you define the inbound rule and for the response, it automatically creates an outbound rule independent of what is defined in that outbound rule. There is no concept of the ephemeral port.

Inbound			
Source	Protocol	Port range	Comments
0.0.0.0/0	TCP	80	Allows inbound traffic to port 80 from the internet
Your public IP range	TCP	22	Allows SSH traffic from the company network
Your public IP range	TCP	3389	Allows RDP traffic from the company network
Outbound			
Destination	Protocol	Port range	Comments
Security Group ID of your MySQL database server	TCP	3306	Allows outbound MySQL access to instances in the specified security group
Security Group ID of your MS SQL database server	TCP	1433	Allows outbound Microsoft SQL server access to instances in the specified security group

Table 3-02: Security Group Set of Rules

Consider you have one web server instance and multiple management instances. In a Security Group, you have an option to create one management SG and add all management instances in it and then allow that SG in Web server SG inbound rule. Therefore, it is easier to handle rather than using NACL, which gives all instances

equivalent access in the web server instance subnet. You can also define instance ID in SG. Hence, if an instance IP changes, it does not affect the working of SG as it uses the instance ID rather than IP. From figure 3-10, you can understand that in this way, management SG has a right to access Web server instance whenever it needs to add an instance in its SG.

Similarly, if you have a list of Active Directory and a large number of instances, and you need to define separate rules for both incoming and outgoing traffic; then it's better to use Security Group. In the Security Group, you define all rules and add the instances in that, so you do not need to manage the complexity of defining separate rules on each instance. In that SG, you define source and destination, so that if this Security Group attaches to another machine, it can also communicate to the instances or any other machine on which Active directory port is attached. This means that all machines in the security group can communicate with each other as well.

In a VPC, default SG itself is defined in incoming traffic, which means that all machines in VPC have open communication.

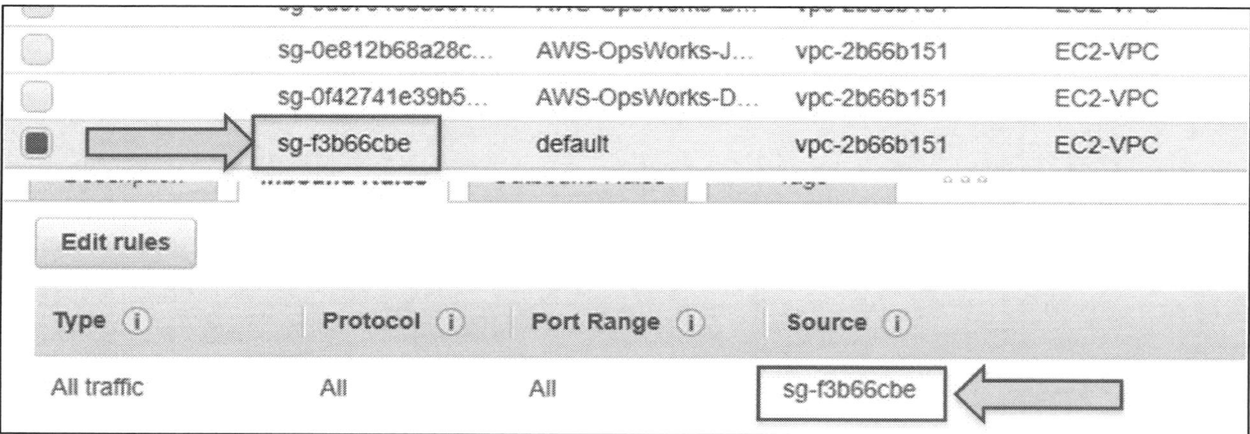

Figure 3-10: Default Security Group

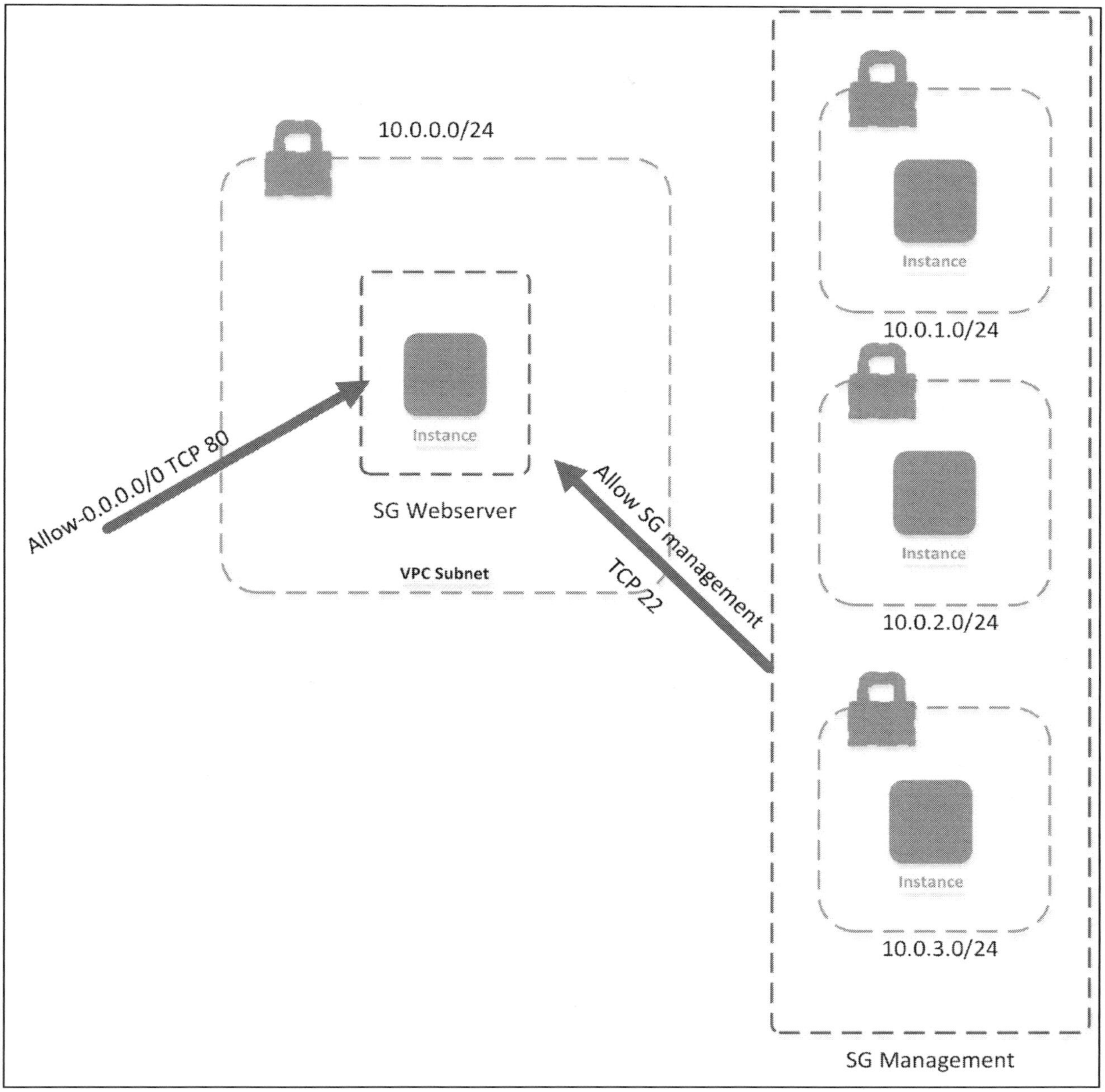

10.0.0.0/24
Instance
SG Webserver
VPC Subnet
Allow-0.0.0.0/0 TCP 80
Allow SG management
TCP 22
Instance
10.0.1.0/24
Instance
10.0.2.0/24
Instance
10.0.3.0/24
SG Management

Figure 3-11: Example of a Security Group inside VPC

The following points are essential to understand for the exam:

- You can add up to fifty inbound and fifty outbound rules to each SG.
- If you need to apply more than a hundred rules to an instance, you can attach at most five Security Groups with every one network interface.
- You can designate "allow" rules but not "deny" rules. This is a critical difference between security groups and ACLs.
- You can specify different rules for inbound and outbound traffic.

- By default, inbound traffic is not allowed until you add inbound rules to the Security Group.
- By default, new security groups have an outbound rule that allows all outbound traffic. You can remove the rule and add outbound rules that allow specific outbound traffic only.
- Security groups are stateful. This means that responses to allow inbound traffic is permitted to flow outbound regardless of outbound rules and vice versa. This is an essential difference between Security Groups and ACLs.
- Instances attached with the same Security Group cannot talk to each other unless you add rules to allow it (with the exception being the default Security Group).
- You can change the Security Groups with which an instance is associated after launch, and the changes will take effect immediately.

Network Access Control Lists (ACL)

Network Access Control List (ACL) is an extra optional layer of security that acts as a stateless firewall on subnet level. An ACL is used to control in and out traffic of one or more subnets. You can set up a network ACL to add an extra layer of security to your instances in a VPC. ACL is a numbered set of rules that AWS assesses in order. It starts with the lowest numbered rule to determine whether the in and out traffic is allowed for any subnet that is associated with this ACL. Upon creation of a VPC, a default network ACL is generated, which you can modify. This single NACL can be applied to many different subnets. This default ACL allows all inbound and outbound traffic. When you create a custom ACL, its default configuration will deny all traffic until you create rules that allow otherwise. Network ACLs are set up in the similar way you do for your Security Groups. Every subnet in your VPC must be associated with a network ACL. NACL process the traffic before it leaves or enters in the subnet as it is at subnet level. By using NACL, you can provide an advanced level of security to all instances in the subnet. Therefore, a subnet has only one NACL at a time.

In NACL we can apply the rules to the traffic depending on the action that is either allowed or denied. In NACL, rules are assigned to a specific number. When a packet matches, the process is stopped and action is applied (either allow or deny). At the end of each rule, there is a mandatory rule, which cannot be edited or removed. This rule in custom NACL denies all traffic to and from any resource that is mentioned in table below with blue. For an incoming packet, it is the source, and for an outgoing packet, it is a destination address.

Rule#	Type	Protocol	Port Range	Source	Allow/Deny
100	SSH	TCP	22	0.0.0.0/0	Allow
200	HTTP	TCP	80	1.1.2.9	Deny
300	HTTP	TCP	80	0.0.0.0/0	Allow
*	All Traffic	All	All	0.0.0.0/0	Deny

Table 3-03: NACL Table

Consider an example of two packets; one packet is http 3.2.3.2 and other is http 1.1.2.9. When a packet enters in a subnet, which has NACL. First, it checks the 1st rule, which does not match as it is for SSH. Then it goes to the 2nd rule, which matches for the second packet and if this rule denies that packet, it will not allow that packet to enter. Now the third rule checks again for the first packet, and here if it allows the packet that is coming from any source, this packet may enter in the subnet. If this rule does not match, then it checks for the mandatory rule and applies the action of Deny.

Ephemeral Port

The ephemeral port is the port that is chosen by the client when it wants to initiate a request to the instances in a VPC. The range of these ports depends on the Client OS. Using this port, the request is generated to the destination address, or in response to this request, sent outside the VPC to the client address on an ephemeral port.

OS	Ephemeral port	Selection method
IOS	49152-65535	TCP sequential-UDP random
Linux	32768-61000	Random
Free BSD	10000-65535	random

Table 3-04: Ephemeral Port

Consider that a client sends a request to the web server in a VPC then it chooses an ephemeral port and sends a request to web server address on port 80. In response to that request, a separate outbound rule is needed to be defined, as NACL is stateless. In that request, we define a destination as a client on ephemeral port selected by the client. So, we have to define two rules separately in inbound and outbound for full communication.

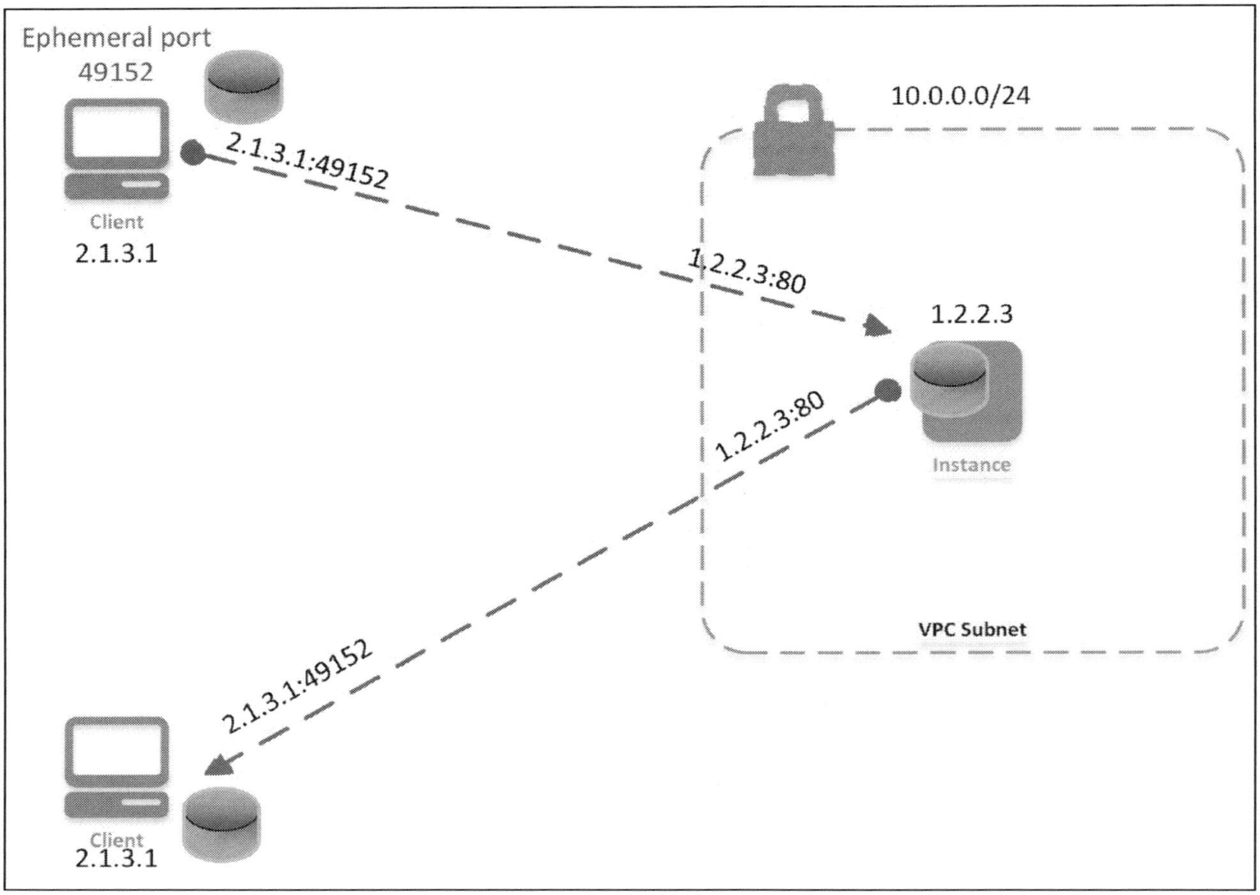

Figure 3-12: Example of NACL inside VPC

Inbound rule for example:

Rule #	Type	Protocol	Port range	Source	Allow/Deny
100	HTTP	TCP	80	0.0.0.0/0	Allow
140	Custom TCP	TCP	32768-65535	0.0.0.0/0	Allow

Table 3-05: Inbound Rule in NACL

The outbound rule for example:

Rule #	Type	Protocol	Port range	Destination	Allow/Deny
100	HTTP	TCP	80	0.0.0.0/0	Allow
120	Custom TCP	TCP	32768-65535	0.0.0.0/0	Allow

Table 3-06: Outbound Rule in NACL

Security Group	Network ACL
Operates at the instance level	Operates at the subnet level
Supports allow rules only	Supports both allow and deny rules
Stateful: Return traffic is automatically allowed, irrespective of any rule	Stateless: Return traffic must be allowed by the rule set
AWS evaluates all rules before determining whether to allow traffic	AWS evaluates rules in number order when determining whether to allow traffic
Applied to independent instances	Automatically applied to all instances in the connected subnets

Table 3-07: Comparison of SG and ACL

Deep Dive - Network Address Translation (NAT) Gateways

NAT is generally a concept of changing source private IP address into a public IP address that is routable. NAT has a record of private to public address translation that is helpful for response purpose as well like if some instance in private subnet sends request to internet for patch then NAT gateway changes instance private IP with Public and brings it to the internet, and then get a patch from the internet and returns it to that instance by changing that object's public address into its respective private IP. Any instance that you launch in a private subnet inside a VPC is unable to communicate with the internet through the Internet Gateway. This could be a problem if the instances need to access the internet from the VPC to download patches, apply security updates or update application software. To resolve this issue, AWS offers NAT (Network Address Translation) instances and gateways to allow such privately deployed instances to gain access to the internet. The NAT gateway provides better availability and higher bandwidth and requires less administration than NAT instances.

NAT Instance:

NAT (Network Address Translation) instance is an Amazon Linux AMI. These instances are designed to accept traffic from instances that are inside a private subnet. To forward

the accepted traffic to the IGW, the NAT instance translates the source IP to the public IP of the NAT instance. Additionally, the NAT instance keeps track of the forwarded traffic to return response traffic from the internet to the appropriate instance in the private subnet. NAT instances can be searched in the EC2 console by their identifier string: *"amzn-ami-vpc-nat"*.

To Make Internet Accessible for Instances Inside a Private Subnet:

- Create a Security Group for the NAT for outbound traffic rules that identify the needed Internet resources by port, protocol, and IP address.
- Launch a Linux NAT AMI as an instance in a public subnet and associate it with the NAT Security Group that is recently created.
- Disable the Source/Destination Check attribute of the NAT.
- Configure the route table attached with a private subnet to direct Internet-bound traffic to the NAT instance.
- Allocate an Elastic IP and associate it with the NAT instance.

The above configuration enables instances that are in private subnets to send outbound Internet communication, but it prevents these instances from receiving inbound traffic forwarded by someone on the Internet.

Consider an example in which you have two AZs with 2 subnets in each. In both AZs' private subnets, there are instances that need to communicate with the internet. So, we have NAT instance in public subnet in one AZ and add a rule for communication. If NAT instance subnet fails, then problems occur. To overcome the problem, create another NAT instance in another AZ and add route towards that. Now, each AZ has its own NAT instance on which their specific private instance is routed. Now, if the NAT instance in one AZ fails, that AZ's private instance does not communicate over the internet as its route table only route private instance traffic towards its own NAT instance. In this way, you need to add some logical configuration that automatically shifts traffic to the available NAT instance, but it has some limitations; like if an instance in private subnet increases, then NAT instance capability of compute decreases. Therefore, in the case where rapid scaling is used or elasticity is needed, NAT instances are not good; hence we have NAT gateway.

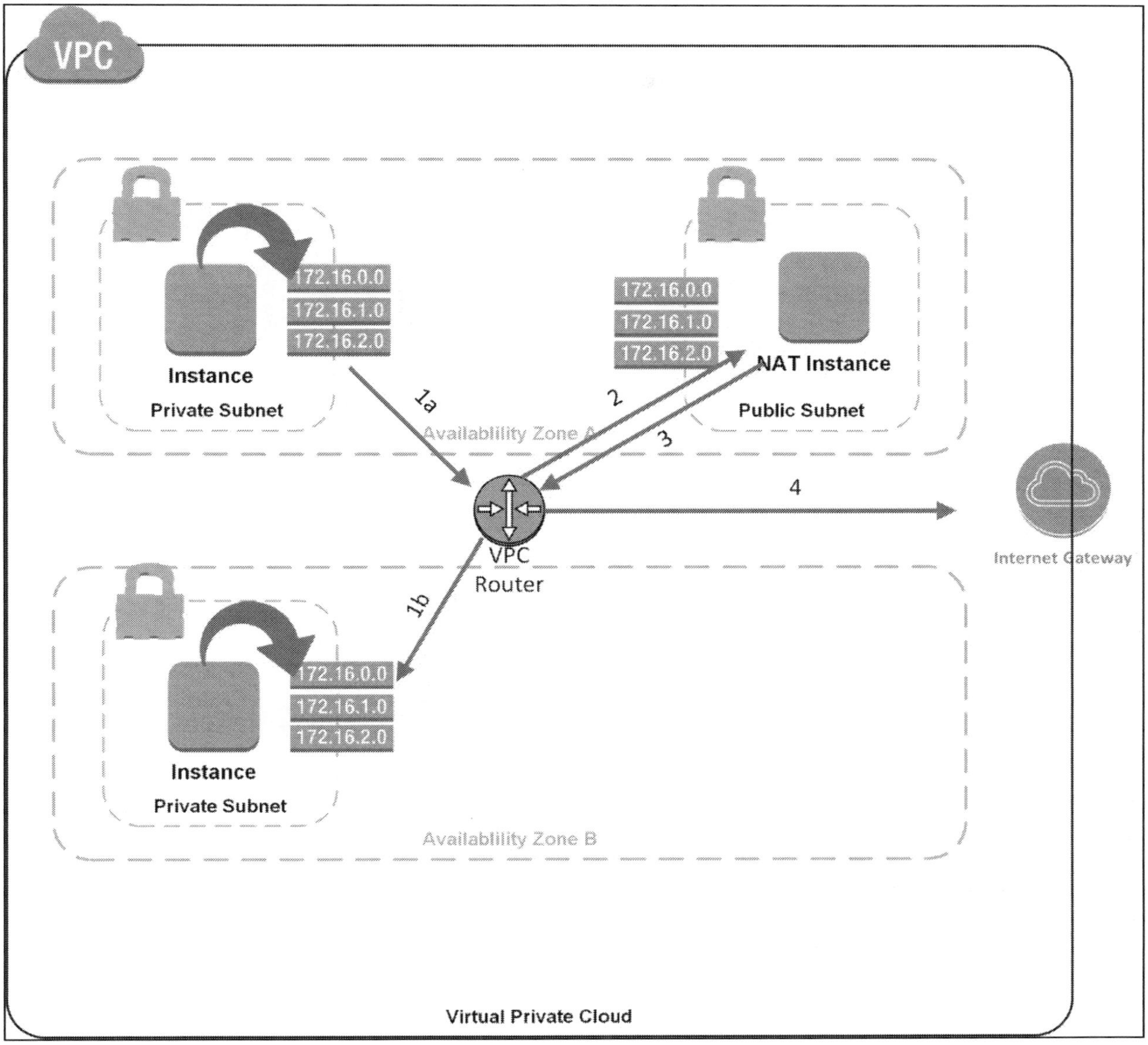

VPC
172.16.0.0
172.16.1.0
172.16.2.0
Instance
Private Subnet
1a
Availability Zone A
172.16.0.0
172.16.1.0
172.16.2.0
2
NAT Instance
Public Subnet
3
4
VPC
Router
Internet Gateway
1b
172.16.0.0
172.16.1.0
172.16.2.0
Instance
Private Subnet
Availability Zone B
Virtual Private Cloud

Figure 3-13: Single NAT Instance Architecture

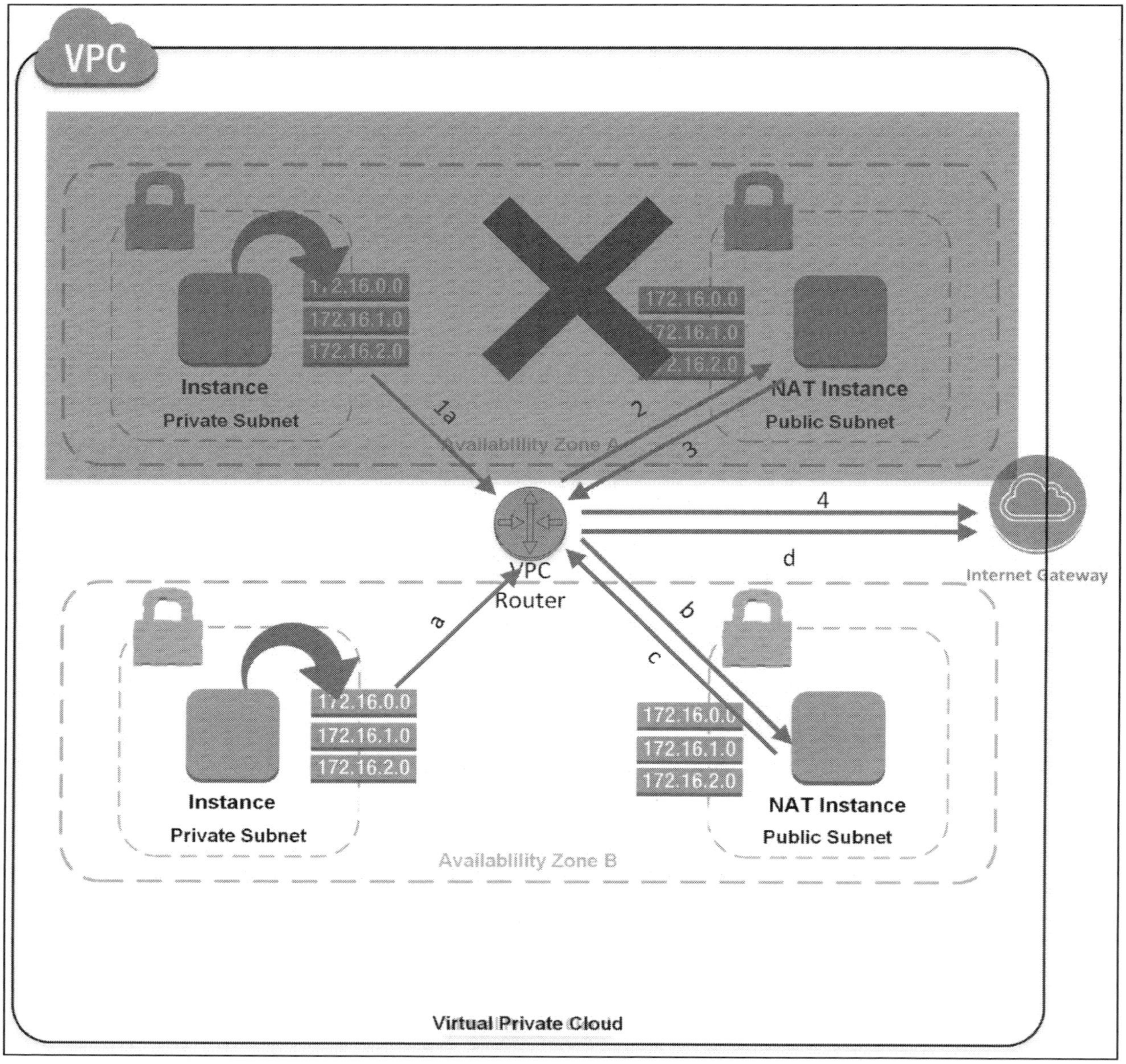

Figure 3-14: Multi NAT Instance Architecture

NAT Gateway

NAT gateways are AWS managed resources that are operated similarly as NAT instances but are more straightforward to manage. These gateways are highly available inside an Availability Zone.

To enable instances that are in a Private Subnet to access the Internet resources via an IGW through a NAT Gateway:

- Configure the route table attached to the private subnet to direct Internet-bound traffic to the NAT gateway.
- Allocate an Elastic IP and associate it with the NAT gateway.
- Now, you have to give reference of level endpoint ID, which you can edit to subnet route tables that we see in NAT instance.

Like a NAT instance, this managed service allows outbound Internet communication and prevents the instances from receiving inbound traffic sent by someone on the Internet. When using NAT gateway, you have intra AZ resiliency or inter AZ's resiliency. NAT gateway is fully elastic and it grows and shrinks with ease; there is no limitation on it. It supports up to 45Gbps scaling. If you require more than that, then you can allocate multiple NAT gateways and distribute allocations across it.

Billing of NAT gateway is charged per gigabyte on per gateway. There is the concept of bastion host, which is used to access private machine within a VPC for administrative purpose. But this bastion host concept is for NAT instance, not for NAT gateway. In NAT gateway, the Security Group is not associated with it because the Security Group is attached to the instance. For controlling the traffic to and from the subnet in which NAT gateway is present, you can use NACL, or you can use a Security Group that is applied to the instance behind NAT gateway, but it is less flexible.

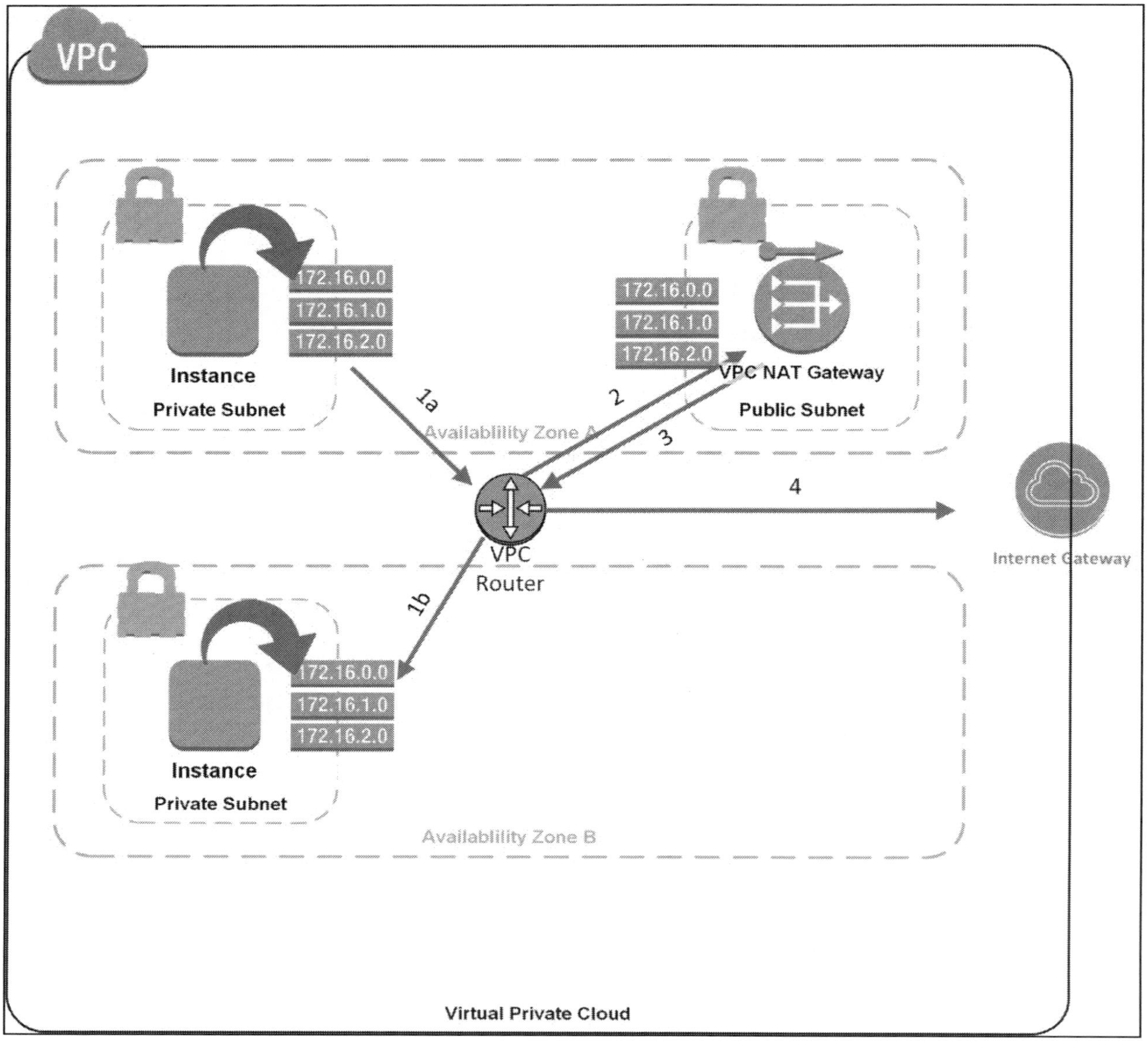

Figure 3-15: Single NAT Gateway Architecture

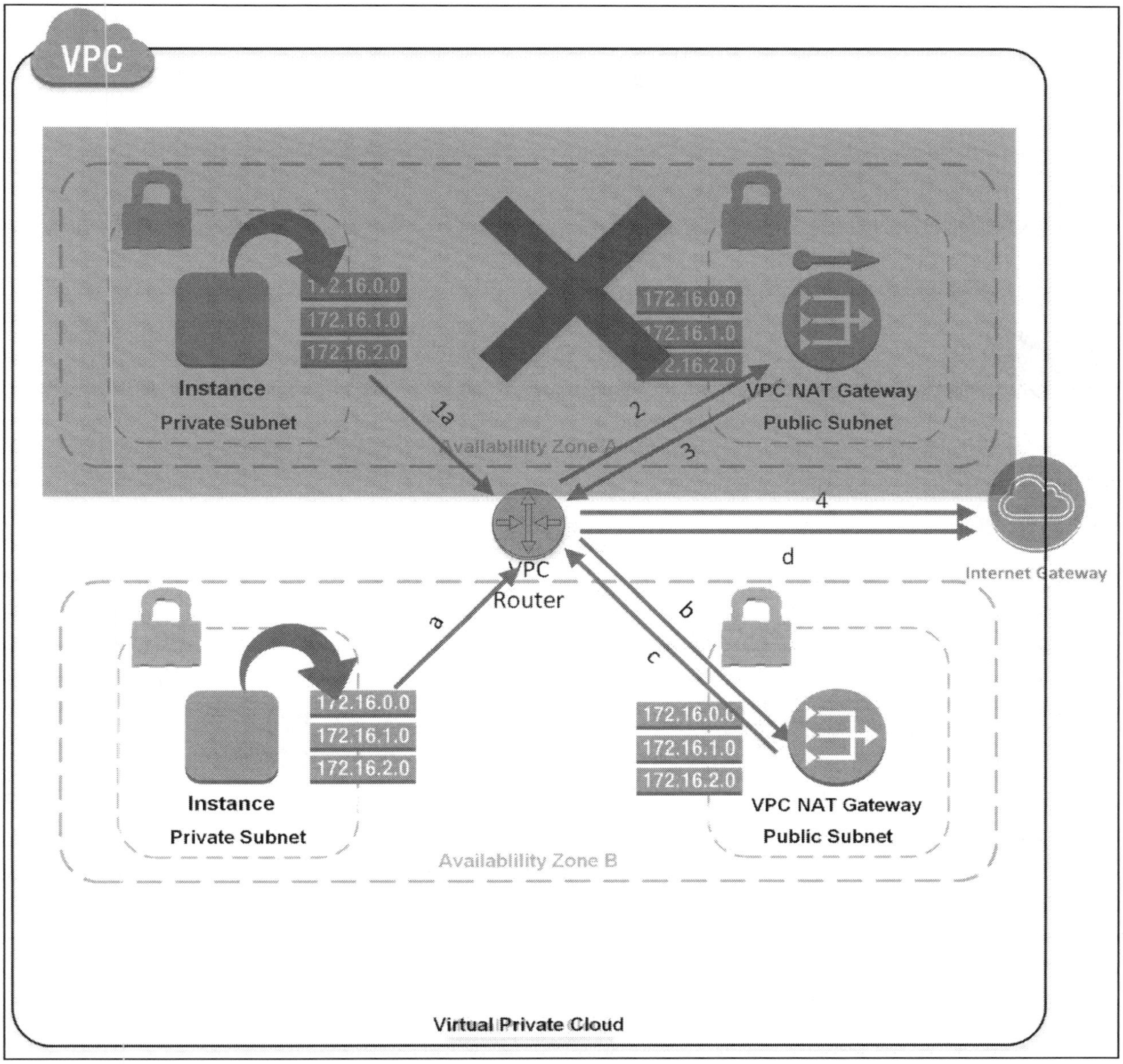

Figure 3-16: Multi NAT Gateway Architecture

EXAM TIP: To create an architecture that is independent of Availability Zones, create a NAT gateway in each Availability Zone and configure your route table to make sure that the resources are using the NAT gateway in the same Availability Zone.

Deep Dive - Virtual Private Gateway (VGW)

Amazon Virtual Private Cloud (VPC) provides two ways to connect your VPC to a corporate network: VGW and CGW.

You can connect an actual datacenter to your VPC using either software or hardware VPN connections. This will make your VPC an extension of the data center.

A Virtual Private Gateway (VGW) is the Amazon VPC side of a VPN connection between the two networks. VGW is same as IGW. You can associate one VGW per VPC, and you have a limit of 5 VGW per region. You can change this limit by sending a ticket to AWS support. VGW is highly available by design. When VPN is created, multiple VPN endpoints are connected to VGW, which means that anything attached to VGW can connect to multiple IP endpoints.

A Customer Gateway (CGW) is your side of a VPN connection between the two networks. A CGW can be a hardware device or a software application.

If you have a VPC and your corporate Data center, place VGW in VPC while CGW in Corporate network then, create a VPN for connecting the on-premises network to VPC. This connection is a connection to VPN endpoint, which is a part of VGW.

VGW knows about both network information; VPC and the corporate network.

Following are the critical points to understand VPGs, CGWs, and VPNs for the exam:

- The VPG is the AWS side of the VPN tunnel.
- The CGW is the user-end of the VPN tunnel. It can be a hardware device or a software application.
- You must create the VPN tunnel between the CGW and the VPG.
- VPGs support both dynamic routings with BGP and static routing.
- The VPN connection consists of two tunnels for higher availability to the VPC.

Consider an example for communication of corporate datacenter to the component of VPC.

- First, route traffic from a data center to CGW to communicate to an instance inside VPC beyond VPN peer. The CGW only knows about that instance because of BGP or static route sharing between CGW and VGW.
- The data from CGW is sent to VGW through VPN with encryption.
- At VGW packet is removed from encapsulation and decrypted.
- VGW sends data to the VPC router.
- Then at last, packet is sent to the instance in the subnet by the information it has in it.
- Likewise, in reverse order, first packet from instance is sent to VPC router then, router checks the route table attached to that subnet to identify the ID of VGW to send data to the corporate data center.
- VPC router sends data to VGW.

- VGW encapsulates and encrypts the data and forwards it to the CGW.
- CGW decrypts and removes encapsulation and forwards it to the server or data center. In case of using VGW, you need to define specific subnet and prefixes that are used in corporate network in the route tables of subnets.

As we know that traffic from VPC routes towards corporate network, you can define it manually in route table by adding a rule in which VGW is defined as target and IP address of corporate network as a destination. However, you have another option of route propagation, which propagates the route by dynamically adding to the route table that is attached to the VGW. Then again, in this propagation, some critical things need to be understood.

- It does not overlap the local route, which is already defined in the route table.
- Static routes are also not overlapped.
- The path defined by DirectConnect or VPN then read after local routes.

VGW also has the capability that it can connect to multiple CGWs on multiple VPN connections.

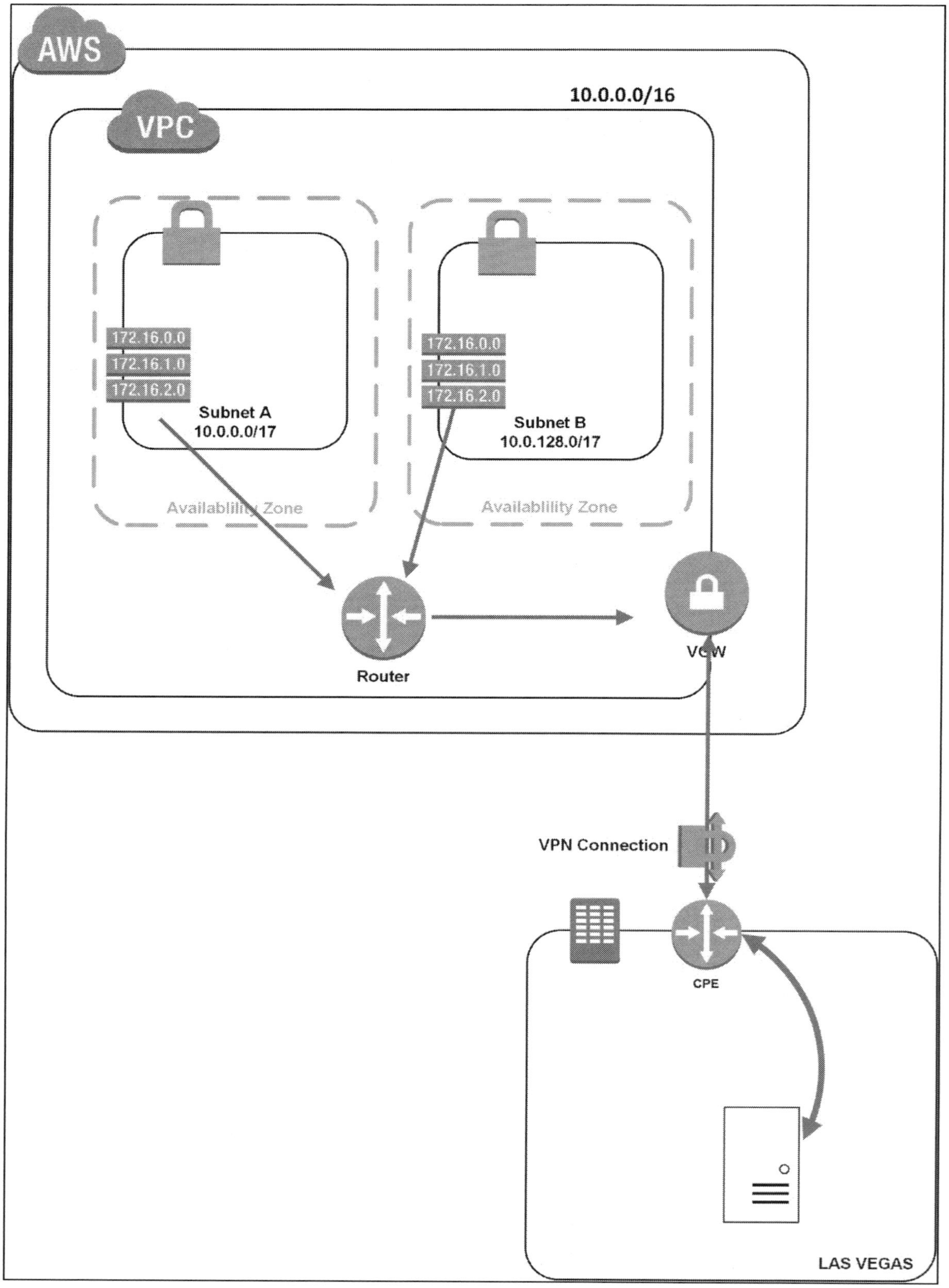

AWS

VPC

10.0.0.0/16

172.16.0.0
172.16.1.0
172.16.2.0

Subnet A
10.0.0.0/17

172.16.0.0
172.16.1.0
172.16.2.0

Subnet B
10.0.128.0/17

Availablility Zone

Availablility Zone

Router

VGW

VPN Connection

CPE

LAS VEGAS

Figure 3-17: VPN Architecture

Subnet Architecture Types

There are multiple types of subnets inside a VPC. We will discuss them in detail.

- **Private Subnet** is a type of subnet in which the traffic does not route towards IGW. It has its route table through which it can communicate to all subnets inside VPC by default. They can communicate or access on-premises or hybrid network via VGW by using VPN or DirectConnect. A private subnet can also connect to other VPCs' subnet via VPC peering. Private does not have any route towards the internet, and it also does not have public IP. Hence, for communication with public entities, private subnet use NAT instance or NAT gateway.
- **VPC-Only Subnet** is another type of subnet, which is more restrictive. It has a dedicated route table. In this route table, only local entries are defined. So it is only capable of connecting to its VPC public and private subnet. It does not use AWS public endpoints, but it uses private endpoints. If the instances in that subnet need to perform software updates, then it is only possible if its VPC has software update server inside VPC.
- **VPN-Only Subnet** is only used in those case when you want an extension of your datacenter on AWS or for auditing and security compliance capability. With this type of subnet, there is no concept of the public subnet. The only route is to the corporate network via VGW. There are no local routes defined in this.
- **Public Subnet** is another architecture type of subnet whose dedicated route table is defined towards IGW. It provides all services inside it; a public address and public access to all AWS public endpoints and internet. They host mostly internet facing facilities like a web server. It can also be used to host NAT instances and NAT gateways. You can design or add the path to communicate with the corporate network.

Deep Dive - VPC Peering

Software VPN mesh is a concept in which on each subnet one instance is running VPN appliance, and is connected to its neighboring subnet within VPC in the same region. However, software VPN makes some additional cost as EC2 software endpoints are running on the instance and for high availability (which also needs some additional cost as HA has to have multiple instances running). Managing of endpoints is also cost dependent. In case of multiple endpoints or large instances, create a performance issue. When using Software VPN, you cannot link the Security Group from another VPC to it. You can only use remote end IP ranges. VPN software can be used between VPCs using IP by resolving AWS hostname of the instance on remote VPC, but it also creates some

problems in connection among VPC internal IPs. To overcome all these issues, VPC peering option is available, which can be handled differently.

For that in the account, there is network component VPC peer. It can be created by defining two points: local VPC and remote VPC. VPC peer works on a pending acceptance concept meaning remote VPC needs to accept the peering request; when you have VPCs in the same account, you use the VPC ID of local and remote VPCs. Once peering is accepted, a network peering object is created with a prefix of pcx in ID. This ID is used as a reference to update the route table to connect to other VPC. We already know that VPC is not transitive property supported. In case of different account VPC, you need to define the account number at creation time of peering.

For VPC peering, we need to add a route of VPC peering by adding its ID in target and destination of other VPC to which we want peering. This route needs to be added to both local and remote VPCs.

VPC peering connection is a network between two VPCs that allows you to route traffic privately between them. Instances in either VPCs can communicate with each other as if they would inside the same network. VPC peering connection can be initiated between your VPCs, or with a VPC in another AWS account, or with a VPC in another AWS region. Cross-region VPC peering is also supported; it is a recent update in AWS VPC peering options. An Amazon VPC peering connection is not a gateway neither a VPN connection and does not introduce a single point of failure for communication.

AWS uses the existing infrastructure of the VPCs to create a VPC peering connection. A VPC connection helps you in smoothening the transfer of data.

Consider an example in which you have two VPCs in different accounts. In one VPC subnet, there is an instance, which has SG that is used in all other SG to allow SSH access. However, if you want to use that SG in other VPC, which is on another account, it cannot be possible without VPC peering. In VPC peering, we simply refer to that SG as a source in other VPC SG. So, by using VPC peering, you can grant SG access across VPC boundaries. But if you have a concept of DNS then by using VPC peering, it is not beneficial because if public DNS of one VPC is accessed by another VPC, it does not resolve the private IP of that VPC. If your web server in one VPC has two IPs: one is public (which has public DNS) and other is private (which has private DNS), then within a VPC public DNS always resolve to the private DNS or IP. But if VPC peering is enabled and the other VPC tries to use public DNS, then it does not resolve private IP. This creates a problem as VPC peering network use private IPs in internal route. Because when peered VPC uses external public DNS to communicate, it is not possible. Therefore, it is better to use IPs in VPC peering rather than DNS.

But if you want to use DNS in VPC peering then you have two options:

1. Allow DNS from Peer VPC means if VPCs are in the different account or same account, then allow remote VPC machines to resolve Public DNS into a private IP address.
2. Allow DNS from local VPC means if your VPC peer is in the same account, it works the same by allowing peered VPC to resolve DNS to a private IP address.

Above options are used when your peered VPCs are on the same account, but the best option is to use the 2nd one as it is quicker than the other. To perform any of the options available, you need to enable DNS resolution, and DNS hostname in VPC peering and for that, enable DNS options in both VPCs. The cost of VPC peering is 1 cent per GB regardless of region and account.

How to Create a VPC Peering Connection?

- Generate a request to peer with another VPC. You can request to peer with another VPC in your account, or with a VPC in a different AWS account.
- For an inter-region VPC peering connection, the request must be made from the region of the requester VPC.
- To activate the request, the owner of the accepter VPC must accept the request. For an inter-region VPC peering connection, the request must be accepted in the region of the accepter VPC.
- If the peer VPC is within the same account, it is identified by its VPC ID. If the peer VPC is in a different account, it is identified by Account ID and VPC ID. The peering request expires in a week if it is not responded to.

A VPC can have multiple peering connections; it is a one-to-one relationship between VPCs, meaning two VPCs cannot have two peering agreements between them. Also, peering connections do not support transitive routing. Peering is a non-transitive relationship, which means each network that you want to connect must be directly linked.

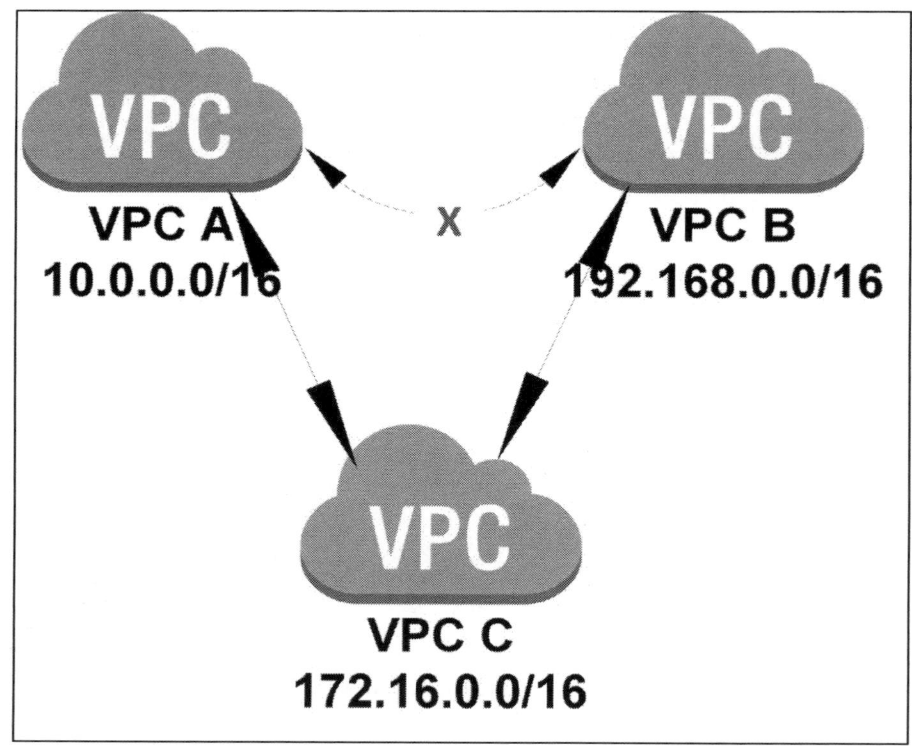

Figure 3-18: VPCs Do Not Support Transitive Routing

Limitations of VPC Peering

When planning to create a VPC peering connection, the following points should be kept in mind;

- VPC peering connection cannot be established between those VPCs that have matching or overlapping CIDR blocks. If IPv6 blocks are different and IPv4 block is same of two VPCs, you cannot create a peering connection between them.
- There is a limit of 50 VPC peers per VPC that can be increased to 125 on request.
- VPC peering does not support transitive relationships.
- You cannot have more than one VPC peering connection between the same two VPCs.
- Any tags that you create for a VPC peering connection are only applied in the region where you created them.
- Private DNS values cannot be resolved between instances in peered VPC. However, you can do this by enabling DNS resolution option.
- Communication over IPv6 is not supported.

Multi-VPC Architecture

Multi-VPC architecture is a concept in which you use multiple VPCs for different purposes and integrate AWS resource between VPCs more easily. Multi-VPC architecture can be applied to the single region or another region.

Consider an example in which you have one shared VPC, which can be used by other VPCs for some usage, in this way you save cost by using single VPC for sharing purpose. The below diagram shows the single to multi-VPC connection in which the main VPC communication to VPC A and VPC B but VPC A and VPC B cannot communicate to each other. In this case, both VPC A and VPC B have different CIDR ranges.

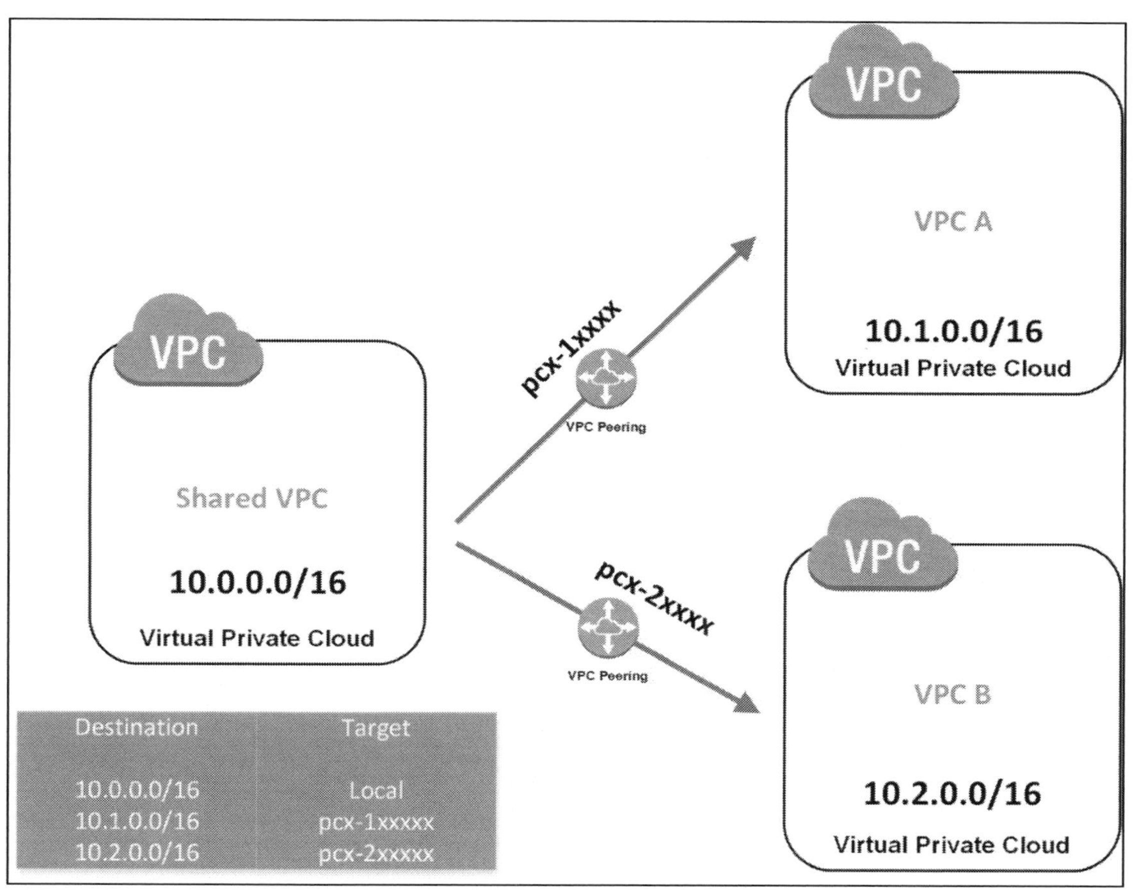

Figure 3-19: Multi VPC architecture with Different CIDR

If we have the same CIDR ranges that are technically possible, then VPC peering is created, but the main VPC route table is confusing as it has two same CIDR ranges with different targets. So for that, define sufficient prefix in route table so that only that prefix's traffic goes to that VPC and the remaining goes to the other. You also have another option by splitting a subnet in shared VPC into two and define individual route

table one for each peer. In this way, you can communicate the VPC with the VPCs that belong to the same CIDR ranges.

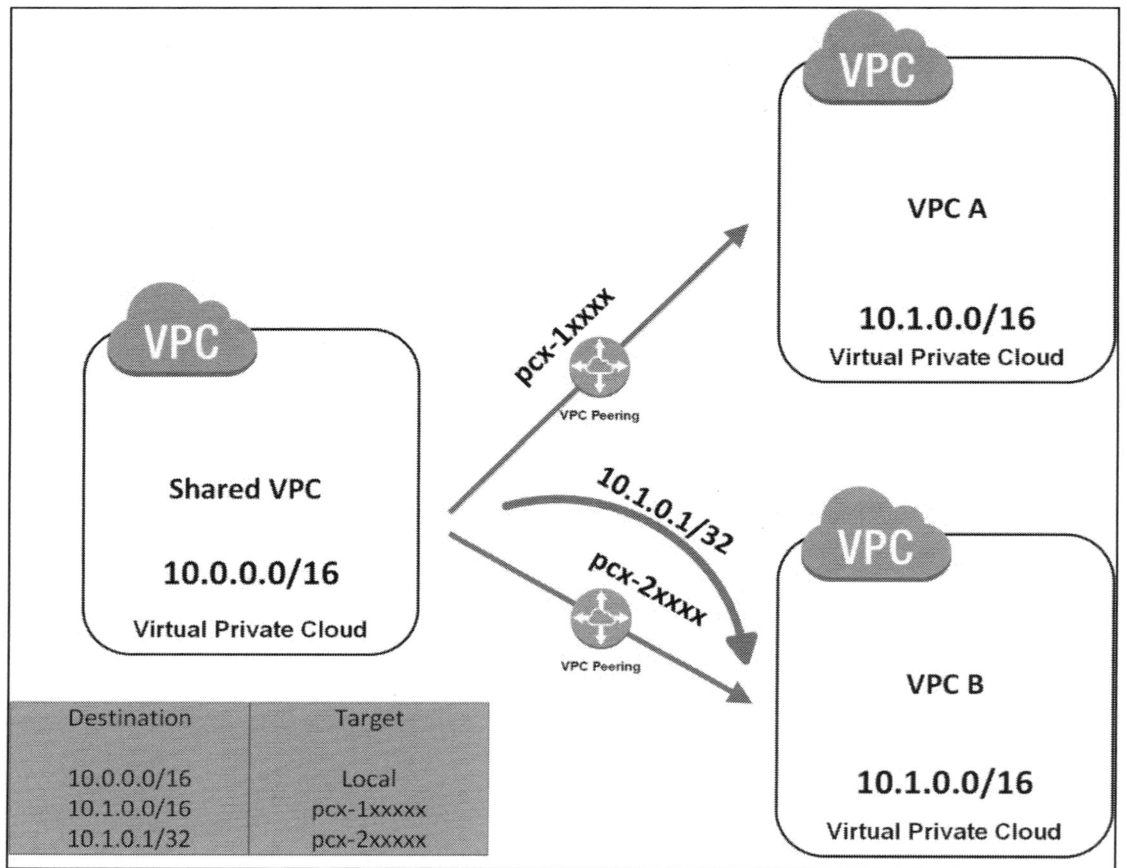

Destination	Target
10.0.0.0/16	Local
10.1.0.0/16	pcx-1xxxxx
10.1.0.1/32	pcx-2xxxxx

Figure 3-20: Multi VPC Architecture with the same CIDR

Consider another example in which because of some organization restriction, organization created a different VPC in each account, with appropriate permissions allowed to that VPC to perform and create VPC peering. In this way, if your production account gets hacked and you assign permission to other VPC that only accept writes and deny deletes/modifies, then all the log files are written into that VPC from production VPC, and it cannot be deleted or changed.

Deep Dive - VPC Endpoints

Endpoints are horizontally scaled virtual devices that are redundant and highly available VPC components that allow communication between instances in your VPC and services without imposing availability risks or bandwidth constraints on your network traffic.

VPC endpoint is an entity within VPC, which is referenced by its ID. In route table, you need to add this ID as a target, and in the destination, you define the public resource that

you want to access. In this way, if your VPC does not have public subnet or internet gateway, then by using VPC endpoint, you can communicate to the public resource (S3 or DynamoDB).

Amazon VPC endpoints allow you to connect your VPC privately with other AWS services powered by *PrivateLink* without an Internet Gateway or via a NAT instance, VPN, or AWS DirectConnect connection. Instances within your VPC private subnet do not require public IPs to communicate with resources in the service. Multiple endpoints can also be created for a single service.

There are two types of VPC endpoints: interface endpoints and gateway endpoints. Always create the type of VPC endpoint required by the supported service.

To create an Amazon VPC endpoint, you must do the followings:

- Prescribe the VPC
- Identify the service (you can specify a service by prefix list in the form *com.amazonaws.<region>.<service>*)
- Specify the policy. You can allow full access or create a custom policy. The specified policy can be changed anytime
- Itemize the route tables; a route will be added to each specified route table, which will state the service as the destination and the endpoint as the target

Destination	Target
10.0.0.0/16	Local
0.0.0.0/0	igw-1ab3c4d

Table 3-08: Route Table with an IGW

The above table is an example route table that has routes directing all internet traffic to an internet gateway and S3 traffic to the VPC endpoint

Destination	Target
10.0.0.0/16	Local
0.0.0.0/0	igw-1a2b3cd
pl-1a2b3c4d	vpce-11bb22cc

Table 3-09: Route Table with an IGW and VPC Endpoint Rule

The above route table will direct all traffic destined for S3 to the endpoint. All other traffic will go to the IGW.

Consider another example in which you have public and private subnet so public subnet follows the path to connect to S3 via IGW while you can also create an alternative path of private subnet's instances to the S3 by using VPC endpoints.

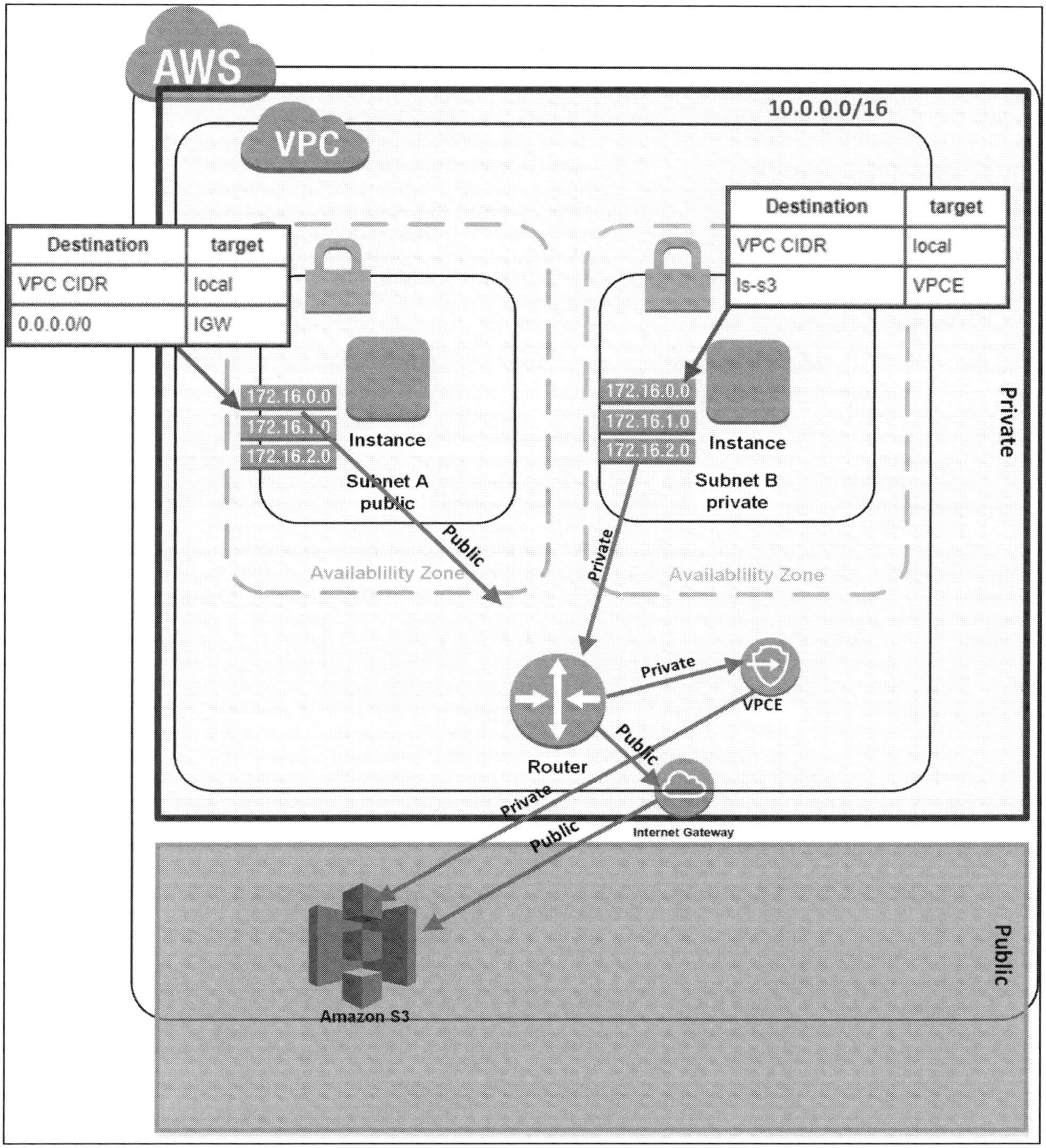

Destination	target
VPC CIDR	local
0.0.0.0/0	IGW

Destination	target
VPC CIDR	local
Is-s3	VPCE

Figure 3-21: VPC Endpoint

Limitation of VPC Endpoints

There are some limitations of using VPC endpoints:

- Endpoints are region specific, which means you cannot connect the VPC of a region to the service in another region.

- Endpoints are restricted to be used within VPC and are not able to extend across VPC boundaries.
- For endpoints working DNS, resolution is required.
- By default, policy in VPC endpoint is unrestricted. However, you can edit the policy to restrict the S3 or DynamoDB.
- Not to use NACL in VPC endpoints.
- Routing on subnets is dependent on the prefix ID of the object, which is defined in the route table.

You can apply restriction by defining policy on either VPC or instance in the subnet. If an instance in a subnet needs software updates by using VPC endpoint, then apply the policy, which allows the specific bucket to access for software updates. Similarly, if you want to restrict access to a bucket from another VPC endpoint, then define a policy in which define the condition and deny action means whatever VPC endpoint wants to access, the bucket does not allow it until VPC endpoint matches with the given condition.

MindMap

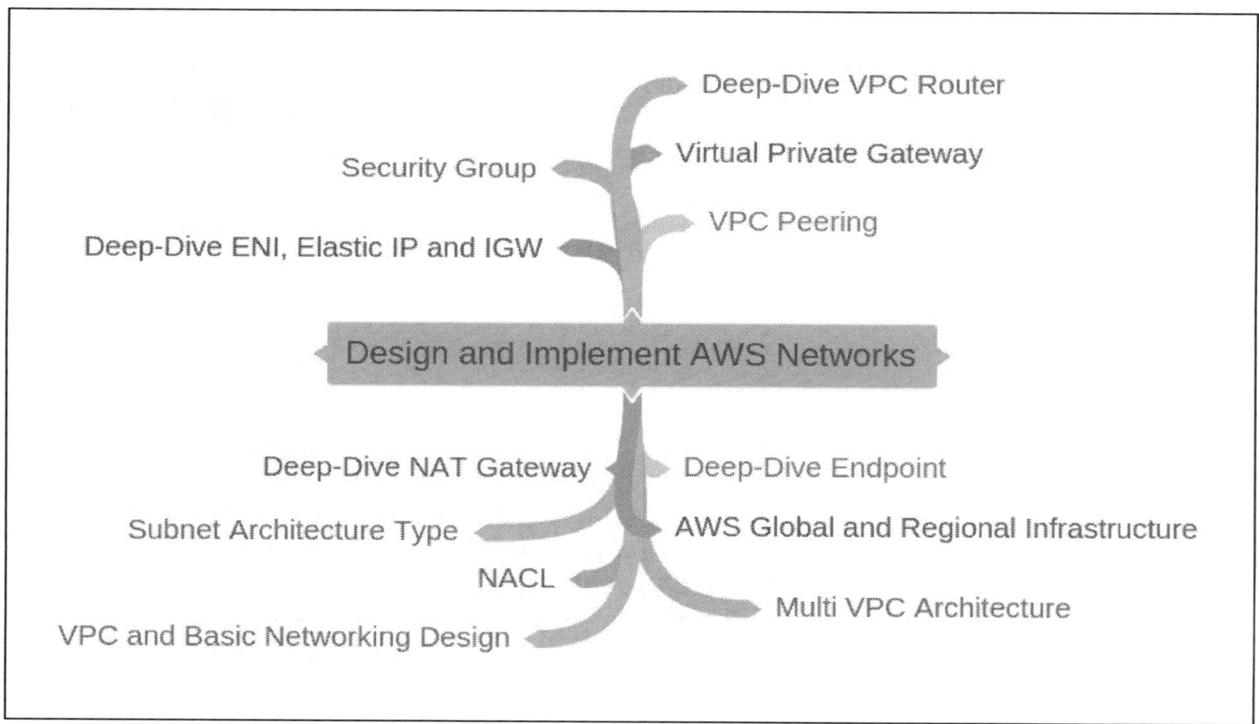

Figure 3-22: Mind Map

Practice Questions:

1. In AWS, which of the following maps to a separate geographic location?
   a) AWS Region
   b) AWS Datacenter
   c) AWS Edge Location
   d) AWS Availability Zone

2. Which one is not a component of VPC?
   a) Route table
   b) EIP addresses
   c) PrivateLink
   d) NAT gateways

3. ______________________ is a logically isolated portion of the AWS cloud where you can launch AWS resources in your defined virtual network.
   a) Edge location
   b) Datacenter
   c) VPC
   d) None of the above

4. In AWS, you can also create your own VPC quickly and easily via AWS console/ CLI/ API. You need to provide three main things. What are they?
   a) CIDR block
   b) Tenancy
   c) Policies
   d) VPC name tag

5. The smallest subnet that can be created is ____ that contains 16 IP addresses.
   a) /24
   b) /16
   c) /0
   d) /28

6. _______ is the Amazon VPC side of a connection to the public Internet.

a) Internet Gateway
b) Route table
c) Subnet
d) NAT Instance

7. Which of the following permissions acts at the subnet level?
   a) NACl
   b) Security group
   c) Roles
   d) None of the above

8. Which VPC component is the core component without which local subnets communication is not possible?
   a) Internet Gateway
   b) Route table
   c) NAT Instance
   d) VPC Router

9. In each subnet CIDR block, ____________ number of IP addresses are reserved.
   a) 5
   b) 4
   c) 3
   d) 6

10. Which is used to be defined as a logical construct within a VPC that holds a set of rules that are applied to the subnet?
    a) Internet Gateway
    b) Route table
    c) NAT Instance
    d) VPC Router

11. An Elastic Network Interface includes the following attributes: (Choose multiple)
    a) MAC address
    b) Dedicated host

c) IPv6 address
d) Source/Destination check

12. Every Amazon VPC must have only one DHCP option set assigned to it.
    a) True
    b) False

13. How are you charged for elastic IP addresses?
    a) Hourly, when they are associated with an instance.
    b) Hourly, even when they are not associated with an instance.
    c) Based on the data that flows through them.
    d) Based on the instance type to which they are attached.

14. What is an IGW?
    a) An IGW can be defined as a logical construct within a VPC that holds a set of rules that are applied to the subnet.
    b) IGW is designed for dynamic cloud computing. It is static, public IPv4 address in an AWS managed pool.
    c) IGW is a horizontally scaled, redundant, and highly available component of VPC that allows communication between the instances in VPC and the internet.
    d) An IGW lets you provision your logically isolated section of the AWS cloud where you can launch AWS resources in a user-defined virtual network.

15. To connect a VPC to your corporate network, which component is needed? (choose any 2)
    a) IGW
    b) VGW
    c) CGW
    d) VPC router

16. In default SG, all outbound traffic is ___________________.
    a) Allowed
    b) Deny

17. In VPC, which AWS component is used to communicate your private instance with internet for software updates?
    a) IGW
    b) VPN
    c) CGW
    d) NAT Instance

18. If your private instances are increasing and compute capacity also increases and you want elasticity, then which component is used for this purpose when your private subnet instances need an update from the internet?
    a) IGW
    b) NAT gateway
    c) CGW
    d) NAT Instance

19. How many VGW can you connect to one VPC?
    a) 2
    b) 1
    c) 5
    d) 3

20. In which subnet architecture there is no concept of the public subnet?
    a) VPC-only subnet
    b) VPN-only subnet
    c) Both
    d) None of these

21. Which AWS service is used to communicate two VPC to each other?
    a) VPN
    b) Direct Connect
    c) Endpoint
    d) VPC peering

22. Which VPC component is used by private subnet to connect to public AWS service

without using NAT?

a) VPN
b) Endpoints
c) CGW
d) VGW

Chapter 04: Design and Implement Hybrid Networks at Scale

Introduction:

In this chapter, we will discuss the Hybrid networks, what it is and how does it function. In addition, we will discuss in detail that how can a hybrid network be designed and implemented with on-site environment and AWS cloud.

Hybrid Network

A hybrid network is a network of computers using several types of connecting technologies or topologies. It is a combination of on-site IT and Cloud services. The reasons for migrating to cloud are grouped into two, i.e., Reactive Reasons and Proactive Reasons.

Reactive Reasons

Reactive reasons are negative or deadline driven. This type of reason generally occurs due to business pressure or any deadline.

Datacenter Extension

Data center extension is the process of extending the existing data center into the AWS cloud. It is always a reactive reason for migration.

Scenario:

An organization has two physical data centers. Both of the data centers are connected to the internet, and they are also connected to each other. The following would be the reason for migration to Cloud:

- When the company grows, it needs more capacity. The space for the data center will eventually have some limit. Therefore, due to the lack of capacity, the company would move to the cloud.
- Due to the increase in the cost of management of data centers.
- Due to unstable weather condition at the location of the data center.

For all these reasons, an organization may want to link its physical data center to AWS, which will solve all the above mentioned problems, and the organization can avail different services at a reasonable price.

Compliance and Regulatory Requirements

The migration to the cloud can be due to compliance and regulatory reasons. The reason of dependency may vary from country to country.

- **Auditing**

Many companies use external compliance or auditing consultancy in which they have to fix the issues immediately after the result of audits that can be expensive.

- **Data Breach**

A data breach is an accident in which the information is accessed without authorization. An organization may face data breach, in which they do not necessarily lose their reputation and quality factor, but they want to prevent that factor from happening again and again.

- **New product launching**

If an organization is launching a new product, which requires more capacity for the data center.

Pro-active Reasons

These types of reasons are related to any technical improvement or positive change in business.

High Availability or DR solution

A traditional high availability or DR requires two data centers; one is primary and other is secondary. The company has to pay for both the datacenters (Operational staff, maintenance, equipment) even when they are not functioning. Whenever any DR event occurs, the standby datacenter will be active. Similarly, for high availability, the standby data center will perform on behalf of the main data center. Therefore, the standby data center will cost more.

AWS provides a flexible and the most cost-effective solution. The organization can continue with the traditional data center, but for High availability and DR events, they can replace the standby datacenters with AWS services in which many of basic services such as VPC and subnets are free of cost. The charges are only applied when services are in use otherwise on standby it will be nearly equal to zero.

Dynamic bursting

Dynamic bursting is a process where your use AWS for providing burst capacity.

Let us say you run an online store, which is hosted in a traditional on-premises datacenter where you sell widgets. You have a new widget, which is one of its kinds. You are

expecting heavy growth in sales. With the increased sale, you need to scale your capacity, but the data center has its limitations. This will cause performance and reliability issues. The traditional approaches to handling these issues are:

1. Increase the DC capacity
2. Add another DC to facilitate the existing DC
3. Use AWS or Hybrid Cloud environment

Solutions 1 and 2 can cause problems like an increase in the running cost of your platform. You can use AWS services in Auto-scaling environments, which can scale automatically according to your load requirements. Using AWS will not be much expensive as you only pay for what you use. In addition to that, you will not have to pay for the hardware and networking equipment as if you would if you were to set up a data center.

AWS *as a Service Model

Modern IT platforms have multiple layers:

Physical facilities: AC system, security, and other environmental controls

Network: Switches, routers, firewalls, etc.

Servers: Physical servers that are hardware

OS: Operating system

DB & Services: Base level services like databases, storage, etc.

APP: Applications or other infrastructure elements

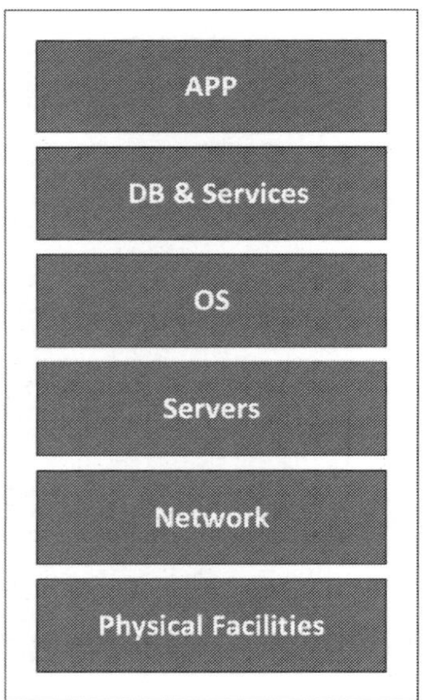

Figure 4-01: IT Platform

For a business, one may have to manage all of these, if not using AWS. The most of the IT budget is based on two things:

- Cost of Hardware of services and networking equipment
- Operational cost

AWS offers services, which handle physical to server layers (Figure: 4-01) known as infrastructure as a server, which is the extension of *as a service (*aas) model in AWS such as platform as a service, function as a service, database as a service and many other. These services cover the three layers in OS, DB, and service layers. AWS offers S3 and EBS as storage as a service product, RDS is a database as a service product, Amazon Workspace is desktop as a service product and Redshift is data warehousing as a service product.

There are several Hardware connectivity options available in AWS.

- Software VPN
- Hardware VPN
- Direct Connect (DX)

Software VPN

Amazon VPC offers flexibility in network routing. This includes the capability of creating secure VPN tunnels for connecting multiple VPCs to a bigger virtual private network between two or more VPN software applications so that the instances on each VPC can connect to each other by using a private IP. It is recommended to use your preferred VPN software provider to manage both ends of the VPN connection to connect VPCs across multiple AWS regions. An internet gateway connected to each VPC is used to ease communication between the VPN software devices.

In the architecture in Figure 4-02, we have the following components:

- An AWS account.
- A VPC is created in two Availability Zones, having one subnet in each AZ with a routing table in both subnets.
- A VPC Router is providing routing services to the private network.
- An Internet gateway to the VPC with a default route to the gateway from both subnets.
- An EC2 instance in one subnet and an elastic IP address is associated with this instance. (Currently, the instance has access to the public internet and assumes that all the Security Groups and network ACL are opened to allow this access.)

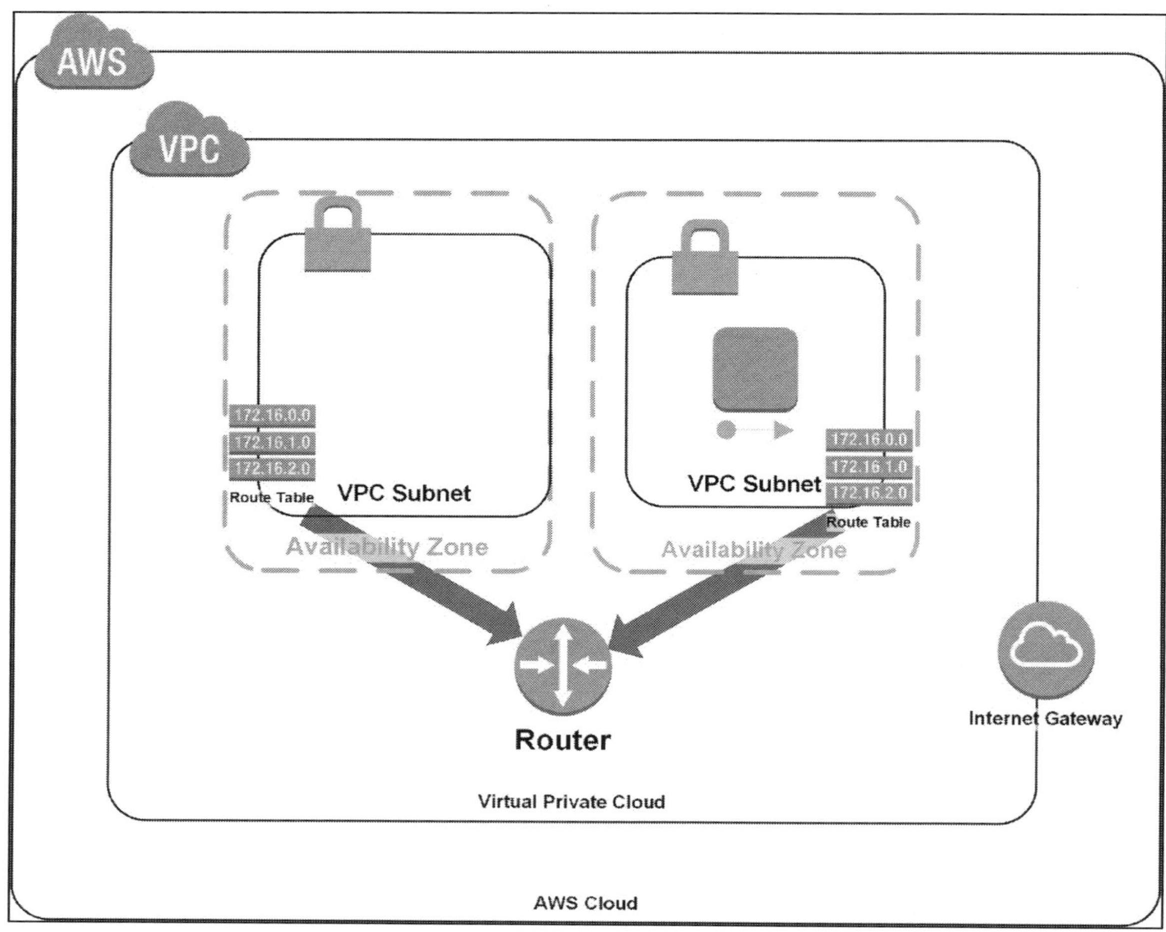

Figure 4-02: AWS Side of VPN

Now the software VPN will use this architecture (Figure 4-02).

Use cases

a) An organization has an existing on-site custom VPN solution due to government (or technical) requirement. This solution is not based on IPSec but it is an open VPN. Now the organization would require an open VPN connection with the AWS site. In this case, AWS IPSec based hardware connection would not be suitable.

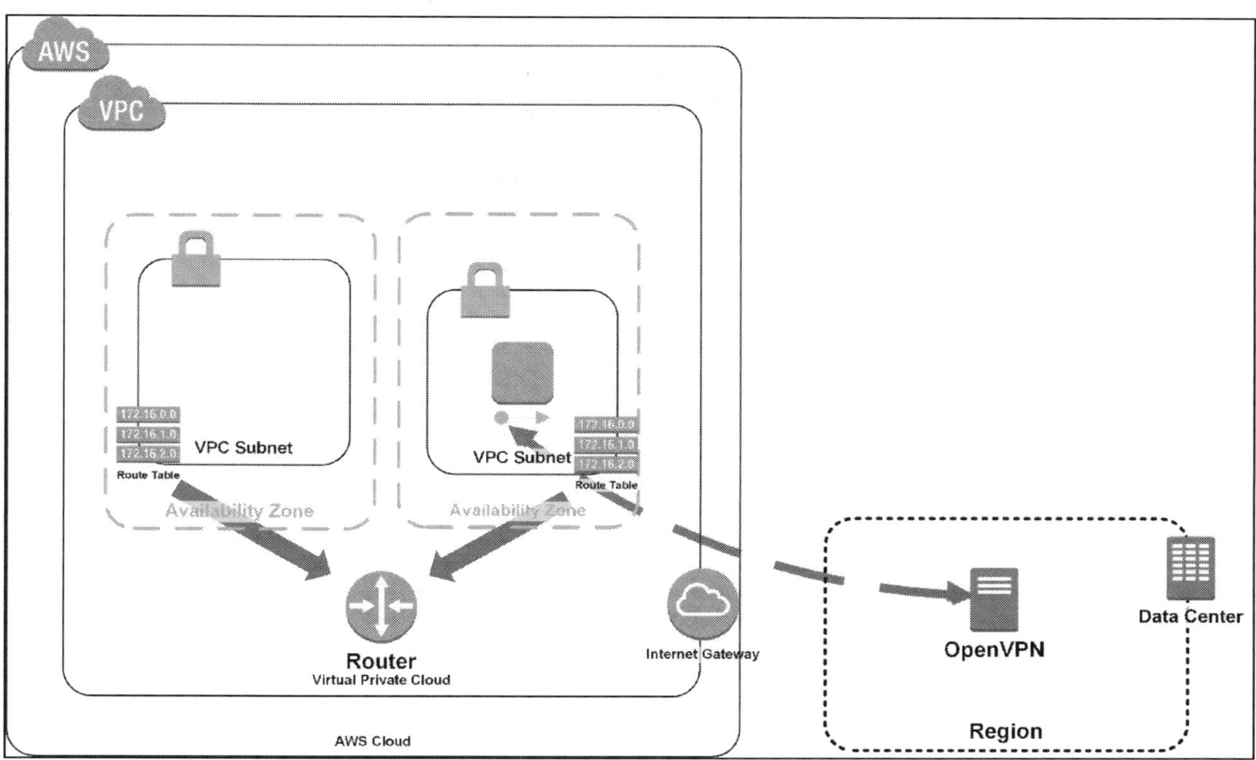

Figure 4-03: Software VPN (Use Case A)

b) Software VPN can be used in connecting two VPCs when these VPCs are in different regions (since 2017, if these VPCs were in the same region, you may connect it by VPC pairing). For this purpose, an EC2 instance with an elastic IP address is added in the remote region to create an appropriate network connection, and then a software VPN connection between the VPN appliances is established to communicate between the local and remote region. From 2018, inter VPN pairing is available to connect VPNs of different regions, therefore; there is no need of software VPN for this case now.

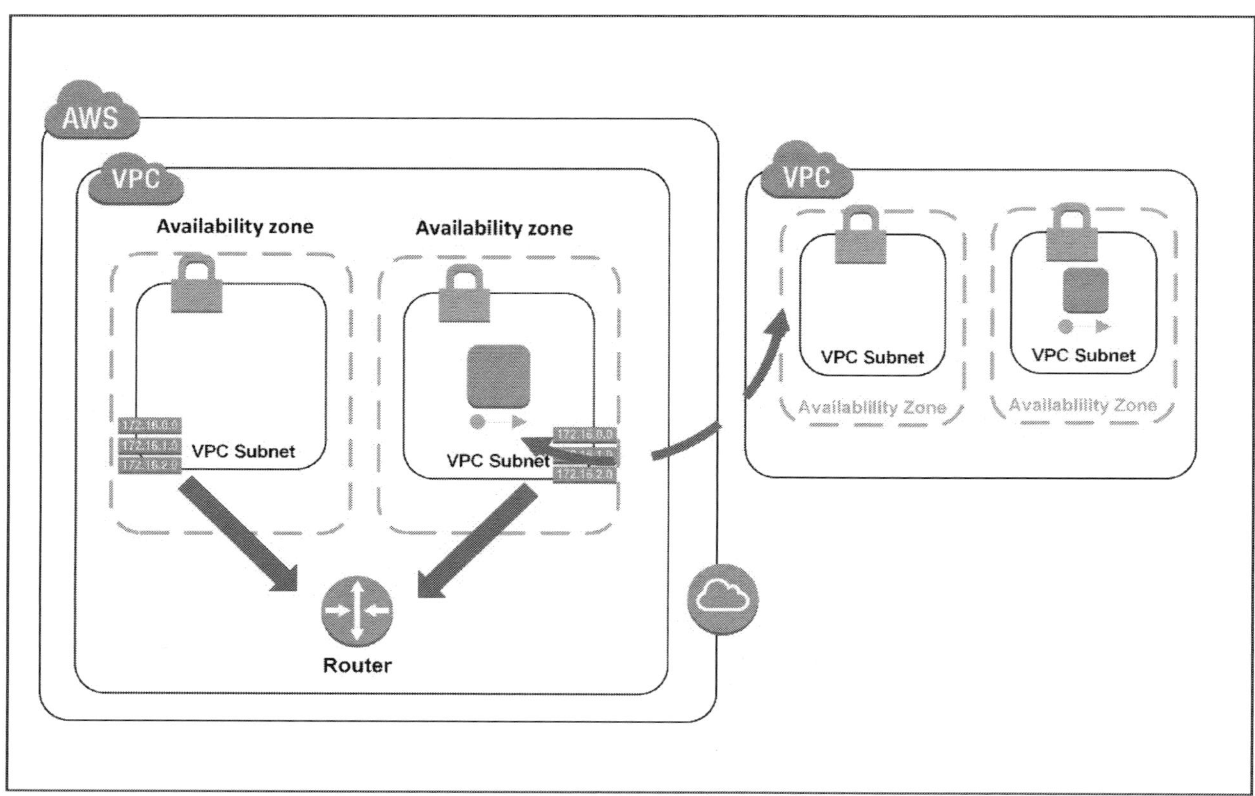

Figure 4-04: Software VPN (Use Case B)

Pros of Software VPN

- It has the widest compatibility that means you can install any VPN software in EC2 instance.
- Quick Configuration because there is no need of any physical installation as it uses software appliances for both remote and local ends.
- It checks the alignment with strict government issues.

Cons of Software VPN

- No IPSec is available
- You have to manage your instances
- You have to manage your installed product or OS
- No default resilience
- Due to the public internet, you can experience uncertain network latency
- Network speed and performance is dependent on the instance

Hardware VPN (VPC VPN)

Hardware VPN is a managed solution for all VPCs. Hardware VPN is a managed and resilient product of AWS. It works across all Availability Zones within the same region. AWS charges VPN services based on two components:

1. Per hour VPN connection charge of the VPN object
2. Data transfer charges

Hardware VPN is the preferred way whenever VPN connection is required, as consistent latency and high performance is not important. It is also a low-cost link. When dealing with a time-critical deployment, use VPN connection. Whenever consistent latency and performance is important, DirectConnect is a better option. If you have a low budget, go for VPN and if you can afford expenses, then go for DX.

Key Logical Components

AWS hardware VPN consists of a number of key logical components, these are as follows:

Customer Gateway (CGW)

It is the logical representation of your Customer Premises Equipment (CPE). It is placed where you specified the external IP address of the CP device, and it defines which type of routing the device is using, i.e. static or dynamic.

Virtual Gateway (VGW)

It is the logical termination of the object of all VPN connection and DirectConnect connection in a VPC. VGW is created in a region and then attached to VPC. The VGW to VPC ratio is one to one, i.e. only one VGW can be attached to one VPC.

VPN Connection

It is the connection used to link one Customer Gateway and one Virtual Gateway.

VPN Connection Configuration

This configuration is produced when a VPN connection is created. This VPN connection contains the IP addressing, IKE information, IP stack information, and optionally BGP information. These configurations are downloadable pre-formatted by AWS for common VPN End Points (VPN EP) so they can be applied on a customer side router.

Route Table in VPC subnet

Route table of VPC subnets needs to be updated with routes for VPNs using static or route-propagation method

Architecture of Hardware VPN

The given architecture (Figure 4-05) includes the following components:

- An AWS account with VPC.
- Two Availability Zones having one subnet each.
- A routing table in each subnet.
- A VPC router
- A Virtual Private Gateway (VGW) is attached to VPC.
- VGW provides multiple resilient VPN points; Two VPN endpoints are in each Availability Zone. These VPN endpoints links with the Customer Gateway (CGW).
- A VPN connection links this infrastructure with the Customer Gateway (CGW).
- The CGW will connect to the VPN endpoints of both AZs in order to make one or two tunnels.

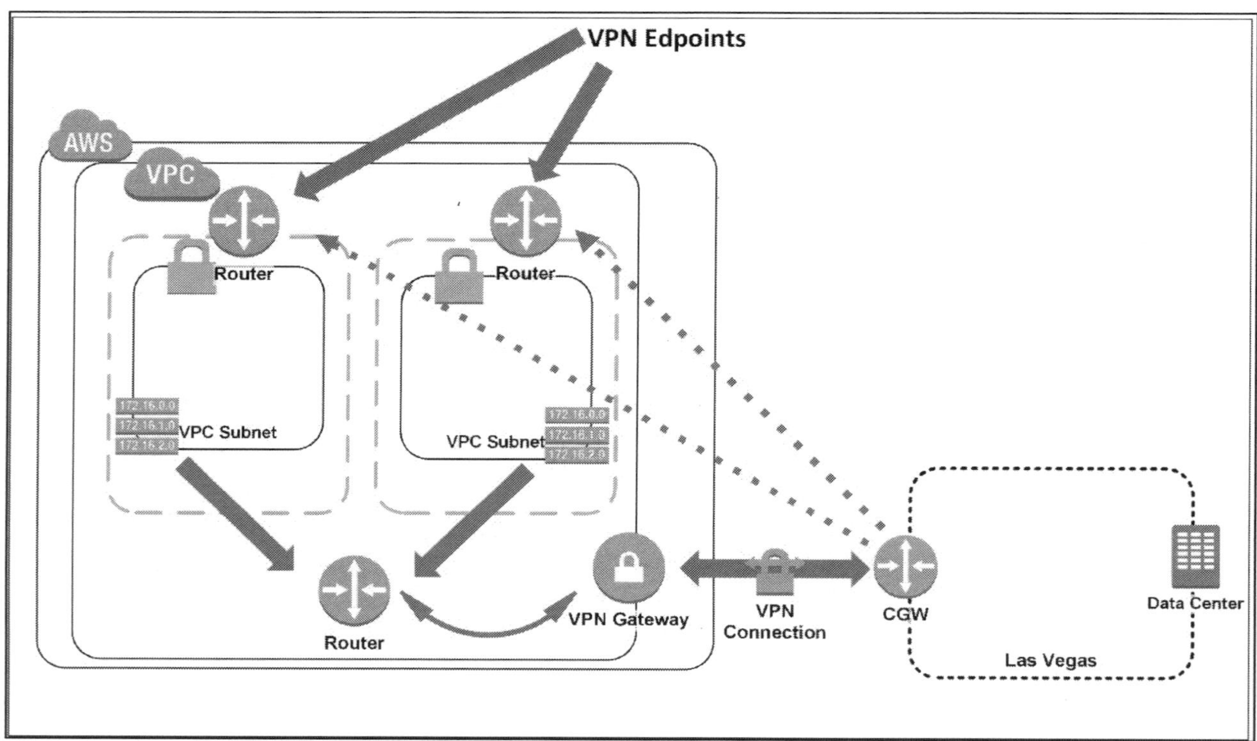

Figure 4-05: Hardware VPN (a)

You can add more CGW in this architecture (Figure 4-06).

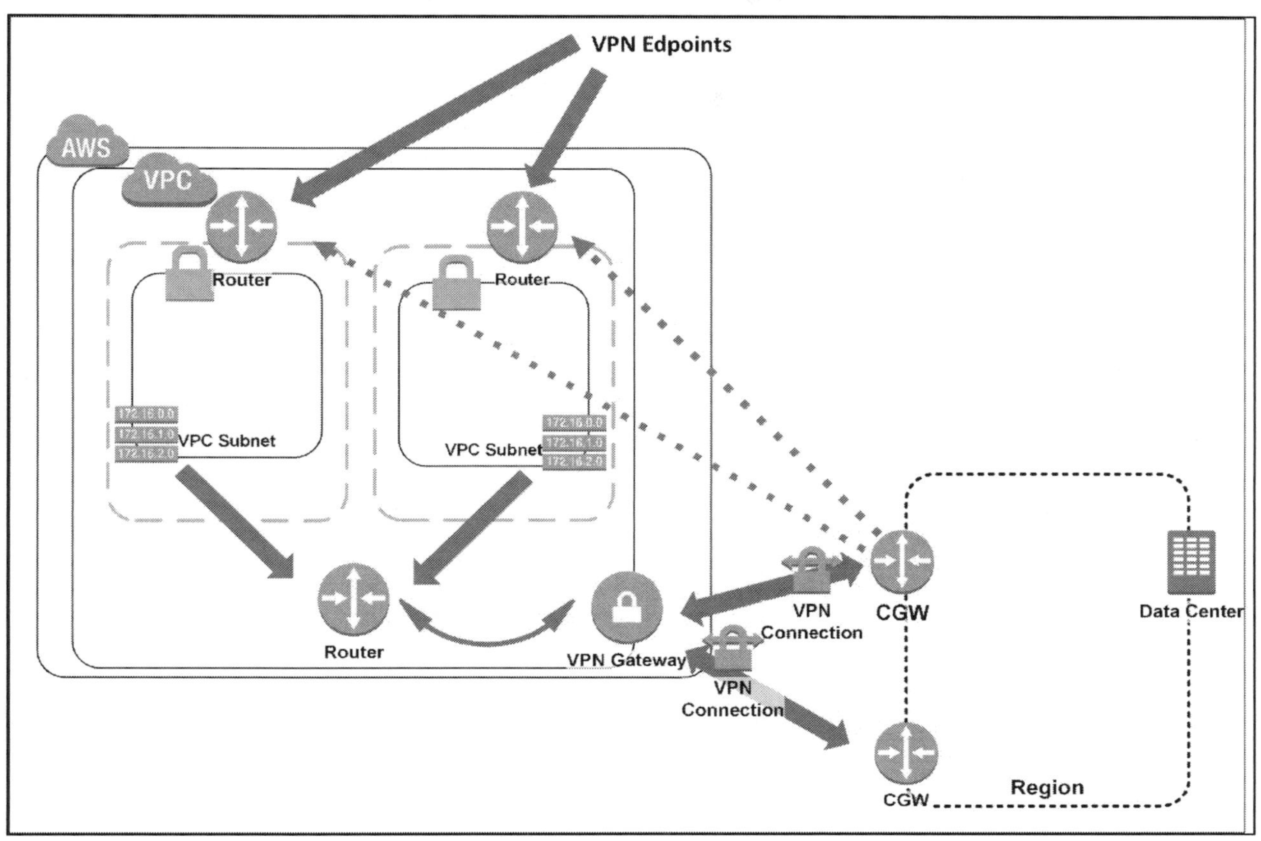

Figure 4-06: Hardware VPN (b)

Pros of Hardware VPN

- It can be configured quickly because it does not require any physical hardware changes or network installation as it only uses the customer hardware.
- It provides multi-AZs or multiple fault tolerance resiliencies by default. You can get access to multiple IP endpoints for the termination of VPN. You can be able to add multiple customer side devices to increase resiliency at the customer side.
- It can be used with DirectConnect connections (DX); therefore, you can use VPN as cheap economical backups to physical connections.
- Hardware VPN can be configured by using the console, CLI or an API, which can allow you to automate the management of your system, so no ongoing management is required.

Cons of Hardware VPN

- Hardware VPN cannot be used to communicate two VPCs; this service is only designed to connect with the customer VPN product with your AWS VPC.
- The connection should be initiated from the client side.

- Tunnel timeout will be automatically down after a certain amount of time passed without any response from the client side hence, any EC2 instances trying to communicate will fail.
- It will face inconsistent network latency.
- Higher level of network performance will be problematic.

Hardware VPN is of two types, depending on the types of routing:

1. Static Hardware VPN
2. Dynamic Hardware VPN

Static Hardware VPN

Scenario: An organization hires an IT engineer for the communication between their VPC subnet in AWS and corporate DC in Las Vegas using Static Hardware VPN.

Considering the architecture in Figure 4-07, there is an AWS account with a VPC (10.0.0.0/16). In VPC there are two Availability Zones, both having one subnet in each, i.e. subnet A (10.0.0.0/17) and Subnet B (10.0.128.0/17). A VPC router is also included by default. Both of the subnets are VPN-only subnets, which mean that they only have access to other VPC subnets. A corporate data center is situated in Las Vegas, which has subnet, i.e. Las Subnet1 (192.168.0.0/24).

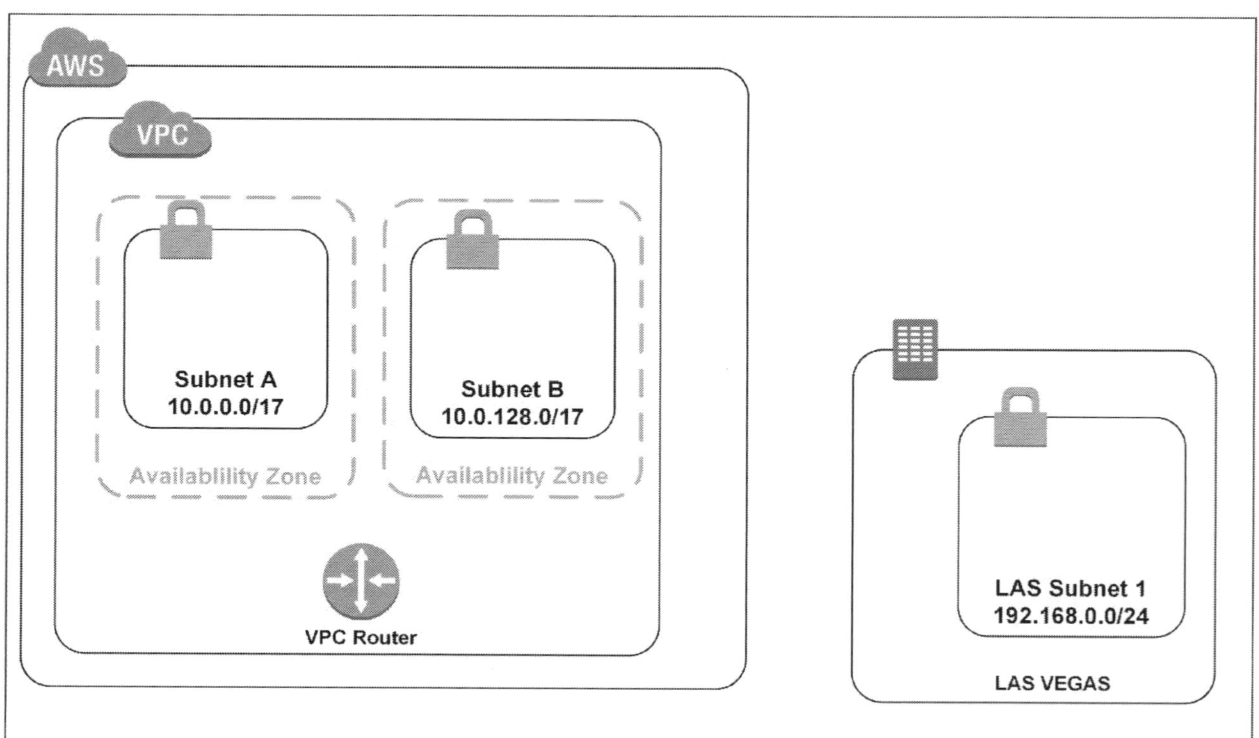

Figure 4-07: AWS Side and Customer Side Architecture

The IT engineer comes up with three connectivity options:

1. Software VPN
2. Hardware VPN
3. DirectConnect

By considering the pros and cons, he decided to use Hardware VPN.

Now further, he has to decide whether to select Static Hardware VPN or Dynamic Hardware VPN. For the conclusion, he looks at the BGP status of the customer router. If the customer router is BGP capable, then one should select dynamic routing otherwise select static routing. The customer router at Las Vegas office does not support BGP therefore, the connectivity should be by using Static Hardware VPN.

Static Hardware VPN Configuration Logical Steps

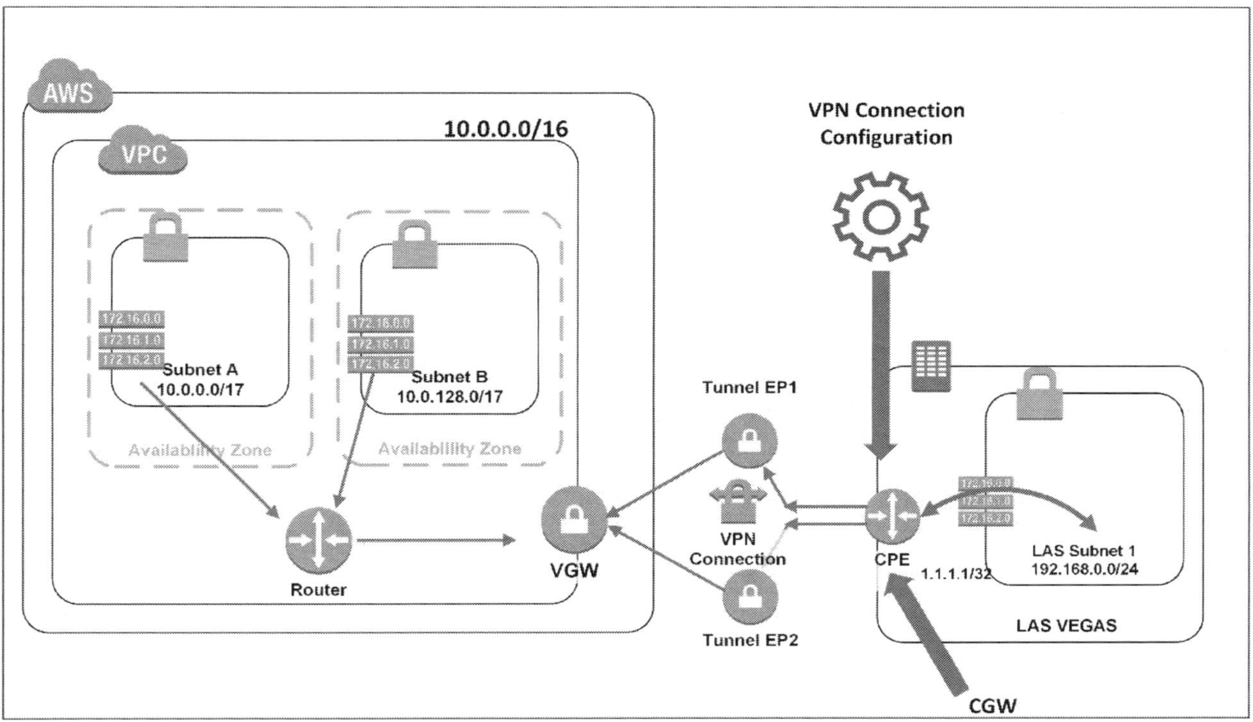

Figure 4-08: Static Hardware VPN Architecture

For static routing, following are the steps (For all steps refer to architecture in Figure 4-08):

Step 1

Determine that Customer Premises Router or Customer Premises Equipment (CPE) is suitable or not (BGP supported and also supports other AWS IPSec requirements). Customer Premises Router (1.1.1.1/32) is suitable here.

Step 2

Create the CGW within AWS, and these represent Customer Premises Router. CGW can be created using Console, CLI or API. In Figure 4-09, this is shown by using the console. Enter the appropriate nametag, which will help in finding the required router from multiple routers. Select the routing type, i.e., static. IPv4 address should be provided of the router's external interface, which is publicly route-able.

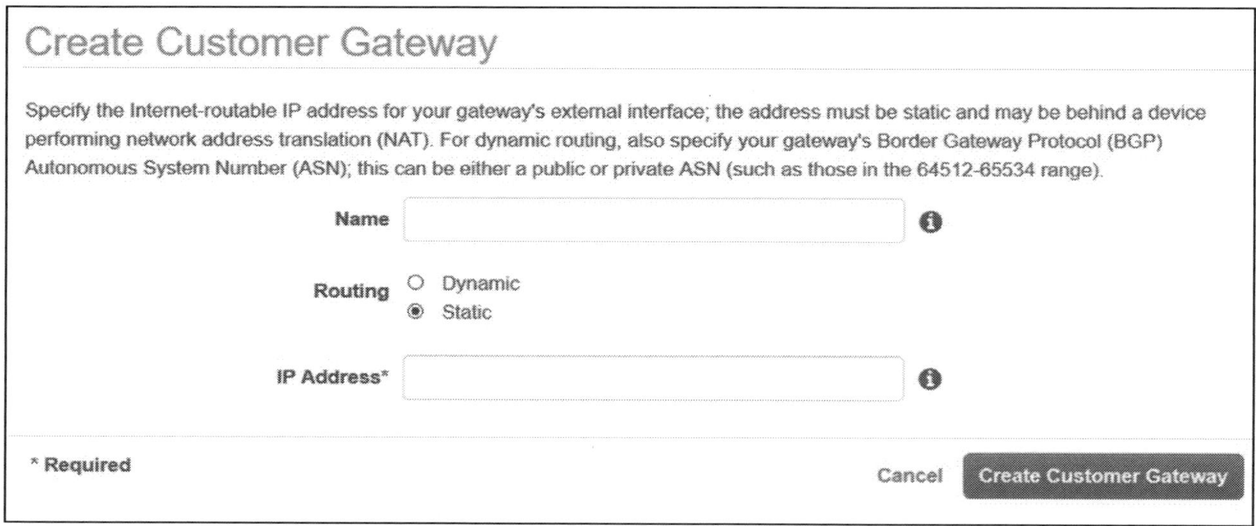

Figure 4-09: Create Customer Gateway using the Console

Step 3

Create a VGW and attach it to the VPC. Once VGW is attached, it becomes reference-able that means in a route table or Security Groups in VPC, VGW can be referred for routing or security decisions.

Note: Single Virtual Gateway can only be attached to single VPC, or single VPC can only have single VGW.

Step 4

Create a VPN connection, which is a link between VGW and CGW. Enter the nametag. The Virtual Private Gateway should be specified. Existing customer gateway can be selected or create a new customer gateway. You have to select the routing method, and for the given scenario, static is selected. Therefore, static IP prefixes should be entered. VPN connection using the console is given in Figure 4-10.

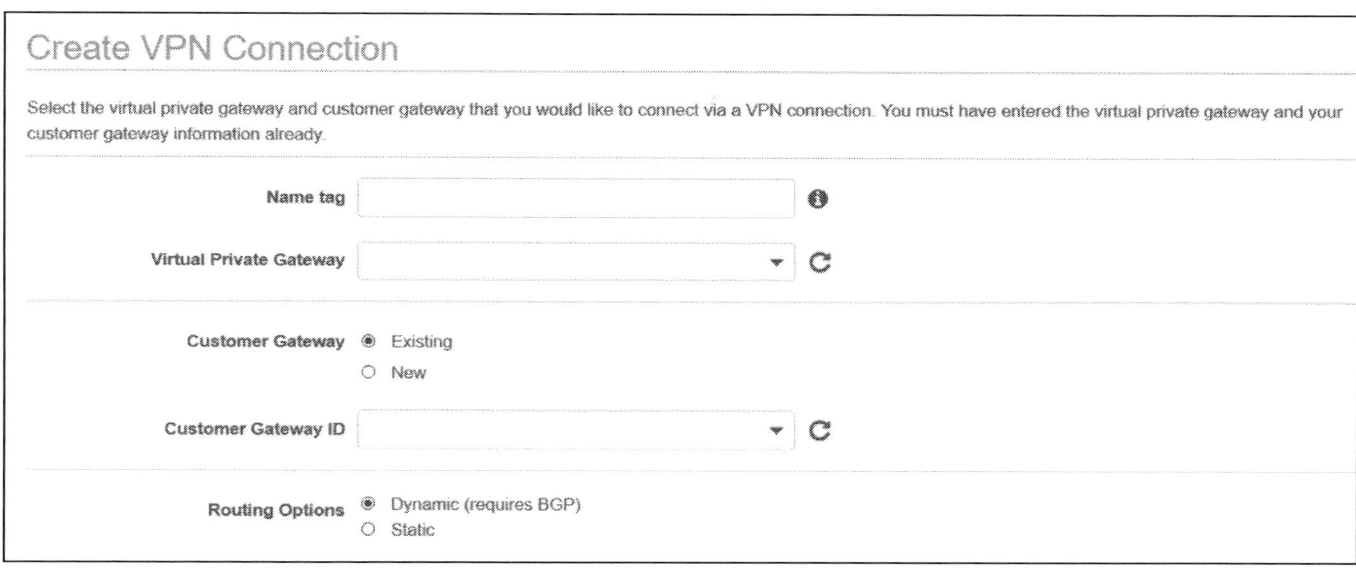

Figure 4-10(a): Creating a VPN Connection using the Console

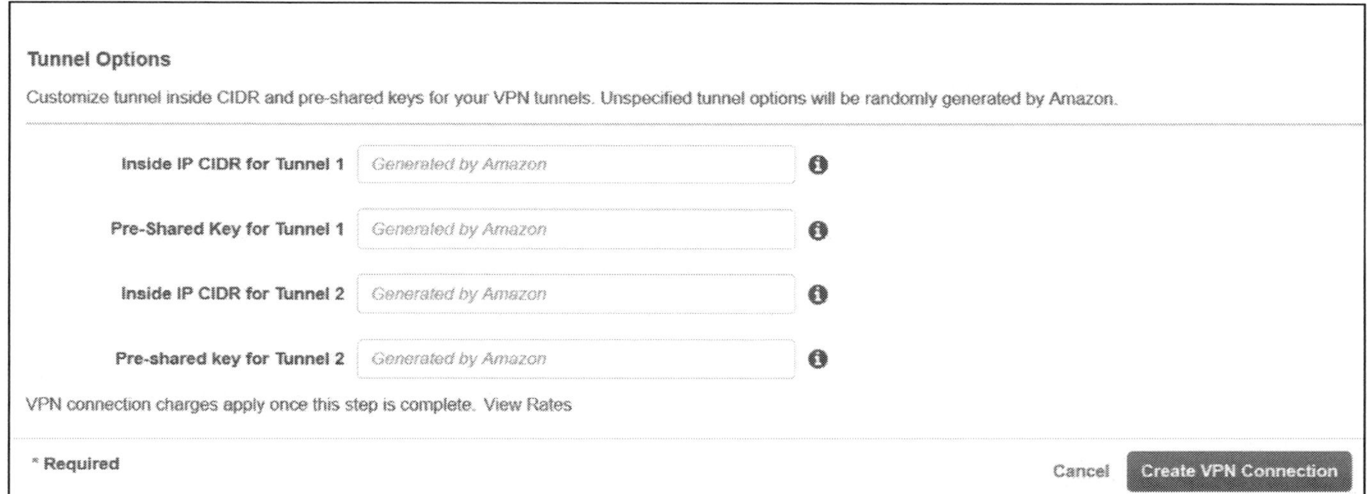

Figure 4-10(b): Creating a VPN Connection from the Console

When a VPN connection is created:

- AWS allocates two externally addressable VPN End Points (EPs), which are used to support the remote ends of two VPN tunnels i.e. Tunnel 1 and Tunnel 2. AWS guarantees to place these endpoints in separate fault domains on separate equipment. These endpoints enable AWS to overcome any failure or maintenance requirements.
- AWS generates VPN connection configuration data. This can be downloaded from AWS in the adjustable format for the various types of CPE (Cisco IOS, Cisco ACI, etc.). This configuration provides the information required for each phase of VPN

(IKE, IPSec, interface configuration and static routes). Configuration details can be directly applied or extracted and run through the automated process.

The configuration file contains:

- The IP config details
- Contains the pre-shared keys
- Encryption or authentication details required for VPN
- Static routing information

The local subnet uses the CPE as default route therefore, now it can reach to the CIDR range of the VPC.

Step 5

Add the route information to the VPC for remote subnets (Subnet A and Subnet B). Either main route table is located or a custom route table is attached. For adding routes to the route table, there are two options:

- Route manually, in this case, a new route is added to each route table with the destination network is 196.168.0.0/24.
- Enable route propagation on AWS VPC subnets route table. This will automatically update the route table with the learned routes of VGW. There is no filtering in this technique because it will add all routes.

Now the VPC router will use VGW for the traffic having the destination of 192.168.0.0/24. When the CPE gets any traffic for AWS VPC, VPN process begins starting from IKE then IPSec and then the tunnels are activated, which are logically terminated at VPC — thus, establishing the connection between AWS VPC and Las Vegas.

Static VPN Requirements

- The connection should be initiated from the customer end for the flow of traffic between AWS and the customer side. There should be "keep alive" thing or similar to it in order to keep traffic as a precaution. If the customer side is down, AWS cannot initiate the connection even if it wants to communicate. Therefore, the connection should always be up.
- IKE security association uses pre-shared Keys. If the organizational standards do not allow the use of pre-shared Keys, RSA digital signatures can be used for this purpose (This alternative is not allowed for Hardware VPN connections).
- IPSec security association should be in Tunnel mode; Policy VPNs is not supported. It means that the traffic should be defined with the help of interfaces and routes, not with the policies of VPNs.

- Endpoints should be AES 128-bit encryption and SHA-1 hashing supported.
- For the compatibility, the router should support Diffie-HellMan Perfect Forward Secret-Group 2.
- If CPE does not respond to AWS due to any reason, AWS will assume that links are dead and in result, it drops the tunnels and security associations. Therefore, the customer device should support Dead Peer Detection.
- Fragmentation of IP packets before encryption.
- 1 unique security association per tunnel.

Security Association Per Tunnel

A one-way policy, which agrees communication primitives between two VPN peers, is known as security association. Hence, for the communication over the VPN tunnels, there should be two security associations. Referring to the diagram, it is from left to right and right to left. So, there is one security association per tunnel.

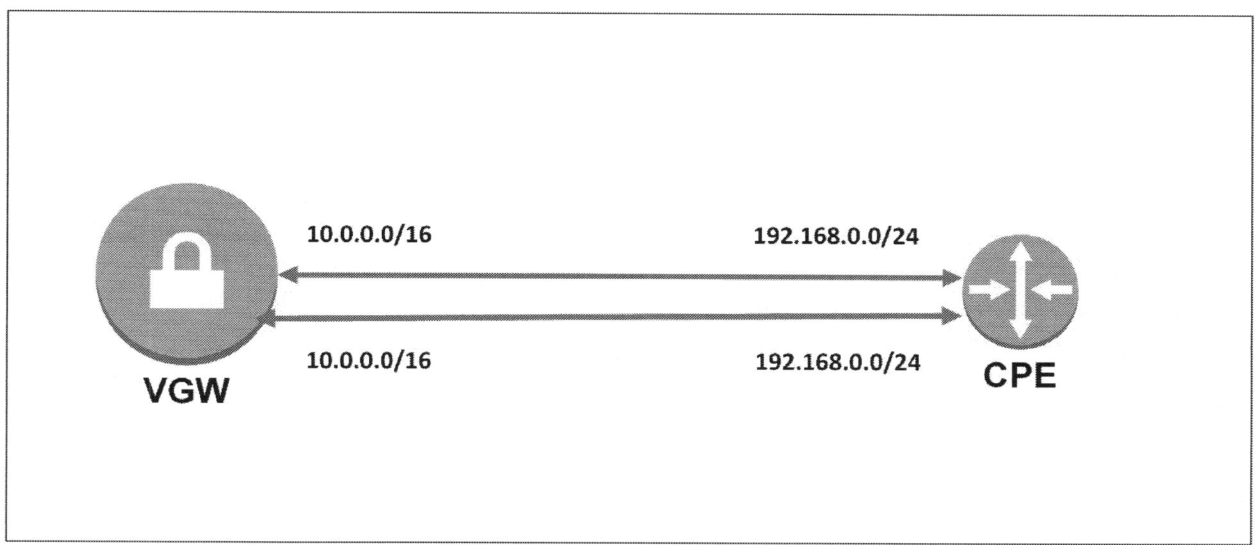

Figure 4-11: 1 Unique Security Association per Tunnel

Route Selection Way in VGW

Highest priority depends on the IP prefix. The most specific prefix is prior. If the system has multiple routes of same specific prefix, then the priority is decided by the routes, which are learned via DirectConnect. This means that routes learned through DX have higher priority over routes learned via VPNs. If the similar specific prefix routes are not related to DX, then the priority decision is taken by routes learned via Static VPN over the Dynamic Routes. The reason for this is that Static Routes are manually defined and Dynamic Routes are automatically learned routes. Routes selection is at last based on the shortest AS-PATH.

This route priority order is for the learned routes. If route propagation is enabled, then the route in route table will appear in this priority order.

Priority	Propagated Route Type
1	Most specific IP prefix 192.168.0.5/32 is preferred over 192.168.0.0./24
2	Direct connect Learnt routes
3	Routes learned via static VPN
4	Everything else BGP-based on shortest AS-PATH

Table 4-01: Priority Route Table

Dynamic Hardware VPN

In Static VPN, routing is static and should be defined on the VPN connection. The static routes can be updated whenever there is an update. If you add or remove any network, you have to update your VPN connection object with Static Routes.

Note: If the VGW is unaware of the CIDR range or a prefix, they will not route traffic to and from the remote VPN pairs for that prefix.

To understand the difference of Dynamic Hardware VPN let us consider that an organization has a single VPC operating in a two Availability Zone region, and they want to connect it to a customer.

Customer Side

The customer is in Las Vegas has two CPE and one subnet (192.168.0.0/24). This subnet is internally connected to a router of local address 192.168.0.1. This internal router exchanges the information to external routers (LACE-A and LACE-B) using IBGP. External routers have external publically addressable routing address, i.e. 1.1.1.1 and 2.2.2.2 respectively (Figure 4-12). These external routers are connected to two different ISPs, which ensure the connection resilience level at both customer and ISP level.

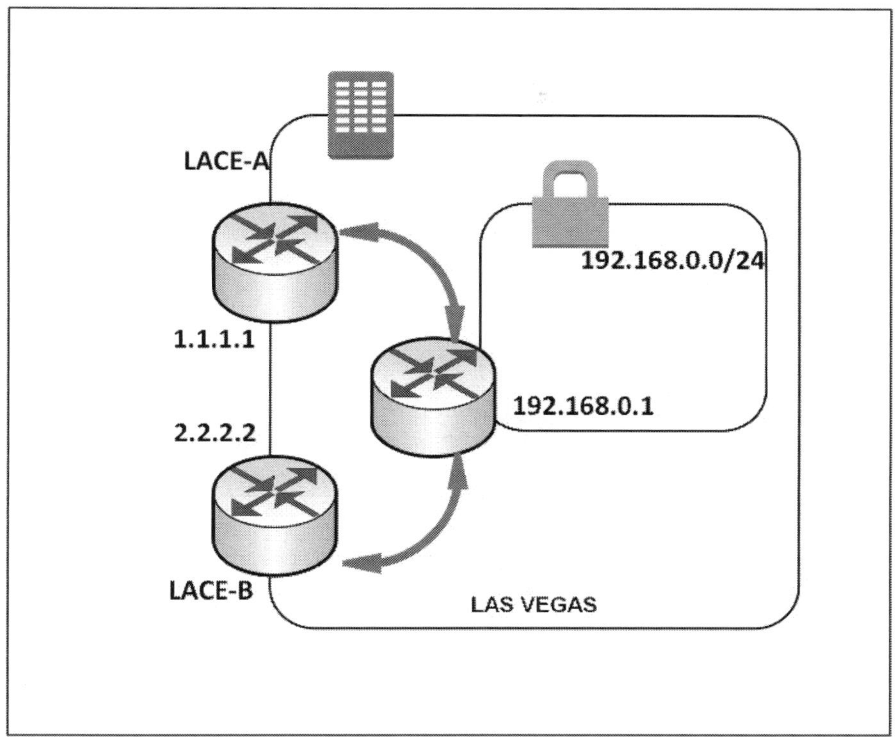

Figure 4-12: Customer Side

AWS Side

VPC is using 10.0.0.0/16 CIDR address range. This VPC is inside two AZ region having two fault domains. Inside these domains, there are two subnets (SN-A and SN-B) with address range 10.0.0.0/17 and 10.0.128.0/17 respectively. Each subnet contains a route-table. The organization has a VPC router.

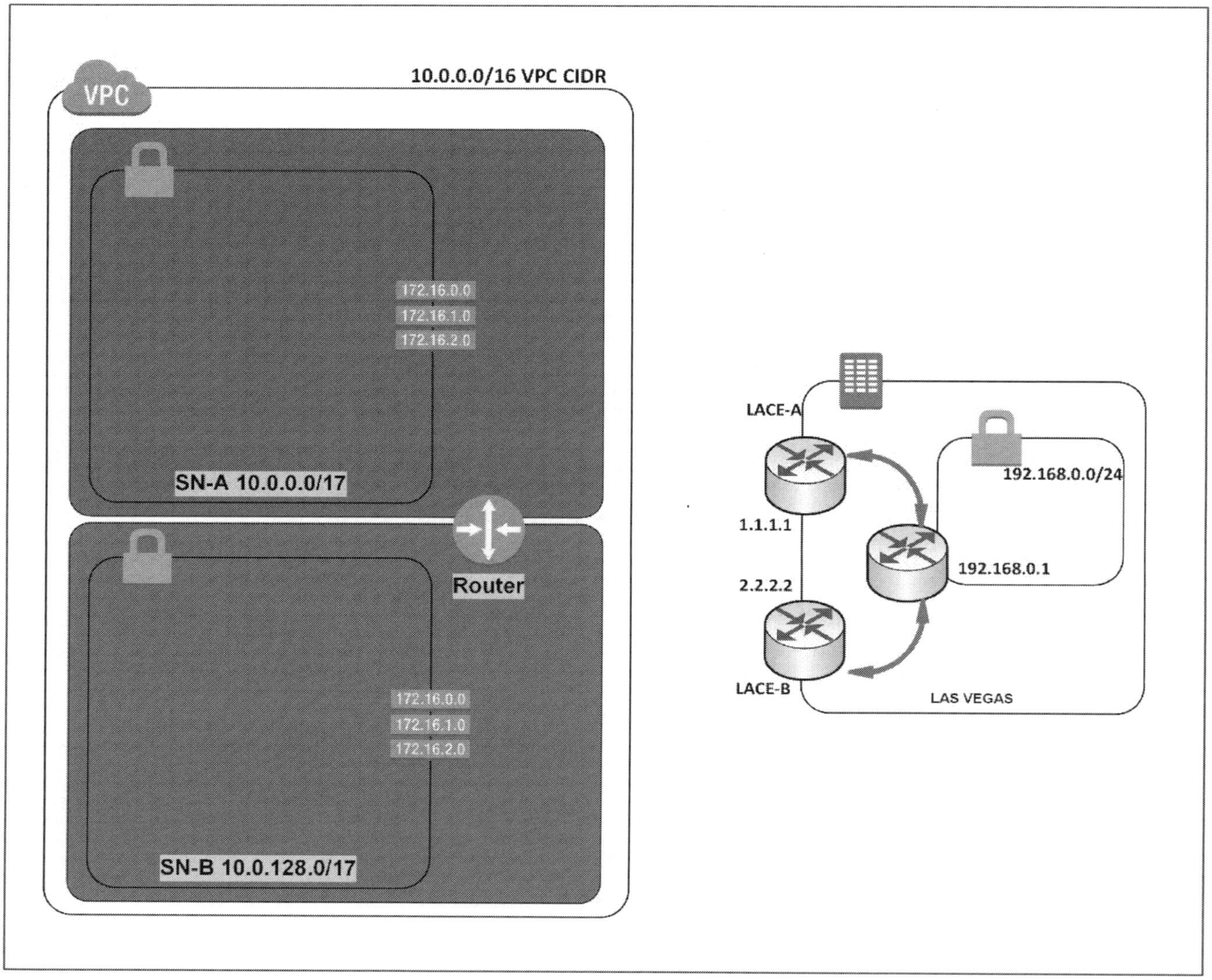

Figure 4-13: AWS Side and Customer Side

Dynamic Hardware VPN Configuration Logical Steps

Following are the logical steps to configure dynamic hardware VPN.

Step 1

Determine whether the Customer Premises Router is suitable or not (is BGP supported and also supports other AWS IPSec requirements). Customer Premises Router is suitable here.

Step 2

Create the CGW within AWS; these represent Customer Premises Router. Specify the AS number or the AS end. An AS number represents a grouping of routing infrastructures managed by one entity, business or person. For creating customer Gateway, choose an

ASN from private number ranges, which is from 64512 to 65535 (recommended). Add a name tag, select the type of routing, and enter the IP address of the router. Similarly, do this for the LACE-B router and choose the same ASN.

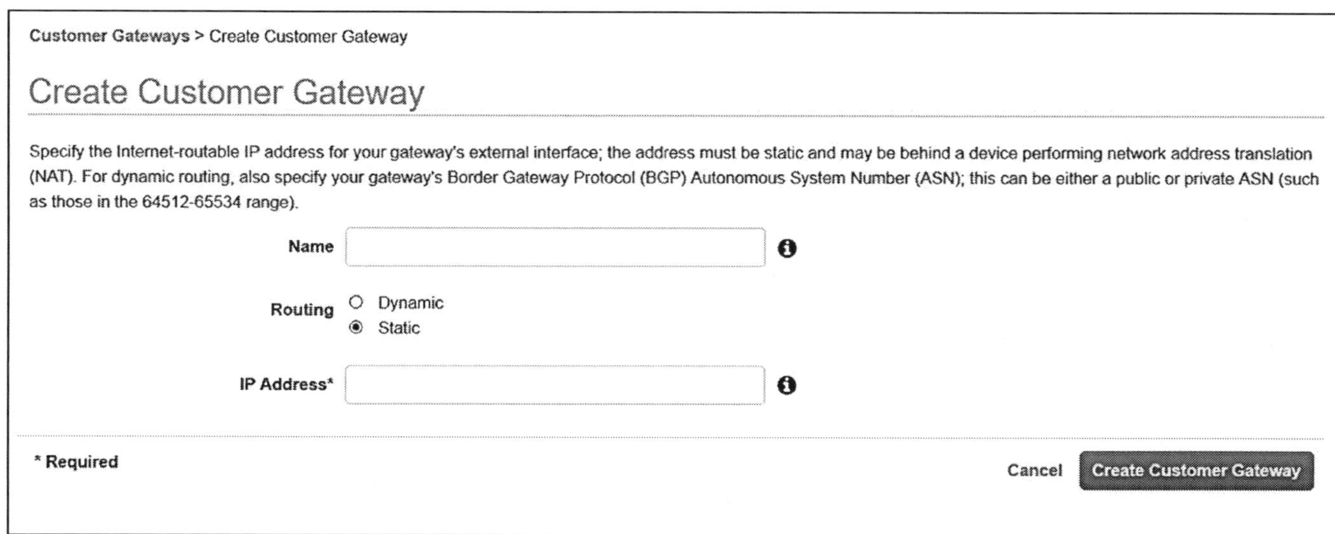

Figure 4-14: Create Customer Gateway

Step 3

Create a VGW and attach it to the VPC, this will create an object, which will be reference-able for routing purposes, and it is the termination point for any Hardware VPN or Direct Connect interfaces of organization VPCs. (Figure 4-16)

Step 4

Create a VPN connection, which is a link between VGW and CGW. In Dynamic Hardware VPN, there is no need to specify the routing information because it directs AWS to proceed to routing via BGP.

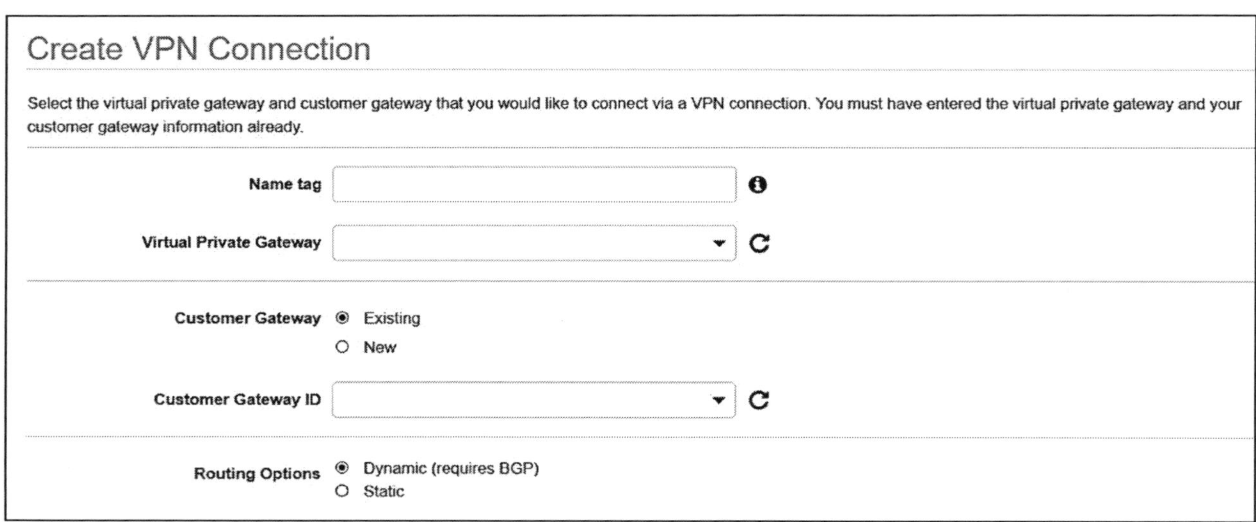

Figure 4-15: Create a VPN Connection

A VPN connection can be created using console, API, and CLI. When a VPN connection is created:

- AWS allocates two externally addressable VPN End Points (EPs). In the discussed case (Figure 4-16), there are EP-A (52.15.180.220) and EP-B (52.15.183.140). These endpoints can be the same, partially the same or completely different for every VPN connection. AWS guarantees to place these endpoints in separate fault domains on separate equipment. These endpoints enable AWS to overcome any failure or maintenance requirements.
- AWS generates VPN connection configuration data. This can be downloaded from AWS in the adjustable format for the customer router. This file can be applied directly, or the information can be entered manually by extracting the information, which will provide the required information to CPE router in order to establish two IPSec Tunnels, one is for EP-A, and the other is for EP-B (T1 and T2). In addition, it provides the information for the tunnel network interface on the Customer side and AWS side. For the given scenario, it is given as below:
    - Tunnel 1 interfaces: Customer side interface, i.e. T1-C (169.254.59.54) and AWS side interface, i.e. T1-A (169.254.59.53)
    - Tunnel 2 interfaces: Customer side, i.e. T2-C (169.254.59.130) and AWS side, i.e. T2-A (169.254.59.129)

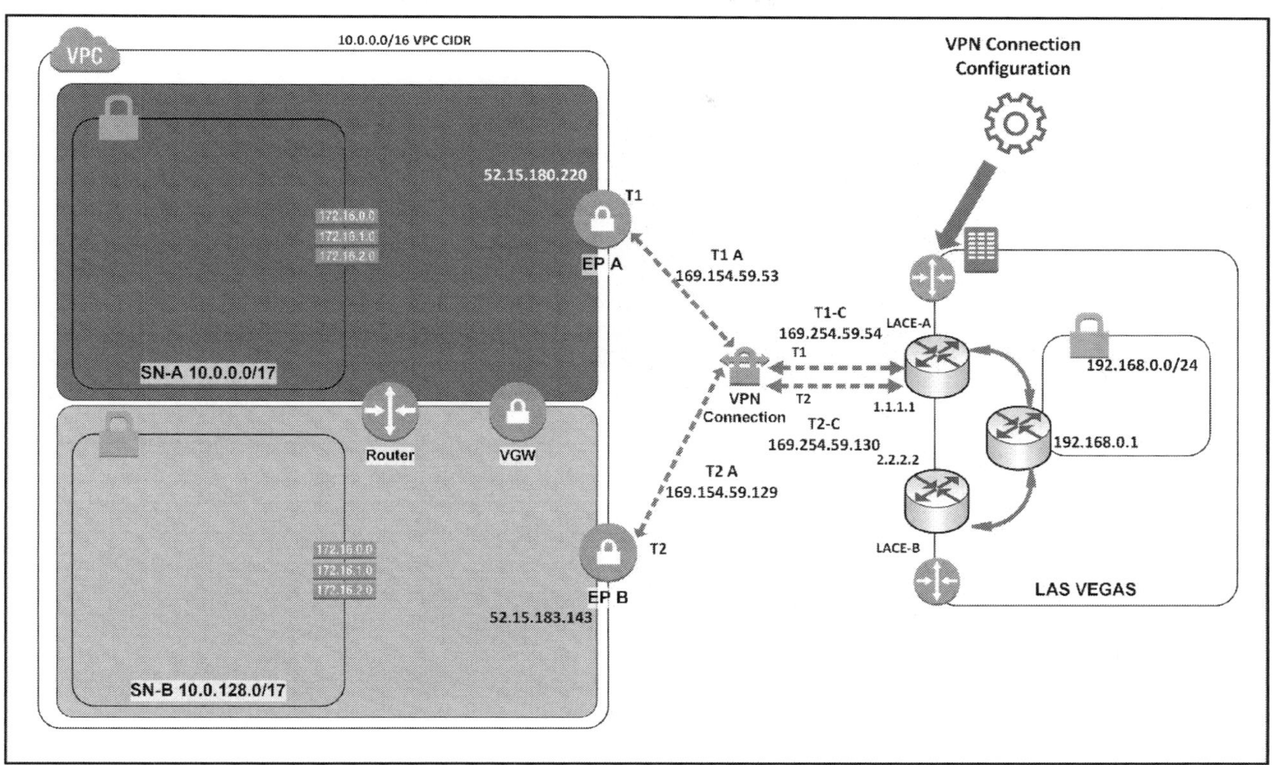

Figure 4-16: Dynamic Hardware VPN Connection Architecture

The configuration file will do the following tasks:

- Configures BGP on the customer side router
- Sets BGP ASN to 65000 (as defined in creating CGW)
- Provides the information about the BGP neighbors (ASN which is always 7224 for AWS VPNs and BGP neighbors IPs, which is the tunnel interface at the AWS side, i.e. in this case 169.254.59.53)

Now, IP connectivity and BGP neighbor configuration's information are available therefore, the system is now able to exchange routing information dynamically between neighbors i.e. between VGW and CPE. For second CPE (LACE-B) there is also a second VPN connection.

Step 5

Add a route-table and attach it to both subnets SN-A and SN-B. Enable route propagation for the routers attachment. The routes learned by VGW via BGP and the routes that are manually set are automatically propagated to both route tables.

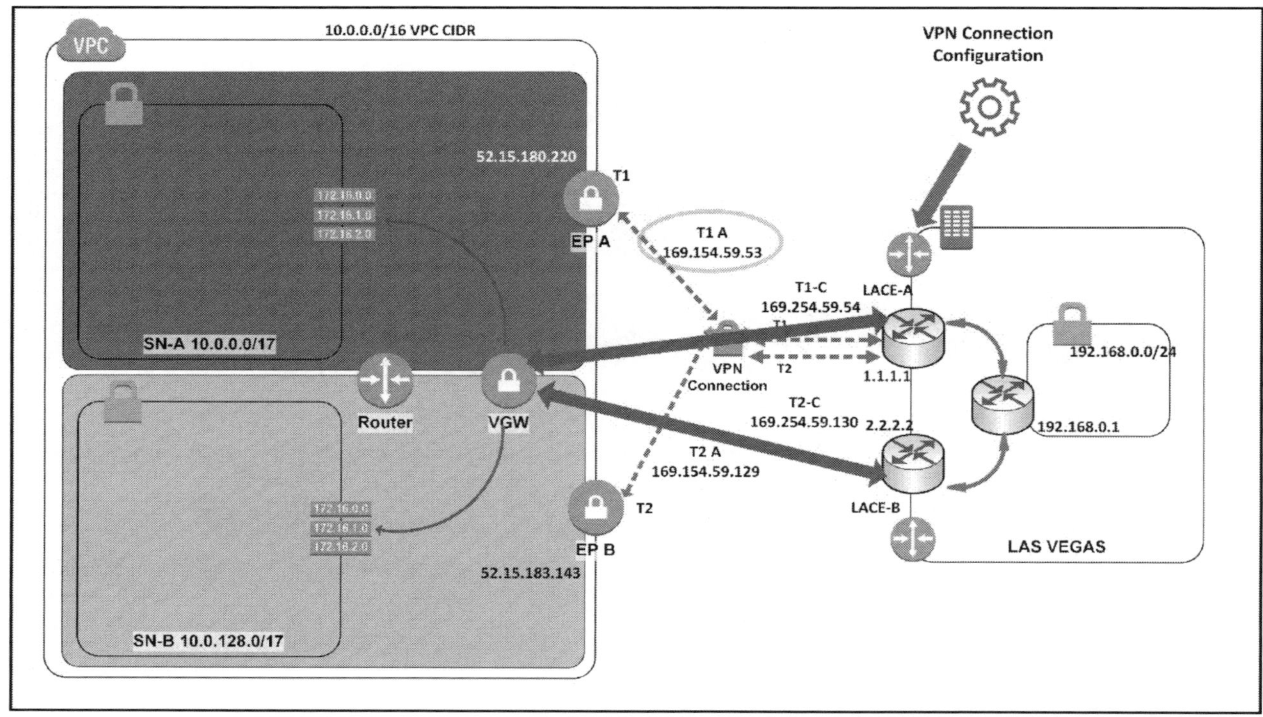

Figure 4-17: Dynamic Hardware VPN Connection Architecture (a)

Now consider the given architecture (figure 4-18), which is similar to the previous architecture (Figure 4-17) but architecturally it is drawn by removing some irrelevant objects. This is the VPN and BGP architecture.

This architecture represents two sides, i.e. AWS side on left and Customer side on right

AWS side

We have the following components:

- A VPC (10.0.0.0/16) with two subnets SN-A (10.0.0.0/17) and SN-B (10.0.128.0/17) using the main route table of the VPC.
- A VPC router
- VGW
- ASN is 7224

Customer side

Customer side has:

- Las Vegas data center region
- A subnet (192.168.0.0/24)
- Internal router
- External router

- ASN is 65000

Both AWS and Customer sides are linked via a VPN connection.

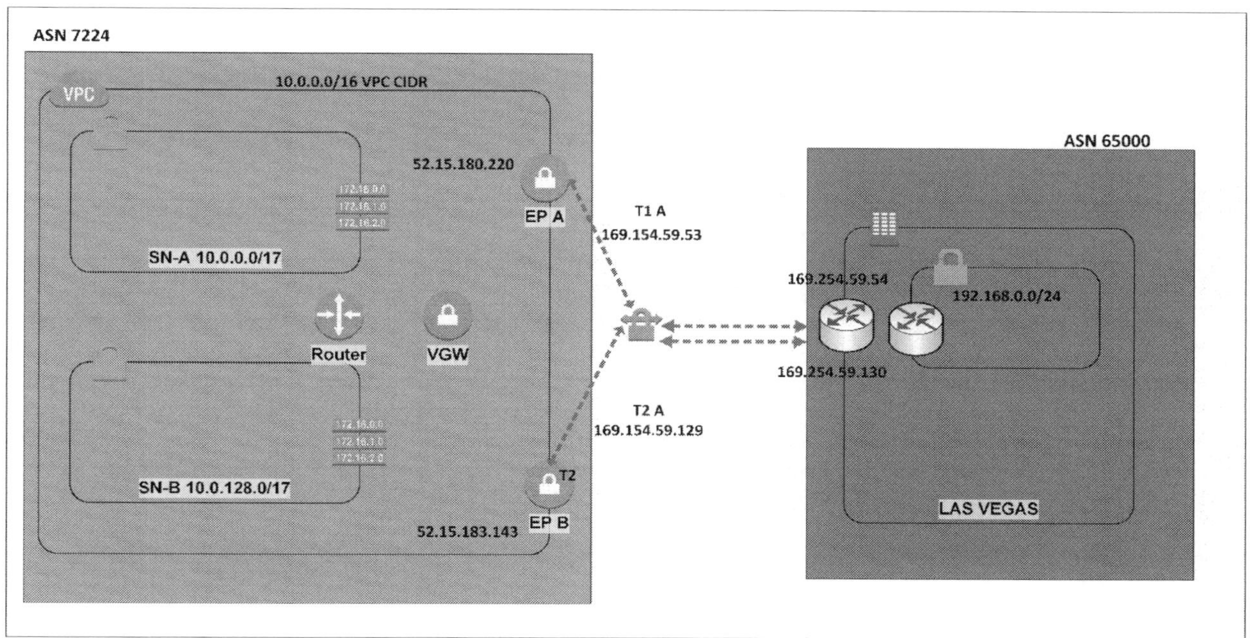

Figure 4-18: Dynamic Hardware VPN Connection Architecture (b)

BGP Route Advertising

This procedure is illustrated using architecture in Figure 4-19.

Customer side route table is Table B, and AWS side route table is Table A.

Customer side route table (Table B.1) initially consists of local subnet. The first column contains network address (192.168.0.0/24), the second column address (0.0.0.0) defines that it is a local subnet, the third column is the wait value, and generally 32,768 is used for locally connected routes. The last column is showing the origin of ASPATH, which defines the route the packet takes for reaching inside the autonomous system or network. In the discussed case, it is "i" representing that the route origin is the internal routing protocol (IGBP, RIP, RIPv2, or locally connected network). Only the customer router knows this network and route, but through BGP, this route is sent to the AWS side (BGP sends the best path to the destination but in our case, we have just one route available 192.168.0.0). So, the router prepends its AS number on to the ASPATH and it advertises the routes to both of its pairs.

192.168.0.0/24	0.0.0.0	32768	I

Table 4-02: B.1

There are two AWS endpoints, therefore, VGW at the termination point has two paths or routes for the same customer-side network for each tunnel. In VGW, route table's (Table A.1) second column has different values (169.254.59.54 and 169.254.59.130)

192.168.0.0/24	169.254.59.54	0	65000,i
192.168.0.0/24	169.254.59.130	0	65000,i

Table 4-03: A.1

Both of these routes are dynamically learned BGP routes. AWS will assume that the user wants to use an active/active configuration for the VPN because, both share the same ASPATH link i.e. user wants to use both tunnels to send traffic to Customer. Organizations have VPC subnets in AWS side. By default, AWS advertises the CIDR range of VPC, not the subnets. The route of VPC is shown in the third row of AWS side route (Table A.2) configurations.

192.168.0.0/24	169.254.59.54	0	65000,i
192.168.0.0/24	169.254.59.130	0	65000,i
10.0.0.0/16	0.0.0.0	-	i

Table 4-04: A.2

This route will be advertised to the both BGP partners connected to VGW, which will add two more routes in the customer side route table (Table B.2).

192.168.0.0/24	0.0.0.0	32768	I
10.0.0.0/16	169.254.59.53	0	7224,i
10.0.0.0/16	169.254.59.129	0	7224,i

Table 4-05: B.2

The traffic will be distributed across both VPN tunnels equally if the BGP multi-pathing is enabled on the Customer side.

Now enabling the route propagation on the main VPC route table will allow all the learned routes of VGW to propagate in both route tables of subnets.

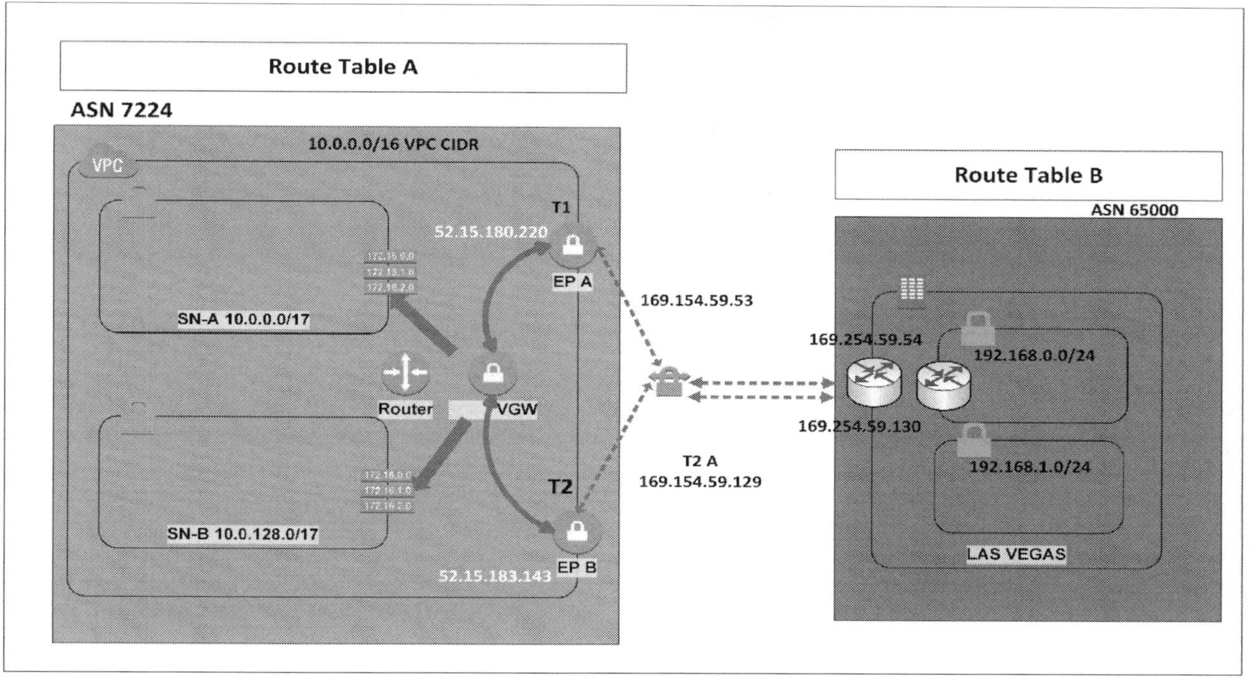

Figure 4-19: Dynamic Hardware VPN Connection Architecture (b) with Routing

If the organization adds one more local subnet on the customer side, this will create two more routes by local routing, which will be then advertised across both BGP peers on the AWS side. These routes are then added to routing information of the VGW. Due to route propagation, the instance running in SN-A and SN-B will get these routes available (Table A.3 and Table B.3).

192.168.0.0/24	169.254.59.54	0	65000,i
192.168.0.0/24	169.254.59.130	0	65000,i
10.0.0.0/16	0.0.0.0	-	i
192.168.1.0/24	169.254.59.54	0	65000,i
192.168.1.0/24	169.254.59.130	0	65000,i

Table 4-06: A.3

192.168.0.0/24	0.0.0.0	32768	i
10.0.0.0/16	169.254.59.53	0	7224,i
10.0.0.0/16	169.254.59.129	0	7224,i
192.168.1.0/24	0.0.0.0	32768	i

Table 4-07: B.3

Local Waiting

All of the learned paths are treated equally by AWS. To influence this, you can use local waiting. Local waiting is a vendor-specific way to influence outbound routing. For example, you can use this to influence routing from Las Vegas into AWS. You can add a wait value for one of the paths; let us say for 10.0.0.0/16, you set the wait value as 500. A higher wait value means higher routing preference. The adjusted wait value can be used to restrict communication from a specific tunnel. Note that the wait value is local to the router, which means that the wait value for a path cannot pass across multiple local routers.

Local Preference

To overcome this, you have another option of using ***Local Preference.*** It is an attribute that can be set within an AS boundary to prefer a specific path throughout a remote Autonomous System. In the given scenario, all routers within Las Vegas will obey the preference value. If you adjust the local preference of the tunnel 2 path, you can make your outgoing active/active communication configured to active/passive with tunnel2 being the active path by setting its preference value. If local preference is not set, the default value will be 100.

AS Path

Finally, you have the AS Path option that can affect inbound routing, i.e. from AWS to Las Vegas. Every time a path is advertised to an AS, the AS number of that path is prepended on to the path once. If you want AWS to use a specific tunnel to send traffic, you can add additional prepends to other path.

Direct Connect DX

Consider the number of locations; some different logical locations can be in same physical space, therefore, take it as logical locations. Refer to the given architecture (Figure 4-20), for understanding, there are the following components:

- An AWS region having a VPC
- Two subnets, each in different AZ
- A route table is attached to each subnet
- A VPC router
- A VGW, which functions as a private router or an endpoint between VPN and DX traffic

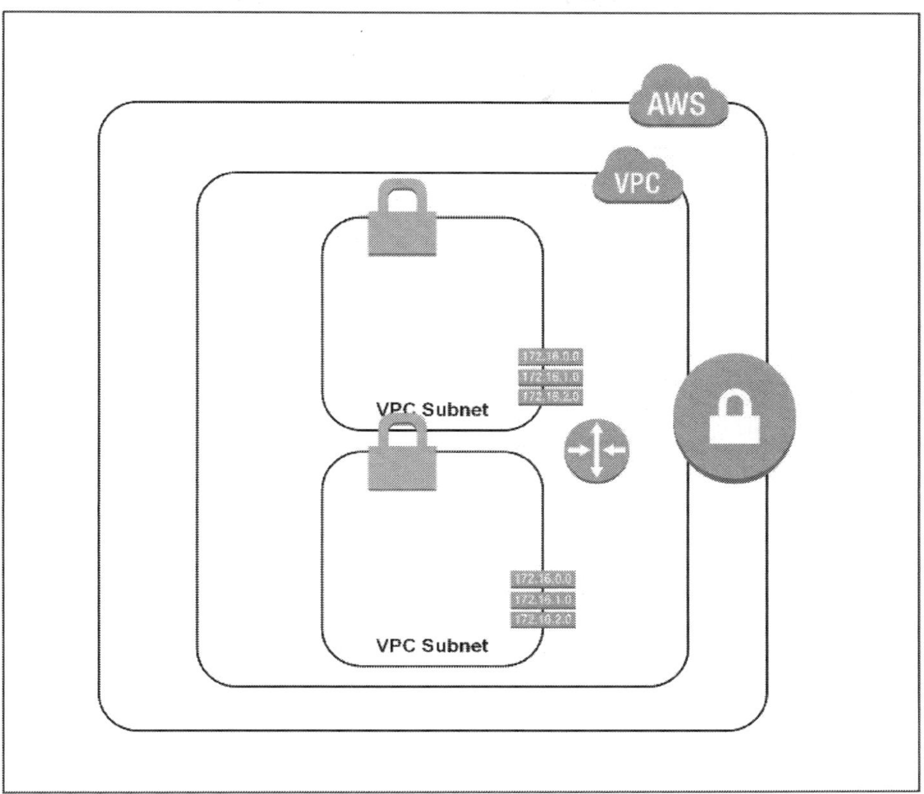

Figure 4-20: AWS Side

While combining the AWS region architecture with DX location, consider the architecture (Figure 4-21) that has following components:

- A DirectConnect Location in a colocation facility; these might be same or different
- One DX location that has same physical location but perhaps on a different flow
- A DX space in a DX location
- DX router; DX router is equipment managed by AWS

This router is connected with the AWS local region by the AWS backbone, a super high-speed low latency network between the DirectConnect location and any Availability Zones in that region. When you place an order for DirectConnect, you are essentially linking your infrastructure in that region with the DX router. This architecture is the basic connection between your AWS things in a region (specifically VGW) and DX router.

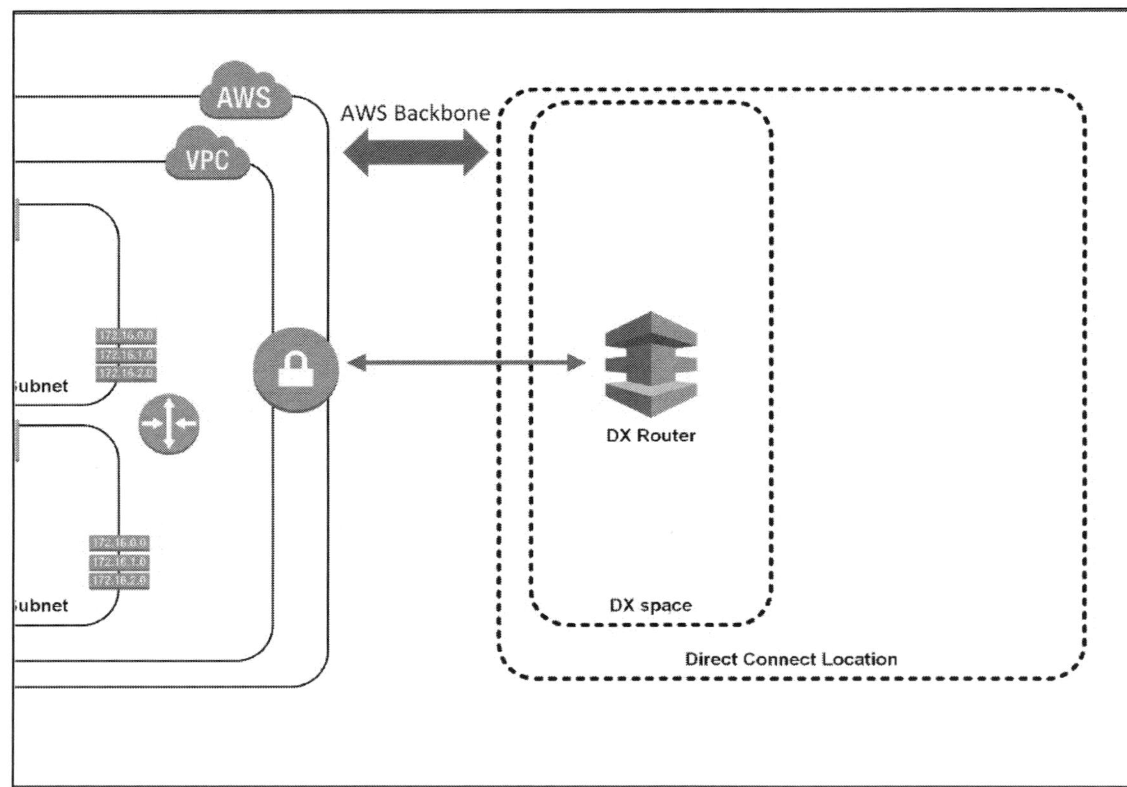

Figure 4-21: DX Location with DX Space

In DX location, there is a customer co-location or customer DC having its router (Figure 4-22). Customer will have all the services here such as servers, storage or might be simple transit facility.

When DirectConnect link is ordered, the end state will be a port in the DX router, which is allocated directly to the customer. This port will allow the customer to arrange cross-connect in a DC facility between DX router and customer router. This connection will be a trunk 802.1 Q multiple VLAN capable link.

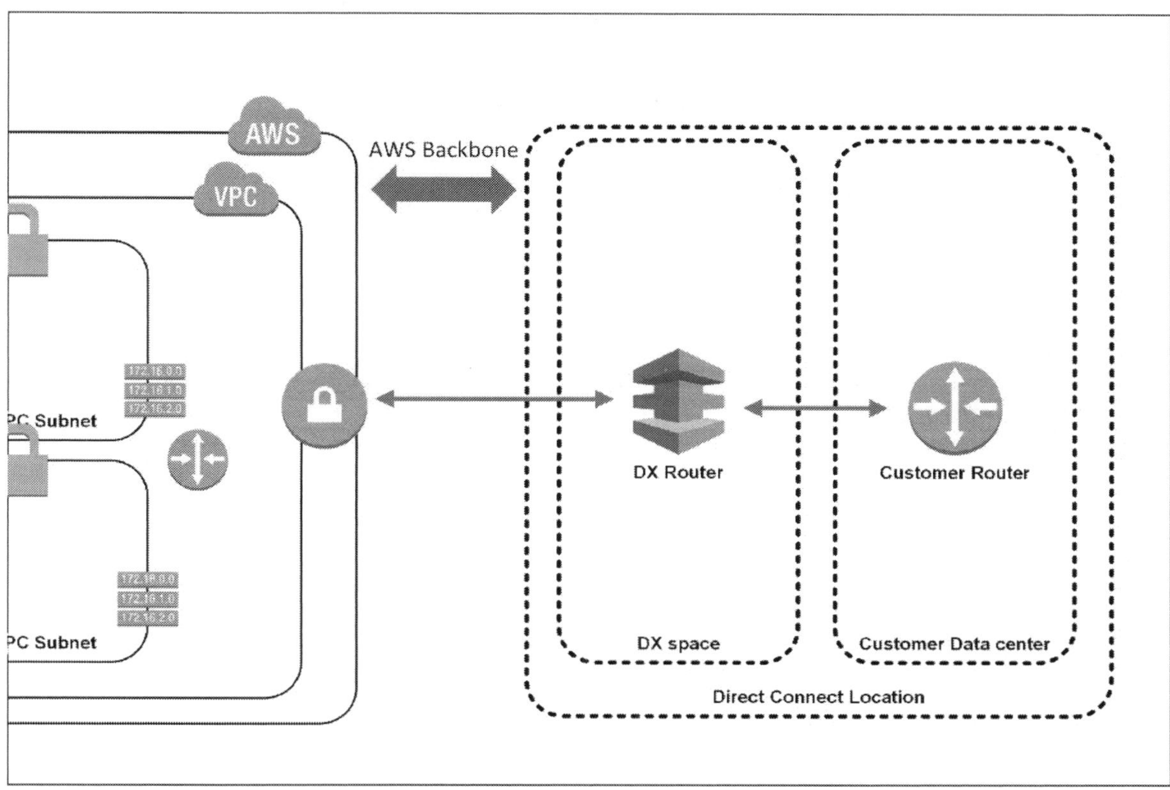

Figure 4-22: DX Connection Architecture

A customer WAN or MPLS can also be included in the above architecture, which would be linked to one or more customer sites.

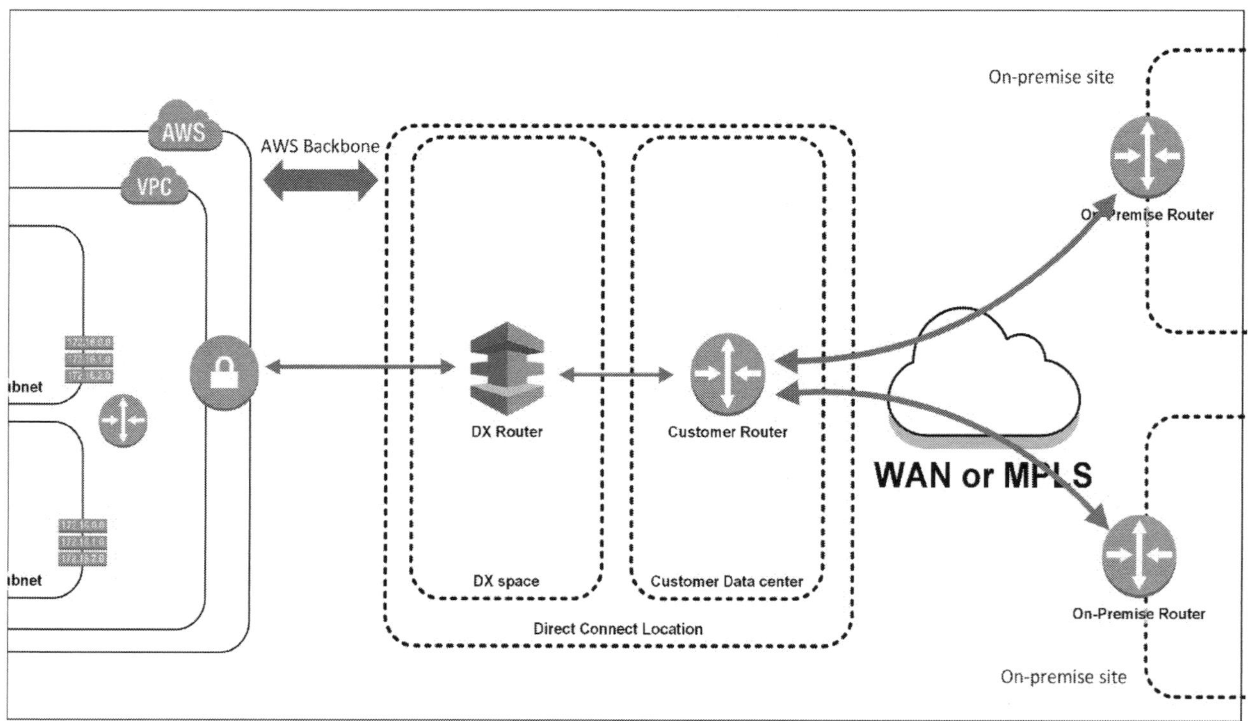

Figure 4-23: DX Connection Architecture

Customer can get DX directly from AWS via a port on DX router and a cross-connect or can get DX via a partner that allows to utilize other locations.

Note: DirectConnect in AWS is only available in 1 or 10 GB/s but you can get all speeds when ordering DirectConnect through partners.

Characteristics of Direct Connect

- Its setup is slow because this connection requires physical installation.
- Due to its physical nature, it is not resilient by default.
- It can be combined with Hardware VPN in order to achieve resilience.
- No ongoing management required because you can achieve automation using AWS console, API and CLI.
- More expensive than Hardware and Software VPN because it includes operational cost, required datacenter space, physical routers.
- Less bandwidth cost.
- Cost is based on port hours therefore; it is cost effective.
- Public internet is not used in this technique therefore; it provides consistent network latency.
- Consistent network performance.
- Single DirectConnect can be split in multiple VPCs or multiple accounts.

- Multiple DirectConnect can be combined if you need more bandwidth and high speed.
- It is not secured by default, if you need security, you have to achieve it by using IPSec VPN over a DX.

Physical Architecture & Installation Process

Basic Terminologies

We have an AWS region in which there might be different Availability Zones (AZ). Within these AZs, we have public AWS services and AWS private services i.e. VPC. In this topic, when any AWS region is referred to, that means Availability Zones, public and private endpoints are there in the regions.

AWS DirectConnect (DX) is a physical location, which is independent on the AWS region. That means DX are located in well-known data center facilities or co-locations. There can be multiple DX locations in a region. You may have some communication equipment or servers. If you do not have servers, you may take some space in the co-location facility for DX link or you may not. Within the DX location, we have AWS cage (AWS site), which is the space allocated for AWS in the co-location facility. At least two DX routers are available in AWS cage. In co-location facility, equipment can already be present, or need to be installed, or there can be an equipment provider. Beside the AWS cage, there is logically a customer space (Customer cage). You might have equipment at one DX location, or you have multiple equipment at that one DX location or multiple equipment at all DX locations. Inside customer cage, there are one or multiple customer routers. For adding more resiliencies in your network, you can add more routers and more DX locations in your region.

Customer WAN/MAN/LAN is a customer Wide Area Network, Metropolitan Area Network and Local Area Network. It is the main part of the customer network not the interface of your network within the AWS. This will include customer's business network i.e. business sites, users, servers etc. Inside Customer WAN/MAN/LAN, there is a customer WAN/MAN router.

Example: In E-commerce business, if it does not use LAN MAN or WAN then there is no need of customer WAN/MAN/LAN segment shown in the rightmost side of the diagram.

If your business has a network outside the co-location, then you need the communication links between the co-location and outside network that will extend your infrastructure in the co-location facility to your customer network. Communication between AWS and co-location facility is a high-speed backbone network that ensures very high bandwidth with low latency connectivity between all AZs in a region.

Actual Connection: DirectConnect is the connection between the AWS account and the DX location. After the connection is created, you have the logical connection entity within your AWS account and you have a port on one DX router in the AWS cage. This port is configured as 802.1 Q Trunk so; it can carry multiple VLAN. LOA (Letter of Authority) document is also provided, which lists the port of DX router. You and your partner can cross-connect by using LOA with the facility management team between the physical port of the DX router and the physical port of you or your partner's router. This physical connection (X-Connection) is the physical fiber connection of 802.1 Q Trunk. You can also establish this physical connection between your customer router and customer network.

Therefore, the connection between AWS and customer network is 802.1 Q trunk.

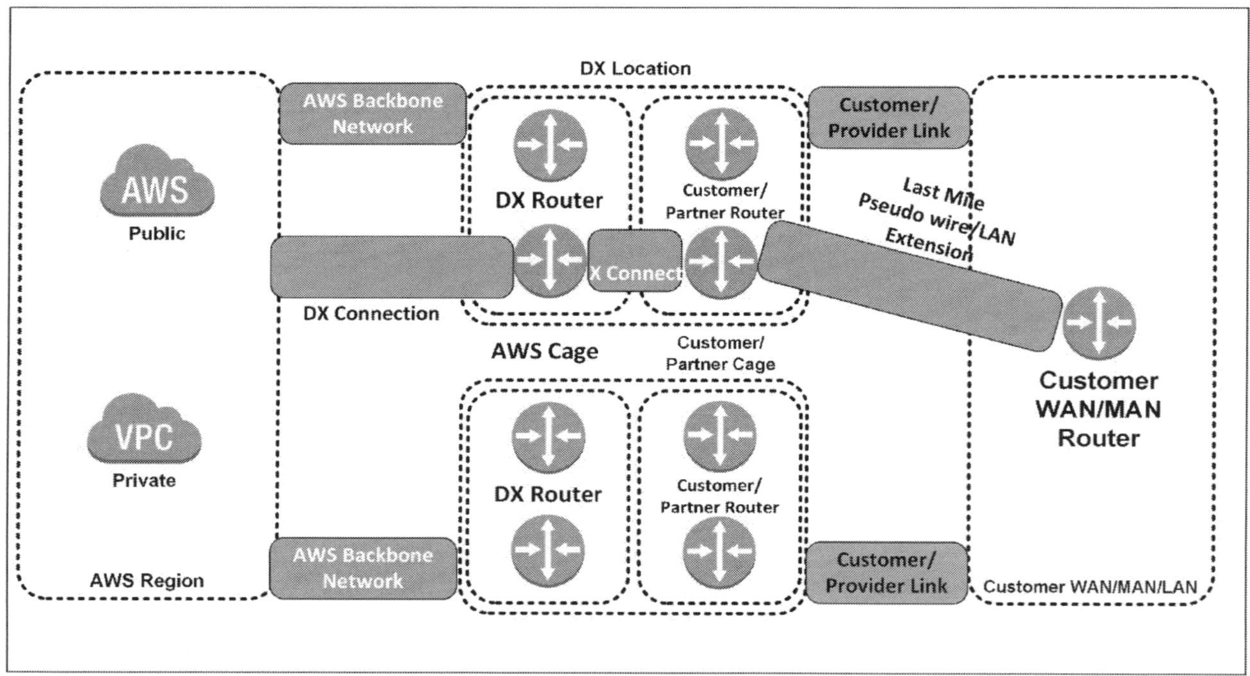

Figure 4-24: DX Physical Architecture Before Creating VIFs

Interfaces can be created in this Trunk. Interfaces are of two types:

- Public interfaces
- Private interfaces

Public interfaces are created to use public services provided by AWS such as DynamoDB and S3 whereas, Private interfaces are created to access VPC.

Virtual interface is the logical AWS construct that is represented by VLAN from OSI layer 2 and BGP pairing between the AWS and customer router.

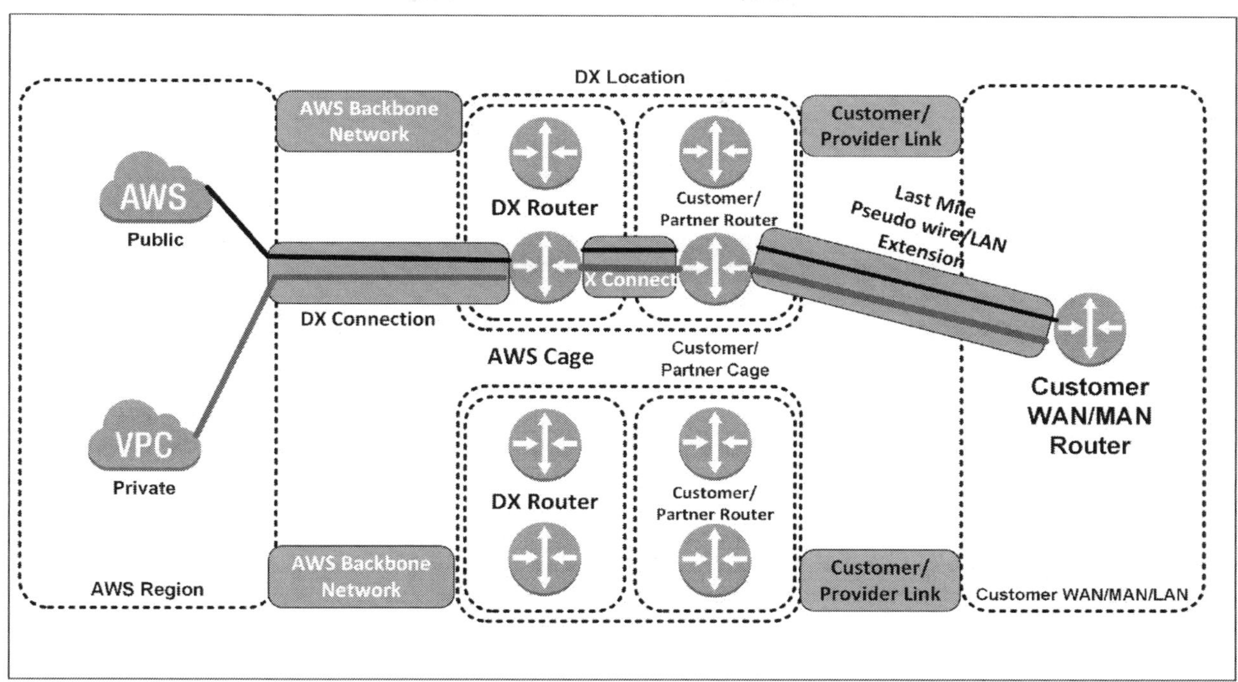

Figure 4-25: DX Physical Architecture with VIFs

Logical Components

AWS account: For direct connection, one should have an AWS account.

DX Connection: It always has a DXConn identifier. It is the connection between your AWS account and DX location. This will provide you the port number on your DX router in your DX location, which is 802.1 Q Trunk. After that port, you have to arrange a cross-connect between your DX router and Customer Router. This connection should be single mode fiber.

Once the DX is terminated within the co-location router, which belongs to you or your co-location partner, then you may arrange connection to your premises or network.

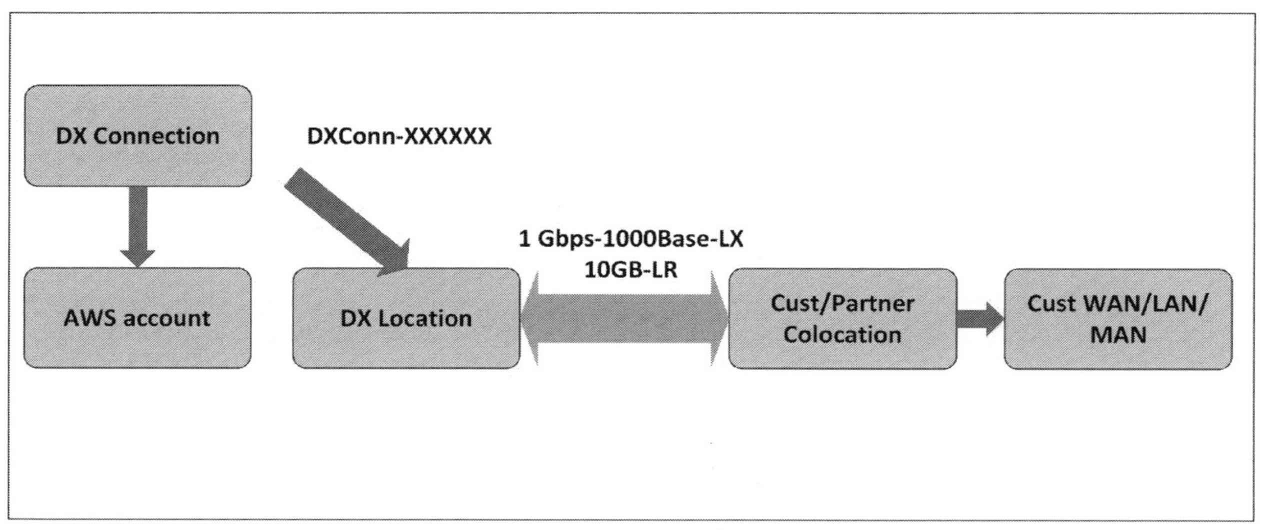

Figure 4-26: Logical components of DX

Physical Installation

Generally, three or four entities are involved in DirectConnect.

- Customer
- AWS
- Location Provider
- Career/ Partner

1. You have set your region correctly; for example, if you want to create DX in Sydney, the region should be set to Sydney.
2. From the DirectConnect area of the console CLI or API, you can create direct connection. You have to select the speed of the connection and the location (DX location).
3. AWS views your request, views the DX location capacity and after that, they allocate your port in DX router in the specified location and it can take 3 days. Then, AWS provides LOA, which is the document that is sent on the root user account or you can also download it from the console.
4. Next step is to arrange the cross-connect. You now have LOA, either you or your partner can allocate the port or either you or your partner can provide your LOA to DX location provider. The provider then confirms the authorization, plans the cabling and physically installing cross-connect. The process is different according to the different locations. Once the process is completed, you are notified for the Cross Connect completion.
5. Depending on your architecture, you can now connect your DX location to the customer network. This can be done by using point-to-point connections or you may

use MPLS, VLAN or encapsulation technology. This process generally takes up to 90 days.

6. In Physical port configuration and physical installation, you have to set the port primitives. According to AWS recommendation, auto-negotiating should be disabled, four duplex is enabled, and port speed and the requested speed from AWS should be same.
7. Interface configuration is a logical process. You have to set VLAN or any BGP authentication to create interface. After its creation, configuration details can be downloaded or the interface can be done manually.

			Customer	AWS	Location Provider	Carrier/ Partner
1	Select Region within AWS account	N/A	X			
2	Order Connection- Specifying 1 or 10 GB and DX location	Depends	X			
3	Arrange DX port on DX router Deliver LOA CFA	3 Days		X		
4	Arrange Cross Connect – provide LOA and your customer port details or your carrier/partner handles	~1-4 Days	X		X	O
5	(Optional) Physical backhaul from carrier to customer	~90 Days				X
6	Port & Physical integration	Depends	X			
7	Interface creation, configuration, integration	Depends	X			

Table 4-08: Responsibilities for a DX Connection

Direct Connect Sub 1 Gbps via a Partner

If you do not have any equipment in DX location, you can use a partner or a network carrier. If you need 50 Mbps OR 500 Mbps, these are not provided by AWS hence, you will require a partner. If you need 1Gbps speed, AWS might not be the best option.

In the above architecture (Figure 4-25), when you have done DirectConnect connection directly i.e. without a partner, the customer (you) is provided with a port on DX router and you arrange a cross-connect to your router in DX location or you get a network partner to extend your network (to the right of the figure4-25). In this architecture, you have the all-time control of physical cables carrying multiple VLANs. Logically you have multiple VLANs or multiple Virtual Interfaces (VIFs) on one DirectConnect trunk.

DirectConnect using a Partner

The cross-connect connection is earned by the partner, which is between DX router and partner's router. Cross-connect is the cable of 802.1 Q Trunk, which is able to carry the VLAN information (Virtual Interfaces). This cross-connect is shared with all the customers of the partner therefore, this cross connect may have multiple VLANs. You as customer have no control or visibility over multi VLAN capable cross connects. You will get the hosted connection (Hosted connection is created by the partner and shared in your account). In this architecture, there is the special hosted connection, which only allows one VLAN. This hosted connection is added to your AWS account, which will look the same as when the connection was ordered directly from AWS, only the difference will be that the hosted connection has pre-assigned VLAN.

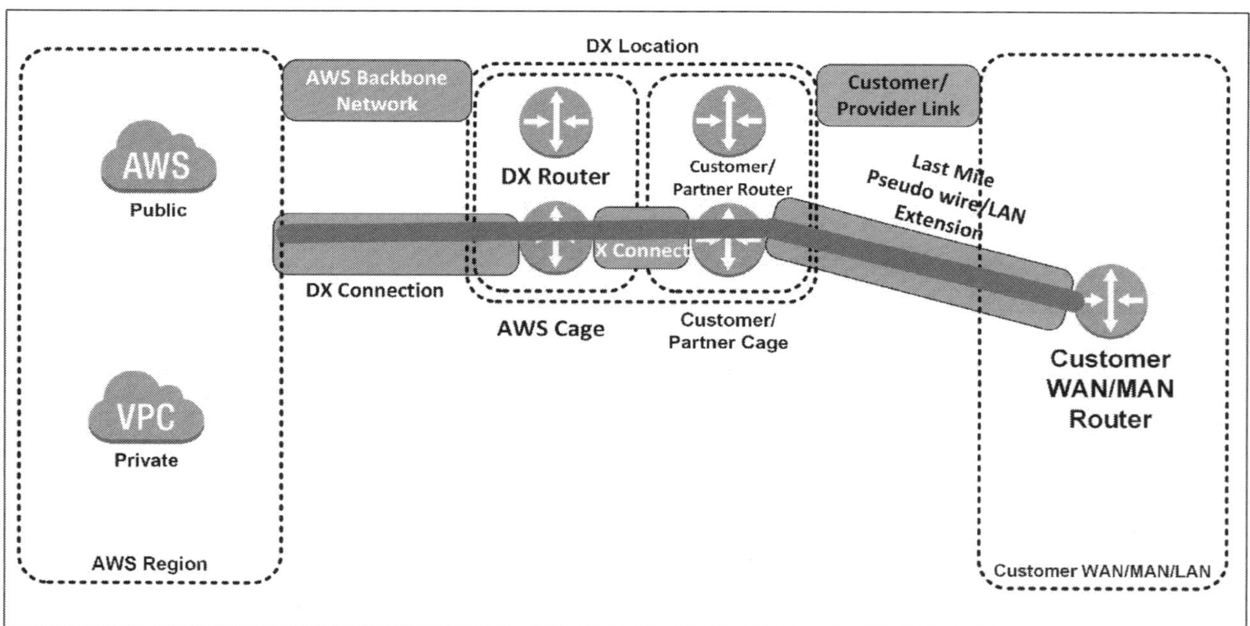

Figure 4-27: DX using Partner without VIF

In addition to this, you can connect a public or private VIF (one private or one public) so you do not have any control over multiple VIF, only single VIF is allowed. If you want more VIF, you have to repeat the procedure for more hosted connections.

Note: You will get a locked VLAN by the provider on which you can get a single Virtual Interface.

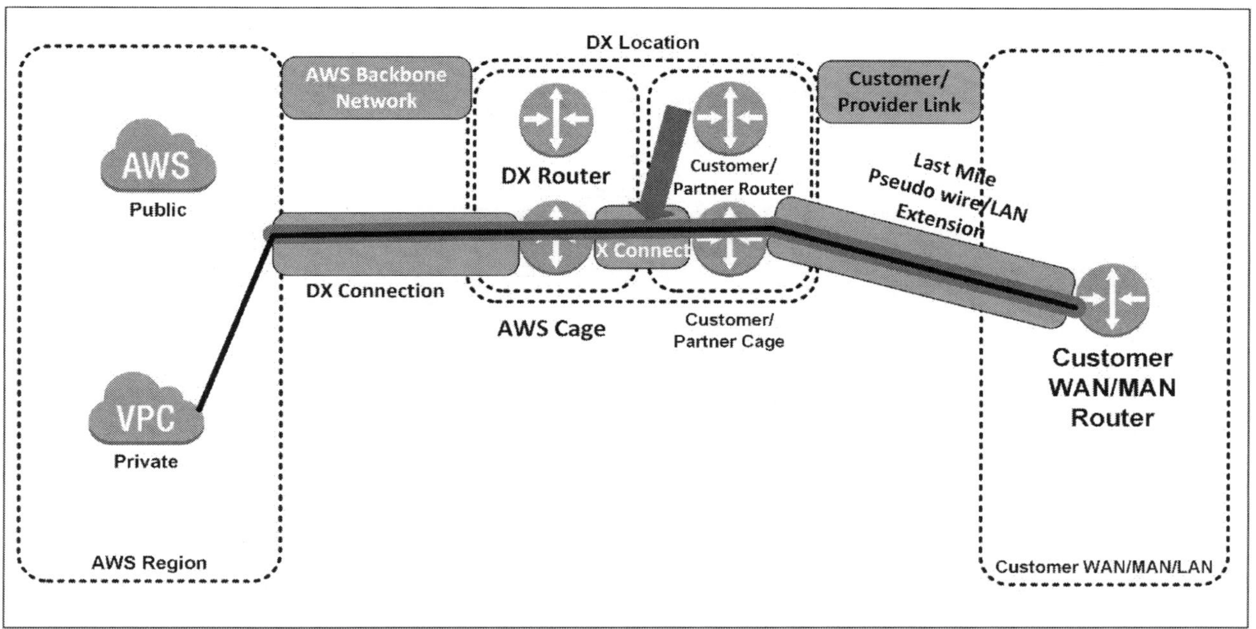

Figure 4-28: DX Architecture using Partner with VIF

Logical Structure of Partner Supplied Connection

AWS account is required where you will earn the hosted connect. AWS account number is provided to the DX partner with the requirements of the speed (1 Gbps).

On the backend, DX partner arranges all the physical equipment required for the cross connect with AWS and it returns two things:

- Physical way for connecting to the network, either directly or using MPLS
- Hosted connection with assigned VLAN that appeared in your AWS account

Further, after getting the hosted connection, you have two options:

- Creation of public or private VIF in the same account as the connection
- Creation of hosted VIF in another external account

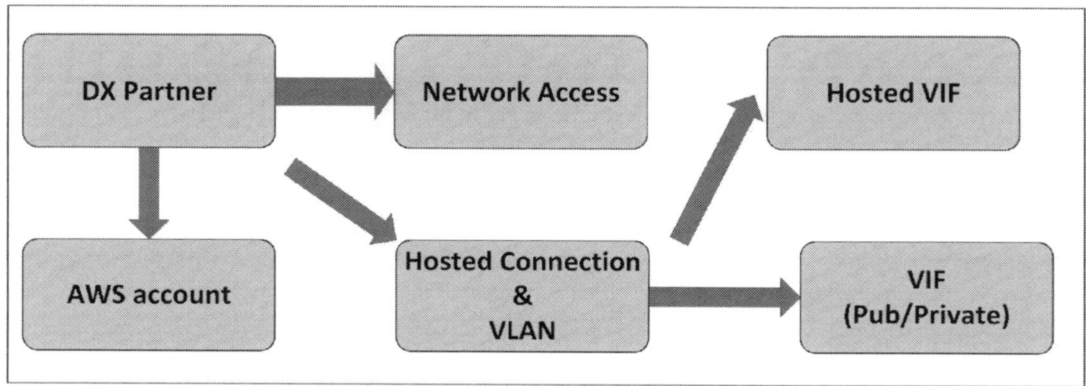

Figure 4-29: Logical Component of DX for Hosted Connection

In Partner provided connection, Partner is free to use any physical connection method. By using AWS, you have only two choices for connection speed (1 Gbps or 10 Gbps) and deliver over a single mode fiber. Partner DX solution provides flexibility in delivery over shared nationwide networks.

Creation of Partner Supplied DX Connection

There are only two entities involved i.e. Customer and Partner.

1. You have to provide your desired speed and the account number to your partner.
2. Accept the connection of your requirement.
3. Now, create a virtual interface (public or private), the options are same as when doing it directly. For private VIFs, you are required the public or private ASN or pair IPs for private VIFs can be auto generated. For public VIFs, ideally you will use public ASN and for advertise you need public IP range or public prefix.
4. At last, you have to perform router configuration and integration. When you download the configuration for the VIF pre-formatted from the vendor platform or you can also apply this manually.

Once the instance is configured, the working will be same as directly using AWS.

			Customer	Partner
1	Request a sub 1 gig connection from APN Partner (DX)	1 week – 3 months	N/A	X
2	Accept the hosted connection	Immediate	X	
3	Create Virtual Interface	*1-2 Days	X	
4	Router configuration & Integration	Depends	X	

Table 4-09: DirectConnect APN Connection

Direct Connect (DX) Private VIF

In the mentioned architecture in figure 4-30, there is a VPC (10.0.0.0/16) in two AZ regions. It has two subnets (10.0.0.0/17 & 10.0.128.0/17), one in each AZ. A VGW is attached to VPC. On the right side, A is the corporate data center with two subnets (192.168.0.0/24 & 192.168.1.0/24) as shown. An external router is attached. For this case, suppose it is a CISCO router, which is capable of BGP and it is physically located in DX location. Consider for this scenario; there is DirectConnect placed already and cross connect between the corporate router and DX router in the AWS cage. Two things happened when you create a private VIF:

- A private BGP session is created, which uses private prefixes. This session is created between customer and DX router.
- A layer 2 primitives of that connection is established i.e. VLAN ID is used between the ports of DX and customer router.

AS number of AWS is 7224 and customer side is, let us suppose you have taken 65000.

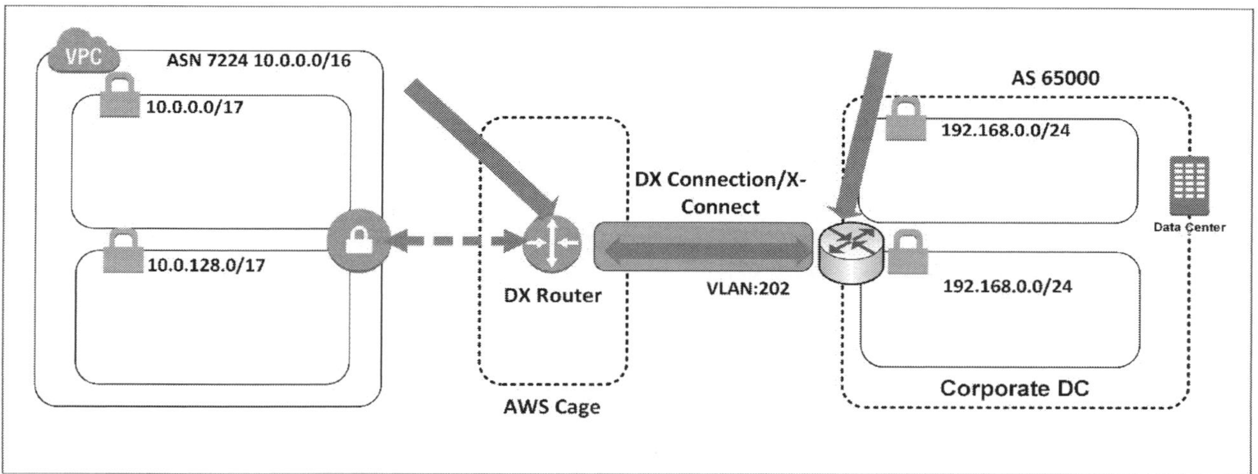

Figure 4-30: DX Private VIF

Creation of Private VIF

Layer 3 details for the BGP session (peer IP addressing). For private VIF the peer IP address should be private. If they were auto generated by AWS, then it would be in 169.x.x.x range. BGP session is authenticated with MD5 key selected by the customer (you) or auto generated by AWS. AWS also advertises the VPC CIDR range to the remote VGP peers rather than the individual subnets. In the mentioned case, 10.0.0.0/16 is advertised to the corporate datacenter router.

Enter the AS number for your corporate data center. If it is private VIF then the address should lie in the range of 64512 – 65535. If you select the auto generated BGP key, then the MD5 key will be auto generated by AWS.

Here, the connection will be DirectConnect connection if you use AWS or it would be the hosted connection if you use Partner Provider. You should select the region. If you are selecting virtual interface owner as My AWS account, then you should be careful for the VGW setting. When creating a private VIF, specifying VGW is mandatory. VLAN field is an important and mandatory field. It provides the link between the physical layer of the customer router and the VIF.

For Private VIFs, auto generated peer IP addresses can be entered, which should be private IPs of any /30 subnet masks.

If you select the "Another AWS account", then that account needs to accept the interface creation request and you do not have to specify VGW additionally; you have to provide the account Id. It will then create hosted virtual interface.

The router can be configured manually or it can be downloaded from the Virtual Interface dialog.

Direct Connect (DX) Public VIF

The public services like S3 and Dynamo DB offered by AWS are accessed via public endpoints. In DirectConnect private VIF, to access these services the traffic has to exit from corporate data center via public internet using AWS public region link. Therefore, using these services through public internet will introduce limitations of public internet i.e. inconsistent latency, limited performance and speed and internet data charges from AWS.

Public interface is the solution for the above situation using some modification in private VIF architecture. The differences are given below:

- The peering relation between DX router and customer router should use the publically routable /30 IP range and should be unique
- The ASN should be public
- The architecture is same as in private VIF with a slight difference of an internet gateway attached to VPC

When you create the VLAN of public interface, the DirectConnect non-internet path to the public services is available. AWS advertises the public IP ranges use for public services to the customer router and you as a customer is advertising public IP addresses your router uses to the network of AWS public service.

Therefore, by this strategy, the traffic is moving via public VIF, which provides you the faster transfer rate due to DirectConnect facility, consistent latency, high performance and speed.

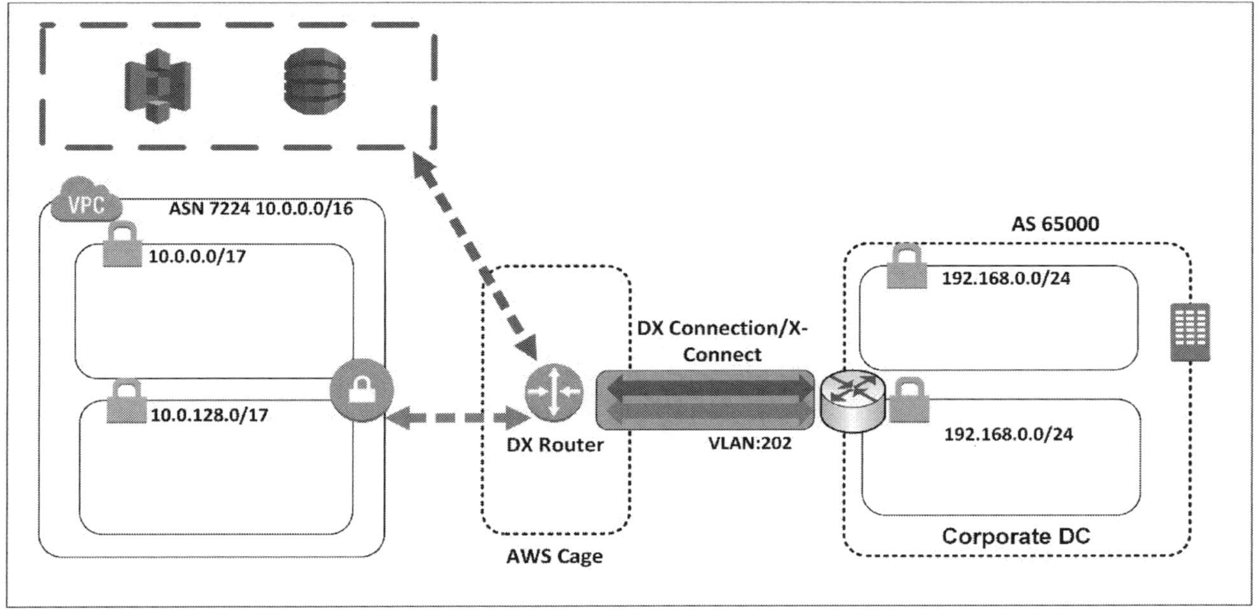

Figure 4-31: DX Public VIF

Creation of Public VIF

1. Select the connection and Virtual Interface Owner. Choosing "This Account" will create standard VIF whereas, choosing "Another AWS Account" will create hosted VIF in an external account.
2. Select the VLAN, VIF interacts with layer 2 of your network through this VLAN.
3. You have to enter BGP peer IP by yourself, it cannot be auto-generated this time. You can take support of AWS if you do not have publically routable IP address, in the result AWS will provide you the correct BGP relationship IP address.
4. Enter the BGP ASN (recommended to be public ASN) and prefixes for advertising. AWS will then verify the IP ranges you specified because incorrect public advertising on BGP system can cause major issues.

   Unlike Private VIF, if you selected other account as an owner, no request acceptation is required. You can download the configuration or you can directly apply it manually by extracting the information.

As we know that DX is a physical connection into the DX location within a region, by considering the given figure below (Figure 4-32), our datacenter is in Sydney and if you have to access the public services in Sydney, you can access them without using public

internet via Public VIF. If you want to access the public services in America, you cannot access these services without using internet because the public ranges that are advertised over the customer router is of Sydney.

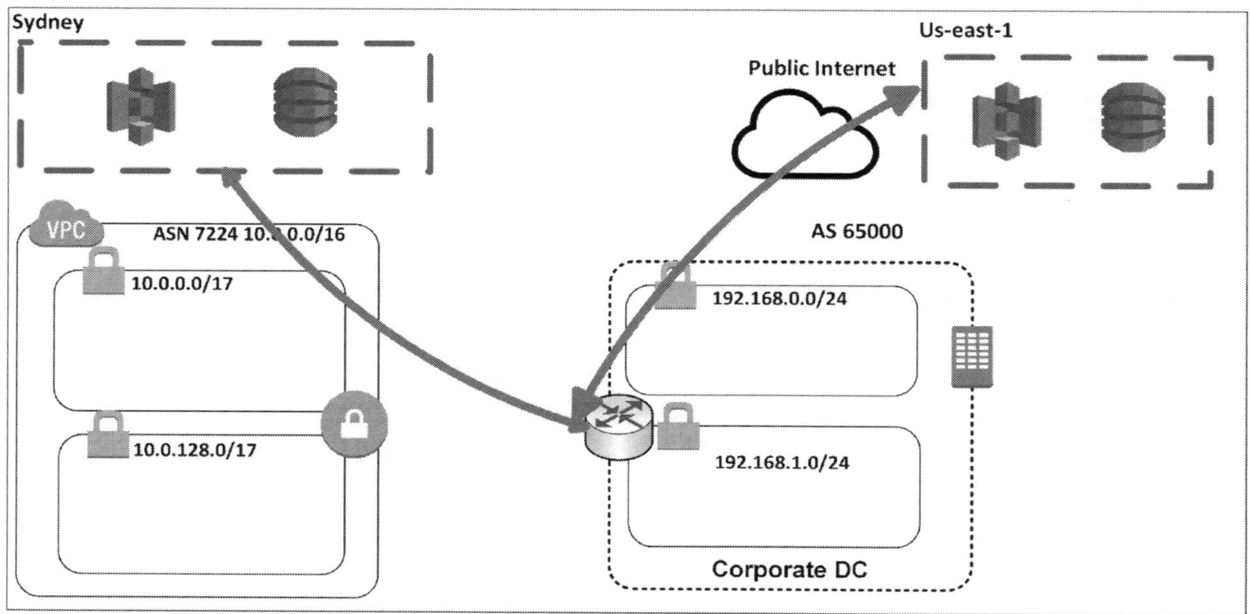

Figure 4-32: Accessing public services using Public VIF

However, if you are in the S region, a concept of inter-region traffic is introduced, which allows the traffic over public VIFs move to other region. To understand this concept, we need to discuss this in detail with the help of an example.

You have a corporate network connected to a DX location in us-east-1. This DirectConnect connection is used for communication between the corporate network and AWS using AWS public endpoints. This is because the public IPs of both sides are advertised to each other. Because you have not defined any prefixes for other regions of US such as us-west-1 or us-east-2, therefore, the traffic to these regions should travel over the public internet.

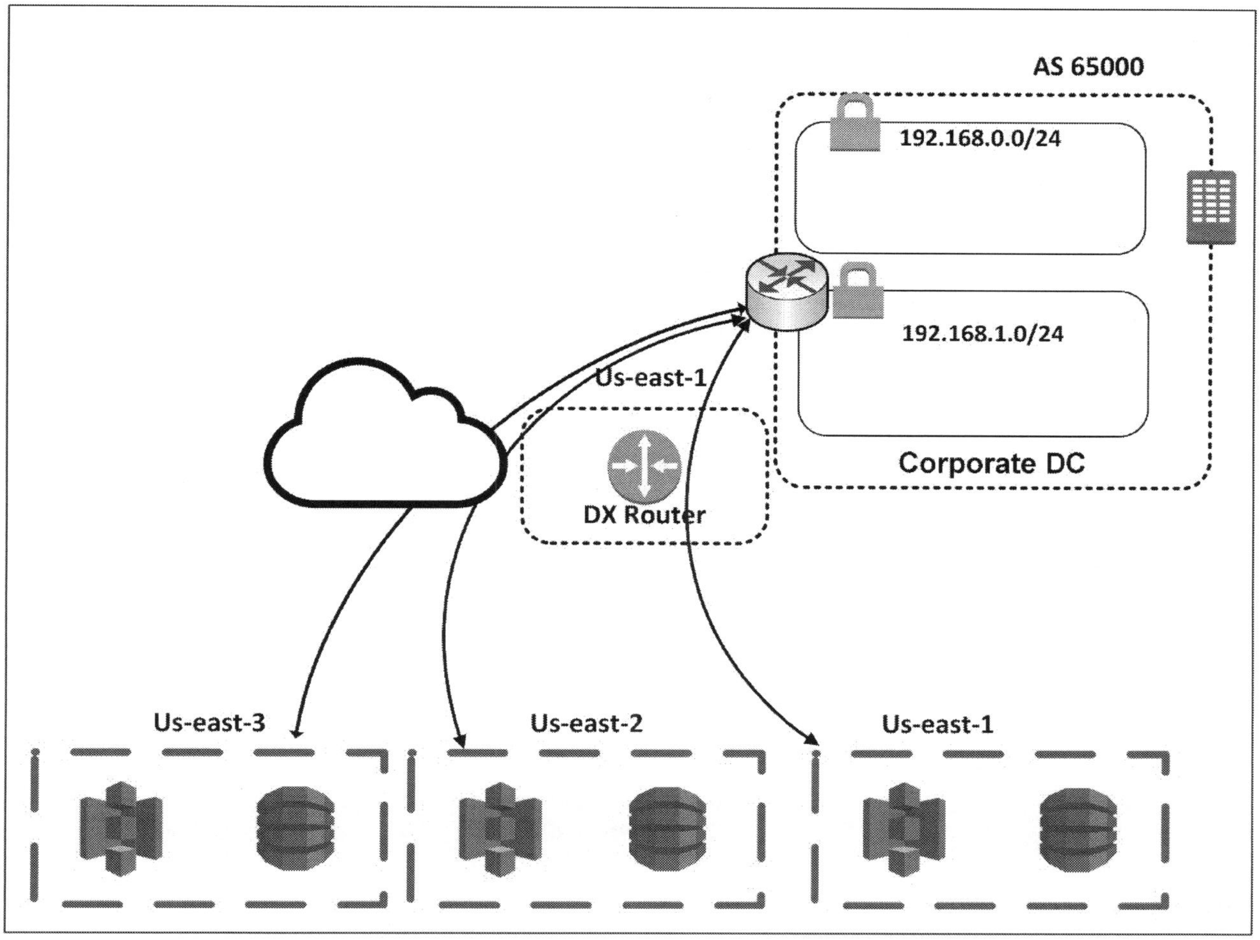

Figure 4-33: Inter-Region Connectivity

However, in US, this is not the case anymore, because of the inter-region connectivity; with a single DirectConnect connection in any location within US, you can access AWS services in all US regions.

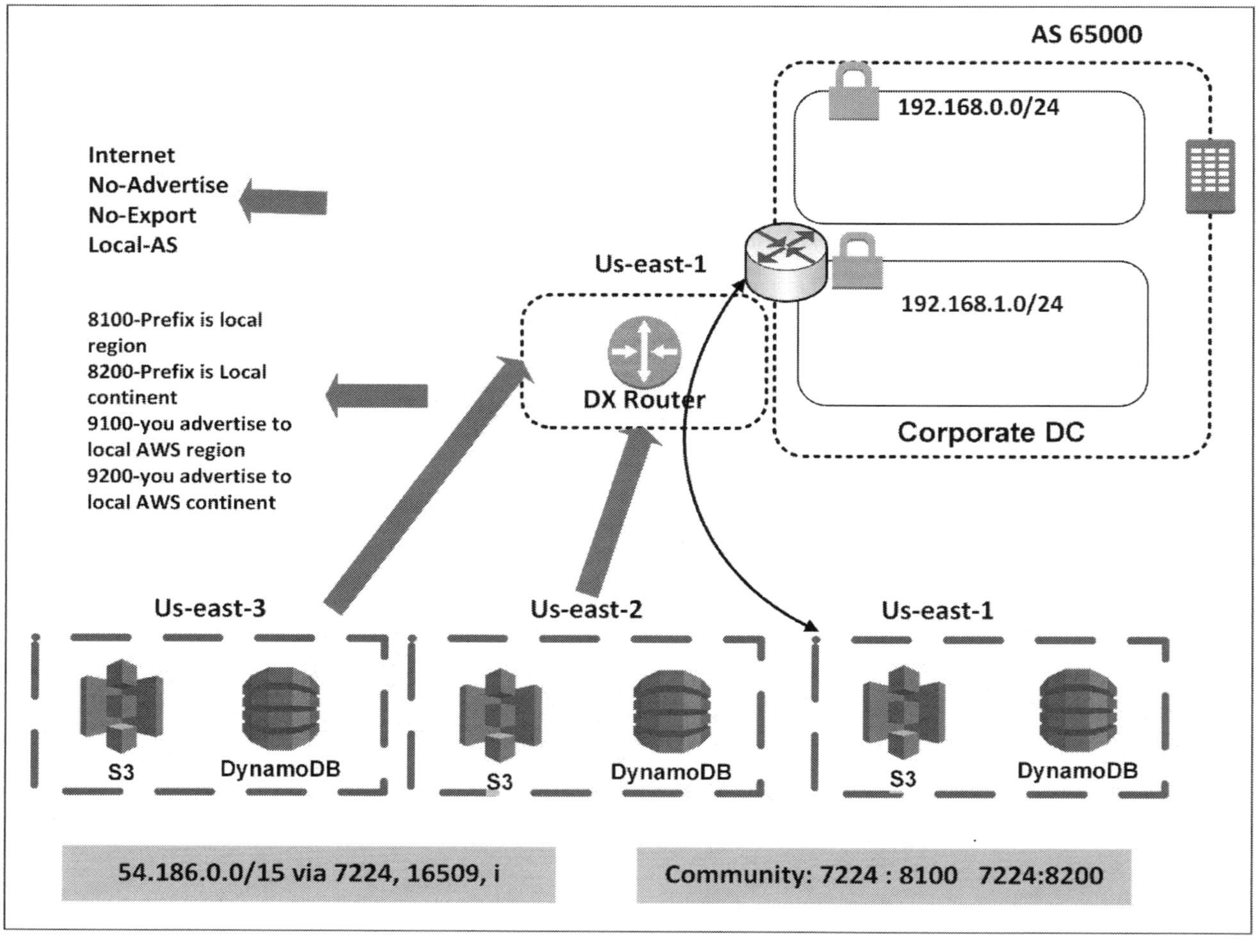

AS 65000
192.168.0.0/24
192.168.1.0/24
Corporate DC
Internet
No-Advertise
No-Export
Local-AS
Us-east-1
8100-Prefix is local region
8200-Prefix is Local continent
9100-you advertise to local AWS region
9200-you advertise to local AWS continent
DX Router
Us-east-3
Us-east-2
Us-east-1
S3
DynamoDB
S3
DynamoDB
S3
DynamoDB
54.186.0.0/15 via 7224, 16509, i
Community: 7224 : 8100 7224:8200

Figure 4-34: Inter-region Connectivity

Securing Direct Connect

In the DirectConnect Architecture (Figure 4-35), A corporate DC is connected to the DC router and a private VIF is used to link the corporate network with VPC (10.0.0.0/16 CIDR range). There are three security zones i.e. zone A, B and C. The security zone surrounding the VPC cloud is medium or semi security zone as it cannot be fully controlled. Corporate DC is surrounded by the fully controlled security zone. The AWS and the facility network in the center of the architecture are also surrounded by the zone, which is insecure because it includes the physical DirectConnect connections.

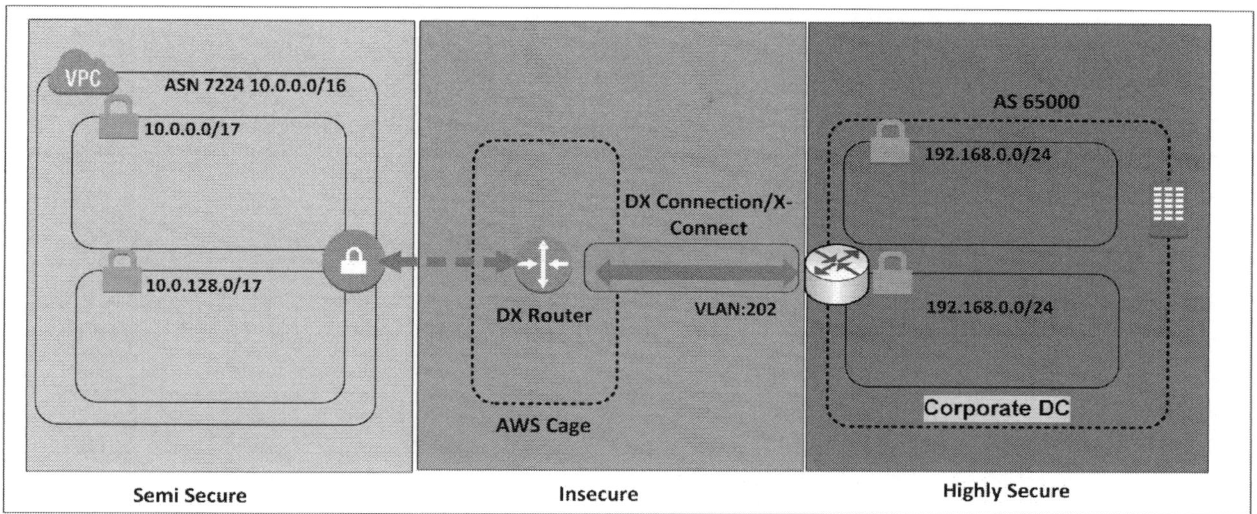

Figure 4-35: Security Zones

As we know that DirectConnect is basically a physical point-to-point connection technology therefore, by default it is not secured. The transferred data is not encrypted and it can also be encrypted by using specific application.

Security in Public VIF

In the case of public VIF, it is not problematic as the data is transferred to or from AWS public endpoints. If the data has to be transferred over insecure network like public internet, then all services will use "https" or any alternative secured protocols in transit.

Security in Private VIF

In private VIF, VPC is connected to corporate DC where traffic is transferred over private WAN or LAN where generally no built-in encryption is available. Therefore, in private VIF, security needs to be introduced.

For minimizing the risks for traffic transit over a DX link:

1. Remove the private VIF.
2. Create a public VIF across DX.
3. Utilize the two public IP endpoints that are provided by VGW, which is attached to VPC and is able to use IPSec VPNs. Set IPSec VPN between the Customer Router and VGW public endpoints via public VIF.

Using this strategy, the data packets will move from the customer router to the VGW public endpoint in a secured protocol (encrypted) and at the endpoints, they are decrypted and moved into the VPC via VGW to the required destination.

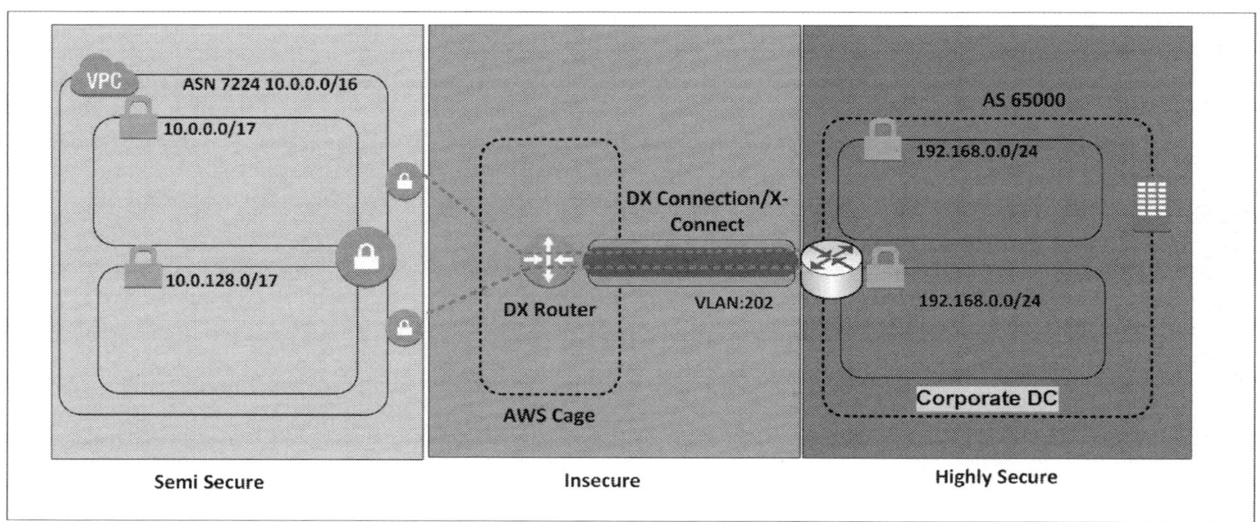

Figure 4-36: Security in private VIF

This will allow accessing the private services using public VIF in a secured way. We have discussed US inter-region connectivity before, using that, AWS advertises the prefixes of all AWS regions to your VIF; you can establish an IPSec VPN to all the regions. This will provide secure inter-region transit over a single DirectConnect connection.

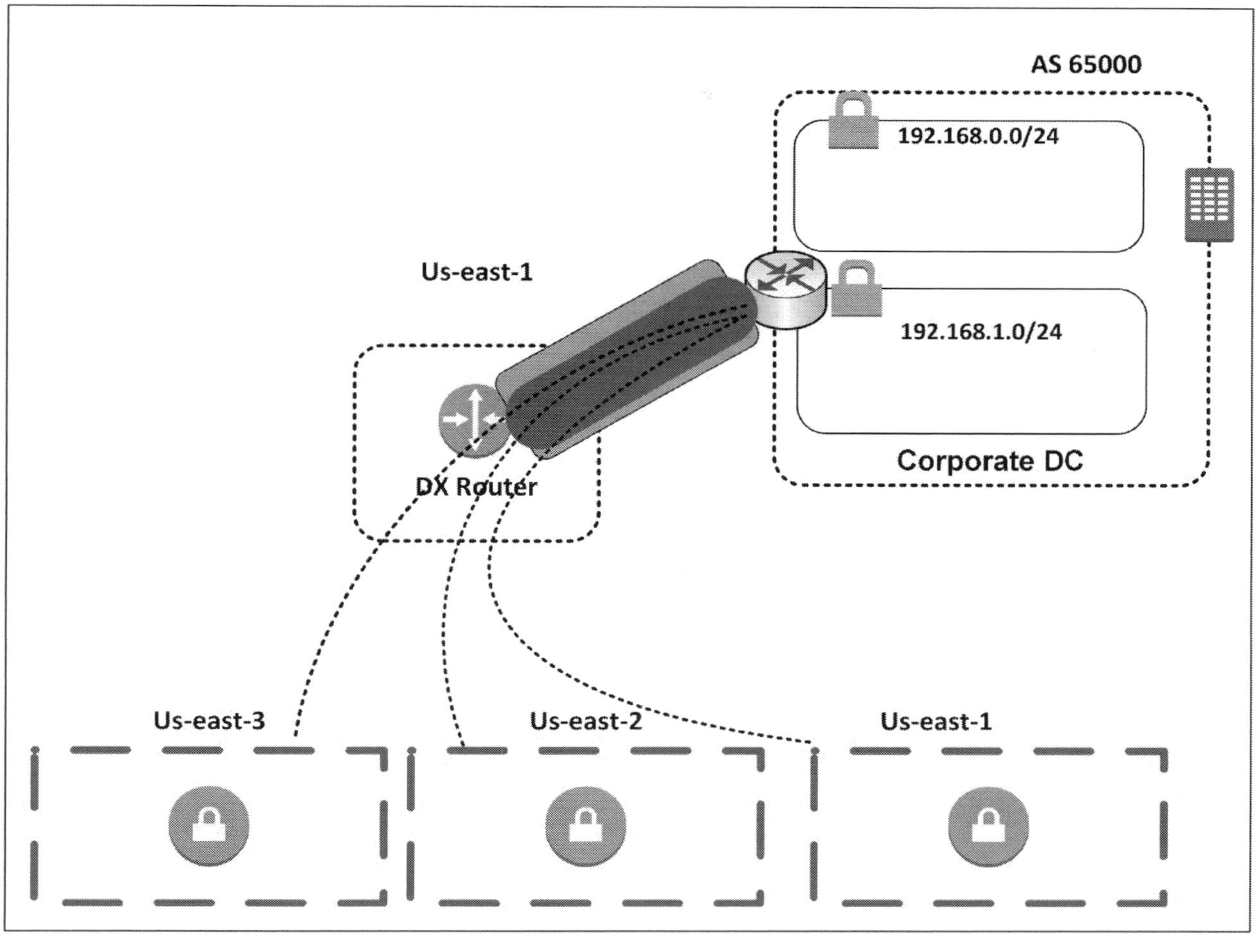

Figure 4-37: Secure Inter-Region Transit

Direct Connect Billing

For the explanation of DirectConnect billing, consider the given architecture in Figure 4-42. Where there are two AWS accounts; one belongs to you and the other belongs to the external entity. Both of the accounts have an S3 bucket and a VPC. VPC contains VPC subnet with an EC2 instance. VGW is attached to VPC for VPN and DX connections. There is your corporate data center on the rightmost corner.

Scenario 1:

You got access to an external AWS account S3 bucket where no DX connection is applied. You are storing your files inside that bucket.

Billing Elements:

- Resources or services charges; the charges are different for different resources. The charges would be paid by the account holder.

- Internet Transfer IN charges are the charges for accessing the internet for the utilization of resource in AWS account. It is a free facility.
- Internet Transfer charges for the data transfer through the corporate center. These charges should be paid by you. The outbound data transfer will be more expensive than the service charges.

Replacing external AWS account by your AWS account:

Billing Elements:

- Resources or services charges
- Internet Transfer IN (Free of cost)
- Internet Transfer charges

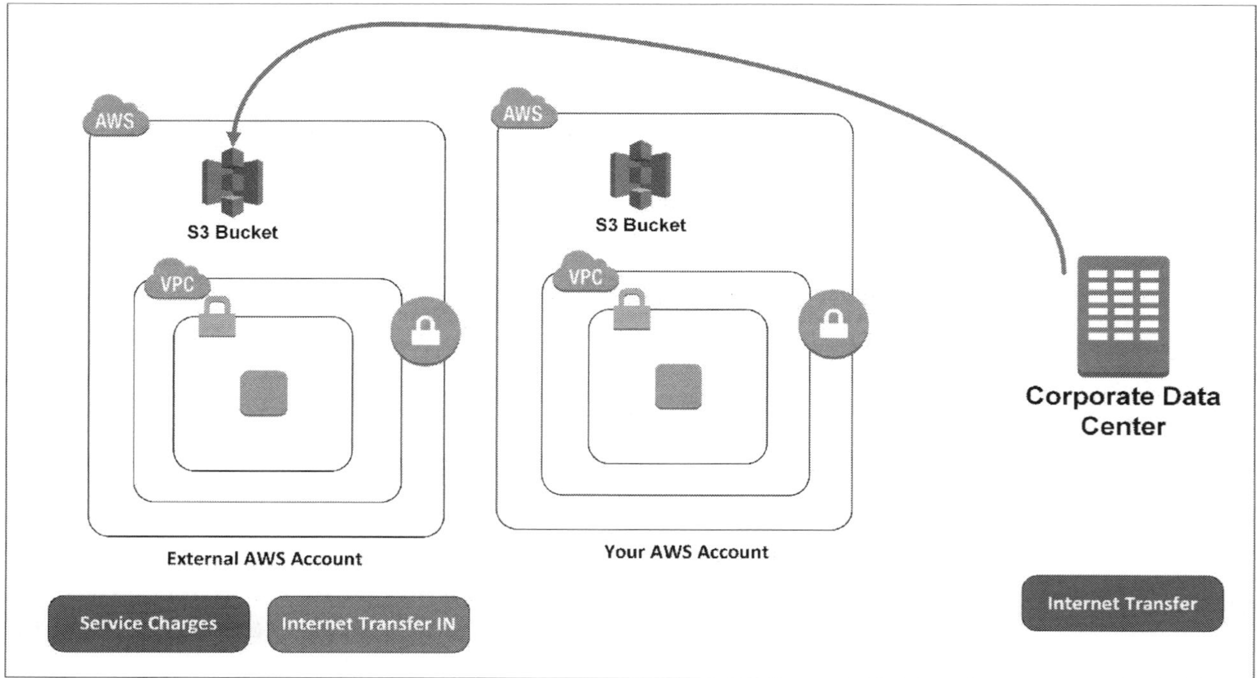

Figure 4-38: Scenario 1

Scenario 2:

For outbound traffic, if you are reading your data from the S3 bucket of external account:

Billing Elements:

- External account owner: Service charges and Internet Transfer out charges
- You: Internet data transfer charges

If you are using your own AWS account, then all the charges i.e. service charges, Internet transfer out and Internet transfer charges.

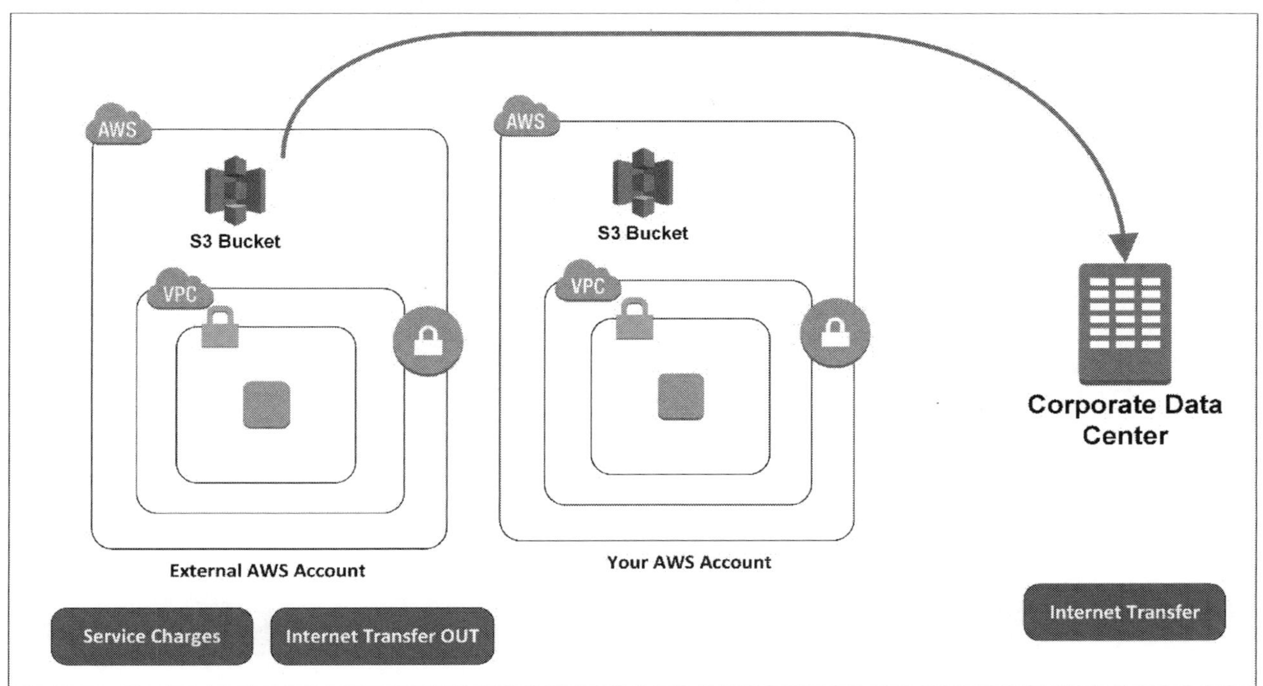

Figure 4-39: Scenario 2

Scenario 3:

External AWS account EC2 instance is using public IP for transferring data to corporate DC. Billing elements are service charges (running EC2 instance) and Internet transfer OUT charges that are paid by external AWS account owner while Internet transfer charges are paid by you. When using your AWS account, you have to pay for all of the three charges.

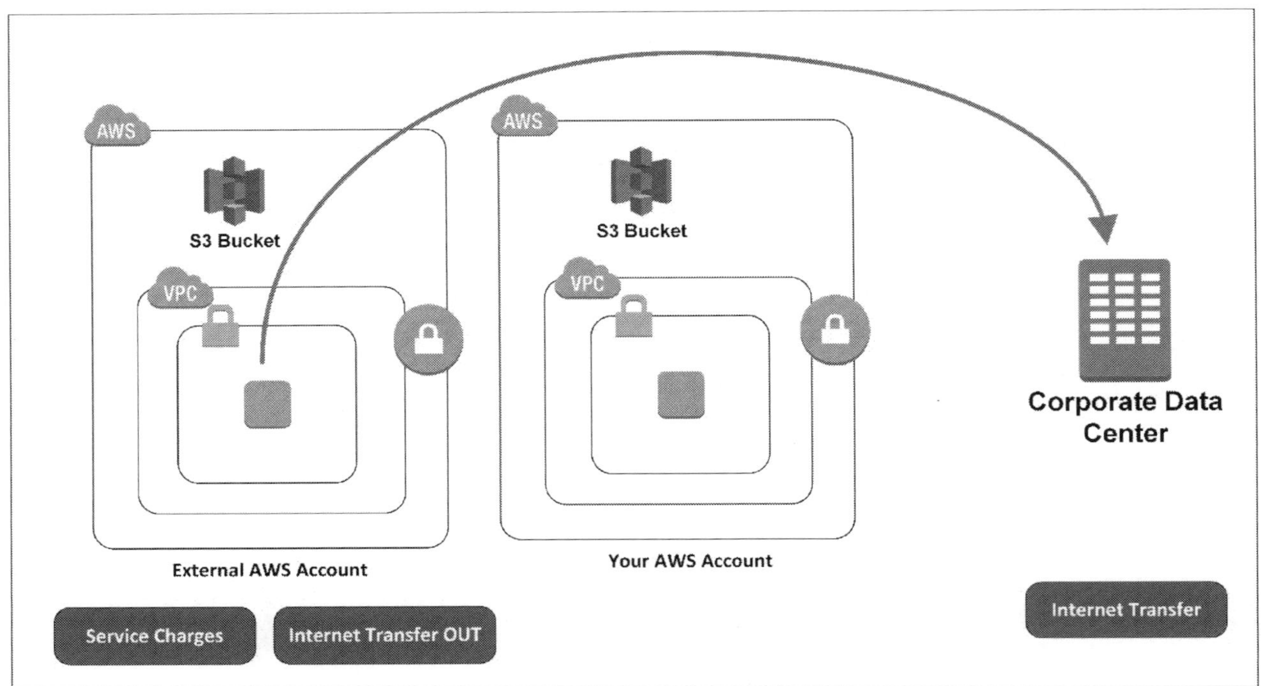

Figure 4-40: Scenario 3

Scenario 4:

You are using IPSec VPN for private access:

Billing Elements:

- Per hour charge for the VPN connection
- Internet Transfer OUT charge
- Internet transfer

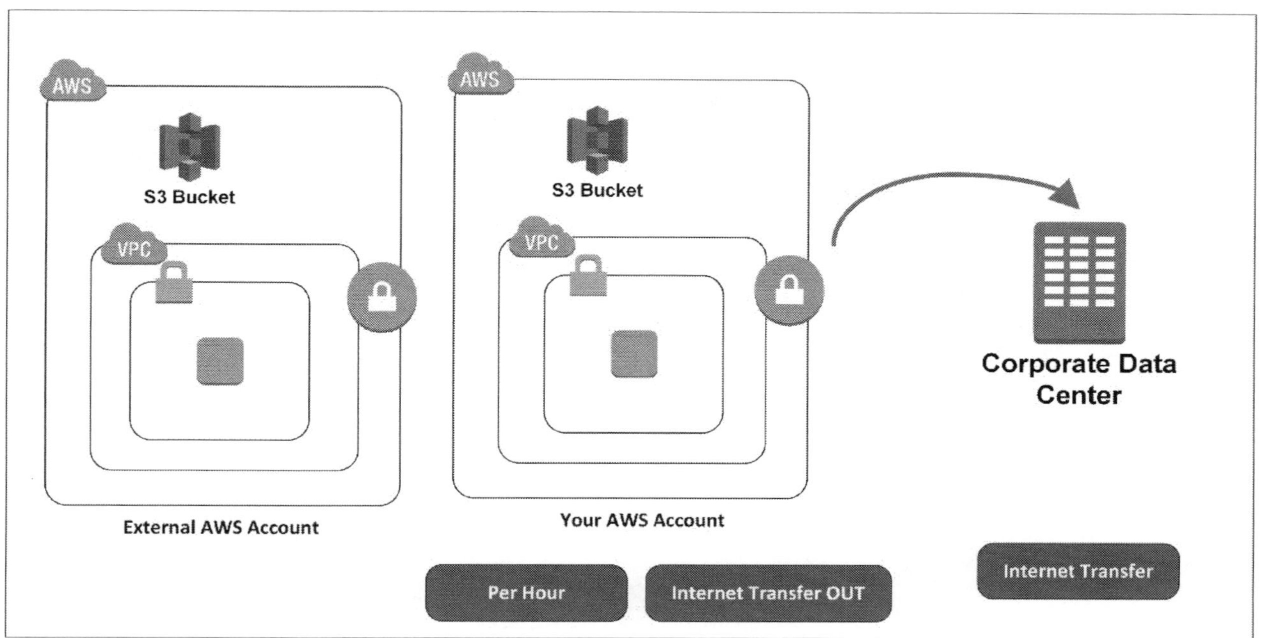

Figure 4-41: Scenario 4

Scenario 5:

Using DirectConnect with public and private VIFs:

Billing Elements:

- Port charges per hour that varies according to the port speed and location. The charges start as soon as your first cross connect is activated.
- VIF charges are paid by the account that owns the VIF, which can be yours or an external account. The VIFs can be shared to the external account then, the external account will be responsible of these charges.
- Data transfer into an AWS account is free for private VIFs i.e. inbound traffic.
- Outbound traffic will be charged according to the per GB of DirectConnect rate that is negligible in front of Internet rates.
- Data transfer charges (inbound and outbound) using public VIFs.
- Resource charges of your own account using public VIFs but, if you are using external public resources, you do not have to pay for it; the external account owner has to pay it.
- Charges for using IP VPN over public VIFs for a secured connection.

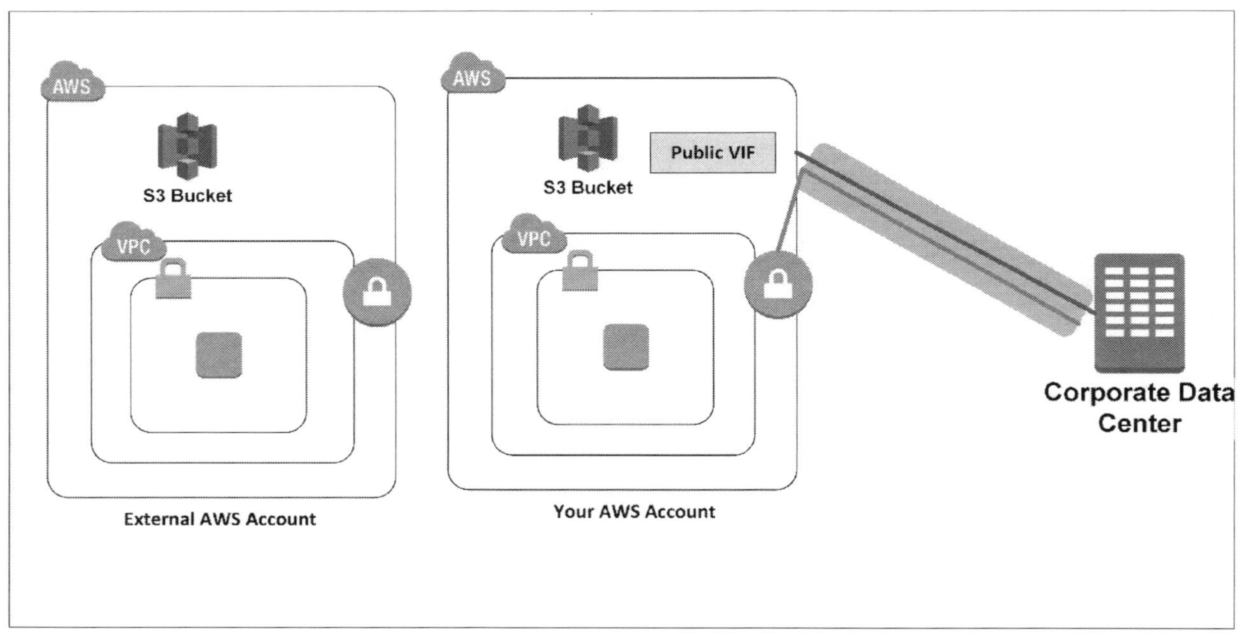

Figure 4-42: Scenario 5

Cloud Hub Architecture

Consider a scenario where your business is spread across five states of the US (Los Angeles, New York, Chicago, Houston, San Diego). You are the IT manager of your business who wants to connect all five sites from IT networking perspective and has to provide internet access to all of these sites.

If considering traditional communication, you will have number of options. First, you may decide to manage your own communication links and have physical links between all the sites and one main site.

Solution 1:

Your company's head office is in New York, therefore, New York is your central site. Internet link from the New York site is shared and available to all other sites. This hub and spoke topology is shown in figure 4-43.

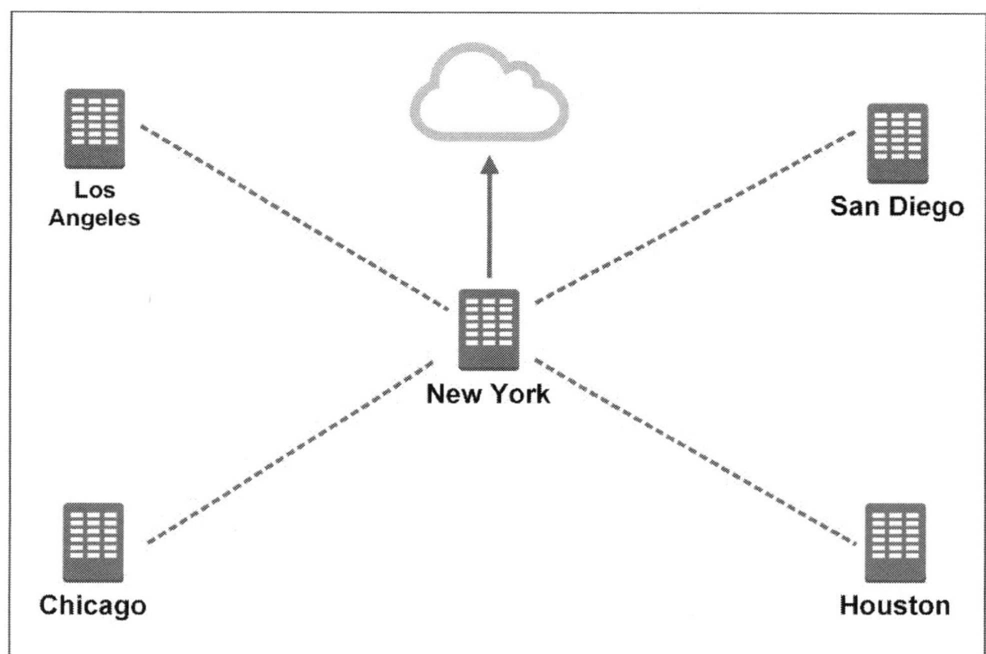

Figure 4-43: Site Connections Solution 1

This can be a good solution but will have number of issues, which include dependency on the New York site that for instance, if the New York site fails for some reason, all of the other sites will lose the connection with each other and will not have Internet access as well.

Solution 2:

You can make the data center facility as a central unit (Figure 4-44). This will reduce the risk of connection loss and a data center is generally more resilient than any office. This solution will increase your expenses. Moreover, in case the data center facility is down, then again you will face the communication and Internet problem.

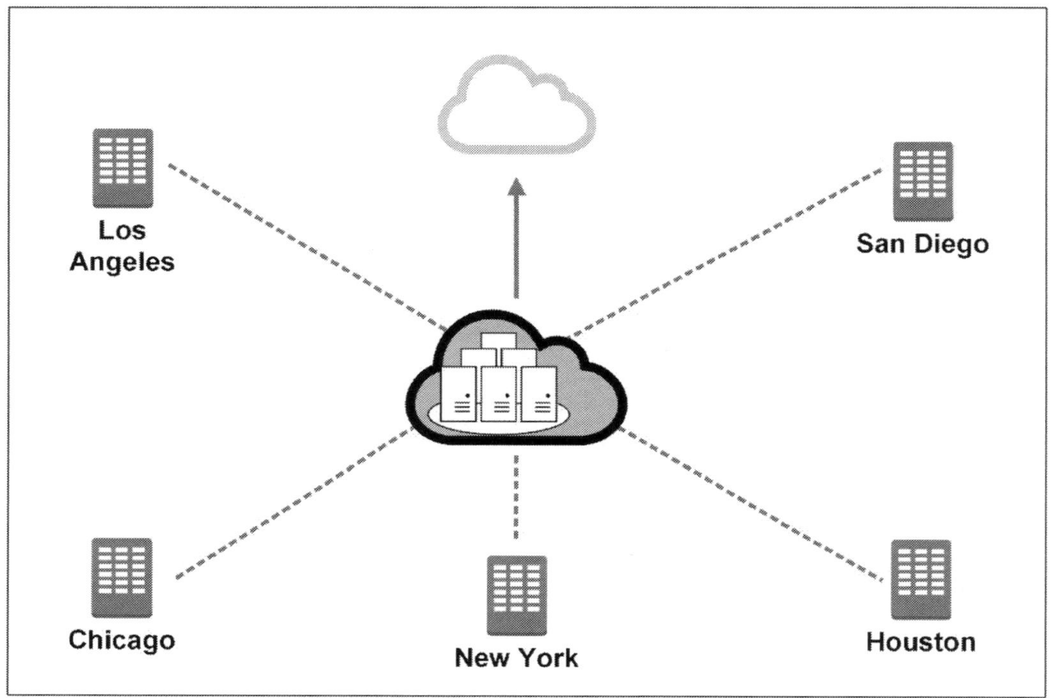

Figure 4-44: Site Connections Solution 2

Solution 3:

Use the Mesh topology in which every site is connected physically to the other site and every site has its own dedicated internet connection (Figure 4-45). This will increase your physical connections. The individual internet links are cheap but the one to one physical connections will be expensive. Each site in this topology will have a fault domain that for example, if your New York site is down for a reason, then still you are connected with the other sites i.e. There is no dependency on a single site or datacenter for communication or internet access.

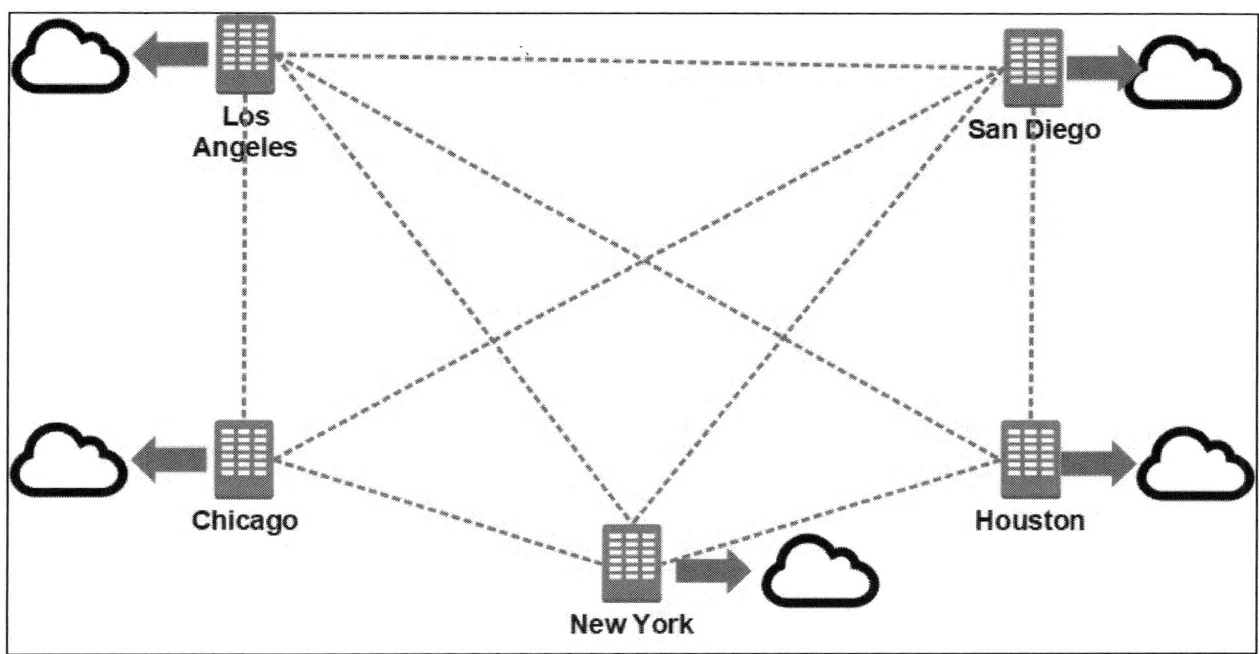

Figure 4-45: Site Connections Solution 3

Possible adjustments on this design are:

- Performance or consistency of communications between sites is in critical.
- You could avoid cost of expensive with wide area network links.

Solution 4:

Establish a VPN mesh network, which will provide separate internet links to all the sites and site-to-site VPN technology such as IPSec for communication between sites can be used. This is a reliable and cost effective solution. This topology needs an administrator for configuring, managing and maintaining the VPN connection.

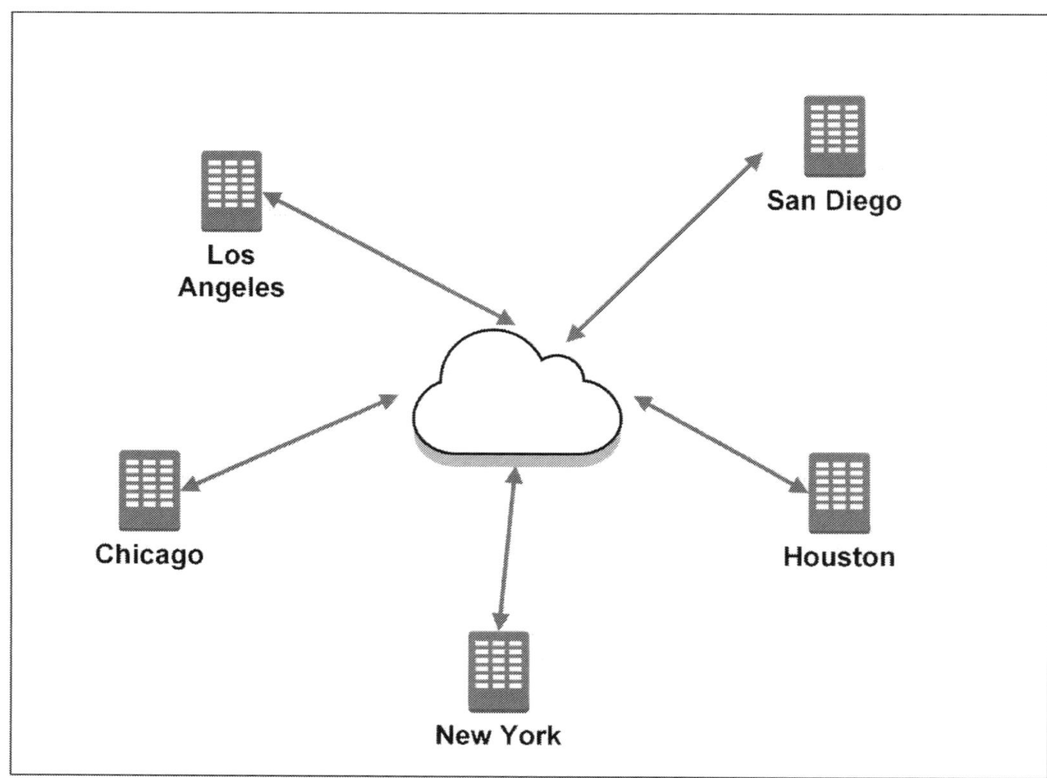

Figure 4-46: Site Connections Solution 4

Solution 5:

Alternative to the administrator, you can apply a managed MPLS network. By this architecture, each site is using a network provided by MPLS. This network is shared network operated by the provider and used by all of its customers. The performance is generally consistent. It is resilient and fully managed by the Telkom provider.

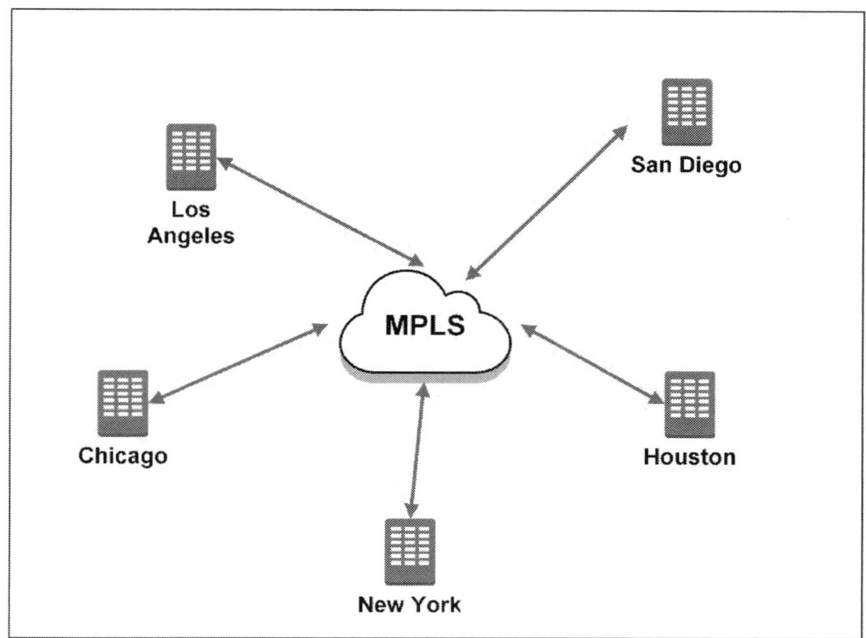

Figure 4-47: Site Connections Solution 5

Solution 6:

AWS provides a service known as Cloud Hub, which combines the benefits of a mesh network with resiliency provided by an Enterprise grade system.

Cloud Hub architecture starts in an AWS environment with a VPC. Considering that, this environment is in a region with two Availability Zones. Both AZs have a subnet in each. VPC that is provided by AWS is aligned with Cloud Hub architecture by default when creating an account. The VPC is constructed across multiple fault domains, that is why it is resilient and highly available by design.

We have public Internet in the center. Using an IPSec VPN, we have connected the VPC to the head office in New York. For VPN connections, we have used VGW at AWS end and CPE at the New York office (Customer end). Dynamic routing is used here therefore; we will be using BGP. AWS ASN is 7224 and New York ASN is 65000 (As we are using BGP). The network of VPC is 10.0.0.0/16 and of New York site is 192.168.0.0/24. Subnet inside VPC have route-table attached to it and route propagation is enabled.

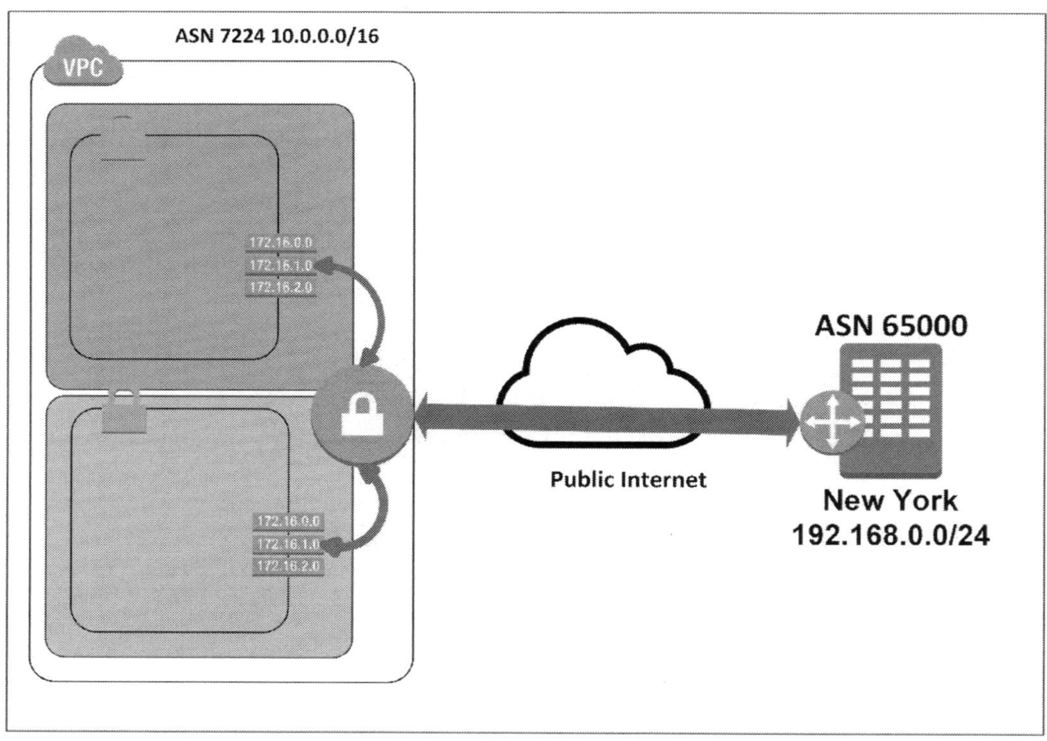

Figure 4-48: Cloud Hub Architecture with Head Office Site

When we add the other sites, we have:

- Houston with a prefix of 192.168.2.0/24 and ASN 65001
- Chicago with a prefix 192.168.1.0/24 and ASN 65000

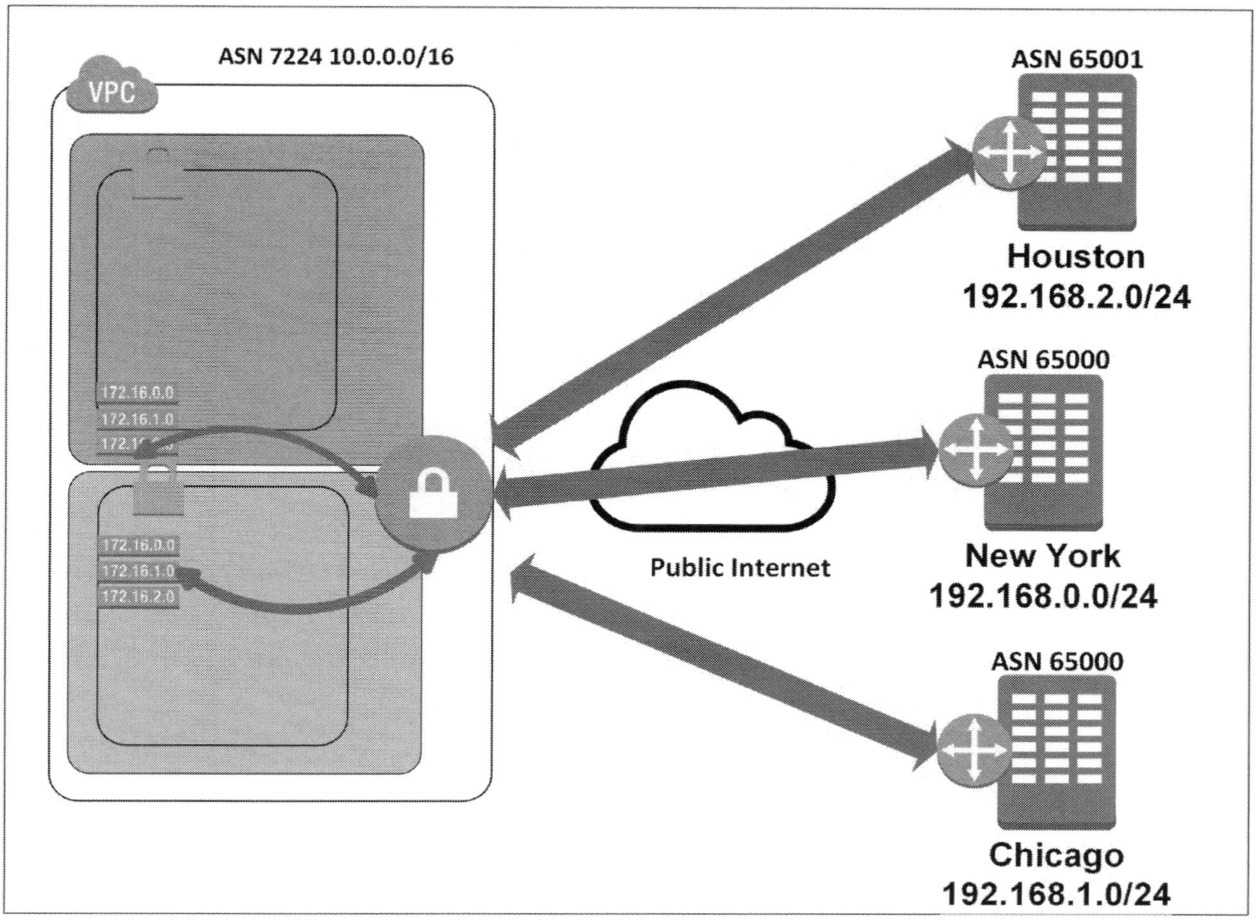

Figure 4-49: Cloud Hub Architecture with Multiple Sites

In this architecture, a single VGW has to handle columns between three remote sites and VPC. The VGW route-table will be like as given below:

Destination	Target
10.0.0.0/16	Local
192.168.2.0/24	Remote Peer IP
192.168.1.0/24	Remote Peer IP
192.168.0.0/24	Remote Peer IP

Table 4-10: VGW Route Table

This table enables the VGW to reach any of the sites using VPN peer IP and the remote sites can reach to VPC via local routes. Each remote site will know two IPs for two tunnels and even more if we have used more than one VPN connection on a single site in order to

increase resiliency. We are using Dynamic VPN and BGP therefore, VGW is advertising the prefixes it knows to its connected neighbors.

For example, in Chicago BGP is operational; it will have the following route table:

Destination	Target	AS PATH
10.0.0.0/16	VGW	7224,i
192.168.2.0/24	VGW	7224,65001.i
192.168.1.0/24	0.0.0.0	I
192.168.0.0/24	VGW	7224,65000,i

Table 4-11: BGP Route Table

It has prefixes of all other sites and VPC. In ASPATH, it is mentioned that the route between the remote sites are via ASN 7224, which is here at the AWS VPC. For this information to be available at remote sites, you have to configure CGW of each site to advertise the network.

In this Cloud Hub architecture, you have Hub and spoke network. Hub is the highly resilient VPN, which works across multiple fault domains. Each VPN has two tunnels to two independent VPN endpoints, which are in different fault domains. You can add multiple VPNs per customer site. Hub site i.e. AWS is perfectly capable of scaling and having its own infrastructure so, you gain the ability to have a Cloud-based network concentration point with infrastructure capacity for significantly less than the cost of its physical relational datacenter design pattern.

If your business requires consistent performance and high bandwidth that cannot be delivered via VPN, you can use DirectConnect in the same architecture instead of VPNs in this case. DX also terminates in VGW for VPC. DirectConnect also uses VPN as a backup. You can use software VPN solution with Cloud Hub.

Suppose that your VPC in this architecture is in US and you have to connect EU based VPC to the network so you can do it by using software VPN connect to the remote VPN server in VGW.

This whole architecture can be built on a low budget.

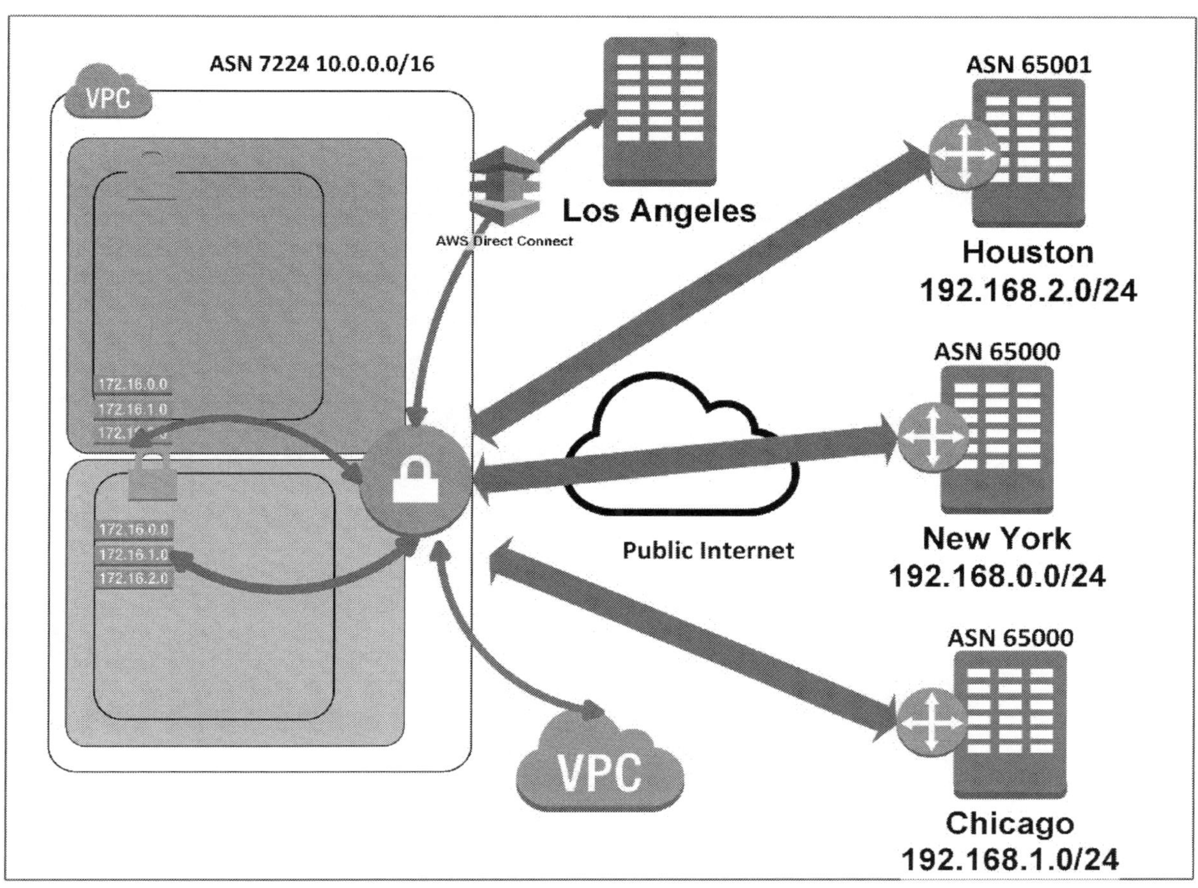

Figure 4-50: Cloud Hub Architecture with DX and VPN Connection

Limitation

The sites cannot have the overlapping IP ranges and each CPE should support the dynamic VPNs (IPSec and BGP).

Extreme Hybrid Network Redundancy & Resiliency

Resiliency can be increased in the Hybrid networks. For illustration, refer to the figure 4-51. An Organization is running a business that has the architecture in figure 4-51. In this architecture, there are following components:

- An AWS account
- A VPC (10.0.0.0/16) with two VPC subnets (10.0.0.0/17 & 10.0.128.0/17)
- A VGW attached to VPC
- Two IPSec Endpoints as a small lock

- A corporate data center with two subnets (192.168.0.0/24 & 192.168.1.0/24) and two Customer Routers (one more for adding resiliency)
- Two Co-location facilities (Equinix SY3 and Global switch SY6); both are in Sydney
- A network partner, because no network equipment is available in co-location facilities.

Network partner is giving the following facilities:

- Providing transits to or from DirectConnect locations or co-locations
- Providing local transit to customer for two offices
- Providing pair of resilient internet connections

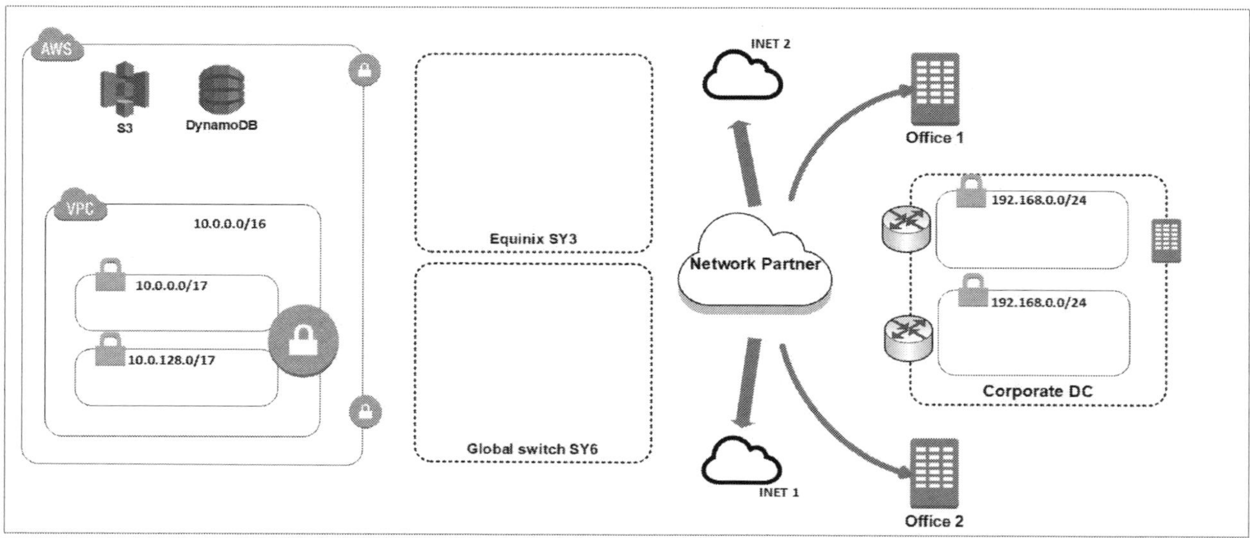

Figure 4-51: Hybrid Network (a)

Linking Network with AWS

In order to link AWS with corporate data center, the business requirements are:

- Establishing connection quickly, as soon as possible
- Consistent Latency
- High Bandwidth between VPC and corporate DC
- Cost effective
- Maximum Resiliency

Some requirements are fulfilled by using IP VPN while, some requirements are the characteristics of DirectConnect and therefore, the concept of Hybrid networking is introduced.

The first requirement is the fast establishment of connectivity, which excludes the use of DirectConnect and it is the property of IPSec VPN.

For the quick connection and resiliency, the architecture in fig 4-52 provides a solution of using VPN connectivity between VPN endpoints and customer router. At the AWS endpoint, the connection is resilient because there are two paths (two endpoints) and for the customer side, using one router will not be resilient as there will be only one path therefore, two Customer Routers are attached in order to obtain resiliency, which introduces the second tunnel path to the endpoints. The paths between VPC and corporate DC are equal in length and the routes are learned from the same device type propagated from dynamic VPN. The multiple BGP pathing should be enabled on both sides. This system is load balanced and fully resilient. In the case of failure of one path, alternative path is present.

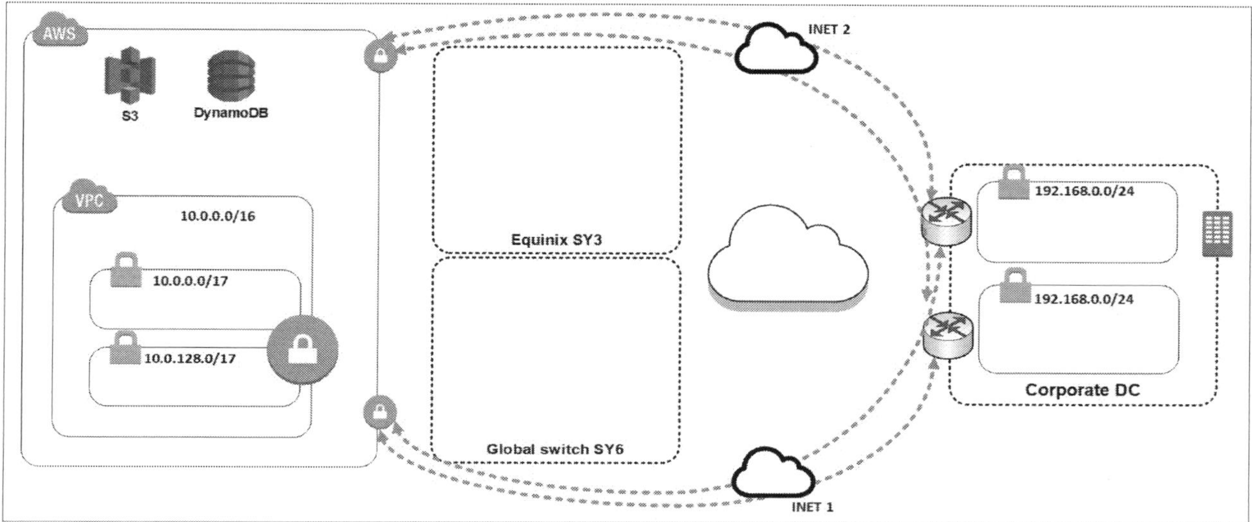

Figure 4-52: Hybrid Network (b)

Now, let us address the other three requirements i.e. consistent latency, high bandwidth and cost effective system. The above architecture (Figure 4-52) is using internet transit, which is expensive, inconsistent and has limited bandwidth so that it cannot be used for the rest of the three requirements. For these requirements, DirectConnect is the solution. For high bandwidth, use a 10 Gbps DX port. There is no equipment in the co-locations so, order a cross connect to the DX router and network link extension to the Customer Router. Public and Private VIFs are created inside these links, which are extended to the corporate data center without data extension. This will provide an economic solution because transfer costs over public and private VIFs are cheap. Setup with DX will provide a high performance and low consistent latency solution. Prefixes learned from DX are preferred over that are learned from dynamic VPN therefore, DX connect will be the primary connection and VPN acts for backup connection. The second same DX are provided in Global switch SY6 for adding resiliency. This connection acts as a backup in case of failure in the connection available in Equinix SY3.

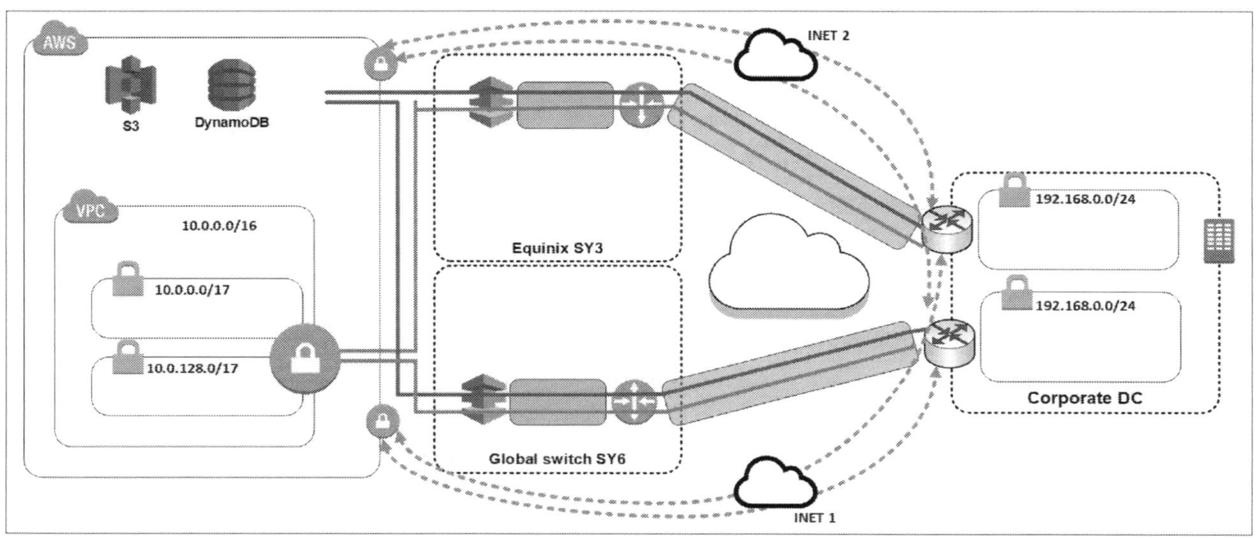

Figure 5-53: Hybrid Network (c)

For extreme resiliency, two more DX connections are established in each co-location. AWS ensures that whenever there are multiple DX connections in the same co-location, they should be terminated at the separate DX routers. This final architecture (Figure 4-54) provides tolerance against the failure of any customer router, DX location or Network partner router.

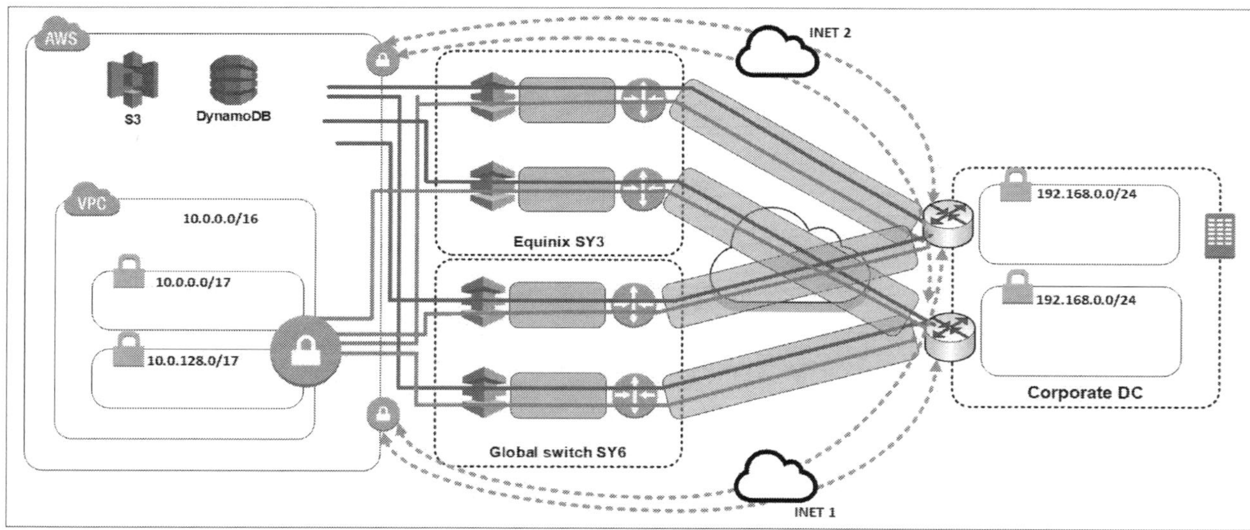

Figure 4-54: Hybrid Network (d)

QinQ-VLAN Stacking

QinQ is a technology, which is also known as 802.1 ad or VLAN stacking.

Access Port is unaware of VLAN and traffic from this port cannot be changed in any way. Traffic at Datalink layer on access port uses 802.3, which is the standard Ethernet. Placing an access port into a VLAN is called per-port VLAN, for doing this; a membership is to be added on the switch for the particular port. In the given figure 4-55, three ports are added to VLAN 100 and three are added to VLAN: 200. Only the switches are aware of this VLAN ports. The multiple switches with VLAN port are inter-connected via trunk port. The devices connected to an access port generate one or more VLAN standard 802.3 Ethernet frames whenever traffic is generated on an access port. These frames are tagged with a VLAN ID (Same as the VLAN ID in which the access port is) when entered in a trunk port. In this way, multiple VLAN Ethernet frames can travel through trunk port and the receiver switch is able to check to which VLAN ID the coming port belongs . This is how QinQ 802.1 works.

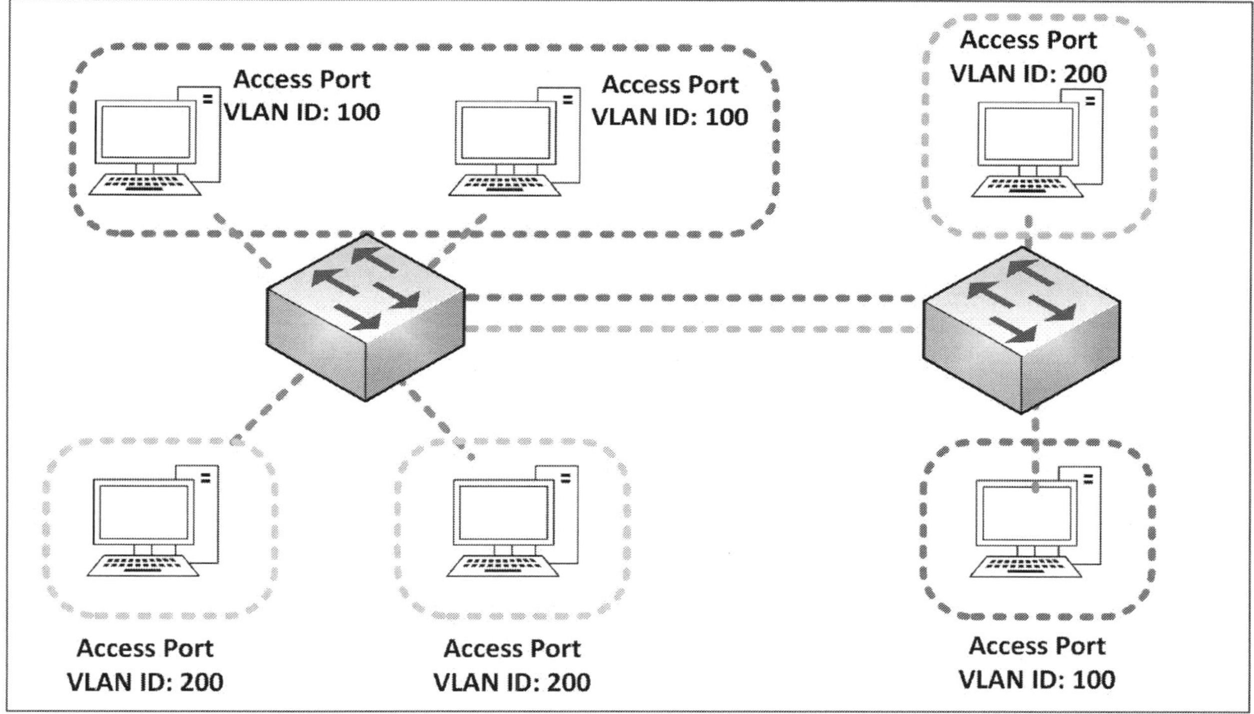

Figure 4-55: Network with Access Port and VLAN ID

In figure 4-56, this is the 802.3 Ethernet type 2 frame, whose length is between 64 to 1518 Bytes. This frame is further divided into the following components:

- MAC or Frame header, which is 14 Bytes in length, which is further divided into destination MAC address (6 Bytes), source MAC address (6 Bytes) and Ether type (2 Bytes), which is generally the encapsulation type or link of the frame.
- Data or payload frame, which is 46 to 1500 Bytes long and consists of Payload, which is mainly the IEP Data but it can be the other protocols that are running on top of the Ethernet.
- 4 Bytes of CRC checksum in order to detect or correct the error.

The extension of Ethernet frame with VLAN tagging is not related to encapsulating 802.3 frame in a VLAN frame for VLAN tagging.

XX XX XX XX XX XX Destination MAC address	XX XX XX XX XX XX Source MAC address	XX XX Either Type	IP Payload	CRC Checksum
MAC/Frame Header (14 B)			Data (46-1500 B)	4 B
802.3 Ethernet Type 2 Frame (64-1518 B)				

Figure 4-56: 802.3 Ethernet Type 2 Frame

802.1 Q adds the VLAN tag in a frame; the minimum size of the frame remains the same while, the max size is increased to 1522 Bytes. The minimum size of payload is reduced to 42 Bytes.

XX XX XX XX XX XX Destination MAC address	XX XX XX XX XX XX Source MAC address	XX XX XX XX 802.1 Q header	XX XX Either Type	IP Payload	CRC Checksum
MAC/Frame Header (18 B)				Data (42-1500B)	4 B
802.1 Q VLAN Tagged Frame (64-1522 B)					

Figure 4-57: 802.1 Q VLAN Tagged Frame

QinQ is the evolution of VLAN tagging which will enable to add multiple VLAN tags into a frame. Multiple VLAN tagging is not representing that the tags belong to different VLANs; this creates the ability of nested VLANs or an inner or outer VLAN, which helps in logical operations like PUSH and PULL at a VLAN level or at layer 2.

The value of ether type is set to ox8100, which indicates that the frame is 802.1Q and has VLAN tags. To change this frame in 802.1 QinQ frame, the ether type field should be set to ox88a8 and the extra VLAN tag can be added. The VLAN tag, which is closer to source MAC address, is the outer tag (Supplier Tag) and the tag close to payload is inner tag (Customer tag).

Destination MAC address	Source MAC address	802.1 Q header Supplier tag (S tag)	802.1 Q header Customer tag (C tag)	Either Type	IP Payload	CRC Checksum
MAC/Frame Header (18 B)					Data (42-1500B)	4 B
802.1 ad QinQ VLAN Tagged Frame (64-1526 B)						

Figure 4-58: 802.1 ad QinQ VLAN Tagged Frame

Two operations can be performed in QinQ frame:

- PUSH
- POP

To understand this, let us suppose that 802.1Q has one VLAN tag and for adding the supplier tag, you have to use the PUSH operation and similarly for removing the tag, perform POP operation. The PUSH and POP operations are performed over the outer tag only i.e. supplier tag. QinQ allows tag nesting. Tag nesting is important in terms of architecture.

QinQ is used generally when you are not in DX location because, if you are in a DX location, you have your own equipment in the DX facility.

Consider the scenario in figure 4-59, where there is DX Router and a Customer Router. A direct connect is created. There are public and private VIFs in the connection with VLAN ID. In order to communicate with VLAN interface, the router requires VLAN ID. Public VIF is using VLAN tag of 100 and private VIF is using VLAN 200.

When DC facility is not available and wants to connect the remote DC premises, a physical fiber cable is required for the VLAN extension and the customer has the control of that cable therefore, VIFs can be extended over that cable.

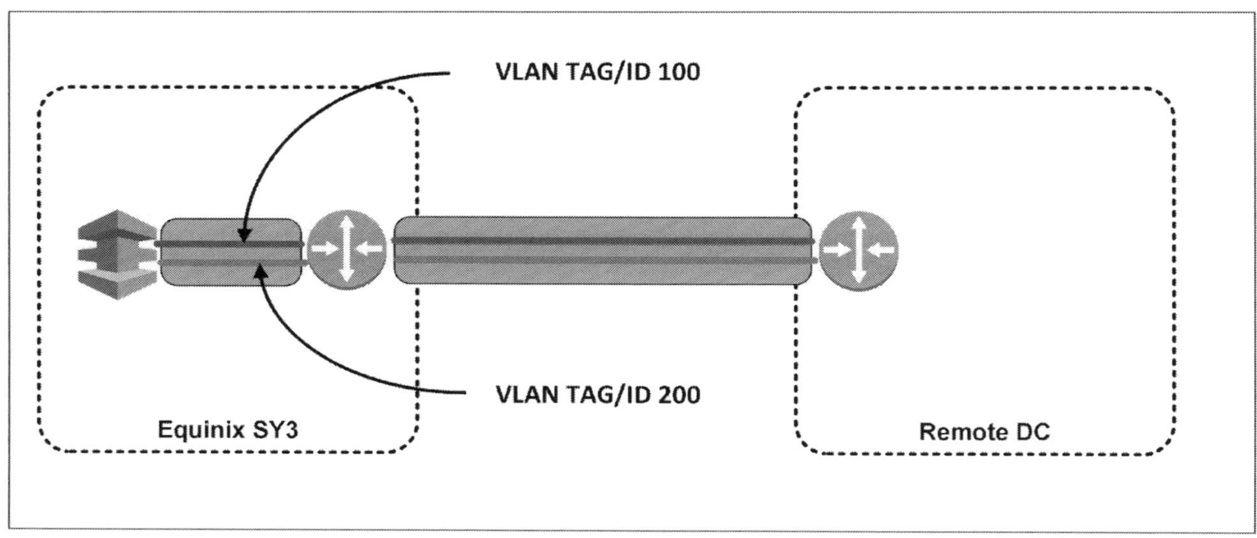

Figure 4:59: QinQ VLAN Stacking

If the case is different in which DX location is in Sydney and the remote DC is very far from Sydney (at any other location for example in Perth, 3300 km away). Now, the physical connection would be very expensive. One remote DC is close to DX location for example, in Brisbane (950 km away).

Following are the problems to be considered in this scenario:

- Long distance to Perth; For which dedicated physical connection is required for the two VLANs for private and public VIFs.
- Multiple site connections, which means more than one physical connection is required.

This will be very expensive and will have high risk of failures, repairing and maintenance costs. For this solution, a large network transit provider can be utilized.

Whenever a National enterprise from large Telco provider is ordered, a dedicated pair of connection is not supplied between your sites and DX location at least, if QinQ or VLAN stacking technology is not involved.

If the company (Figure 4-60) connections are ordered by Telco enterprises then they are provided with the layer 3 connectivity between Equinix SY3, Perth and Brisbane. Each of the sites are provided with the switch or router provided by Telco provider, which is a layer 3 capable device. Telco provider demands for standard 802.3 Ethernet frames (without VLAN tagging) and these frames should contain layer 3 Payload i.e. the source and destination IP address. The provided routers are the default gateway to the local sites. Generally, the Telco provider provides the IP ranges of your site or it can be defined by the customer with mutual agreement.

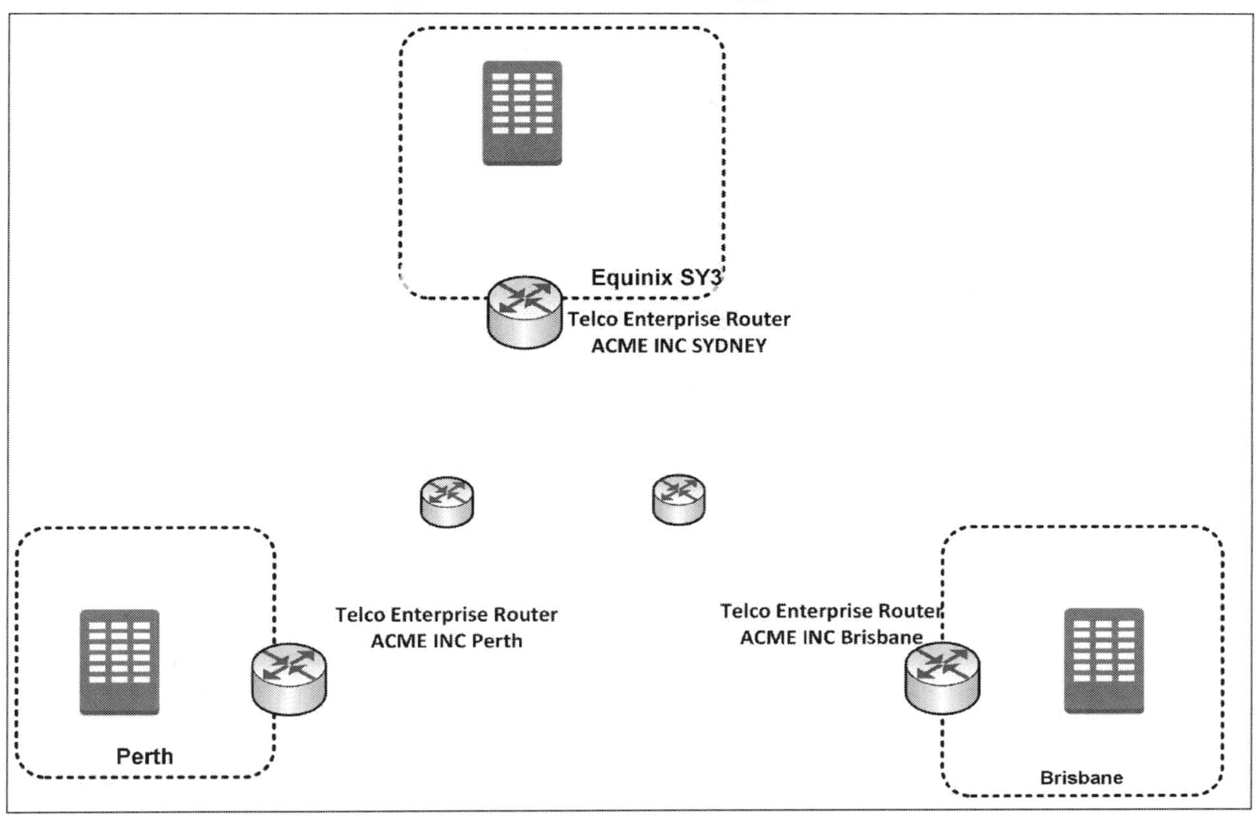

Figure 4-60: Data Transfer using 802.1 Q Technology

Considering the given figure 4-60 , data can be transferred between all the sites. Let us say, a data of 802.3 frame is generated in Perth. This data contains the IP details, which is transferred to the router at Perth provided by Telco provider. The services provided by Telco are managed so there is no need to know how the data is transferred.

Generally, the steps involved in the data transfer are as follows:

- When the data reaches the router, it is tagged with a customer VLAN ID.
- The router knows that at which IP address this data is to be transferred, so it routes that data to the destination with the help of multiple Telco routers.
- When the data reaches the destination, the edge router knows that this data is for which network; it removes the customer VLAN tag and passes this data to the required network.

For moving the traffic between different locations, Telco uses 802.1Q because the path is shared with other customers also and the customers may use the same IP ranges therefore, the supplier uses VLAN tagging. Therefore, if the supplier uses VLAN tagging, then the customers are unable to use tagging for their separation of networks purposes. To solve this problem, QinQ is designed.

AWS has DirectConnect equipment in Equinix SY3 (DX location). A Direct connect is ordered to connect AWS with Equinix SY3 and a port is allocated on DX router. A cross connect is created between the DX router and the ACME Inc. router in Sydney. In order to use QinQ, a VLAN (Supplier VLAN or supplier tag) should be allocated for ACME Inc. (in this case, it is 100).

You can only interact with the edge of the router because you are not the owner of the device. The created cross connect is managed by Telco provider. You have to create a public VIF, which gives a VLAN ID of 1001. The VLAN ID assigned to this VIF is referred as a customer tag. Create a Private VIF and give it VLAN ID 2001.

The requirement is that C tag 1001 is needed in Perth while C tag 2001 is needed in Brisbane. BGP session termination should be configured on the premise equipment and on the DX route or Telco Enterprises can be also used to terminate the BGP session on provider edge equipment.

For understanding Tag stack working for the required connectivity, consider the situation where a workstation in Brisbane needs to communicate with EC2 instance in AWS VPC. It generates the data (IP Payload), which is in 802.3 Ethernet frame having destination address of VPC. It is then tagged with a customer VLAN ID 2001 and then sent to the edge router. Then the S-tag is added in the frame by ACME Inc., the frame is changed to QinQ frame. This frame moves to Sydney where the Sydney router strips the S-Tag and the frame is then in 802.1 Q form when it enters in the network. This frame is then transferred to the DX router and DX router passes it to AWS. By using QinQ and the supplier network, a layer 2 tunnel is created across the supplier network or you can say that the port in DX location is extended to the Brisbane site. This Tunnel or extension is used to carry AWS VLAN 2001. This extension cannot be possible without using QinQ Technology. Similar procedure can be used to transfer data between Perth site and Equinix SY3 but with different customer tags.

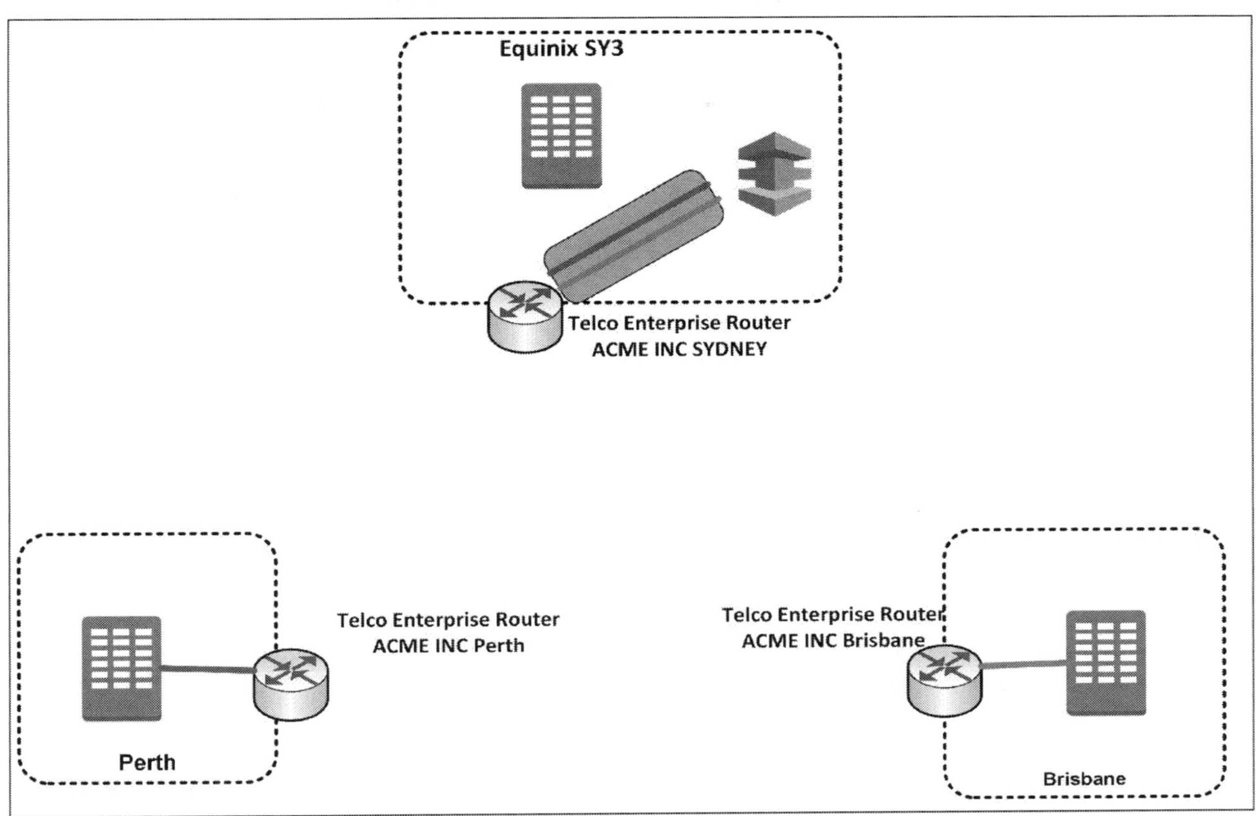

Figure 4-61: Data Transfer using 802.1 and QinQ Technology

QinQ is the technology, which is used when a network provider is utilized and this provider uses layer 2 network sharing with multiple clients. You also use VLAN and want to extend it over multiple sites.

Mind Map

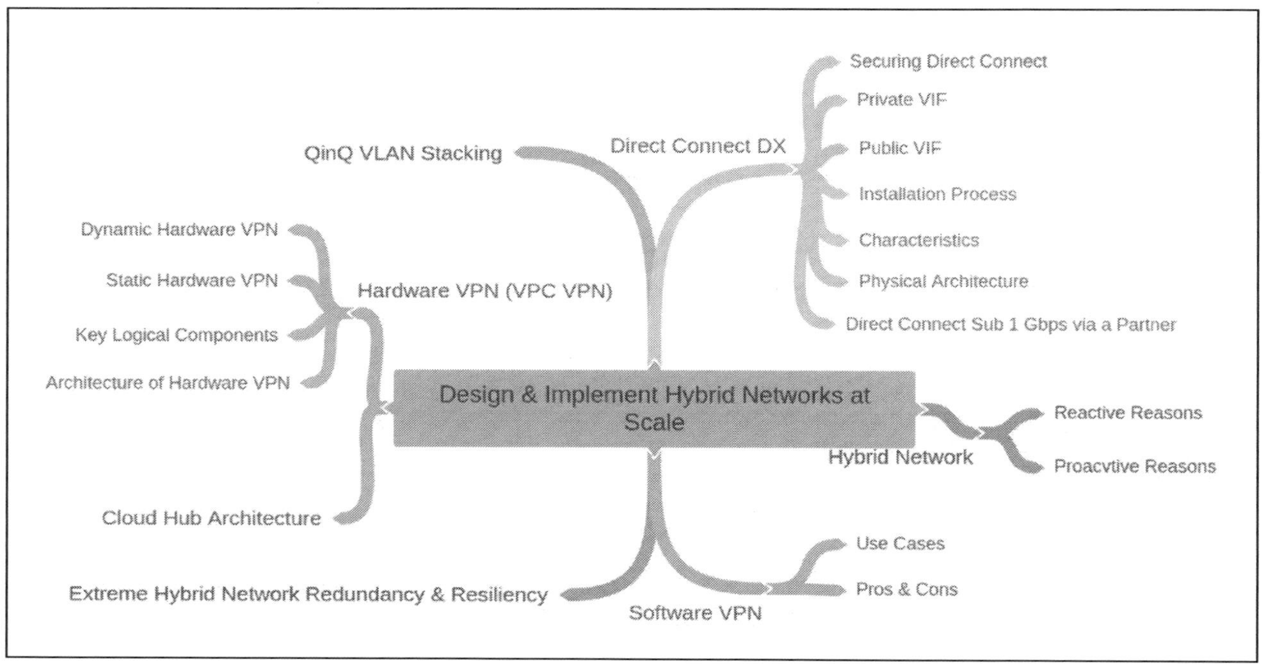

Figure 4-62: Chapter Mind Map

Practice Questions

1. Reasons for migrating to cloud can be of two types, select the correct options. (Choose 2 answers)
   a) Invalid Reasons
   b) Reactive Reasons
   c) Proactive Reasons
   d) Temporary Reasons
   e) Active Reasons

2. Which of the followings is not the supported Hardware connectivity option in AWS?
   a) Indirect Connection
   b) Direct Connection
   c) Hardware VPN
   d) Software VPN

3. Which is the logical representation of Customer Premises Equipment?
   a) VGW
   b) CGW
   c) DX
   d) IKE

4. Choose the two types of Virtual interfaces available in Direct connect.
   a) Hybrid Virtual Interface
   b) Public Virtual Interface
   c) Custom Virtual Interface
   d) Private Virtual Interface

5. Which of the following advantages cannot be availed by using Software VPN.
   a) Widest compatibility
   b) Fast Configuration
   c) Checks the alignment with strict government issues
   d) Consistent Latency

6. AWS charges VPN connection on the basis of:
   a) Minutes
   b) Month

c) Hours
d) Days

7. You are hired by a company and want to connect there AWS VPC with the corporate data center. You have to provide a cost effective solution for the connectivity. Which of the followings would you select?
   a) Software VPN
   b) Hardware VPN
   c) Direct Connect
   d) All of the above

8. Which of the following information is provided by VPN connection configuration file?
   a) IP addressing
   b) IKE information
   c) IP stack information
   d) BGP information
   e) All of the above

9. Which of the following connectivity options will you choose in order to connect two VPCs?
   a) Hardware VPN
   b) DX
   c) Software VPN
   d) None of the above

10. An IT Engineer is working to connect AWS VPC and Corporate DC where CPE is BGP capable. The budget of the company does not allow expensive solutions. Choose the best connectivity solution.
    a) Software VPN
    b) Static Hardware VPN
    c) Dynamic Hardware VPN
    d) Direct Connect

11. An IT Engineer is working to connect AWS VPC and Corporate DC but this time CPE is BGP incapable. The budget of the company does not allow expensive solutions. Choose the best connectivity solution.
    a) Software VPN

b) Static Hardware VPN
c) Dynamic Hardware VPN
d) Direct Connect

12. LOA stands for:
a) Letter of Authentication
b) Letter of Authority
c) Language of AWS
d) Layers of AWS

13. Which type of connection is cross connect?
a) Physical connection
b) Virtual connection
c) Hybrid connection
d) Interfaces

14. VIFs created in external account are known as:
a) External VIF
b) Outer VIF
c) Hosted VIF
d) None of above

15. Which of the followings is a connection without using public internet?
a) Software VPN
b) Hardware VPN
c) Public VIF
d) All of the above

16. In order to secure private VIF, which of the option is used?
a) Hardware VPN
b) Software VPN
c) Public internet
d) Public VIF

17. Which of the followings is the free facility in AWS in terms of Direct Connect?
a) Transfer Out
b) Transfer IN
c) All resources

d) VPN connection

18. To connect multiple sites for IT networking and providing internet access to all, which of the following techniques is best?
    a) Mesh topology
    b) Hub and Scope
    c) Cloud Hub
    d) None of the above

Chapter 05: Configure Network Integration with Application Services

Introduction

In this Chapter, we will discuss Route53, and its routing policies, VPC DHCP, Classic Load Balancing, S3 content delivery, and CloudFront local and global content delivery. After completing this, you will have enough information regarding the networking concept and you will be able to appear in the AWS Network Specialty Exam.

Route 53

To understand Route53, you need to understand DNS in detail, which was discussed in chapter 2. Hopefully, you have understood DNS and its record types. Now, let us move towards Route 53. Route 53 is a service of Amazon which provides highly available and scalable cloud DNS web service that implicitly connects user requests to IT infrastructure running on AWS such as EC2 instances, Elastic Load Balancers, or Amazon S3 buckets. It can also be used to route end-users to systems that are outside of AWS. DNS (Domain Name System) is a globally distributed service that translates human-readable domain names like www.ipspecialist.net to the numeric machine-readable IP addresses like 192.0.2.1 that computers use to connect to each other.

Amazon Route 53 traffic flow makes it easy for you to manage traffic globally through a variety of routing types, including latency-based routing, Geo DNS, and weighted round-robin, all of which can be combined with DNS Failover to enable a variety of low-latency, fault-tolerant architectures.

You can use Amazon Route 53 to register new domains, transfer existing domains, route traffic for your domains to your AWS and external resources, and monitor the health of your resources.

> EXAM TIP: Amazon Route 53 is named 53 because the DNS port is port 53. It is a DNS service and allows you to map the domain to EC2 instance, load balancer and S3 bucket.

Routing Policies

When you create a recordset, you select a routing policy that determines how Route53 will respond to queries. AWS supports multiple routing policies for Amazon Route53, such as:

Simple Routing Policy

This is the default policy for newly created resources. Use this policy when you have a single resource that performs a given function for your domain or for querying a record. This is the simplest routing policy. For better understanding, consider an example in which DNS client requests a local resolver for www.ipspecialist.net. Think that it is a recursive query, which is at background and DNS resolver finds an authoritative server for this domain. It first goes to the root server then, going to another non-authoritative server, it reaches to the authoritative server. This authoritative server is Route53, which returns the response of this query with IP against that domain. This response is a single A record. This routing is known as a simple routing policy. You can extend this routing policy by adding multi-value against that domain. This means that a record or a record set represents the same domain. However, this not for failure or load of traffic, it is merely providing an alternative IP address when a request for the same domain occurs.

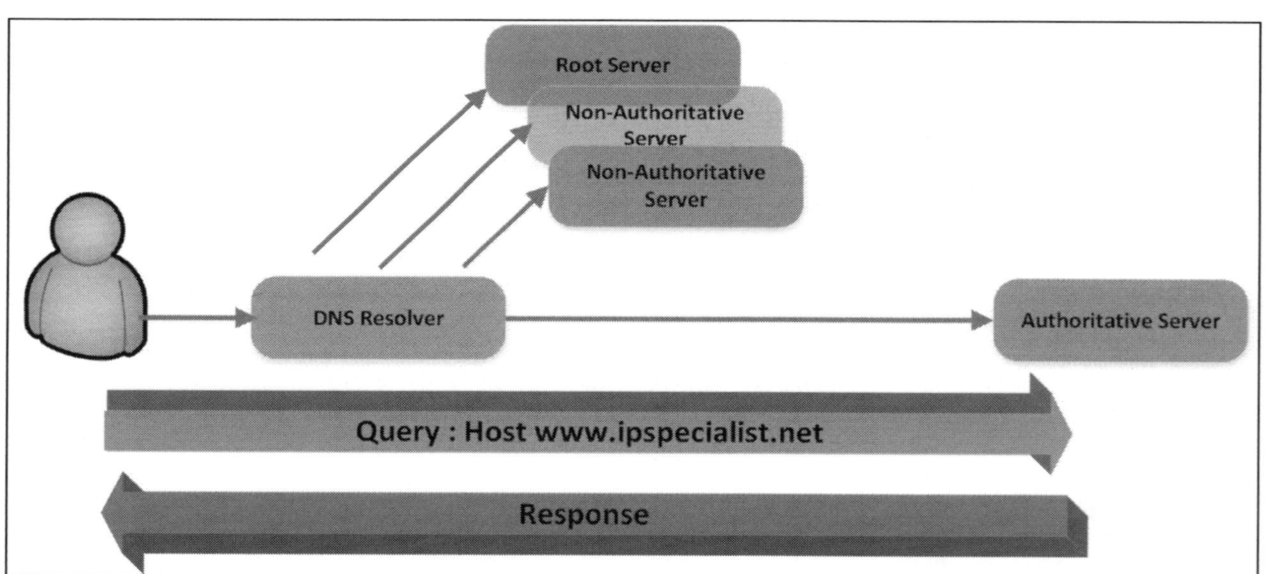

Figure 5-01: Simple Routing Policy

Weighted Routing Policy

You can use a weighted policy when you have multiple resources that perform the same function. This is the extension of the round-robin. Round-robin is a technique, which assigns multiple values or IPs to the same hostname that we can do in simple routing

policy extension. However, in simple routing, this round-robin is not for failure or load as we discussed above so, by using weighted routing policy, you can distribute the load. In weighted routing policy, you have multiple records over the same hostname, and each record has a unique set ID to identify. Each record set also has some weighted value between 0-255. By this value record response, if you a defined weight value of 0, then traffic is distributed equally to each record set.

Consider an example; you have domain "www" to which you associate five recordsets with their weighted value. Then sum all weighted value example shown in figure 5-02. So, the 5th record set's response is 7 out of 14, or if 5th record set is unhealthy, it specifies only via health checks then this record is removed so overall weight of record set is changed and the response depends on basis of this change.

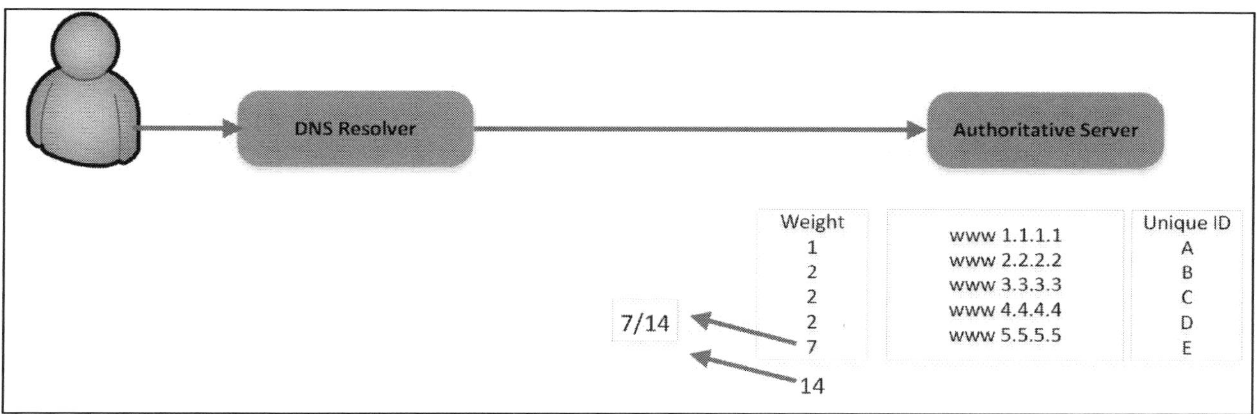

Figure 5-02: Weighted Routing Policy

Failover Routing Policy

Use failover policy when you need to configure active-passive failover. Meaning that one resource takes all the traffic when the other is not available.

Consider an example in which you set two record sets of the same host. One declared as primary, and the other one is secondary. Health checks are also applied, so if the primary record is healthy 100% traffic is routed towards it. If the primary is unhealthy, then 100% traffic is routed towards secondary and if both declared as unhealthy then primary is used for 100% traffic routing.

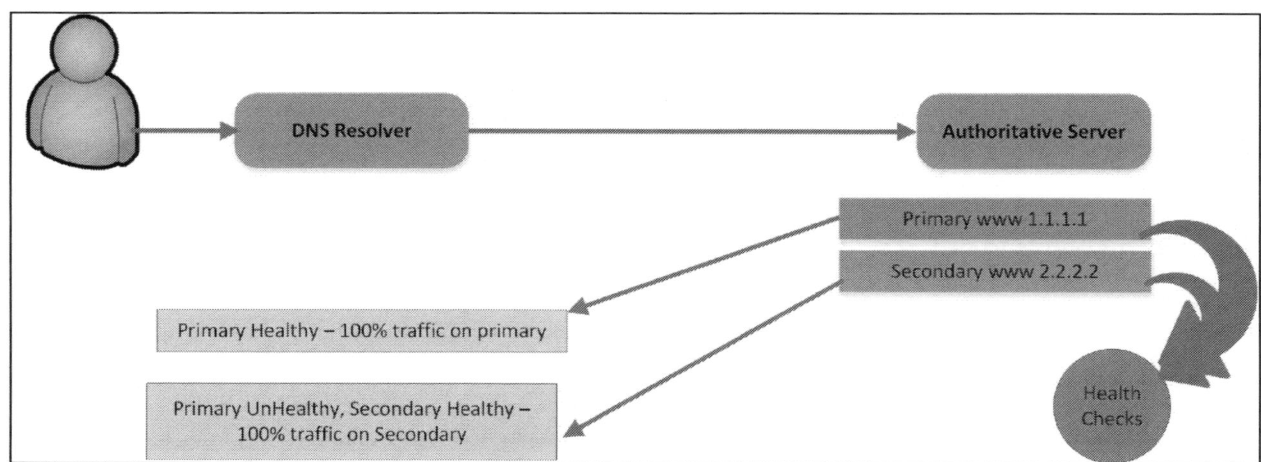

Figure 5-03: Failover Routing Policy

Latency Based Routing Policy

You can use latency-based policy when you have multiple resources in different regions, and you want to direct the traffic to the region that provides the best latency. For Latency Based Routing, AWS continuously checks for latency. With this routing policy, you need to select the region. In this way, by using latency-based routing, you can improve performance by providing that resource to the user with low latency. With Latency Based Routing, you can also define health checks for the record. If any record health check is unhealthy, then it routes traffic towards the next best low latency.

Consider an example; you have created two latency records and a user sent a request from the Ohio region. Route53 Latency Based Routing will check user latency with the created two records and from whom it received the lowest latency. It routes traffic towards that record and gets a response from it.

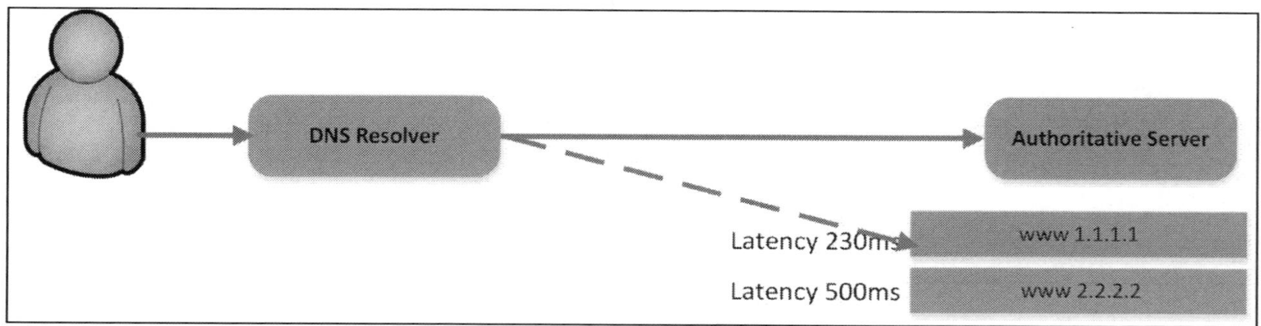

Figure 5-04: Latency Based Routing Policy

Geo-location Routing Policy

Geo-location policy will send your traffic based on the geographic locations of your users rather than using latency. It is used in those scenarios where specific location based stable

routing is needed. Geo-location routing policy can be applied by country, by state, or by continent. By using this routing policy, you can define whether the request generated from end-user is routed to the defined record region or the endpoint DNS.

Consider an example in which a user from California is the request initiator. Route53 using Geo-location routing will forward the DNS request to the record set in that region. If it is not in that region, then to the United States, if here, it does not match, then it goes to the North American continent. After all this, if it still does not match to the endpoint, then it will go to default routing.

In routing, if you want the end-user of a specific region to be restricted to that specific region recordset, then do not specify the default record as it does not restrict your end-user to its region. In case, if the record set in that region, country, or continent is unhealthy, then due to not defining the default record, you can restrict your end-user to its region. Location of end-user is based on DNS resolver IP, but if you are using ISP based resolver, then it does not give an accurate location. To overcome this issue, AWS provides an extension to DNS, which is “edns-client-subnet” that forwards the truncated version of client IP in DNS request. This truncated version of IP contains subnet of client or end-user as DNS query. So routing decision becomes more specific.

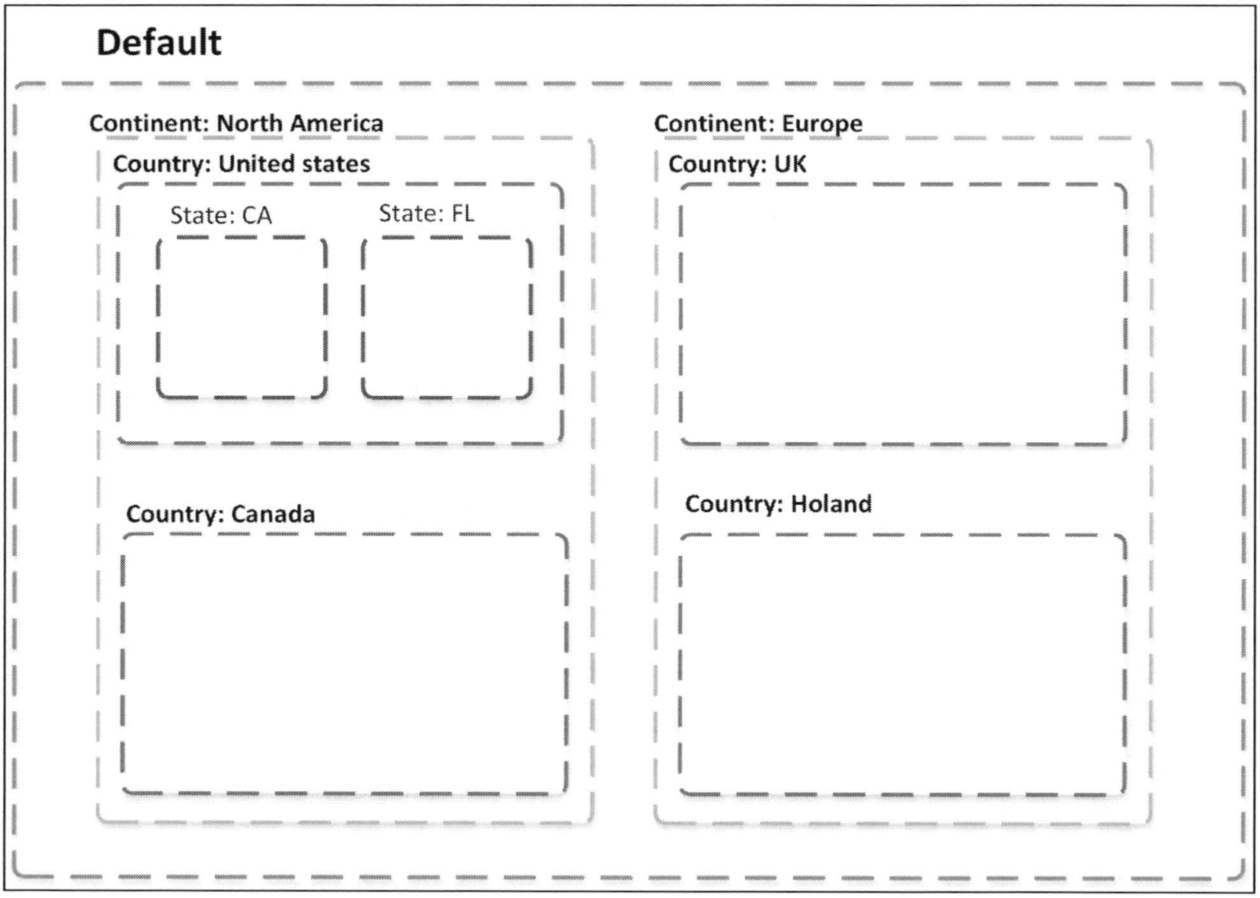

Default

Continent: North America

Country: United states

State: CA

State: FL

Country: Canada

Continent: Europe

Country: UK

Country: Holand

Figure 5-05: Geo-location Routing Policy

Route53 Routing and Resolution Trees

Above, we have discussed all routing policies in Route53, and for all of them, there are DNS health checks. These health checks are used to define health checks of record sets. For making a complex Route53 routing tree, you can use all of the routing policies together. In Route53, there is an Alias record, which is used to point to another record or record set. Alias is used for pointing ELBs as they have Dynamic Addressing. As we know that for DNS root or apex or naked domain we use A record, but as ELB is using Dynamic addressing, you need to refer to it by its DNS hostname, so you can use CNAME, which points to a subdomain. By using CNAME, you will lose some property of the domain, which causes a problem. To overcome these issues, we use Alias record.

In Alias record, you can point to a group of record sets considering them as a single block rather than individual record sets.

Consider an example in which you need to provide worldwide distribution of traffic across the AWS region and define a failover option in case of disaster recovery or failure

of any main component of infrastructure. You have the domain "ipspecialist.net" in Route53, which uses Failover routing policy, and it has primary Alias recordset, which points to a group of record sets that have record sets using Geo-location routing policy while secondary Alias record points to the website-hosting-enabled bucket. In Geo-location group of record sets, we have one recordset in default and one in Europe, and both have health checks as well.

- The first user of UK wants to resolve ipspecialist.net so, from Route53, it points to primary record set as in failover routing policy primary record set is considered as a priority.
- From the primary record set, it goes to the Geo-location group of record sets.
- Now at Geo-location group of record sets, it checks for the record set in the UK, but if we do not have the record set in the UK region, it goes to Europe.
- If Europe record set health check fails, then when the user reaches Geo-location group of record sets, it points to a default recordset.
- In the group of record sets, if any one recordset health check is successful, then this group of record sets is considered healthy.
- Now consider both of the record sets in a group of record set fails, it means health check will fail and then the Alias record pointing to this group of record set will also fail.
- Now the user moves forward towards the secondary Alias record, which points to the bucket that has a static page of failure. In this way, we use both failover and geo-location routing policies together.

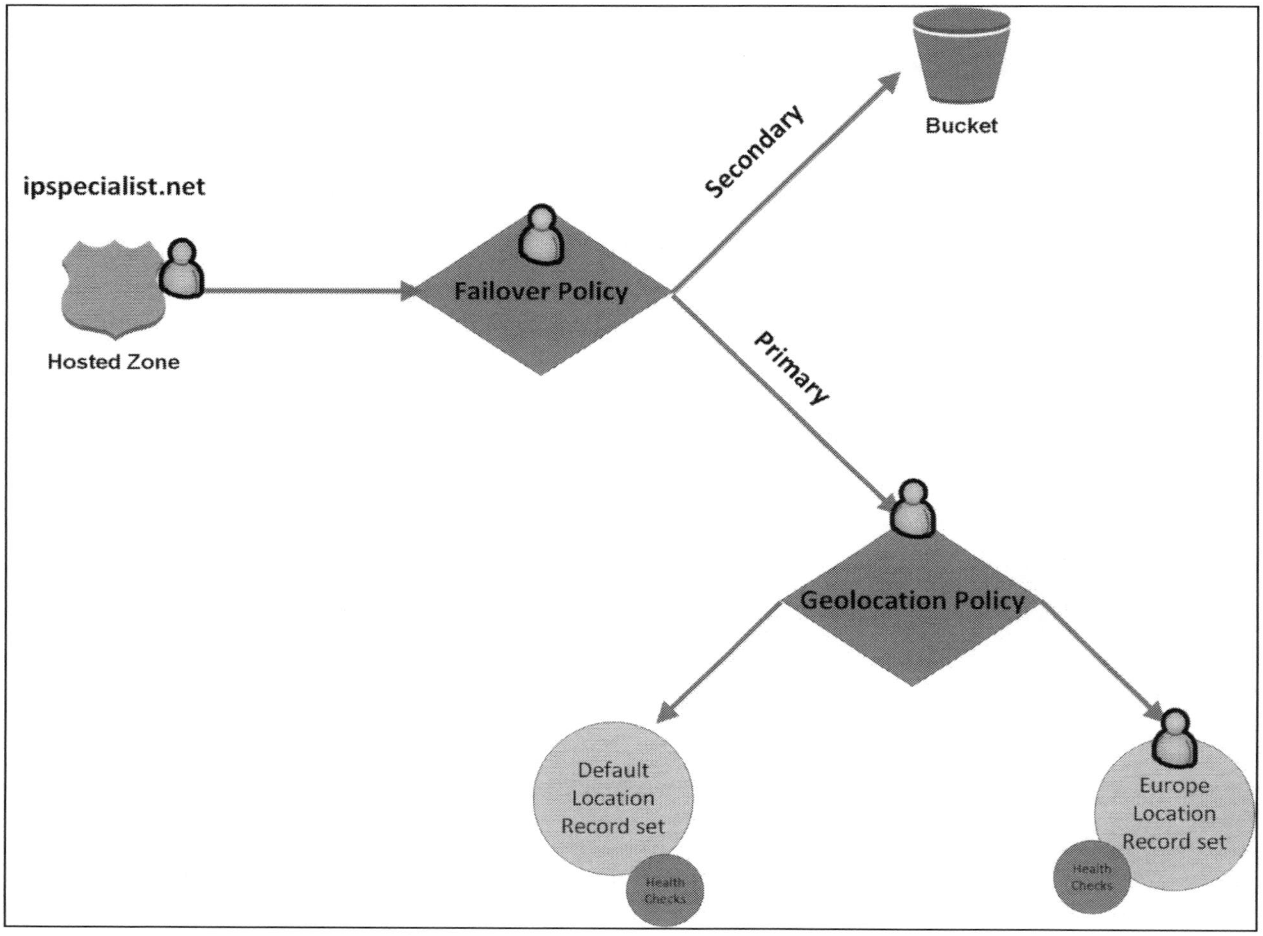

ipspecialist.net

Hosted Zone

Failover Policy

Secondary

Bucket

Primary

Geolocation Policy

Default Location Record set

Health Checks

Europe Location Record set

Health Checks

Figure 5-06: Resolution Tree (a)

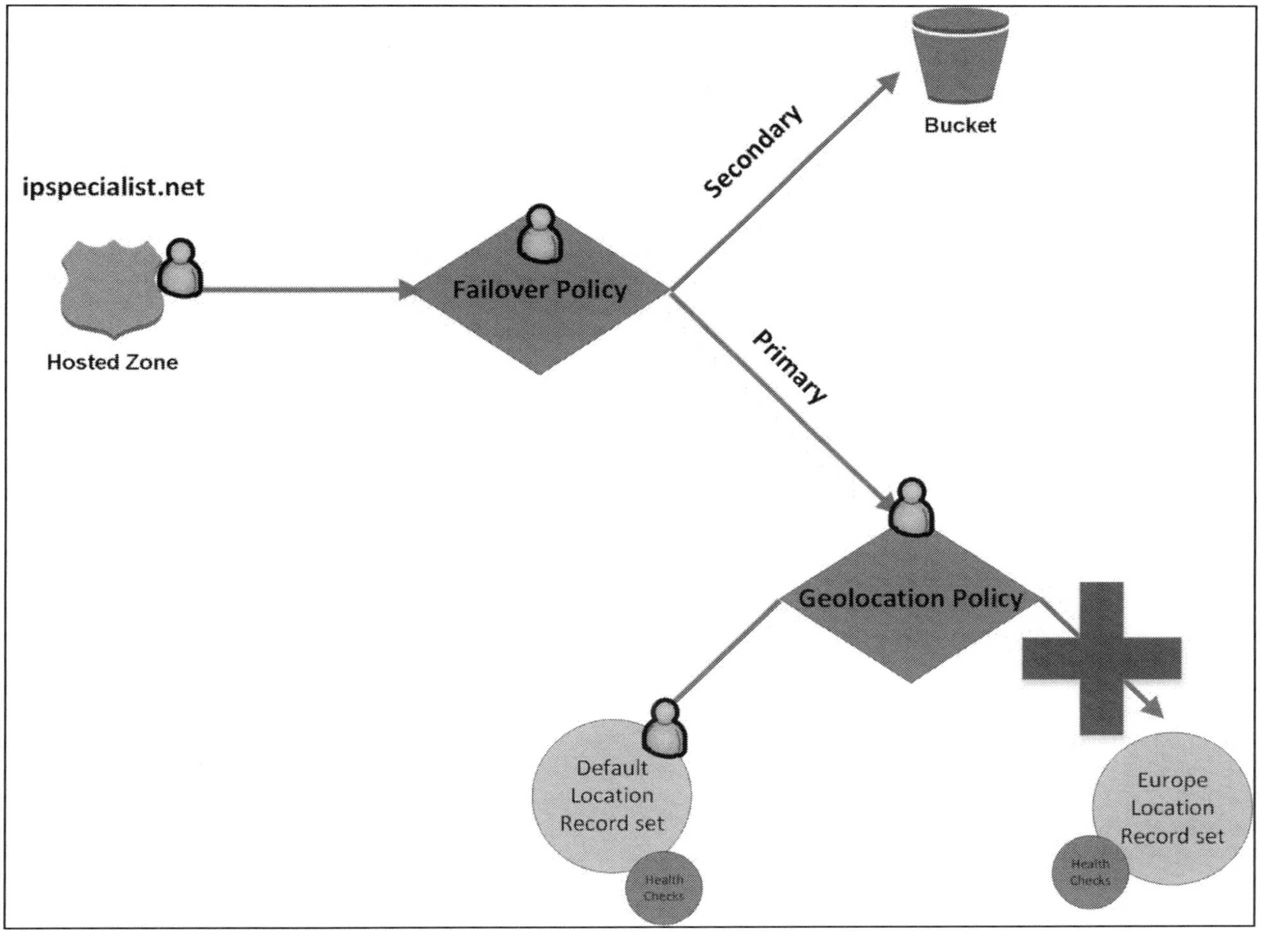

ipspecialist.net
Hosted Zone
Failover Policy
Secondary
Bucket
Primary
Geolocation Policy
Default Location Record set
Health Checks
Europe Location Record set
Health Checks

Figure 5-07: Resolution Tree (b)

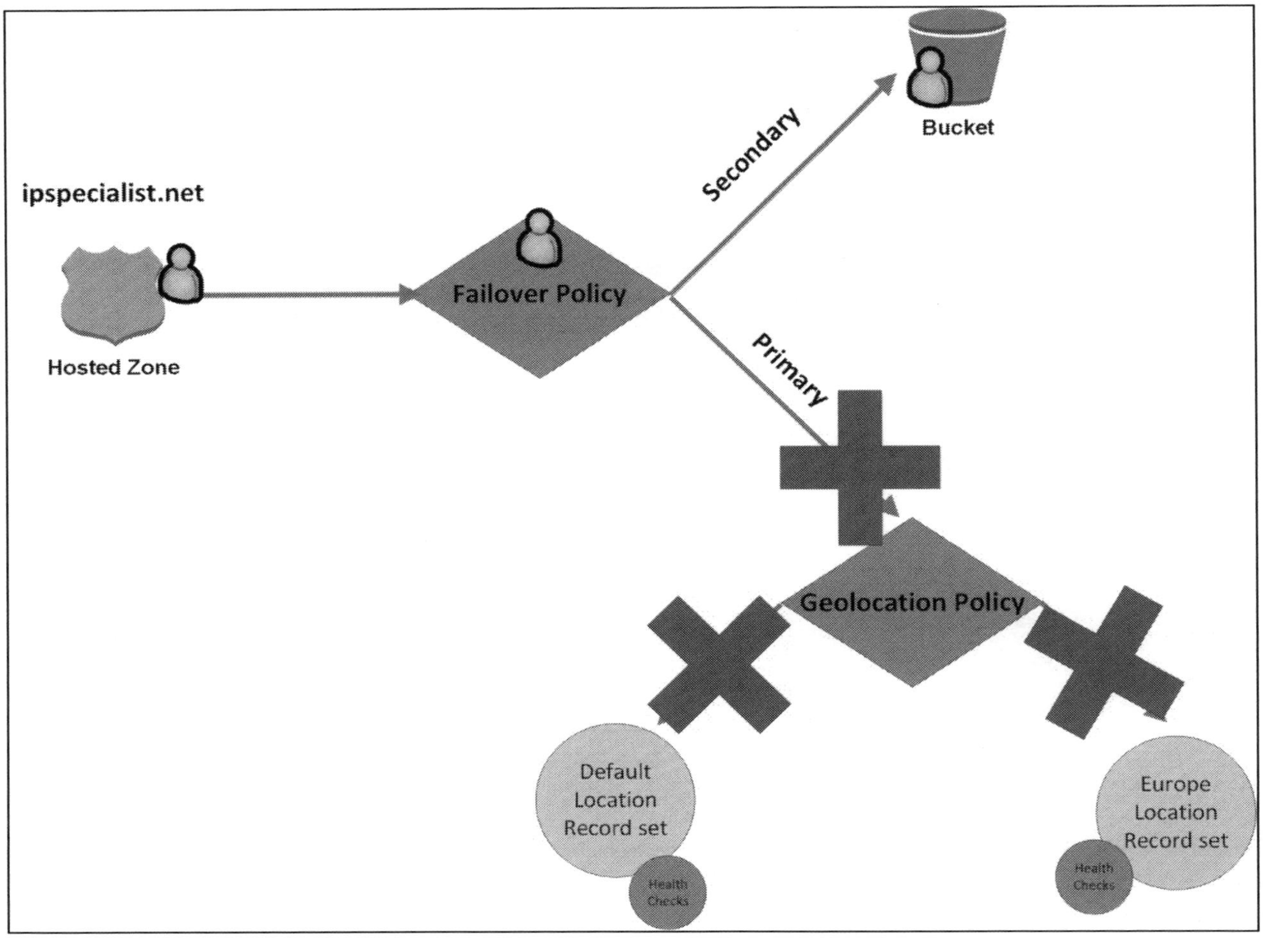

ipspecialist.net

Hosted Zone

Failover Policy

Secondary

Bucket

Primary

Geolocation Policy

Default Location Record set

Health Checks

Europe Location Record set

Health Checks

Figure 5-08: Resolution Tree (c)

> EXAM TIP: Alias is another type of record set, which is a reference as Alias target to point to ELB, S3, CloudFront and record set groups.
>
> Health checks are also enabled individually on each record set. If they fail or are unhealthy, then this record set is considered as disabled. Alias record checks its target health by considering its health check status.

Route53 Private Hosted Zone

Let us discuss a Private Hosted Zone, which is an additional product in Route53. To understand a Private Hosted Zone, you need to understand Public Hosted Zone.

Consider a public internet and private VPC. There is a VPC, which resides between both public and private subnet and has only one instance with public and private IP. On this instance, we enabled DNS hostname; so to this instance, the public hostname is mapped

over public IP while, the private hostname is mapped over private IP. If you are using a resolution of public DNS outside the VPC, then it points to public IP, or if you are using DNS resolution within VPC, then public DNS points to private IP.

Now, assume we have Route53 external hosted zone, which is in public and points to public IP of AWS or public IP of non-AWS service or you can also point to private IP of AWS. This Route53 external hosted zone is accessible over the internet, but the private IP, which is pointed by recordset is not routable over the internet. This is all about the externally hosted zone.

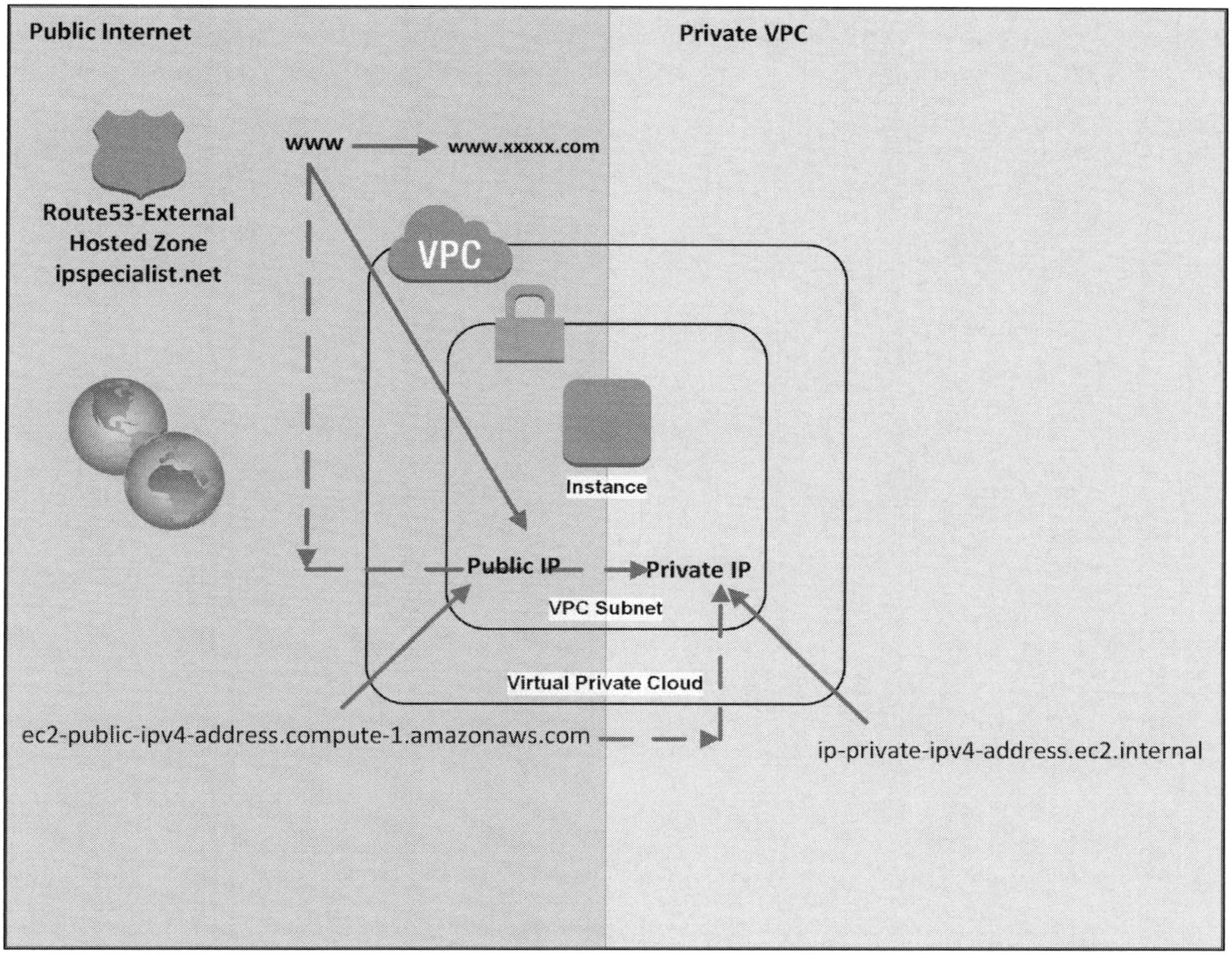

Figure 5-09: External Hosted Zone

Now, consider Route53 internal hosted zone, which is in private VPC and during its creation, it points to VPC. After creation of an internal hosted zone, you can point it to more additional VPCs within the same account of the hosted zone. When record set is created for this hosted zone, then it is only resolvable within those VPCs to which it is

associated. For external VPC association, you can use CLI or API for the hosted zone by using the following commands:

1. create-vpc-association-authorization
2. associate-vpc-with-hosted-zone

First command is used in the account where hosted zone reside while the second command is used in the account where external VPC resides.

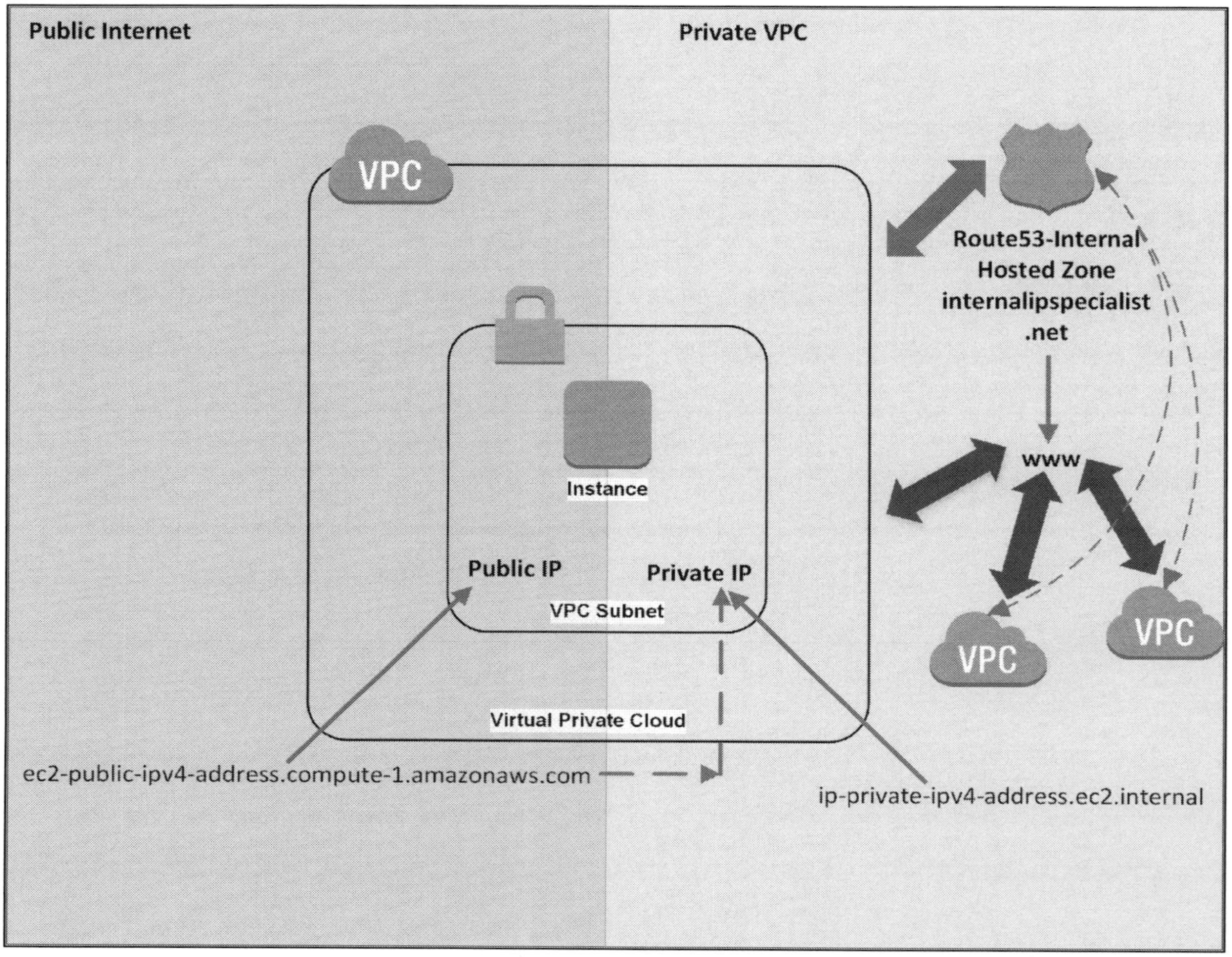

Figure 5-10: Internal Hosted Zone

Route53 Split View/ Horizon DNS

This technique is used to maintain both the internal and external version of the website. This architecture contains both the externally hosted zone and an internal hosted zone. In general architecture, the externally hosted zone is visible to DNS client or internet client while internal hosted zone is visible to internal instances in VPCs. Therefore, if an internal client wants both the internal and external version, then you can use this

technique, even if the domain name is overlapping or different for both hosted zone. This architecture is used in complex DNS resolutions.

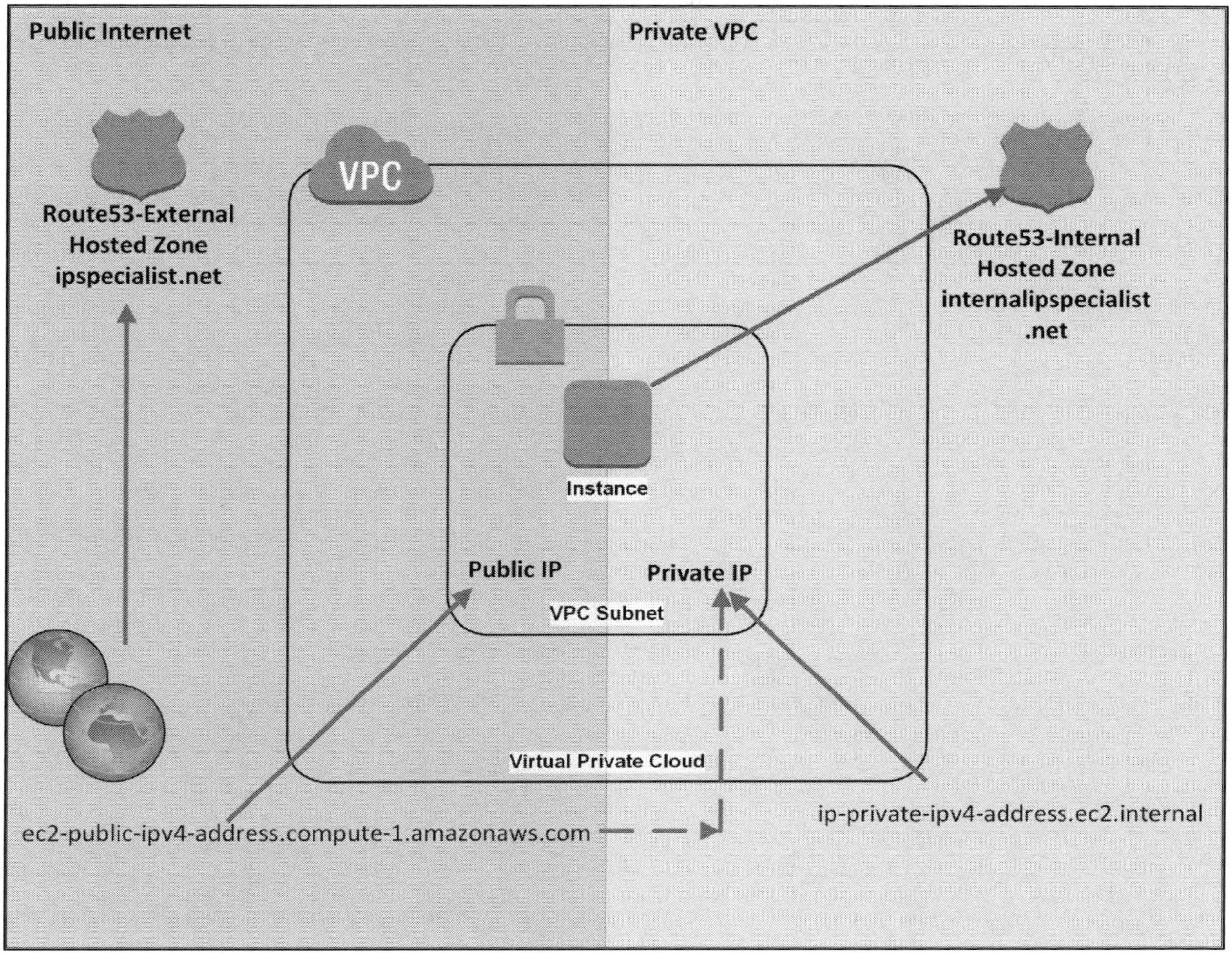

Figure 5-11: Split View/Horizon DNS

Hybrid DNS- Corporate to AWS

When you have architecture on AWS VPC and on-premises, AWS VPC has an EC2 instance to which IP address is assigned from CIDR of the subnet inside VPC. As we know, each subnet has ".2" address, which is Reserved for mapping to the Amazon Provided DNS. This DNS resolver performs queries on behalf of EC2 instance and then communicates to Route53. Now Route53 has a connection to internal hosted zone or external hosted zone or non-Route53 hosted zone.

In the on-premises data center, there is a server, which communicates to an internal resolver for a big production company or to the ISP resolver for small businesses. Then this resolver communicates to internal authority, which may be an AD that has certain

domains. To incorporate data, the center resolver can also communicate to the Route53 external hosted zone, or other DNS hosted zones.

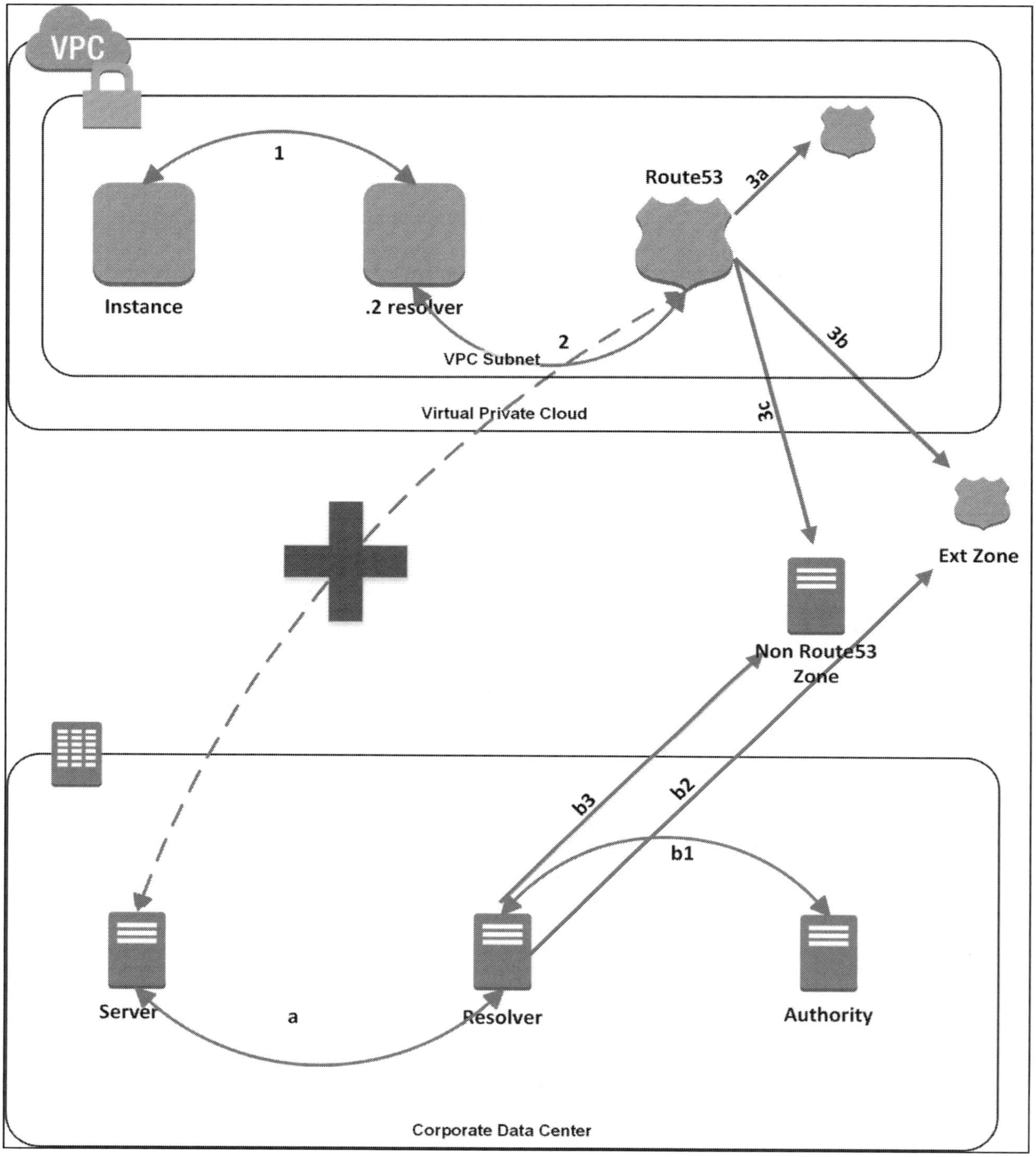

Figure 5-12: Basic Architecture of AWS and Corporate Network

In both of the architectures, there is an issue that internal servers of the corporate network cannot resolve the internal records for VPC. Also, VPC resource does not have any connectivity to the internal authority of the corporate network. Now, here the uses of hybrid DNS technology came that uses Route53 with the conjunction of an on-premises platform like AD.

For hybrid DNS, you will have to create an IPSec VPN tunnel between both networks and point the local server to ".2" resolver, but this resolver will not be able to be accessed outside the VPN even when DirectConnect or VPN is established. Therefore, for resolving to that resolver, you can add intermediate DNS forwarded which, maybe self-build or the AWS Directory Service. Now the flow of the process is:

- the server sends a request directly to DNS forwarder
- DNS forwarder sends a request to ".2 resolver".
- .2 resolver routes to Route53. Then, Route53 points to an external public hosted zone.

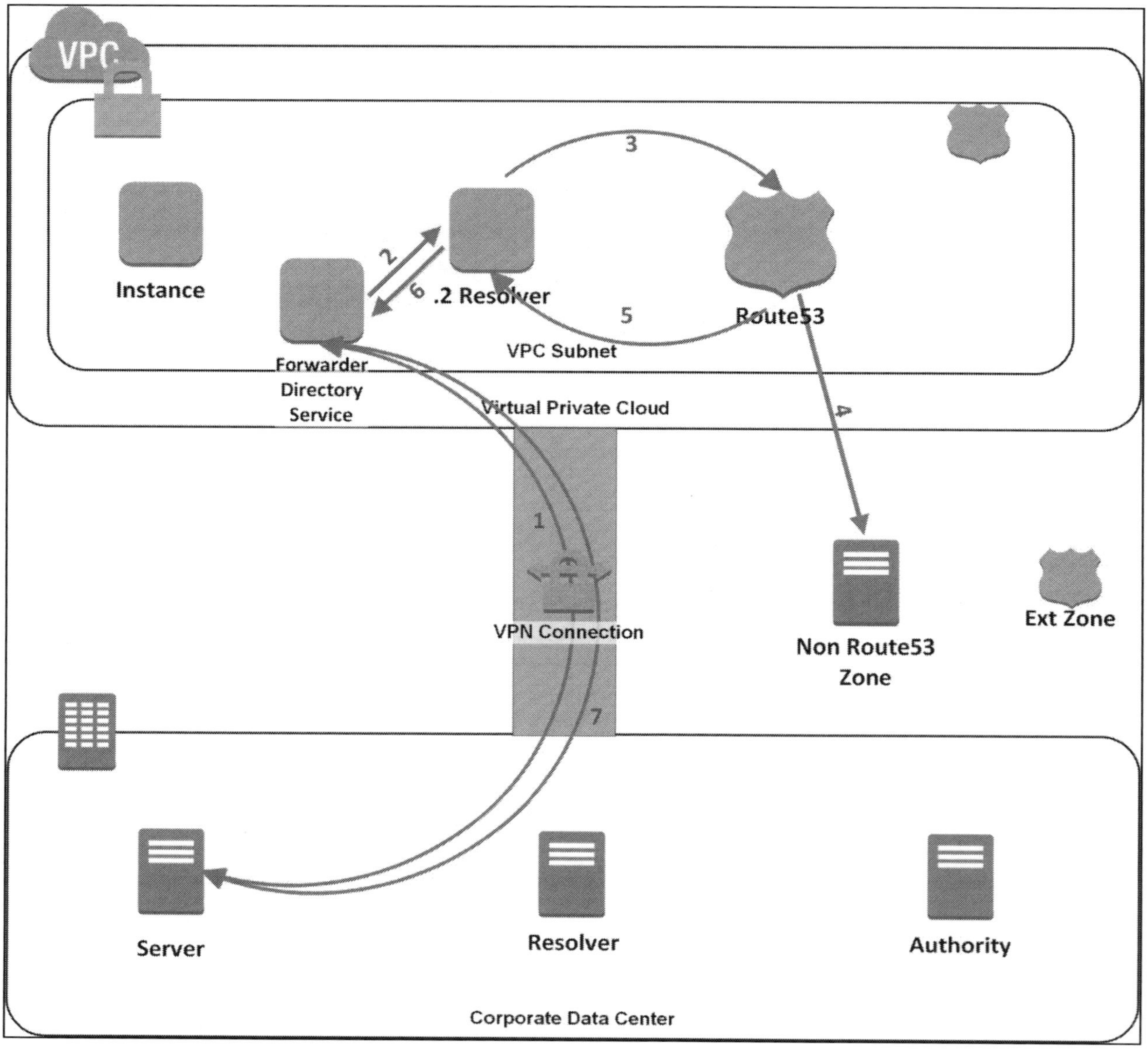

Figure 5-13: Use of Forwarded Directory Service in Hybrid DNS (a)

However, by doing this, internal resolver and authority is not in use, so we must design the architecture in such a way that the request is sent to internal resolver where it identifies either its internal hosted zone or public hosted zone or zone hosted by Route53. Then, on the basis of this, it forwards the request to the respective path.

- If the request is for an internal hosted zone, then it goes to internal authority where authority responses to the resolver then, from the resolver to the client.
- If the request is for public hosted zone or zone hosted by Route53, then resolver sends the request to the DNS forwarder of VPC. This forwarder then talks to ".2" resolver on behalf of the internal resolver. Now from ".2" resolver, it

follows the same path as it did above. The response of this request follows the same path as the request sent.

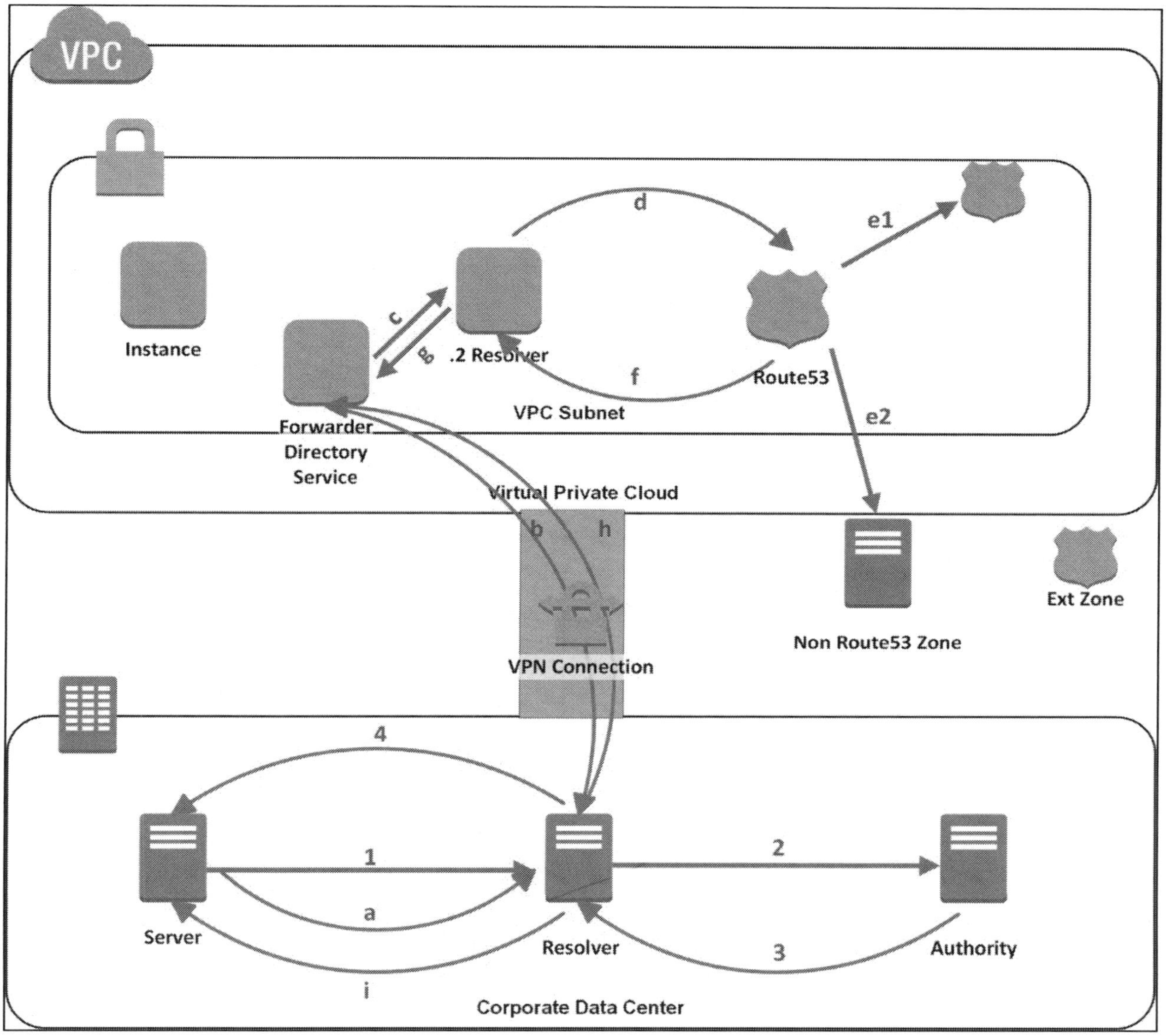

Figure 5-14: Use of Forwarded Directory Service in Hybrid DNS (b)

However, as we discussed in the above example, the EC2 instance in VPC still will not be able to communicate to internal authority or internal hosted zone. Hence, for that, ideally there is a concept, but because of some limitations, this is not possible. The concept is to create STUBZONE inside VPC. This is a system introduced in the VPC where the small number of records, which is named server records are placed. These records point to the server, which is authoritative for that domain. Thus, the communication begins in this way.

- Instance requests the ".2" resolver, then from the resolver to Route53.

- Route53 checks the STUBZONE for the record and sends a response to the ".2" resolver.
- ".2" resolver sends response to the instance.

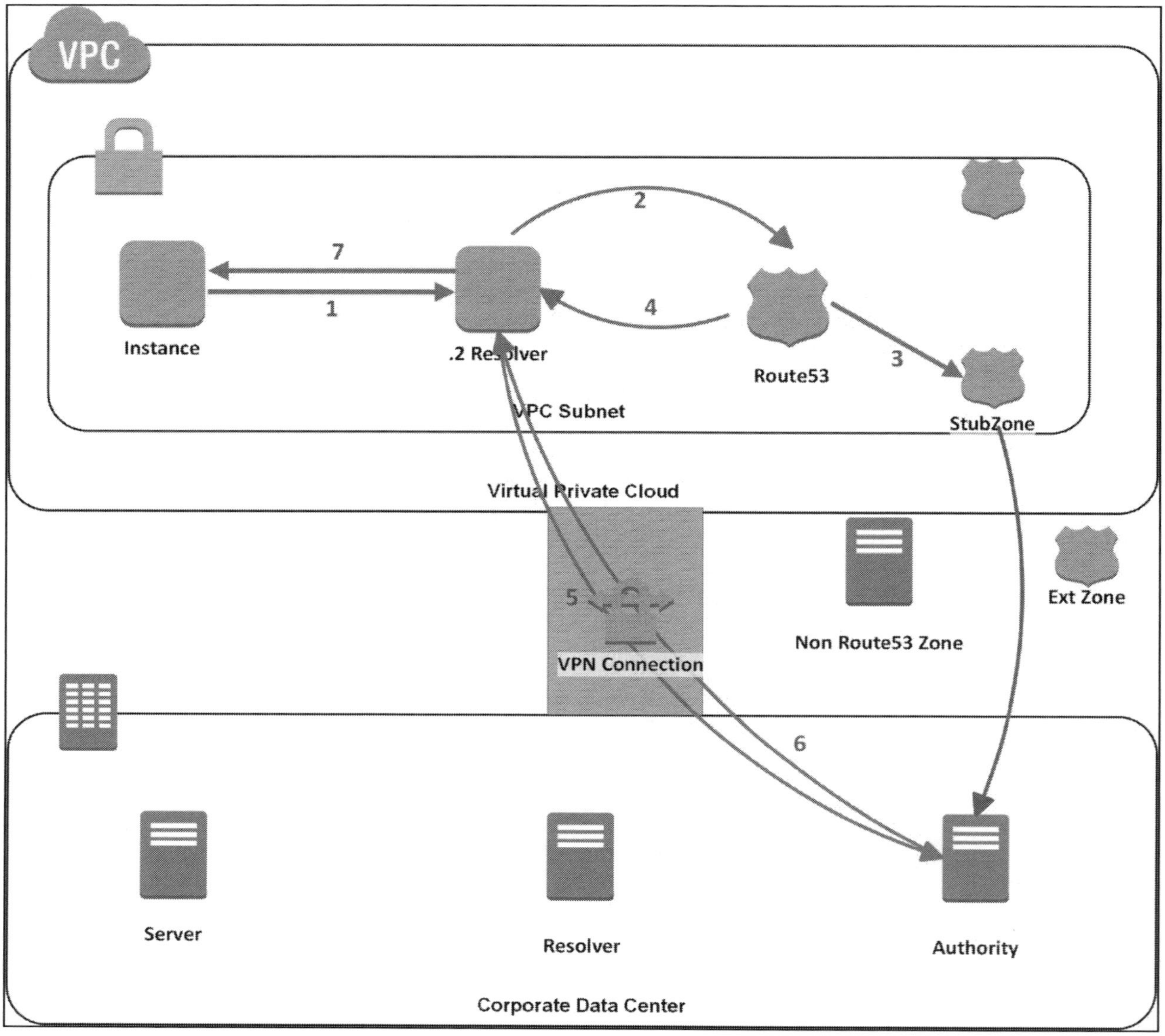

Figure 5-15: Stub Zone in Hybrid DNS

As this concept is ideally good but due to some causes is not recommended, two other ways are defined to use rather than using StubZone.

1) First, create a private hosted zone inside VPC and synchronize it with the hosted Domain server by regularly copying data into that private hosted zone. The instance sends request to ".2" resolver, then the resolver sends it to the Route53.

Route53 communicates with the private hosted zone and sends a response to the instance via ".2" resolver.

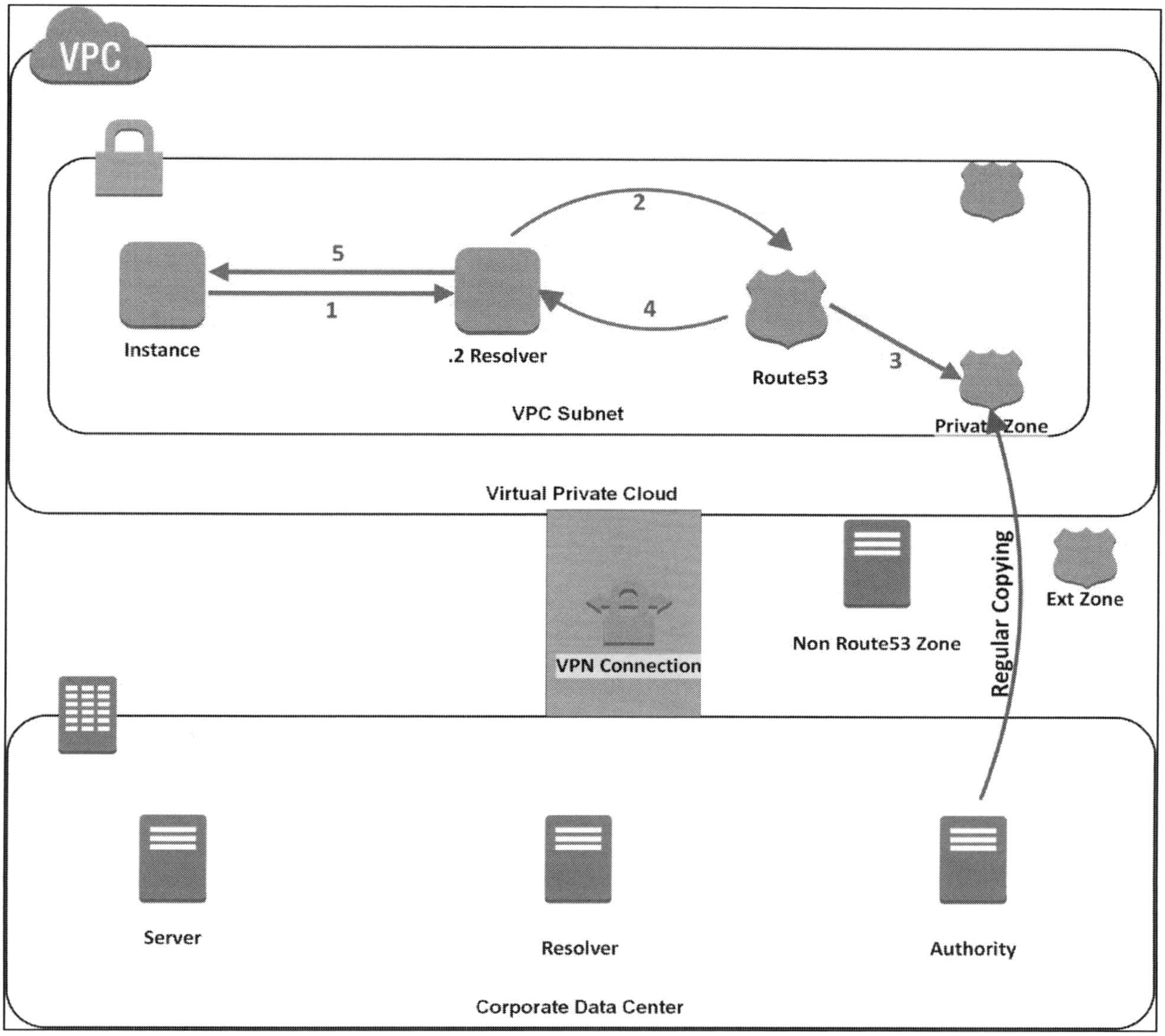

Figure 5-16: Private Zone in Hybrid DNS

From the above method, there is an inconsistency between VPC and private hosted zone. So, to mitigate the inconsistency, you need to ensure that regular copying is entirely overwritten of records from the internal authority to the private hosted zone in VPC. However, potential inconsistency still may occur as there is the direct entry of the client into the hosted zone. To resolve all problems, another method is introduced. It is complex, but it will overcome all problems.

2) In this architecture, we provide on-premises resolver as DNS resolver to all VPC base resources via VPN/DirectConnect by using DHCP option set.

i) If instance request is for the internal hosted domain, then from the on-premises resolver, it goes to the internal authority.
ii) If a request is not for internal hosted zone, then from on-premises resolver, it goes to the DNS forwarder in VPC, then to ".2" resolver, then finally to Route53. From Route53 it checks for the internal/external hosted zone of Route53 and public hosted zone. Now, the response from the specific zone is sent to ".2" resolver via Route53. ".2" resolver then sends this response to the DNS forwarder and then to the on-premises resolver. Now, from the on-premises resolver, it sends a response to the instance.

This architecture is dependent on the VPN/DirectConnect connection while, the first one architecture design is independent of the VPN/DirectConnect connection. So use this new architecture when you have resiliency on VPN/DirectConnect connection.

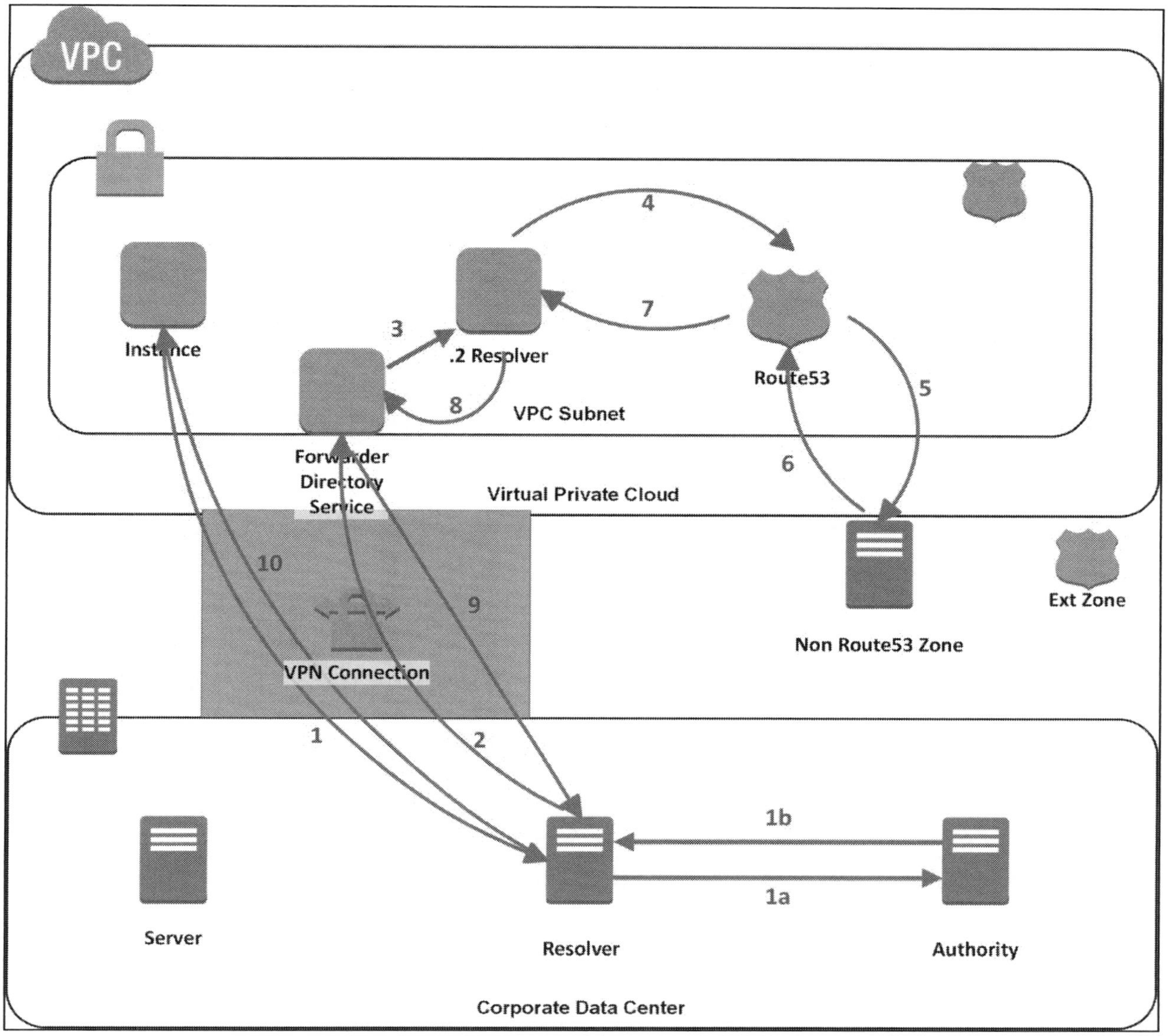

Figure 5-17: Hybrid DNS Resilient Architecture

VPC DHCP

To understand VPC DHCP, you need to understand DHCP. As we know, DHCP is a protocol, which allows the machine to perform L2 broadcast asking for IP and other configurations automatically. The DHCP server is a virtual or physical segment that responds to the request of broadcasting. This protocol allows the dynamic configuration of the machine. It not only gives IP addresses but also provides other information like DNS, local Gateway, subnet mask, VOIP and servers.

DHCP communication between client and server is connectionless, UDP and uses port 67 and 87. There are four phases in communication, which are:

- **Discovery**- This phase is where the client is asking for DHCP lease. In this phase, broadcasting is requested from the client machine via using the broadcast address, i.e., 255s. This is open-ended broadcast, which is received by local entities of subnet where any DHCP server inside subnet is allowed to respond.
- **OFFER**- This phase is where the DHCP server who want to respond, checks the MAC address of the client from its broadcast address and other configuration. Now consider that the IP inside the subnet is reserved and the DHCP server offers that IP in the form of LEASE.

Note: LEASE is temporarily assigning an IP for certain duration with a start and end time. When the duration expires, you need to assign the IP again.

- **Request**- The third phase is the request phase where the client receives the request from one or more DHCP server and then picks any one request and responds to the request that the client wants. The LEASE request may be unicast or broadcast.
- **Acknowledgment**- This phase is where the DHCP server replies to the client in response to their request. The LEASE IP is now stored in DHCP DB with a start and an end point with some other configurations.

Note: Another configuration is known as DHCP option set, which is variable information and may be one or more than one.

[option code] [number of Octets] [vendor specific data]

Option code defines the functions of an option code; some octets define the specific number of octets that are reserved for data and vendor specific data is the data, which is stored.

The above DHCP working is general. Now, let us discuss DHCP in VPC. Consider a VPC with CIDR block 10.0.0.0/16 with 4 subnets in it; 10.0.0.0/18, 10.0.64.0/18, 10.0.128.0/18 and 10.0.192.0/18. As we discussed previously in this book, in each subnet CIDR block, 5 IP addresses are reserved. For DHCP leases in VPC subnet, ".2" is set for DNS server. Therefore, the available range for each subnet is;

- 10.0.0.0/18 –> 10.0.0.4 - 10.0.63.254
- 10.0.64.0/18 -> 10.0.64.4 – 10.0.127.254
- 10.0.128.0/18 -> 10.0.128.4 -10.0.191.254
- 10.0.192.0/18 -> 10.0.192.4 – 10.0.255.254

DHCP in AWS is configured at VPC level. DHCP is controlled by an object called "DHCP options set". It is created via API, CLI or UI. You have multiple options in that as shown in the figure.

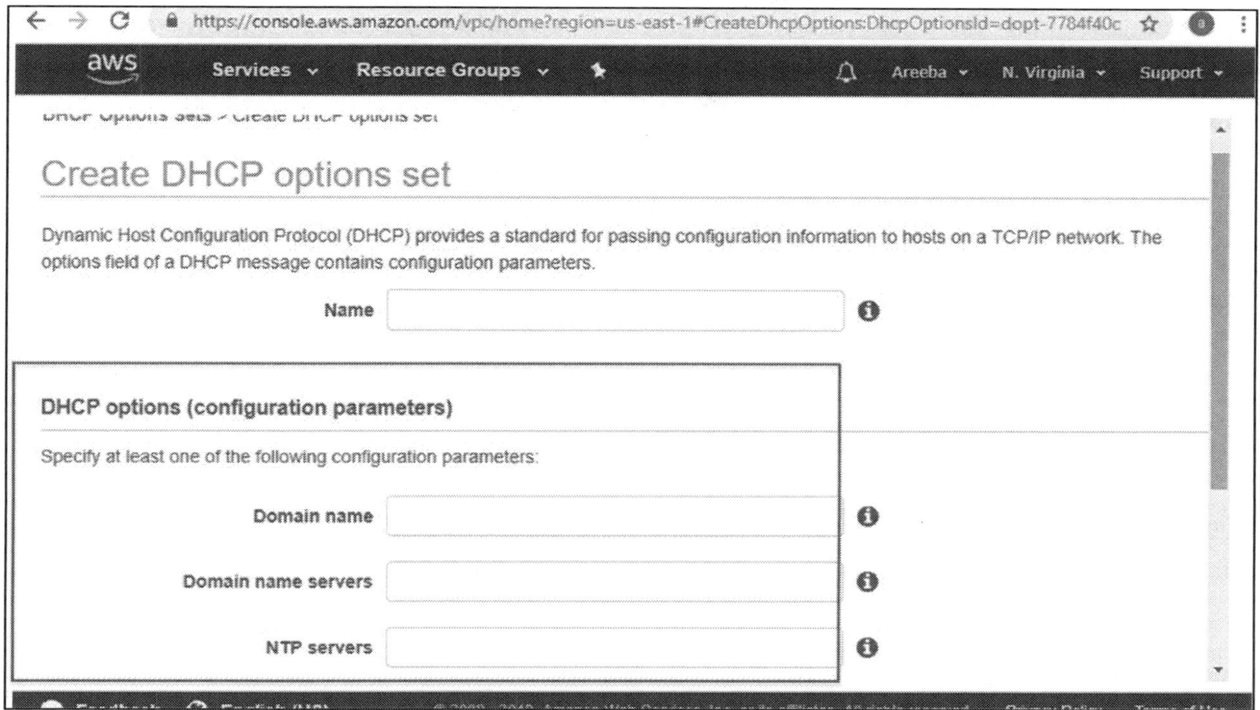

Figure 5-18: DHCP Options Set

- **Domain Name**- it is given to the internal host domain component.
- **Domain Nameservers**- are the own DNS servers that you provided. However, rather than giving the DNS servers locally, use "AmazonProvidedDNS", which is more preferable as it ensures that the DHCP option sets go to the incorrect DNS of VPC and subnet.
- **NTP servers**- this is used to define explicit time server in VPC.

Once the DHCP option is created, you cannot change them, and these remain static like launch configuration. DHCP option set is assigned to multiple VPCs, but VPC only has one DHCP option at a time. You can change the allocation of DHCP option set, which takes immediate effect on VPC.

Elastic Load Balancer

It is an advantage in cloud computing to have access to a large number of services, such as Amazon EC2 instances, that provides a consistent experience for the end users. A way to ensure the consistency, is to distribute request load efficiently across multiple servers. A load balancer is a mechanism, which automatically balances or distributes traffic across multiple EC2 instances. You can manage your virtual load balancers on Amazon, and you can also use the AWS cloud service called Elastic Load Balancer that provides a managed Load Balancer for you.

With Elastic Load Balancer, you can distribute your traffic across a group of Amazon EC2 instances in either single or multiple *Availability Zones* that enables you to achieve high availability for your applications. Elastic Load Balancer automatically scales to the vast majority of workloads. Elastic Load Balancer supports load balancing of Hypertext Transfer Protocol (HTTP), Transmission Control Protocol (TCP), Hypertext Transfer Protocol Secure (HTTPS), Secure Socket Layer (SSL) and routing to Amazon EC2 instances. Single Canonical Name record (CNAME) is the entry point for Domain Name Service (DNS) configuration. It also supports both internal application-facing and Internet-facing Load Balancers. To ensure that the traffic is not routed to the unhealthy and failing instances, ELB supports health checks for Amazon EC2 instances. Elastic Load Balancer can be automatically scaled by collected metrics.

Classic Load Balancing

Classic Load Balancer is the legacy Elastic Load Balancer. You can load balance HTTP/HTTPS applications (with some limitation and use layer 7-specific features, such as X-forwarded and sticky sessions. You can also use strict Layer 4 load balancing for the applications that rely purely on TCP protocol.

Classic Load Balancer has the following advantages over an Application Load Balancer;

- Support for EC2 Classic instances
- Support for TCP and SSL listeners
- Support for sticky sessions using cookies that are generated by applications

EXAM TIP: AWS recommended best practice is referring to a Load Balancer always by its Domain Name System (DNS) name, instead of by the IP address of the Load Balancer to provide a single and stable entry point.

Internal Load Balancer

It is often used in a multi-tier application to load balance between tiers of the application such as an Internet-facing Load Balancer, which might receive and balance traffic to the web or presentation tier whose Amazon EC2 instances send its request to the Load Balancer of the application tier. Internal Load Balancers can be used to route traffic to your Amazon EC2 instances in VPCs with private subnets.

External Load Balancer

External Load Balancer is public or Internet-facing Load Balancer. It is used by clients to communicate to public subnets of VPC. Consider an example; you have VPC with four subnets. Therefore, external ELB is at the border of VPC. Logically, it is a device in which

subnets are homed, meaning that there is an ELB instance or node in each subnet; they are not visible. These ELB nodes perform load balancing for their subnet. However, some limitations are needed for the subnet.

- Size of the subnet is at maximum /27 or less.
- Subnet inside VPC must be public.
- Each subnet has at least eight free IPs that are used for the scale-out purpose. As we know, in each subnet, 5 IPs are reserved; at least 8 IPs need to be free, so if /28 is being used, then the only subnet has 2 IPs for use, which is not feasible so, better to follow these points, while creating VPC.

When ELB is created, it is allocated with a domain name, which is an A record.

"name.region.elb.amazonaws.com"

By using this domain, the named client reaches to front end ELB. As we discussed earlier in this book, A-record uses round-robin functionality, so the different client that uses this domain name reaches to a different ELB node.

While using internal ELB, you need to place this ELB in private subnet for the same VPC where the instances of public subnet communicate to instances in private subnet via this internal ELB. This internal ELB is only accessible from internal resources.

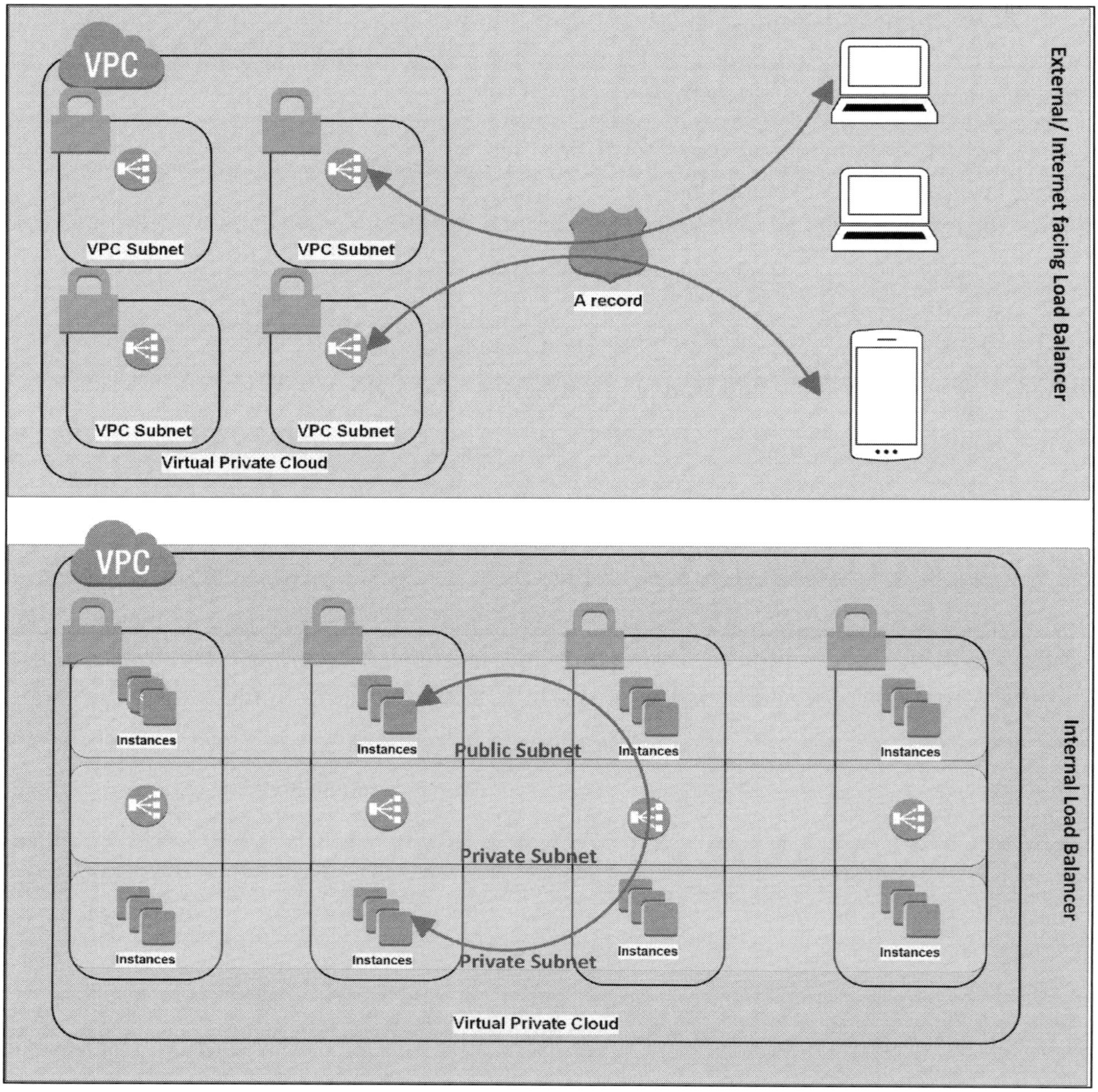

Figure 5-19: ELB External and Internal Load Balancer

All the figures above show the uses of ELB as the frontend. Now, let us discuss the backend concept; consider the same example of VPC where each subnet has an instance, or instances belong to different instance sizes and compute types. The distribution of traffic across these subnets is the same, i.e., 25% as we have 4 subnets but here, we have instances of different sizes so, if we have one large instance in subnet B and 4 large instances in subnet D, then both subnets assign the same traffic amount but, as subnet D has 4 instances, traffic is distributed among them. Again, to overcome this issue "cross-

zone load balancing" is introduced in AWS where load balancing is allowed to all registered instances. In cross-zone load balancing, each subnet is linked at the backend to all registered instances in that VPC. In this way, the traffic distribution is done at the instance level rather than at the subnet level. When using cross-zone load balancing, the best practice is to use instances of the same instance type.

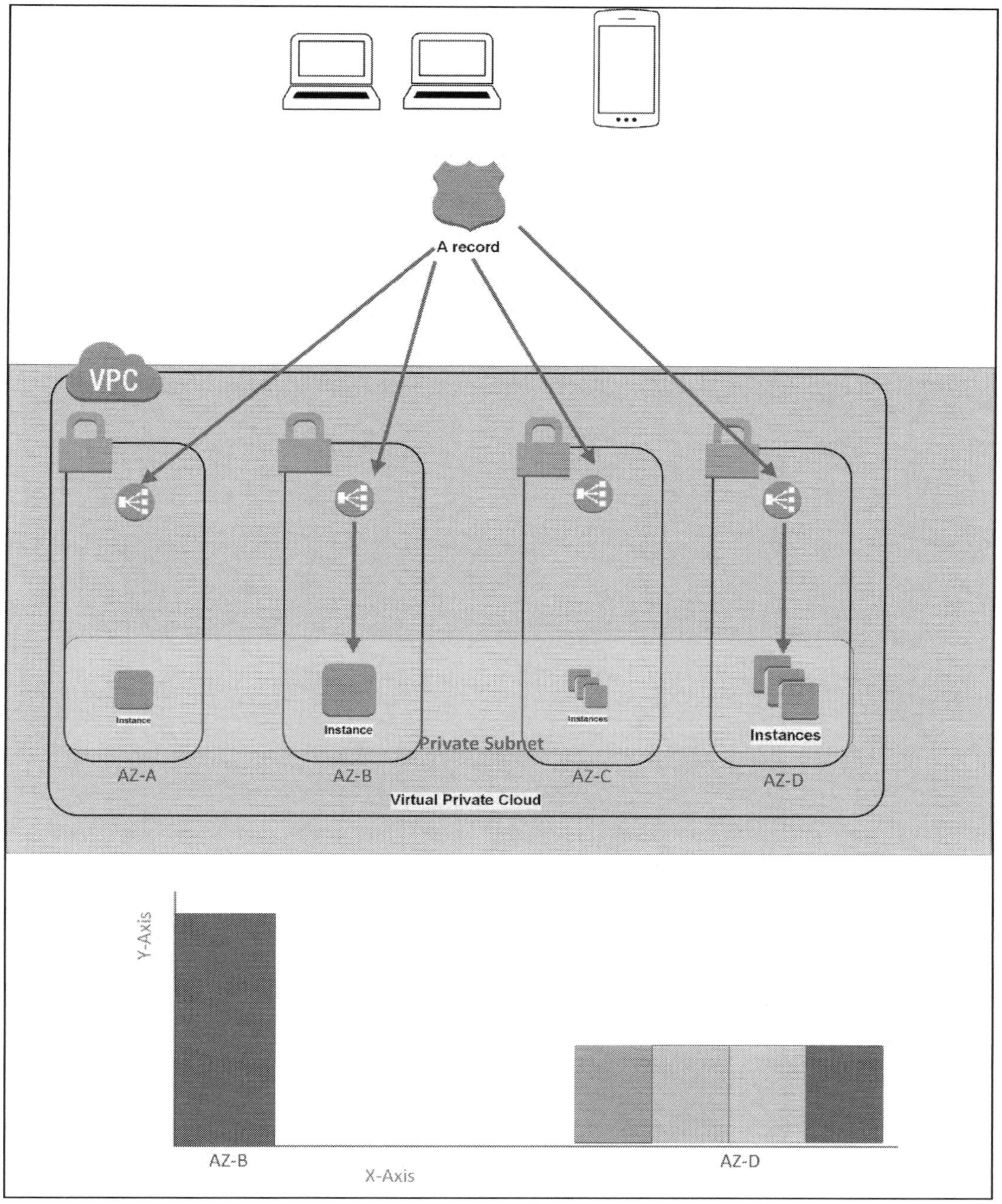

Figure 5-20: Load Distribution via External Load Balancer

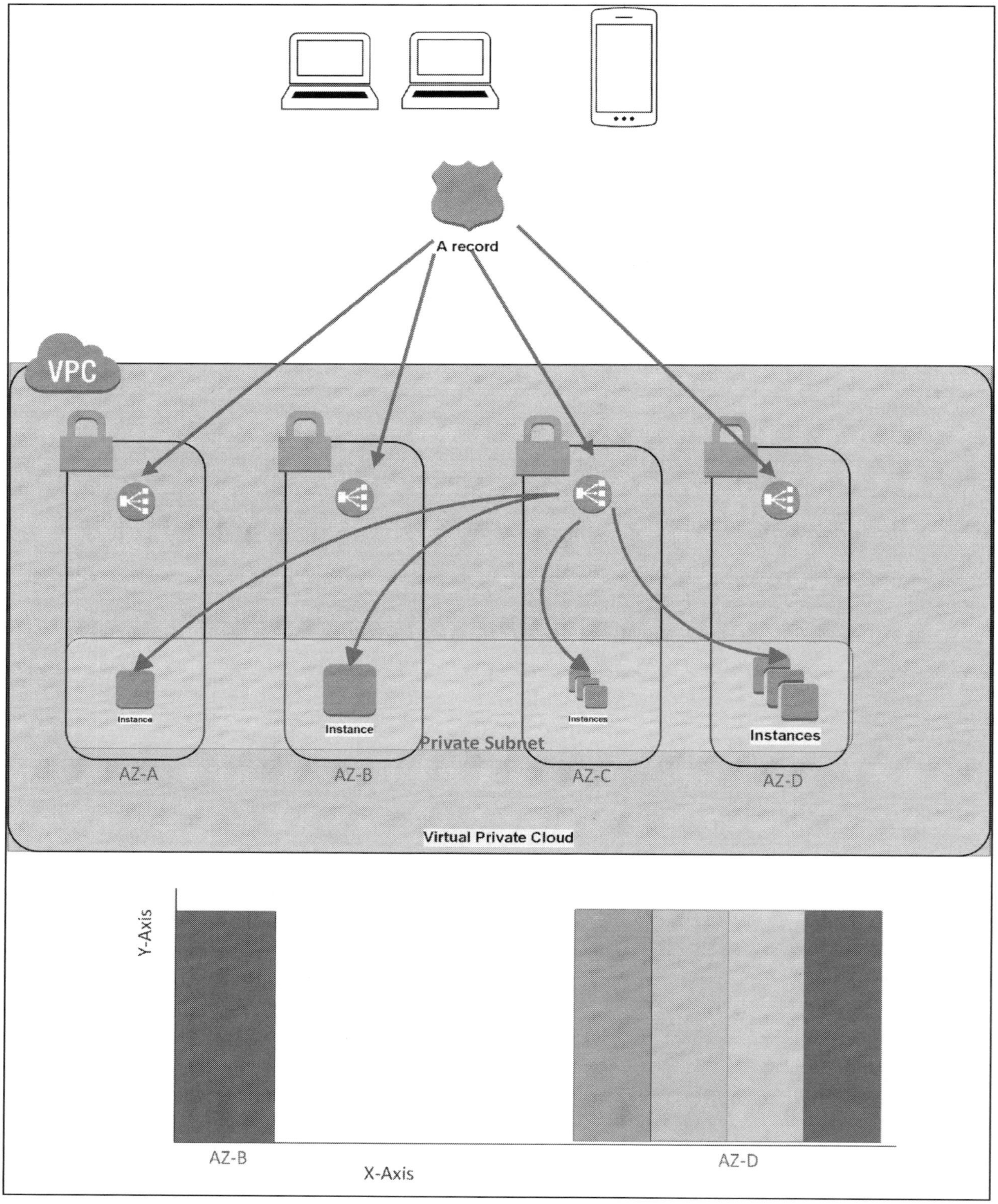

Figure 5-21: Load Balancing via Cross-Zone Load Balancing

Working of Elastic Load Balancer

In ELB, you can add instance as registered instance manually by using Console or API command "register-instance-with-load-balancer". You can also add instances by adding Auto-scaling group, so whenever an instance is added or removed; it will be registered or de-registered automatically. ELB also checks the health of the instance as it has an option to stop traffic on that instance, which is unhealthy. By default, in ELB, it is done with EC2 perspective, but later on, we will discuss more options.

Let us discuss an example in which communication between client and Load Balancer is front-end while communication of ELB with instances is back-end. Within ELB, there is configuration known as Listeners. The Listener is configured with the port (Client to Load Balancer) and protocol for the back-end, and a protocol and a port for a front-end (Load Balancer to Amazon EC2 instance) connection. Every Load Balancer has multiple *Listeners* configured; each for front end protocol like HTTP, HTTPs, SSL or TCP. Listeners can be added during the creation of Load Balancer or after creation.

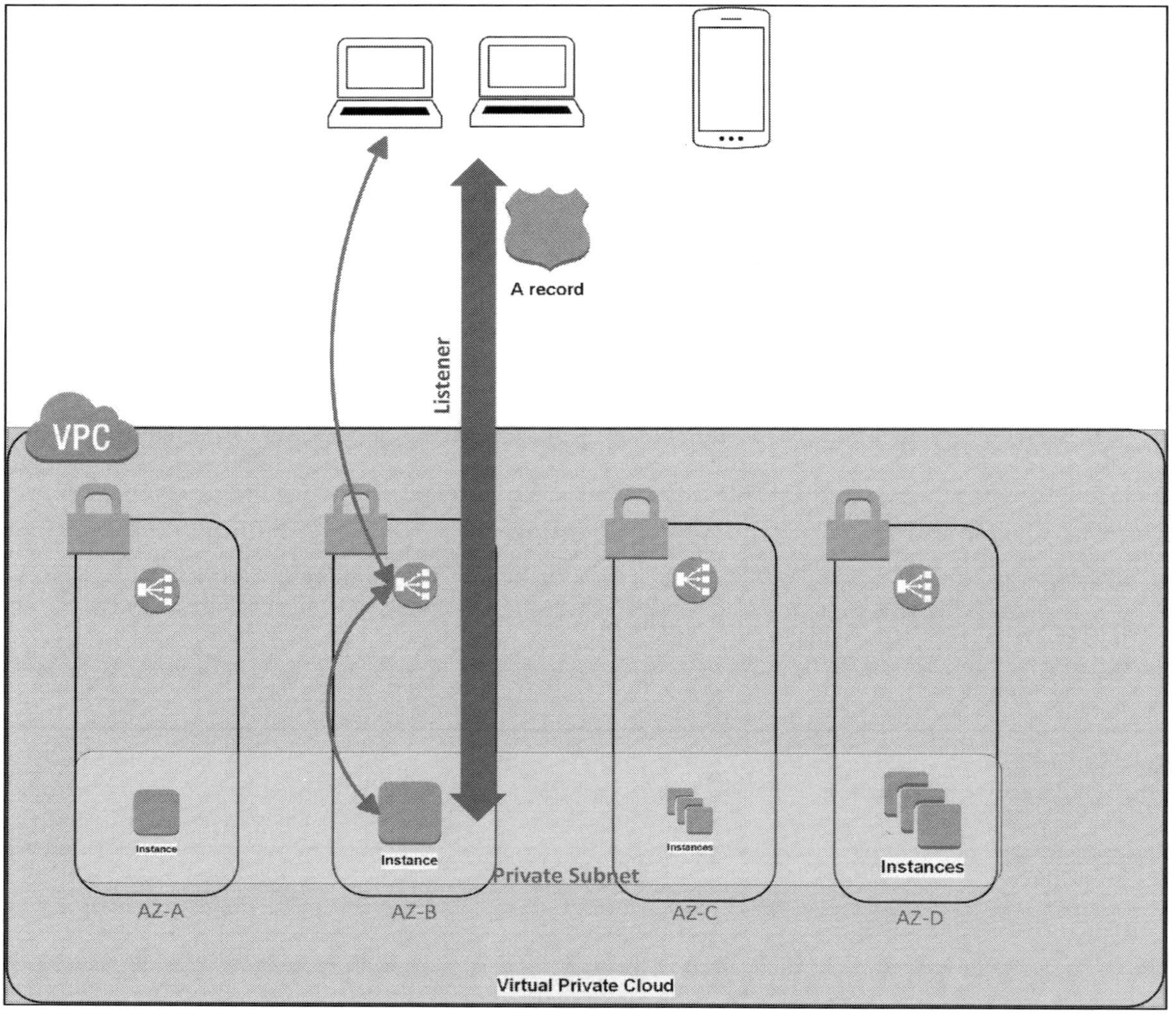

Figure 5-22: Working of ELB

As we discussed the Listener configuration earlier, we know that it has two parts. So for each layer, there are two protocols, one is secure, or another is unsecure. Classic Load balancer operates mainly at layer 4, so TCP is the unsecured protocol, and SSL is the secured protocol of this layer. While it takes some functionality of Layer 7, HTTP and HTTPS are considered as unsecured and secured protocols respectively. For communication, you need to define a protocol of the same layer, it may be secure or unsecure but belong to the same layer; otherwise, the connection is not possible. For example, the TCP/SSL connection is possible, but the HTTP/TCP connection is not possible.

Consider an example of TCP layer 4 ELB where the client initiates a request via using port 80 to the ELB then ELB sends this request to backend server via the same port TCP/80. If the request is from HTTP port, then it ignores it and sends this request without any filter to the server as it does not know about it. In this TCP, connection server does not know about the client, for server ELB is the client. Now, the feature that is known as a proxy protocol, which is a human-readable string provided to the server before TCP connection "PROXY TCP4 CLIENTIP PROXYIP 35646 80/r/n" in this protocol Client IP is of client and proxy IP is of ELB while "35646" is client port and "80" is ELB port. This protocol is passed to the server from ELB, so it knows about that. Proxy protocol feature is enabled via CLI or API. You cannot enable this feature from the console. This protocol is only enabled on TCP/SSL Listeners.

Load Balancers can be created, which uses the SSL/TLS (Transport Layer Security) protocol encrypted connections that also known as SSL offload. You can encrypt the traffic between the client that initiates the TCP session and your Load Balancer and also for the connection between your back-end instances and your Load Balancer. Elastic Load Balancer provides pre-defined SSL negotiation configuration's security policies that are used to negotiate connections between the load balancer and the client. You must install an SSL certificate to use SSL on the Load Balancer, which is used to terminate the connection and decrypt the request before sending a request to the back-end Amazon EC2 instance from the client. Enabling authentication on your back-end instances is optional. Elastic Load Balancing does not support (SNI) Server Name Indication on your Load Balancer that means you will need to add (SAN) Subject Alternative Name for each website if you want to host more than one website on a fleet of Amazon EC2 instances, with a single SSL certificate behind the Elastic Load Balancing to avoid site users seeing a warning message when the site is accessed. This use of SSL certificate at ELB is also known as SSL offload as you do not need to manage SSL certificate at the backend.

As we have already discussed TCP and SSL ELB Listeners now, we let us move to HTTP Listeners that are at layer 7. When a client sends a request with TCP port 80 along with HTTP connection, then ELB forwards it to the server by using a proxy TCP connection. As we know, Classic Load Balancer supports are limited to Layer 7. Now the response from the server is sent back to the client via the same path. The connection between client and ELB using HTTP Listener is over HTTP using TCP while using TCP Listener, the communication is at TCP level and passes HTTP to the server. In HTTP Listener, we are a proxy element, so it allows only validated HTTP communication.

For HTTPS communication, use of the connection is the same as the use of SSL layer between TCP and HTTP with Cypher and certificate at ELB end to reduce the overhead of certificate and cipher at server end by keeping standard HTTP and TCP with use of SSL Listener at the backend. In this way, admin overhead is reduced.

With Classic Load Balancer, there are some specific features of HTTP/ HTTPS Listeners. As we know that not all features of HTTP/HTTPS are supported, the header feature is

used with HTTP/HTTPS Listeners to carry HTTP information along with HTTP message. The headers, which HTTP/HTTPS Listeners use are;

- X-Forwarded-IP: this carries the IP of Client to the server with HTTP element
- X-Forwarded-Protocol: it carries the protocol, which is used by the client to ELB. In this way, the server has visibility of protocol at ELB side
- X-Forwarded-Port: it defines the port used between ELB and Client

These three headers are provided as Layer 7 alternative that you can use in TCP/SSL Listener as proxy protocol.

If your application is using non-standard methods and you want to pass the HTTP layer without any viewing, then use TCP Listeners.

Another feature of HTTP/HTTPS Listener is distributed backend connection, which means that load is distributed at the server end. In this type of Listener, the record of current active connection is on each server and then by this active connection it distributes the load. The server with the least active connection will prefer first to route any new connection.

Sticky Session

The third and last feature of the HTTP/HTTPS Listener is session management. You can use a sticky session feature, which is also known as session affinity that enables the load balancer to bind the user's session to the specific instance. If the instance is unhealthy, then the session is reassigned to another instance.

The sticky session is controlled in two ways:

- **Duration based session stickiness**- the duration of the cookie is defined in seconds. When the client initiates the request, it goes to ELB and checks the cookie for first time request. If no cookie is present, it is forwarded to the server by default routing of the request. Now the response from the server is sent to ELB, then from ELB to the client with a cookie.
  A cookie is defining to which the client is mapped in backend instance.
- **Application control session stickiness**- in this the flow is the same but in response from the server to ELB, it is along with appcookie, which defines the application session state. From ELB to client ELB, cookie along with appcookie is sent. In this way, both cookies are at the client end, and the duration of the ELB cookie depends on the appcookie.

In this way, we can say that the duration based stickiness does not need integration with the application while application control stickiness needs application integration.

Note:

- Certificates and ciphers are defined in HTTPS or SSL Listeners.
- Listener support 1 certificate as ELB, it does not support ENI.
- You can select custom or pre-defined security policy.
- Certification can be done via externally or manually, but in both cases, you are responsible for its purchase, renewal, and replacement.
- Better to choose AWS Certificate manager that performs renewal and replacement automatically but it is only valid for ELB not for server, meaning this should be used in SSL-Offloading.

Access Logs

In ELB, there is a problem of login as in connection with the server. ELB is a client, not a client IP. Therefore, to overcome this proxy protocol in TCP and X-Forwarded for a header in HTTP, Listener is used. By using these two protocols, ELB sends a request to the server with some information about the Client. ELB has by default access logs that are forwarded to S3 bucket. Depending on an interval, these logs are forwarded to S3 bucket. It may be 60 or 5 minutes. Attributes of the logs depend on the Listener protocol and layer. Attributes include a timestamp, ELB name, Client-IP and port, backend-IP and port, request_processing_time, backend_processing_time, response_processing_time, sent bytes and received bytes. Request_processing_time in TCP is the duration when it starts receiving data from the client and sends 1byte of data to the server, while in HTTP, it is the duration from initial contact to request first arrive at an instance. Backend_processing_time in HTTP is the duration when a request arrives at the backend and starts responding to backend while in TCP, it is the total time required to establish a connection with the backend server. Response_processing_time in HTTP is the total time when ELB starts receiving a response from backend instance and starts sending it to the client while in TCP, it is the duration when ELB receives the first byte of response and starts sending it to the client.

In HTTP, there are some extra attributes like ELB status code, backend status code, Request (request URL) and User Agent (detail of requesting browser and device). In SSL/HTTPS, SSL cipher and protocols are defined as an attribute.

When using ELB access logs, you do not need any proxy protocols and X-Forwarder, you have client detail in access logs. It has a separate security policy, which saves them from any exploitation.

Health checks

Health checks are supported by Elastic Load Balancing to test the status of Amazon EC2 instances behind an Elastic Load Balancing Load Balancer. At the time of the health check, the status of the instance that is healthy is *InService,* and the health status of any instance unhealthy is *out of service.* To determine the health of an instance, Load Balancer performs health checks on all registered instances. You can set a threshold for multiple consecutive health checks' page failures before an instance is found unhealthy.

Health checks are composed of four parts: definition, interval, healthy threshold, and unhealthy threshold. The valid value for the interval is 5-300 sec with default 30. The threshold default value is 2 for healthy and for unhealthy 2-10. For health checks, the ping protocol used is HTTP, HTTPS, SSL, and TCP. For ping protocol, you need to define the port, which is also attributed in health checks while for HTTP/ HTTPS, you need to define the path, and also you need to receive 200 status checks on that port. Response timeout is also an attribute where you need to define the time before which the health check is considered healthy or unhealthy. The default value is 5 seconds for that but is valid from 2-60 seconds. But, make sure that response time must be less or equal to the interval so that before starting next health checks, it can identify the status.

S3 Content Delivery and Storage

AWS Simple Storage Service (Amazon S3)

The most secure, reliable and highly extensible cloud storage is Simple Storage Service (S3). We can easily store and fetch data from anywhere on the web through this object storage with web service. You only need to pay for what you are using in Amazon S3, so in this way, one does not need to worry for capacity and traditional storage space.

Amazon S3 can be used with other AWS cloud services because of its high association with other AWS services, or you can use it alone. The most commonly used application is Amazon S3, which is flexible and highly organized storage. There is no concept of subfolders in buckets.

Buckets

In Amazon S3, a *bucket* is a container for storing objects. So, objects are contained in a bucket. S3 Buckets are global, and you can manage them at that level, meaning that any other AWS account cannot use your bucket name because it has to be unique. You can access your bucket by your DNS as well. You can create multiple buckets as well.

Objects

Objects are the fundamental entities stored in Amazon S3. Objects consist of object data, metadata, and unique identifier. The data portion is the actual data that is anything you want to save to Amazon S3. The metadata describes who created that object, what type of info is it, for what purpose that data will be used, and many other contextual information. An identifier is an address through which object will be uniquely identified within a bucket, through this we do not need to know the physical location of the object.

Keys

In Amazon S3, each object stored in the bucket can be identified by a unique identifier, which is known as a Key. The size of the key can be up to 1024 bytes of Unicode including embedded slashes, backslashes, dots, and dashes. Object key uniquely identifies an object in a bucket. Key is unique within the single bucket, but objects with the same key can be obtained in different buckets. The combination of the bucket, key, and version ID uniquely identifies an Amazon S3 object.

Access Control

Access Control lists are one of the best access policy options that can be used to manage the accessing of your bucket and object. Each bucket and object has an ACL attached to it as a sub-resource. Amazon S3 ACL provides specific permissions: READ, WRITE or FULL CONTROL. ACLs are suitable for particular scenarios like enabling bucket logging or making a bucket that hosts a static website be world-readable. ACL describes which group or AWS account has access to and what type of access. When you first create a bucket or object, it has a default ACL that gives the owner full access over the resource.

Version

This portion in the object is defined as a version of the object, which is useful when using versioning. Through versioning, you can save, retrieve, and restore every version of every object stored in your Amazon S3 bucket. This allows you to recover from both unintended user actions and application failures easily. It is a great backup mechanism. With the help of versioning, you can go back to your previous version.

S3 Pricing

Amazon S3 is a web service, which provides storage in the cloud. The Simple Web Service's interface can be used to store and retrieve any volume of data, from anywhere at any time on the web. The following factors should be considered while estimating the cost of Amazon S3:

- *Storage* - The number and size of objects stored in your Amazon S3 buckets plus the type of storage used.
- *Requests* - The number and type of requests; for example, GET requests charges to cost at different rates than other requests, such as PUT and COPY requests.
- *Storage Management* – It includes inventory, tagging of objects and Analytics.
- *Data Transfer* - The amount of data transferred out of the Amazon S3 buckets. Whereas, Data Transfer In is free of charge.
- *Transfer Acceleration* – For optimized transferring of data, use of CloudFront.

Amazon S3 Storage Classes

Storage Classes for Frequently Accessed Objects:

- ***Standard S3:*** This storage class is suitable for the storage of the data that is frequently accessed. It delivers data with low latency and high throughput. The ideal use cases for this storage are cloud applications, dynamic websites, content distribution, gaming, and data analytics. In Standard S3, pricing include:
    1. $0.023 GB/m for storage
    2. Data transfer between S3 and CloudFront is free
    3. Transfer out charges after free tier is $0.09-$0.05 GB
    4. Transferring from one region to another is $0.02GB
    5. Request rate is $0.005 per 1000 puts and $0.004 per 10,000 gets
- ***Reduced Redundancy Storage:*** In this storage, you can store the data with lesser redundancy than the Standard storage class for noncritical, reproducible data. Its durability decreases to four 9s while its cost is less.

Storage Classes for Infrequently Accessed Objects:

- ***S3 Standard* – Infrequent Access:** Ideal for data that is accessed less frequently, such as long-term backups and disaster recovery, but at the same time requires rapid access when needed. Costs lower than S3 Standard but charges higher to retrieve or transfer data. Its pricing is $0.0125 GB/m, which is half of the price of S3 standard.

Amazon Glacier

Amazon Glacier is an exceptionally low-cost storage service, which offers durable, secure and flexible storage for data archival and long-term backup. Users can store any amount of data reliably for as low as $0.004 per gigabyte per month, which results in significant savings as compared to on-premises solutions.

Pricing for expedited is $0.03 GB, a standard is $0.01 GB, and bulk is $0.02 GB.

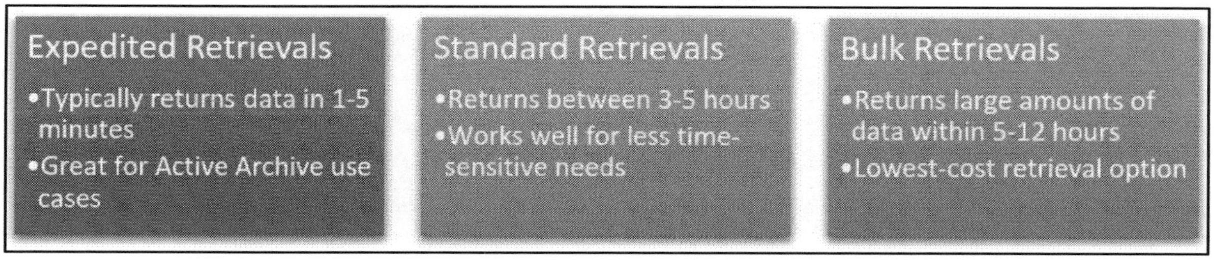

Expedited Retrievals
- Typically returns data in 1-5 minutes
- Great for Active Archive use cases

Standard Retrievals
- Returns between 3-5 hours
- Works well for less time-sensitive needs

Bulk Retrievals
- Returns large amounts of data within 5-12 hours
- Lowest-cost retrieval option

Figure 5-23: Amazon Glacier Types

	S3 Standard	S3 Standard-Infrequent Access	Reduced Redundancy Storage
Durability	99.999999999%	99.999999999%	99.99%
Availability	99.99%	99.99%	99.99%
Concurrent Facility Fault Tolerance	2	2	1
SSL Support	Yes	Yes	Yes
First Byte Latency	Milliseconds	Milliseconds	Milliseconds
Lifecycle Management Policies	Yes	Yes	Yes

Table 5-01: Comparison Between S3 Standard, IA and RRS

Pay Model for S3

Normally, when you create a bucket in S3, you pay for data transfer and data storage. Based on your utilization, charges are added to the Amazon Web Services account linked with the bucket. Amazon gives an option in which you can configure your bucket as Requester Pays bucket. Whenever you configure a bucket as a Requester Pays bucket, the requester pays for the requests they initiate to upload or download data or files in the bucket. You will just have to pay for the cost of the files or data you store in S3.

- You can allow Requester Pays on a bucket when you need to share the data or files, but do not want to be charged for the requests received for operation uploads and data downloads.
- When you allow Requester Pays, Amazon Web Services do not allow you to facilitate anonymous access going on the bucket.

- All requests sent to Requester Pays buckets should be authenticated. When you allow authentication, S3 can identify requesters and charge them for their respective usage of the bucket.
- If an application or system makes requests by assuming an identity and accesses management role, Amazon Web Services charge the account where the assumed role belongs.
- If you create calls to the bucket using the third party, the request must include "x-amz-request-payer" in the header section.
- Requester Pays buckets do not support anonymous, SOAP, and Bit Torrent requests.

Accessing of the S3 bucket

S3 bucket can be accessed via three ways;

1. Using security credentials of AWS by using S3 API or endpoints or CLI. Using Security access key or Access key ID via IAM. Authenticated method of access.
2. Via the internet, like static web hosting that allows HTTP request for the bucket is accessing, but you cannot use this method in Requester pay bucket.
3. Accessing bucket via Bit Torrent seeds, in which object in bucket splits into pieces and bit torrent users download these pieces or other users download the pieces from that user as it becomes seed or they download it directly from S3. In this, there is distributed downloading of objects from seed, and you only charge for downloading from S3. In this way, using Bit torrent, you reduce the cost of downloading files from the bucket, as in that only the first seed is downloaded and the remaining of users download from that seed.

Transfer Acceleration

With this feature of S3, you can transfer files in a fast, easy, and secured way over long distances between your S3 bucket and the end users. From Amazon CloudFront's globally distributed edge locations, transfer acceleration takes advantage. As the data reaches an edge location, the data is routed to Amazon S3 over an optimized network path. When transfer acceleration is enabled for the bucket, its URL changes and then this URL is used by the user all over the globe.

For example, if users want to upload an object to a bucket at a particular location, with S3 transfer acceleration enabled, the users can upload it to an edge location nearest to them. When the edge location receives that object, it will then upload it to the particular storage location using Amazon's internal backbone network. This can dramatically increase the speed of uploads because the users no longer need to upload it directly to the storage location. Instead, they upload it to the server closer to them.

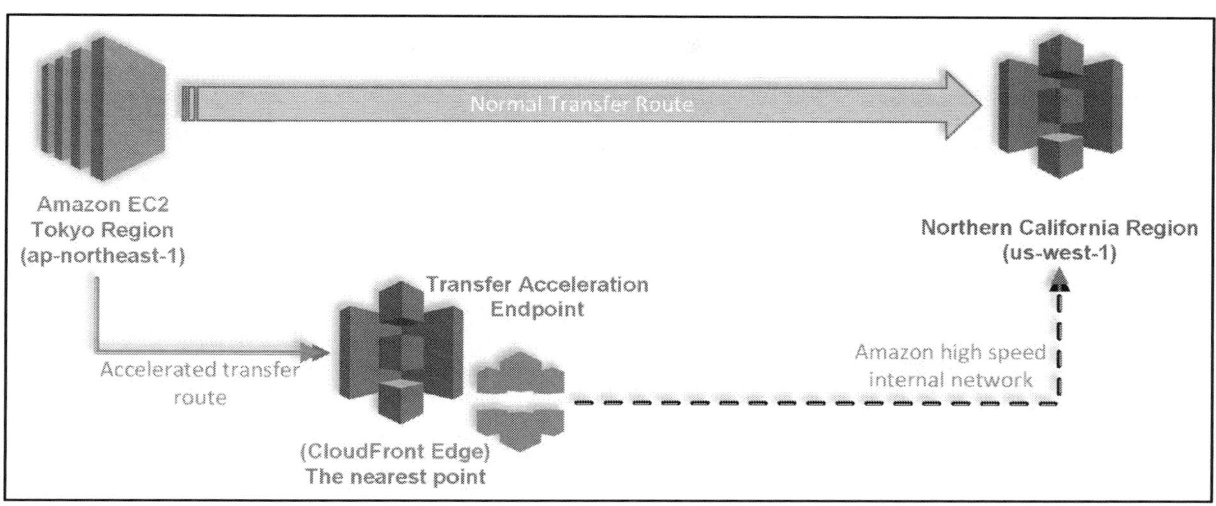

Figure 5-24: Amazon S3 Transfer Acceleration

Pricing of transfer acceleration depends on the AWS Edge location, which is used for transfer. The charges of this are in addition to data transfer, but if the transfer of object is not faster than the normal transfer of S3, then you will not be charged for the transfer acceleration.

Cross-Region Replication

You can replicate the contents of one bucket to another bucket automatically by using cross-region replication. Through this replication, you can replicate new objects simply into any other AWS Region for reduced latency, compliance, security, disaster recovery, and few other use cases. But this replication is not for existing object replication. In a replicated bucket, you can perform filtering by source prefix. Source and destination bucket must be in a different region, and it is one to one concept meaning you can replicate from one source bucket to one destination bucket. For replication, an IAM role is also needed to be defined. For replication to destination bucket, you can change the storage class. During the copying of data, its metadata and ACL are also copied. Cross region replication is good for disaster recovery.

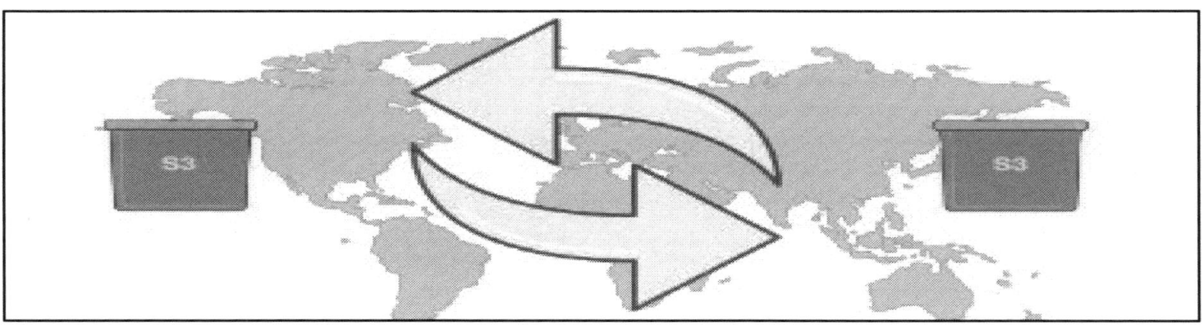

Figure 5-25: Cross-Region Replication

Pre-Signed URLs

When bucket needs to be accessed, then there are two ways of accessing an object in bucket anonymously or authenticated. In anonymous access, the bucket is accessed by HTTPS client. This client does not provide any authentication ID that is why it is anonymous. In authenticated access, accessing of the bucket is via SDK or Pre-signed URL. When request initiates for authenticated access, you need to add a header in the request. This header includes the hashing algorithm, credentials, signed header, and signature.

```
GET /photos/puppy.jpg HTTP/1.1

Host: johnsmith.s3.amazonaws.com

Date: Tue, 27 Mar 2007 19:36:42 +0000
```

Request after adding the header in reqeust is;

```
Authoization: AWS4-HMAC-SHA256 Credential=xxxxxxx/20190202/us-east-1/iam/aws4_reqeust, SignedHeaders=content-type;host;x-amz-data, Signature= vjbyPxybdZaNmGa%2ByT272YEAiv4%3D
```

Signature in this is created via hashing algorithm and Secret access key. Now on AWS side, when this request is accepted, then from request, the header takes access key ID, gets a secret access key and recreates a signature to check it with the provided signature. If it matches to that, the request is authenticated.

When the user is anonymous and is trying to access the bucket resource but it has no credentials (as the user is using web application), then creating individual IAM users for each web app user or sharing access key ID or Secret Access Key. However, these are not the best way to share your storage publically. So Pre-signed URL is used for sharing your object with others. By using a pre-signed URL, you can make bucket privately accessible to the authenticated user. Now web application communicates with S3 and creates pre-signed URL. Your security credentials, bucket name, which you want to share, object key,

specific duration and method to download the object are required while creating the Pre-signed URL, which needs to be defined.

```
"https://s3.amazonaws.com/#{S3_BUCKET}/#{path}?AWSAccessKeyId=#{S3_ACCESS_KE
Y_ID}&Expires=#{expire_date}&Signature=#{signature}"
```

Now, this URL is used for direct access to S3 bucket. You need to define PUT and GET method in separate URLs. When creating a pre-signed URL, the user, which is used to generate it, needs to be authenticated. This feature is enabled by default.

CloudFront Local and Global Content Delivery

Here, we will discuss Amazon CloudFront but not in deep-dive. Let us discuss "What is CloudFront?". Amazon CloudFront is a service that gives developers and your business an easy and cost-effective way to distribute data with high data transfer rate and low latency without any limitation of users. A Content Delivery Network (CDN) is a system of distributed servers that deliver the web pages and other web contents to the user depending upon the geographical locations of users, content delivery server and the origin of the web page. DNS (Domain Name System) is used by CDN to determine the Geographical location.

Amazon CloudFront is an AWS global CDN. Once a user requests for the content that Amazon CloudFront is serving, the user is moved towards the edge location where the content is cached. You can get the content in the best possible way with lower latency, if the content is in an edge location, it will be delivered to the user but if it is not in edge location, it will be taken from the origin. Origin is the origin of all the files that are distributed by CDN. It may be an S3 bucket or a web server where the original files are saved. Amazon CloudFront can work as origin servers and as non-origin servers. As an origin server, it includes Amazon EC2, Amazon S3 bucket, and Elastic Loud balancing or Route 53. As a non-origin server, it includes on-premises web servers.

Followings are some key termonologies for CloudFront:

Edge Location- Edge location is the nearest location where content is cached and can be written or Content delivery service of CloudFront is present. There are two types of Edge locations: Global Edge Location and Regional Edge Location. Global Edge Locations are spread across the globe and small in size as compare to Regional Edge Locations. The Regional Edge Location is in the different region and sits behind the Global Edge Location.

Origin - It is the origin of all the documents that the CDN will distribute. Origin can be an S3 bucket, an Elastic Load Balancer, Route 53, or an EC2 Instance.

Web Distribution- Is typically used for serving web content.

RMTP- Is used for media streaming.

Consumer- It is the user to which content needs to be served or the user requesting for content.

Distribution- Distribution is the name given to the content delivery network, which contains a collection of Edge Locations. In distribution, it defines how data is processed, what way it will be cached and distributed, and how they control with many other settings — all these known as a configuration that is specified in Distribution.

Let us discuss the working of CloudFront.

1. First, the consumer sends a request to CloudFront for content via DNS of distribution. Now, the session between consumer and nearest Global Edge Location is created.
2. If data is already present in Edge Location, then it delivers to the consumer otherwise, Global Edge Location concerns to the Regional Edge Location.
3. If in Regional Edge Location data is present, then it is forwarded to the Consumer via Global Edge Location.
4. If in Regional Edge Location data is not present, then Global Edge Location sends a request directly to the relevant Origin.
5. Now Origin responds to the Global Edge Location from where content is delivered to the consumer.

The delivery of content worst case scenario is delivery via optimized content Delivery Network and best case is to deliver to the nearest Global Edge Location or Regional Edge Location, so content delivers with high Bandwidth and Low latency.

Regional Edge Location is only available for Customized Origins like EC2 instance and external servers; it is not available for S3.

Now, we will discuss some configuration setting controls in CloudFront by distribution.

- Domain Name, which is the primary name of Distribution to interact with Regional or Global Edge Location. E.g., abcdef.cloudfront.net
- CNAME is an alternative of the Domain name. They need to be directed at distribution by creating DNS name and pointing that at the distribution domain name. Now, the content can use that name.
- Logging is also available to keep log files in a bucket with a prefix.
- Price class is where you define at which Edge Location the distribution will be hosted.
- Management of origin means you can add or remove origins.

- Management of behavior is where the origins are controlled. It defines how CloudFront behaves in specific situations.

CloudFront GeoRestriction

CloudFront also supports Geo-restriction on the content that is cached. This feature needs to be understood for real-world usage. Geo-restriction is assigned to distribution and distribution can only have one geo-restriction. By default geo-restriction is disabled, but when you enable it, you need to define geo-restriction type. There are two types of restriction:

- Whitelist is where by default all countries are blocked, and you need to define which country needs to be whitelisted (meaning allowed for access distribution).
- Blacklist is where by default all countries are allowed, and you need to define the blacklisted country, which you need to block for distribution.

To understand this, consider an example where a user from the US is trying to access content via distribution and distribution has whitelisted the UK. When the user sends a request to the closest Edge Location, then Edge Location checks distribution content where it is not allowed to access content, so it sends a 401 forbidden error to the user.

CloudFront 3rd Party Geo-Restriction

As we discussed above, the geo-restriction is at the country level and there is only one set of configuration per behavior. Then what about the restrictions, which we want at the state, town, or zip code level or any complex restriction? The option is to use third party geo-restriction. In third party GeoRestriction, you can apply restriction on a physical location base like using longitude and latitude. All of this restriction is an extension of Geo-restriction.

If you have S3 bucket as the origin and you want to restrict the bucket but it is only accessible via distribution, then make the bucket private by OAI (Origin Access Identity). OAI is used for restricting the S3 bucket to a specific Amazon CloudFront user link with distribution so, in that way, the data in the bucket is only in access of Amazon CloudFront. Therefore, if a user from the UK accesses the web application, the web application sends IP of the user to the third party geo-location service so it responds with the location information of IP like the town, longitude/latitude or zip code. Then by this information, web application either allows access or deny. It allows access to content via pre-signed URL or signed cookies via CloudFront. This access is time limited to avoid sharing of URL and cookies. Accessing directly the origin is also denied, as it is restricted via OAI.

Behaviors

CloudFront also has a configuration setting called behaviors, which defines the behavior of CloudFront response of incoming requests. There is default behavior, which is created at the time of creation of distribution. Behavior includes:

- Origin
- Protocol Policy- by default it is HTTP and HTTPS
- HTTP method- by default GET, HEAD
- A forward header- it defaults none, meaning that if the request is coming from a client with a header, then it is not forwarded to the origin. If you have two requests that differ from each other from the header's perspective, then only one request is cached. If the forward header is set to all, then it can differentiate the request from the header's perspective and cache both of them.
- Object caching- it is used to maintain the duration of the object in the cache.
- Restrictive viewer access- it allows access to content privately via signed URL, cookies or 3rd party geo-location.

Private Content

In Amazon Cloud Front, you can restrict access to the specific user in the network and make your content private. The following tools are available for this purpose:

1. **Signed URLs:** These URLs are from specific IP addresses and are only available for certain time limit.
2. **Signed Cookies:** These require authentication through public and private key pairs.

They both work in the same way as they work for S3. By using this, you provide security in the operation of accessing the content. Via this, you allow an internet user to access content and CloudFront allows authorization and identification based on the Signed URL and cookies.

Web distribution supports Signed URL and cookies while RTMP only supports Signed URL. Signed URL is also used by the embedded application, as they are not supported cookies. Signed URL is capable of controlling individual files. Signed URL may change your URL but using Signed cookies; your URL is not changed. Signed cookies provide control over a group of files, but HTTP stacks need to be supported for cookies.

Up until now, all the settings that we discussed for distribution is enabled per behavior basis, but internally they are mapped at the origin. If you want to enable a different setting on a different section of an s3 bucket, then you need to use two origins using the

same S3 bucket with different origin paths. When you enable any type of restriction, whether Signed URLs or cookies, then you need to enable trusted signers on the account.

SSL Configuration

SSL is enabled on CloudFront Distribution to access distribution via HTTP or HTTPS. The configuration is needed to be done on distribution. It will be done in two ways.

1. The communication path between viewer and CloudFront has two options for SSL. First is using default CloudFront certificate and second is using a custom SSL certificate. The custom SSL certificate may be obtained from Trusted CA, ACM and Self-signed.
2. A second communication path is between CloudFront and Origin, in which domain name of origin must match the SSL certificate, which origin is using.

Note: When the origin is ELB, then you can use ACM and Trusted CA because Self-signed is not supported by ELB. While for Non-ELB origin, you can use Trusted CA.

CloudFront Optimization and Cost

There are various elements that need to be considered from the optimization and cost perspective. The first one is price class, as we know it is where you choose which Edge Location will host your distribution. The price class needs to be selected at the creation of distribution. It has 3 options:

- 100- the US, CA, and EU (Edge Locations)
- 200- includes all 100 class Edge Location + Asia (Edge Locations)
- All- includes all 200 class Edge Location + SA and AU (Edge Locations)

AWS has the authority to go beyond the price class to serve content, but you do not need to pay for that. You are only required to pay for the chosen price class. For more optimization, you need to look into reducing the latency of using all price classes v/s of using reduced cost for more specific price classes like 100 and 200. Like other AWS products, there are no long-term contracts or minimum monthly usage commitments for using Amazon CloudFront. You pay only for as much or as little content as you actually deliver through the content delivery service.

The delivery of content from origin to Edge location is free while from Edge Location to viewer depends on price class; the cost between the Edge Location and viewer is although less than the price of S3 to internet delivery.

Local and Global Resiliency Strategies using AWS Products

In this topic, we will discuss the local and global resiliency using the different products of AWS. Here, we bring all the tools that you already know about the topic.

Let us consider you have a web server on EC2 instance and provide access to the user on this web server. As we have only one instance, if its AZ fails, the users are unable to access the web server so for that you can use the Multi-AZ feature. In this way, you have two same web servers and by using ELB or Route53 round-robin DNS, you can provide the user access to any of the web servers. For resiliency, the use of Route53 is not suitable, so with the use ELB, you can allow the user access to a web server that has files stored in it.

Although the above architecture is good, it has two problems:

- If you have two files, one in each instance, then you need synchronization between this instances, which increase overhead.
- If you create instances manually and statically and any one of the instances fails, there is no replacement of that instance automatically.

In order to overcome these problems, you can use S3 bucket, hence the data is offloaded from the instance to the bucket. In this way, sync issue is resolved. You need to integrate the bucket with the instances as it is highly available and resilient, so the user can send a direct request to the S3 bucket for the content rather than ELB or EC2. As for the other problem of the manually created instance, you can create an AMI of the instance as all data of web server is stored in S3, you only need to create AMI of the instance with a configuration which, is used along with auto-scaling group in launch configuration option. You also need to enable ELB health checks as it stops sending traffic to unhealthy instances, the auto-scaling group terminates that instance and re-creates the other instance from the AMI. Locally, this architecture is good but what happens if the entire region goes down?

Although it happens rarely, it may be possible so for global resiliency, you can use Route53 for a hosted zone with the current configuration and point that to the specific region application. For extension of architecture to another region you can use AMI that you created in previous architecture for migrating into a new region. Then use the Route53 Geo-location routing policy to direct the user to its closest region record set. Health check also needs to be enabled so that if that region record set fails, it routes to the default recordset or any other closest recordset.

You can also use the Failover routing policy with Geo-location routing policy in the same way as we discussed above in Route53 routing and resilience.

For more resiliencies at a global level, you can use CloudFront for the user that is out of AWS data center. Via CloudFront, you can serve the content using Edge Location nearest to the user with reducing latency and cheaper cost as compared to S3 directly.

As we discussed the architecture, in which we use S3 to offload files; you can use another S3 bucket for the static web content of web server. In this way, the only application is running on the web server and management overhead is also reduced.

If you have business logic, then you can use AWS Lambda along with AWS API gateway. In this, user can access S3 static web hosting bucket, then from API gateway receives connection from user and invokes Lambda function to perform tasks like generating pre-signed URLs for accessing private bucket content when Lambda function is created then it will be used by the user to access private buckets content.

Now in this architecture, web server is no more in use, the architecture is dependent on AWS managed services. This architecture is known as server-less architecture.

AWS Workspaces

AWS Workspace is a fully managed desktop as a service product by Amazon. It is configured to provide fully available and dedicated Windows 7 or Windows 10 desktop in a few minutes. This desktop is accessible via PC on IP software or hardware. The way Workspace is implemented is difficult to understand as it is partially in your account and partially on the on-premises infrastructure.

Let us discuss the deployment of AWS Workspaces. For deployment, you need two AZs in VPC, as there is a requirement of minimum two subnets for AWS Workspaces. You also need a Directory service, which is configured, and for that, you need two EC2 instances, on which directory service is running. These instances are in separate AWS managed VPCs. On instances, you do not have the visibility, you only know about the directory service. To this Directory service, ENI is also added in order to deploy the directory on subnets. The need for directory service is because Workspaces use Microsoft Windows for virtual desktop and there is a number of users; so to handle a large number of Microsoft connections, authentication it is used.

Now at the backend, there is the use of PCoIP (PC over IP) protocol to get the method of mouse click and keyboard press on Workspace from you and sound, server and another configuration settings from Workspaces to Client.

When you set up Workspaces, AWS creates a managed VPC on your behalf, which has PCoIP infrastructure. This infrastructure has two Gateways; one is a Management Gateway that handles user and AD communication, and the other is a Streaming Gateway

that facilitates the worker connections between PCoIP client devices and Workspaces. Now AWS Workspaces has two network interfaces; one is Management Interface, which is responsible for management of Workspaces and homed in managed VPC. It also manages and handles streaming data to and from PCoIP endpoint, and you are not charged for data to and from the Management Interface. The second interface is the primary interface and each is in one subnet, which is associated with Workspaces. This primary interface is used for to and from communication with the internet, directory service, and other private network connectivity.

By default, in AWS Workspaces, there is no internet connectivity, but you can add internet connectivity in two ways depending on the security requirements of the network.

1. Enable internet access via public IP, this is done by directory and applying on all workspaces. However, this Workspaces need to be running on a public subnet, which has a default route towards the Internet Gateway. For a more restrictive security, you can also use NAT Gateway and NAT Instances in the subnet of Workspaces for internet access.
2. The alternative environment is where DirectConnect and AWS VPN are used with a default route to get back data to the corporate network before going out to the internet.

In AWS Workspaces, you can also use DNS service on instances in directory service via DHCP option.

Restrictions

- Directory service is by default highly available, but you need a minimum of two subnets for directory service.
- For Workspaces you need minimum /28 and /17 subnet mask. /16 is not able to use as it does not fulfill the HA of directory service.
- 1 IP in each subnet is for Directory service.
- Directory service is supported in a few AZs in specific regions.
- You can associate multiple directories to subnet but Workspaces only associate with 1 directory.
- Workspaces are in 1 subnet /AZ as it is highly available.

Directory types

1. Simple AD (small) is for 500 users and 2000 objects.
2. Simple AD (large) is for 5000 users and 20,000 objects.
3. For bigger Schema Extension or trust, you can use Enterprise AD.

4. AD Connector is also used, which is authentication proxy. This requests back to the proxy of the on-premise or VPC environment Directory.

Correct operation of Workspaces is required for connecting AD connector to on-premises or VPC environment directory. For correct operation, VPN or DirectConnect needs to be used.

WorkSpaces Security

As we know, Workspaces has two network interfaces. Management Interface from the interface perspective needs some rules to allow inbound and outbound traffic. Although from AWS management perspective, you do not have any right.

First, you need to allow inbound TCP 4172 for establishing the UDP connection and up 4172 for user input. TCP 8200 is required for management and configuration of Workspace and for outbound UDP, 55002 for PCoIP streaming.

For primary interface, a large number of ports is involved as it needs free communication on those ports. TCP 53, UDP 53, TCP 88, UDP 88, UDP 123, TCP 135, TCP 137-138, TCP 389, UDP 389, TCP 445, UDP 445 and TCP 1024-65535. All these ports need to be allowed between Workspace and Directory Service.

WorkDocs

It is an enterprise file management and file storage product like Dropbox. In WorkDocs, there are a number of components to be discussed:

- WebApp- it is document management and document viewing application.
- Mobile App- it allows reviewing while remote and mobile.
- Workstation synchronization application- it runs on machines like home-based machines.
- Browser extension- it allows clipping of web page into Word Docs.

WordDocs can be accessed globally as it has a public endpoint, but directory service is also required with that. In AWS Workspaces, Single Sign-on (SSO) is also available to login into Workspace without login to Work Docs service by defining it in settings of the directory.

Workspace user also gets 50 GB free for sync storage to and from the Workspace storage.

Mind Map

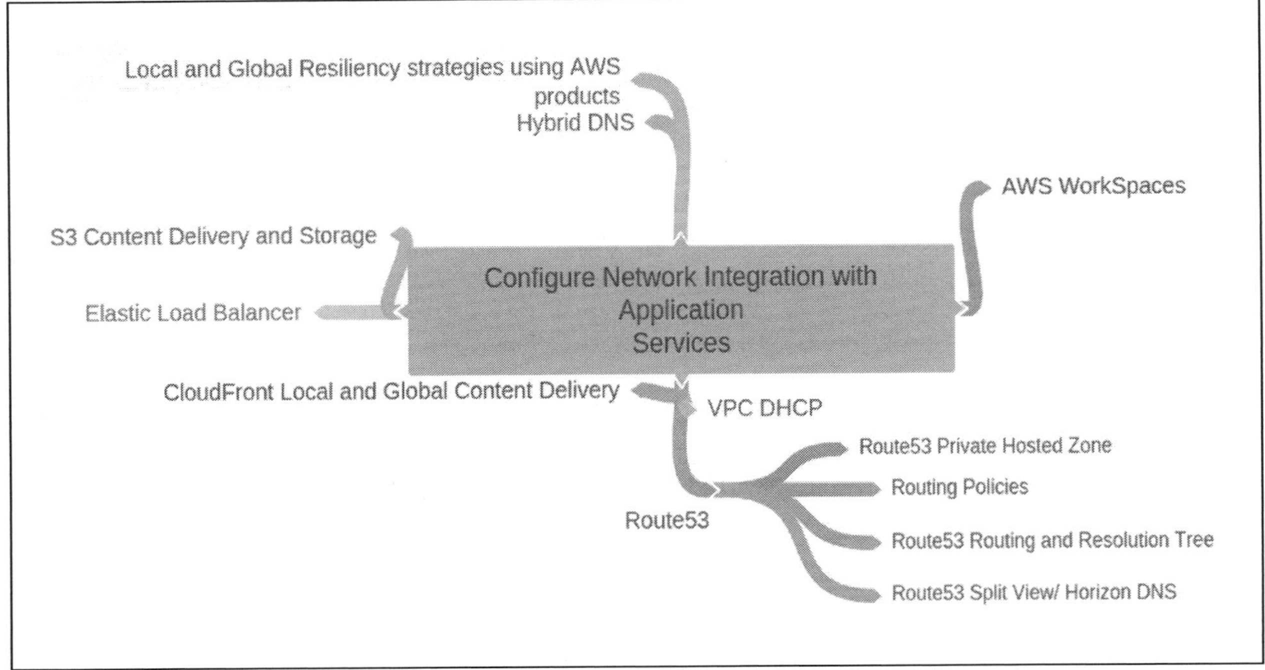

Figure 5-26: Chapter Mind Map

Practice Questions

1. In AWS, which service is used as DNS service?
    a) AWS EC2
    b) Lambda
    c) Route53
    d) CloudFormation

2. Your web application is hosted in multiple AWS regions across the world. Which routing policy should you apply to provide your users with the fastest network performance?
    a) Geo-location
    b) Simple
    c) Failover
    d) Latency-based

3. If a user from the UK region accesses the application, which is in the UK region, then they can access it. When London based user tries access the London based application, they can access it. Which Route53 Routing policy can you use for region-specific routing?
    a) Geo-location
    b) Simple
    c) Failover
    d) Latency-based

4. If you want to use on-premises platform with Route53, then which feature is used?
    a) Hybrid DNS
    b) Health checks
    c) Split view
    d) None of the above

5. Amazon route 53 does not perform:
    a) Health checks
    b) Domain registration
    c) Load Balancing

d) DNS services

6. Amazon Route 53 is named 53 because:
   a) Microsoft has Route 66 registered.
   b) It was invented in 1953.
   c) Only marketing people know this secret.
   d) The DNS port number is 53.

7. If a company wants to know the IPv4 address of its end user, which technique will be used to identify it?
   a) By tracing it
   b) By exploring it through malt ego
   c) Through X-Forwarded for header
   d) None of these

8. Elastic Load Balancing supports routing and load balancing of
   a) Hypertext Transfer Protocol (HTTP)
   b) Hypertext Transfer Protocol Secure (HTTPS)
   c) Transmission Control Protocol (TCP)
   d) All of the above

9. Which Load Balancer type is an internet facing Load Balancer?
   a) Internal
   b) External

10. For external Subnet, which size is the minimum allowed size for the subnet?
    a) /16
    b) /20
    c) /17
    d) /27

11. When ELB is created, it is allocated with a domain name which is an_________
    a) AAA record
    b) A record

c) MX record
d) None of the above

12. If you want load balancing across all registered instances inside subnets, then which feature of ELB is used?
    a) Health checks
    b) Cross-zone load balancing
    c) Sticky session
    d) None of the above

13. If you want to bind user session to a specific instance, then which feature of load balancing is used?
    a) Health checks
    b) Cross-zone load balancing
    c) Sticky session
    d) None of the above

14. In load balancing, what is the default value for an interval of the health check?
    a) 30
    b) 20
    c) 15
    d) 10

15. From which storage service can you easily get data on the web from anywhere?
    a) Amazon Glacier
    b) Amazon S3
    c) ECS
    d) Storage Gateway

16. Amazon Glacier is used for ___________.
    a) Optimizing of Archiving data
    b) Static web hosting
    c) Frequent Access
    d) Accessing data on the web

17. What type of storage is Amazon S3?
    a) Object storage
    b) File storage
    c) Block storage

18. The key size of an object is ___________.
    a) 64 bytes
    b) 32 bytes
    c) 2048 bytes
    d) 1024 bytes

19. In S3 pricing, you need to pay for ____________ and _____________. (choose any 2)
    a) Data transfer in
    b) Data transfer out
    c) Storage
    d) None of the above

20. When you need to share the data or files, but do not want to be charged for the requests received for operation uploads and data downloads, which feature do you need to enable on the bucket?
    a) Versioning
    b) Bucket policy
    c) Requester pays
    d) Transfer acceleration

21. How do you replicate the contents of one bucket to another bucket automatically?
    a) ACL
    b) Cross region replication
    c) Transfer acceleration
    d) None of the above

22. By using which feature of S3 can you allow private access to the bucket to only the authenticated user?

a) Pre-signed URL
b) Versioning
c) Transfer acceleration
d) None of the above

23. Which feature from the following option is used to restrict the user of accessing the content at the country level?
a) Geo-restriction
b) Failover
c) ACL
d) None of the above

24. If you use ELB as origin, then which service is used for a custom SSL certificate?
a) Trusted CA
b) ACM
c) Self-signed
d) A and B

25. In which CloudFront Price class the Edge Location is in the US, CA, and EU only?
a) 200
b) 100
c) all

Chapter 06: Manage, Optimize, and Troubleshoot The Network

Introduction

In this chapter, we will discuss the management of AWS networks. For this, we will have a detailed discussion on VPC flow logs that monitors the IP traffic going to and from your VPCs. We will also be discussing network cost and how to manage and optimize it. Furthermore, you will learn the AWS enhanced networking and at the end; we will be discussing the optimization of network performance.

Introduction to VPC

Amazon VPC lets you provision your logically isolated section of the AWS cloud where you can launch AWS resources in a user-defined virtual network. You have full control over your virtual networking environment, including a selection of your IP address ranges, the generation of subnets, and configuration of route tables and network gateways.

A Virtual Private Cloud is a cloud computing model, which offers an on-demand configurable pool of shared computing resources allocated within a public cloud environment while providing a certain level of isolation from other users of the public cloud. Since the cloud (pool of resources) is only accessible to a single client in a VPC model, it, therefore, offers privacy with greater control and a secure environment where only the specified client can operate.

You can comfortably customize the network configuration for your VPC. For example, you can create a public-facing subnet for your web server that has access to the Internet, and place your backend system such as a database or application server in a private-facing subnet that cannot access the internet. You can hold multiple layers of security, including Security Groups and network ACLs, to help control access to Amazon EC2 instances in each subnet. You can also build a hardware Virtual Private Network (VPN) connection between your corporate datacenter and your VPC and leverage the AWS cloud as an extension of your corporate data center.

You can create multiple VPCs within a region. Each VPC is isolated even if it shares its IP address space. When you create an Amazon VPC, you have to specify the address range by choosing a CIDR (Classless Inter-Domain Routing) block, such as 10.x.x.x/16. You cannot change the address range after the VPC is created. The Amazon VPC address

range can be as large as /16 (65,536 available) or as small as /28 (16 available). This range should not overlap the network with which the VPC is to be connected.

Amazon VPC is the networking layer for Amazon EC2. It was released after the EC2 service. EC2-classic and EC2-VPC are two different networking platforms that are available within AWS because of VPC. (EC2 classic is only available for those accounts, which were created before the launching of VPC).

VPC Flow Logs

With the increase in complexity of web applications and networking, AWS has increased support for monitoring all of the rich data that could be generated by the networks hosted on the AWS cloud. VPC flow log features allow you to collect the IP traffic information going to and from the network interfaces in your VPC. You can publish the data collected by the flow logs to either Amazon CloudWatch or Amazon S3. These logs are helpful in several tasks; such as, you can troubleshoot if specific traffic is not reaching an instance. Alternatively, you can use flow logs to monitor the traffic that is reaching your instances. Remember that flow logs capture the data related to IP traffic; this does not mean that you can get the IP data, but it provides you the ***metadata*** of the traffic under monitoring.

Overview

A flow log can be created for a VPC, subnet, or network interface. If you create a flow log for VPC, all network interfaces within that VPC will be monitored; same is the case with subnets but, creating flow log for a specific interface will only provide information about the attached interface.

VPC flow logs monitor Ingress and Egress traffic for the entity (VPC, subnet, ENI) that they are attached to. Flow logs can monitor traffic for all traffic or can be restricted to accepted or rejected traffic only. This configuration is done when you are creating a flow log. Keep in mind that this configuration cannot be changed, if you want to modify a flow log, you need to create a new flow log with the new configuration and delete the old one.

To create a flow log, you need to specify a resource, the type of traffic, i.e., accepted, rejected, all traffic, and a destination where you want to publish the log data (CloudWatch, S3). When a flow log is created, it takes some time to start collecting and publishing data to the destination that you have set.

Publishing log data to CloudWatch or S3 requires an IAM role. By default, flow logs do not have permission to write data to CloudWatch or S3. There must be an IAM role with

proper permissions so that the flow logs can assume that role in publishing data to the storage that you have chosen.

Note: Flow logs do not capture real-time data.

Some AWS services such as ELBs, RDS, ElastiCache, and WorkSpaces create network interfaces; you can create flow logs for these interfaces too. However, for all that, you cannot use service consoles or APIs to create flow logs, only EC2 console or API can do this for you.

If a flow log is not required anymore, it can be deleted. When you delete a flow log for a resource, the flow log service is disabled, and no log records are created or published to the destination. However, deleting a flow log does not affect the existing records and streams.

Flow Log Records

Flow log data for a monitored resource is a ***flow log record,*** a flow log record is a log event, which consists of fields describing the network flow. Each record is a 5-tuple, and for a specific capture window. 5-tuple is a set of values specifying the source, destination, and protocol for an IP flow. Capture window is the duration for which the flow log service aggregated the data prior to publishing it. The capture window is roughly ten minutes, but can take up to fifteen minutes.

<version> <account-id> <interface-id> <srcaddr> <dstaddr> <srcport> <dstport> <protocol> <packets> <bytes> <start> <end> <action> <log-status>

Figure 6-01: Example Flow Log Record

Figure 6-01 is an example of a flow log record. It contains all the fields that are displayed in a record. We will discuss each field in the following table.

Field	Description
version	The VPC Flow Logs Version
account-id	The ID of the AWS account from which the flow log was created
interface-id	The network interface ID for which you are recording the traffic
srcaddr	The source IP address; IPv4 address of the network interface is always its private IPv4 address

dstaddr	The destination address; IPv4 address of the network interface is always its private IPv4 address
srcport	Source port of the traffic
dstport	Destination port of the traffic
protocol	IANA protocol number of traffic
packets	Count of packets transferred during the capture window
bytes	Count of bytes transferred during the capture window
strat	The start time of the capture window in UNIX seconds
end	The end time of the capture window in UNIX seconds
log-status	The logging status of the flow log: • OK: Data is normally logging to the chosen destinations. • NODATA: During the capture window, there was no network traffic to or from the network interface. • SKIPDATA: During the capture window, some records were skipped may be because of an internal capacity constraint, or an internal error.

Table 6-01: Description of the Flow Log Records Fields

You must be able to interpret the flow log records. It is important for not just the exam, but also, it is necessary to be able to read the log records to be able to identify and troubleshoot the problems that may occur anytime in your network, which is hosted on the AWS cloud.

Note: If a field is not applicable for a specific record, the record displays '-' for that entry.

Examples

- **For Accepted Traffic**

```
2 123456789010 eni-abc123de 172.31.16.139 172.31.16.21 20641 22 6 20 4249 1418530010 1418530070 ACCEPT OK
```

Figure 6-02: Accepted Traffic Flow Log Record

Figure 6-02 is a flow log record showing allowed SSH traffic to network interface ***eni-abc123de*** in account ***123456789010.***

- **For Rejected Traffic**

```
2 123456789010 eni-abc123de 172.31.9.69 172.31.9.12 49761 3389 6 20 4249 1418530010 1418530070 REJECT OK
```

Figure6-03: Rejected Traffic Flow Log Record

Figure 6-03 is another flow log record depicting rejected RDP traffic to network interface ***eni-abc123de*** in account ***123456789010.***

Network ACLs and Security Groups

Being an advanced networking specialist, you are already aware of the stateful-ness of Security Groups. If specific traffic is allowed on a security group, the responses to this traffic are also allowed, even if your Security Group rules do not permit it. On the other hand, network ACLs are stateless, meaning that the responses to allowed traffic are subject to the network ACL rules. This information recap is necessary if you are using flow logs to monitor an overly restrictive or permissive Security Group or network ACL rules.

Let us consider an example; you are ***pinging*** your instance from your home computer. The inbound rules of your Security Group allow ICMP traffic and the outbound rules do not allow ICMP; because of the stateful-ness of Security Groups, the responses to your ping will be received on your home computer. On the other hand, your network ACL allows inbound ICMP traffic but does not allow outbound ICMP; because of the stateless-ness of network ACLs; response to your ping will be dropped and will not reach your home computer. The flow logs will display two flow log records for this activity: one Accept Record and one Reject Record.

The Accept Record is generated because your ACL and Security Groups allow ICMP traffic, therefore, it is accepted in the flow logs. The network ACL does not allow ICMP

outbound, therefore, the reply to ping is blocked and that is the reason for the Reject Record.

Restrictions of Flow Logs

When using flow logs, you must be aware of the limitations of this feature. Following is a brief discussion of what you cannot do with flow logs. Many questions in the exam focus on VPC flow logs, hence, it is better to understand the topic completely.

- As we have discussed before, you cannot change the configuration of flow logs. Changing the configuration (let us say assigning a different IAM role to your flow logs) is not possible. For this, you need to create a new flow log with the required configuration.
- You cannot Tag a flow log.
- Flow logs do not work for the network interfaces that are in the EC2-classic platform.
- Flow logs cannot be used for VPCs that are peered with your VPC. It can only be done if the peered VPC is within your account.

Flow logs do not acquire all IP traffic. Certain types of traffic are not logged. This includes the followings:

- DHCP traffic
- Traffic from instances to Amazon DNS server
- Metadata traffic to and from 169.254.169.254
- Amazon Time Sync Service traffic to and from 169.254.169.123
- Traffic to the default VPC router

Network Cost – Management & Optimization

AWS runs with a pay-as-you-move pricing method for nearly 100 cloud offerings. Even as the range and types of offerings supplied by using AWS have accelerated dramatically, the philosophy of pricing has no longer modified. At the cease of every month, you pay simplest for what you use, and you may start or stop the use of a product at any time. No lengthy-time period contracts are required.

AWS is based totally on the approach of pricing every provider independently to provide customers with superb flexibility through allowing them to choose the services they need

for his or her assignment and to pay handiest for what they use. AWS pricing is comparable to the way you pay for utilities like water or strength. You only pay for the offerings consumed without extra fees or termination fees once you forestall the use of them.

For the topic under consideration, we will use a network diagram, which is part of the open guide to AWS; a community project of designing and publishing documentation related to AWS and its usage.

At the same time as the usage of the AWS Cloud platform, there are three essential traits you are charged for:

- Compute
- Storage
- Data Transfer Out

Since we are talking about the network cost and its management, our focus will be more on data transfer out. As per your business requirements, if there is significant network traffic, a major portion of your AWS expenses is around data transfer. Moreover, the data transfer pricing varies significantly if it is within Availability Zones, within regions, between regions, and into and out of AWS and the internet; depending on your deployment choices.

Some of the most common cost incurring reasons are as follows:

- **AZ to AZ Traffic**
  The EC2 traffic between AZs is the same as between regions. For example, deploying a cluster in different AZs is good for high availability; but can increase network cost.
- **Using Public IPs**
  Usage of an EIP or public IP of an EC2 instance will incur more network cost, even if it is accessed locally within the AZ.

Data Transfer Cost

See figure 6-04 below; it is an overview of the network data transfer costs.

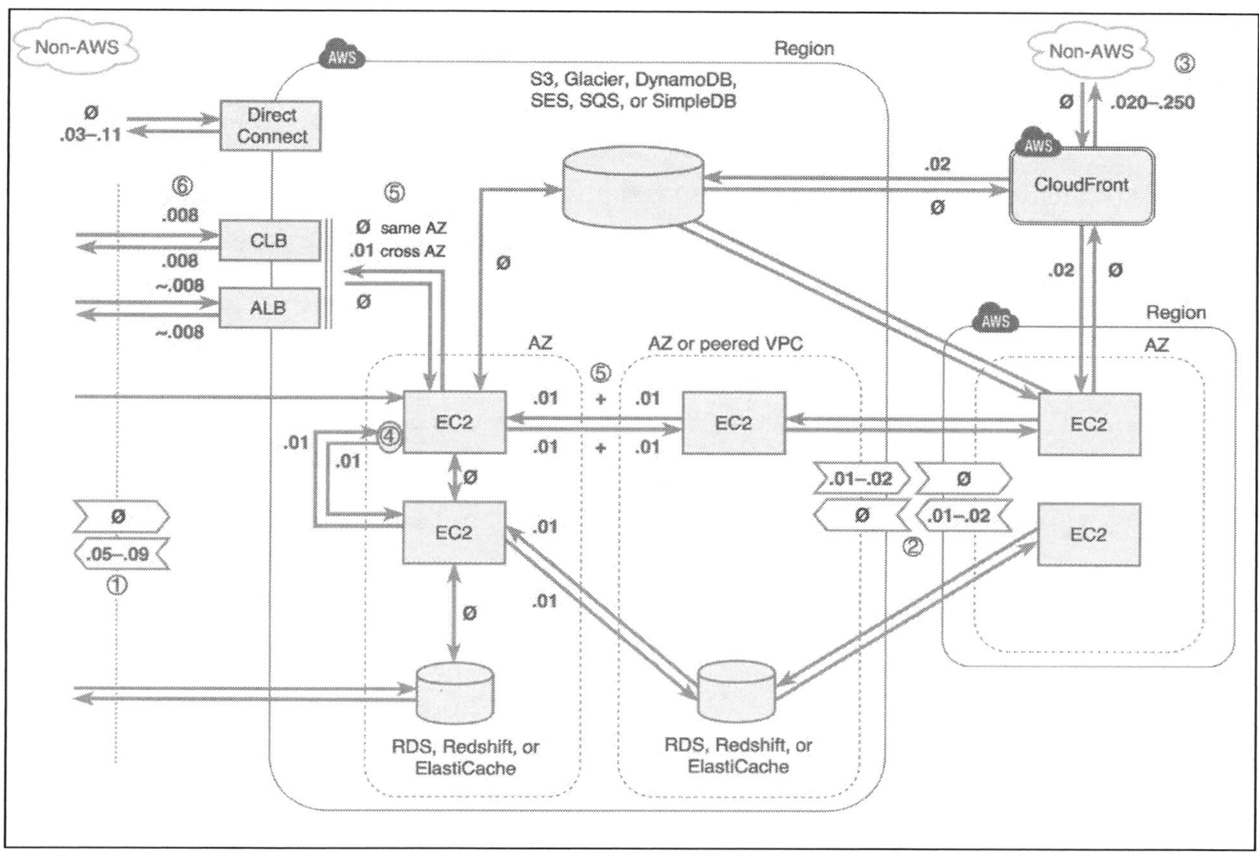

Figure 6-04: AWS Data Transfer Costs

Depicting figure 6-04:

- Numbers are data transfer cost in $/GB.
- Ø means free. Inbound traffic is free in most of the cases; you pay on the way out.

Now look at the numbers pointing different stages of the data flow.

1) First 1 GB is free; direct outbound data starts at $0.09/GB for less than 10 TB.
2) For the given services; Region to Region traffic is $0.02/GB when it exits a region. Between us-east-1 and us-east-2, the charges are $0.01/GB.
3) Outbound CloudFront prices vary by geography and regional edge cache; starting at $0.085/GB in the US and Canada.
4) With public and Elastic IPs, internal traffic incurs additional fees in both directions.
5) Cross-AZ EC2 traffic costs the same as region to region traffic. ELB to EC2 traffic is free except outbound crossing AZs.
6) A classic load balancer is charged per GB. Application load balancer costs are not in $/GB; these are in LCUs.

Note: Prices shown for in and out are for US regions. Prices for some transfers can be higher with the regions.

Knowledge of the cost architecture is essential for the Advanced Networking exam. It is really helpful in designing and troubleshooting networks. You must know how costs are applied and to which account these are applied. You should know all the pricing of network components. Internal traffic is not always free; sometimes you are billed on both directions.

Enhanced Networking

Before we talk about enhanced networking on AWS, let us recall the concept of virtualization. Using virtualization, we create multiple environments from a single, physical hardware system. A software called Hypervisor is attached to the physical server. The hypervisor lets you split one machine into multiple separate, distinct, and secure environments that are known as VMs (Virtual Machines). In this model of virtualization, all the traffic flows between the virtual network interfaces of the VMs and the physical network interface of the host machine via the virtualization layer. Therefore, the CPU of the host machine receives all the traffic and acts accordingly. However, it can be a problem if the data flow is heavy. The hypervisor is a software and software is less consistent. Using this model will be less consistent, and there will be high latency when there are high bandwidth and huge data flow.

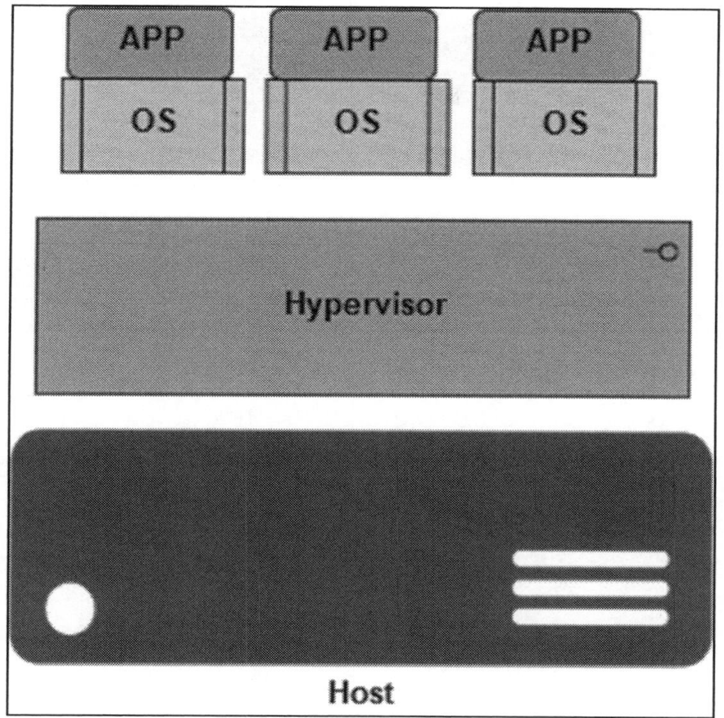

Figure 6-05: Virtualization

Enhanced networking on AWS uses SR-IOV (Single Root I/O Virtualization), which avoids the virtualization layer for data processing. SR-IOV provides high performance networking capability on supported instance types. In comparison with traditional virtualized network interfaces, SR-IOV provides higher I/O performance with lower CPU usage. Enhanced networking provides higher bandwidth, higher PPS (Packets/Second) performance, and lower inter-instance latency.

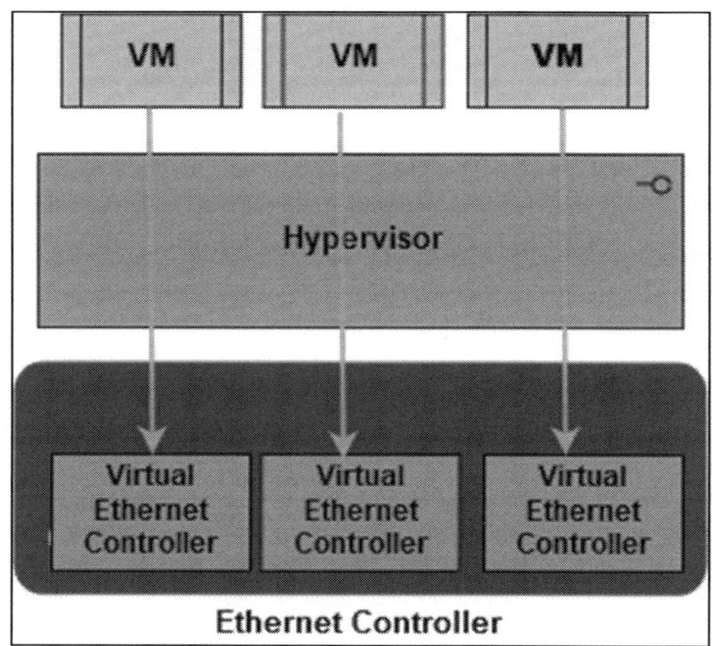

Figure 6-06: SR-IOV

Requirements for Enhanced Networking

For proper functioning, enhanced networking requires three things. First, as mentioned earlier, enhanced networking cannot be enabled on any instance, there must be an instance that supports enhanced networking. Second, the instance should have an Intel or ENA drive, and finally, the AMI that you are using should be tagged as the AMI prepared for enhanced networking.

NOTE: For enhanced networking, the instances must be in a VPC. The EC2-classic platform cannot be configured for enhanced networking.

Types of Enhanced Networking

As mentioned in the introduction, Enhanced networking is supported by specific instance types. According to the type of your instance, you can set up enhanced networking using one of the following ways;

- **Elastic Network Adapter (ENA)**
  ENA supports at maximum, 25 Gbps of network speed. C5, C5d, F1, G3, H1, I3, m4.16xlarge, M5, M5a, M5d, P2, P3, R4, R5, R5a, R5d, T3, u-6tb1.metal, u-9tb1.metal, u-12tb1.metal, X1, X1e, and z1d instances use the ENA for enhanced networking. The Elastic Network Adapter (ENA) supports network speed of up to 100 Gbps for supported instance types.

- **Intel VF (Virtual Function) Interface**

  Intel 82599 VFI supports up to 10 Gbps of network speed. C3, C4, D2, I2, M4 (excluding m4.16xlarge), and R3 instances use the Intel 82599 VF interface for enhanced networking.

Optimizing Network Performance- Placement Group

Here, we will discuss the optimization of EC2 instance's performance at Network level. For that, Placement Groups are used; but before understanding the Placement Group, you need to understand the visual overview of EC2.

As per traditional virtualization, multiple virtual machines have one physical server. EC2 instances are also virtual machines, therefore, they have one physical server. In AWS, you have no visibility of the physical server. This server is in the data center, and you also do not have visibility on this datacenter; they are managed by AWS. In these data centers, physical services of AWS are hosted, and at a granular level on this data center, there is the rack. A rack is a group of services or network components that work together. The grouping of the rack is known as the floor. In a single data center, you may also have multiple floors. In AWS, as you know, you are not able to see the data center, you may see AZ. AZ represents an entity constructed from one or more data centers. In the region, if this architecture is completed, then you have 2 or more AZs depending on available AZs in that region.

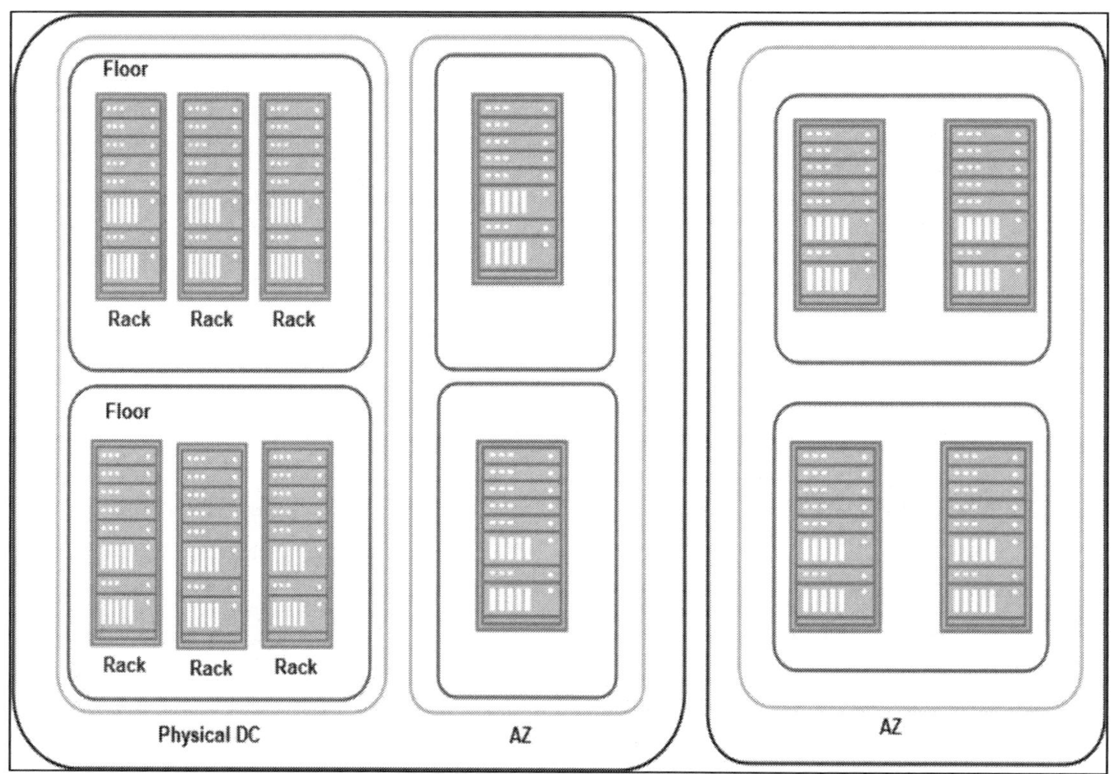

Figure 6-07: AWS Region's Compute Architecture

Placement Group

Placement Groups are logical grouping or clusters of instances in the selected AWS region. Placement groups are specifically used for launching cluster compute instance types. (e.g. c2.8xlarge.) You can launch or start times in a placement group, which determines how times are placed on the underlying hardware.

By default, when launching an instance, you can specify the specific subnet and the availability to launch an instance. Or in the case of default VPC, no preference is specified, and this provides AWS a free range to perform the capacity management and assign an instance to any of the free availability zones. Therefore, when the first time you launch an instance, it might be in the one rack and the next could be in different AZ or may be in the same AZ but in a different datacenter. By default, you allow AWS to place the instance in any of the physical server, any physical datacenter and in any AZ. The placement is just a random placement. You may have an option to specify the AZ and specific subnet limit.

When you provision an instance, you can launch a large number of small instances that can spread over different racks. (Racks as in Figure 6-07), or, you can launch a huge instance that alone can use up all the available capacity of a physical server.

Different EC2 instances have different performance characteristics. An m4.large instance can have a maximum bandwidth of 450 Mbps and can provide a throughput of 56 MB/s; but, with a large instance, these maximum values can be much higher. With a 32.x larger instance, you can get one GBps bandwidth and 1250 MBps throughput. Keep in mind that these values depend heavily on the underlying infrastructure. To achieve the required network speed, you must have the supporting components to get you through with a slower instance. First, you need to provision large instances to get the required bandwidth for communication and you also need to enable the enhanced networking. If you need consistent top speed and latency with your EC2 instances, you will need three things to get it done:

- The size and type of the instances that you are using
- Enhanced networking should be enabled
- Use a Placement Group

While you create a Placement Group, you specify one of the following strategies for the institution:

Cluster – clusters instances into a low-latency group in a single AZ.

Partition – spreads instances throughout logical partitions, making sure that instances in a single partition do now not share underlying hardware with instances in different walls.

Spread – spreads times throughout underlying hardware.

Cluster Placement Group

A Cluster Group is the logical grouping of the instances inside a single AZ. A Placement Group can span peered VPCs within the identical location. The chief gain of a Cluster Placement Group, further to a ten Gbps drift limit, is the non-blockading, non-oversubscribed, completely bi-sectional nature of the connectivity. In different phrases, all nodes inside the placement group can communicate to all other nodes in the placement group at the total line fee of 10 Gbps flows and 25 aggregate without slowing down due to over-subscription. Cluster Placement Groups are recommended for packages that take advantage from low network latency, high community throughput, or each, and if most of the people of the network traffic are among the instances inside the organization. To offer the bottom latency and the highest packet-in line with-2nd network overall performance for your Placement Group, pick out an example type that helps getting a superior networking.

If you receive a capacity error when launching an instance in a Placement Group that already has running instances, forestall and start all of the instances in the placement group, and try the release again. Restarting the instances might also migrate them to hardware that has the capability for all of the asked times.

Partition Placement Group

A Partition Placement Group is a set of instances spread throughout the partition. Partitions are logical groupings of instances, where contained times do not percentage the identical underlying hardware across distinct partitions. The times in each partition do now not percentage underlying hardware with the times within the other partitions, prescribing the effect of hardware failure to handiest one partition. Partition Placement Group may be used to spread deployment of big disbursed and replicated workloads, along with HDFS, HBase, and Cassandra, across distinct hardware to reduce the likelihood of correlated screw ups. When you launch times into a Partition Placement Group, Amazon EC2 attempts to distribute the instances flippantly throughout the number of partitions that you have specified. You could also release times into a selected partition to have greater manipulation over wherein the instances are positioned. Similarly, Partition Placement organizations provide visibility into the partitions—you can see which times are wherein walls. You can percentage this fact with topology-conscious programs, consisting of HDFS, HBase, and Cassandra, which use this information to make smart statistics replication decisions for growing statistics availability and durability.

A Partition Placement Group will have a most of 7 partitions in keeping with Availability Zone. The quantity of instances that can be launched into a Partition Placement Group is restricted to simply using the limits of your account. Partition Placement Group can also span more than one Availability Zones in the same location. In case you start or release an instance in a Partition Placement Group, and if there is particular insufficient hardware to satisfy the request, the request fails. Amazon EC2 makes more distinct hardware to be had over the years so that you can try your request again later.

Partition Placement Group are currently only to be had via the API or AWS CLI.

Spread Placement Group

A Spread Placement Group is a collection of times, which might be placed on the underlying hardware. Spread Placement Groups are recommended for packages, which have a small number of crucial instances that should be kept separated from each other. Launching instances in a Spread Placement Group reduce the danger of simultaneous failures that would occur when instances proportion the identical underlying hardware.

Spread Placement Groups provide entry to the underlying hardware, and are therefore suitable for mixing example sorts or launching instances through the years.

A Spread placement group can span a couple of Availability Zones, and you may have a most of seven running instances according to Availability region in line with the organization.

In case you begin or launch an example in an expansion placement organization, and there is inadequate unique hardware to fulfill the request, the request fails. Amazon EC2 makes greater hardware available through the years so that you can try your request once later.

Keep in mind, you have got some different zones and statistics to switch factors. To keep the excessive performance, compute utility needs is reliant to a few matters. The primary issue is the dimensions and form of the times, which you are launching, secondly the presence of the Enhanced Networking functions after which eventually the usage of the Placement Group. The overall performance institution ensures the overall performance between times as it ensures a local proximity

Limitations & Requirements of Placement Group

- Placement Groups cannot span in multiple AZ. When you create a Placement Group, you cannot put an Availability Zone, but when you first create an instance and pick a Placement Group, the Placement Group is allocated to the AZ in which you launched the instance.
- The name of the Placement Group must be unique across the region. The name of the Placement Group must be unique for the region within your AWS account.
- Reserved instances offer a capability reservation for EC2 instances in a selected Availability Zone. The capacity reservation may be used by times in a Placement Group. However, it is not feasible to explicitly reserve capability for a Placement Group.
- Stick to the same instance type and same size of the instance within the single Placement Group. Otherwise, this increases the likelihood of the capacity issues, and you will not be able to launch the additional instances into an existing Placement Group. Similarly, you cannot move an existing instance in the Placement Group, and you can merge the Placement Group.
- For instances that are enabled for enhanced networking, site visitors between instances inside the identical vicinity that is addressed the use of IPv4 or IPv6 addresses can burn up to five Gbps for single-flow traffic and up to twenty-five Gbps for multi-waft visitors. A glide represents a single, point-to-factor network connection.

- Ideally, launch all instances in the beginning. The Placement Group can work over VPC Peers, but the speed is very limited.

Mind Map

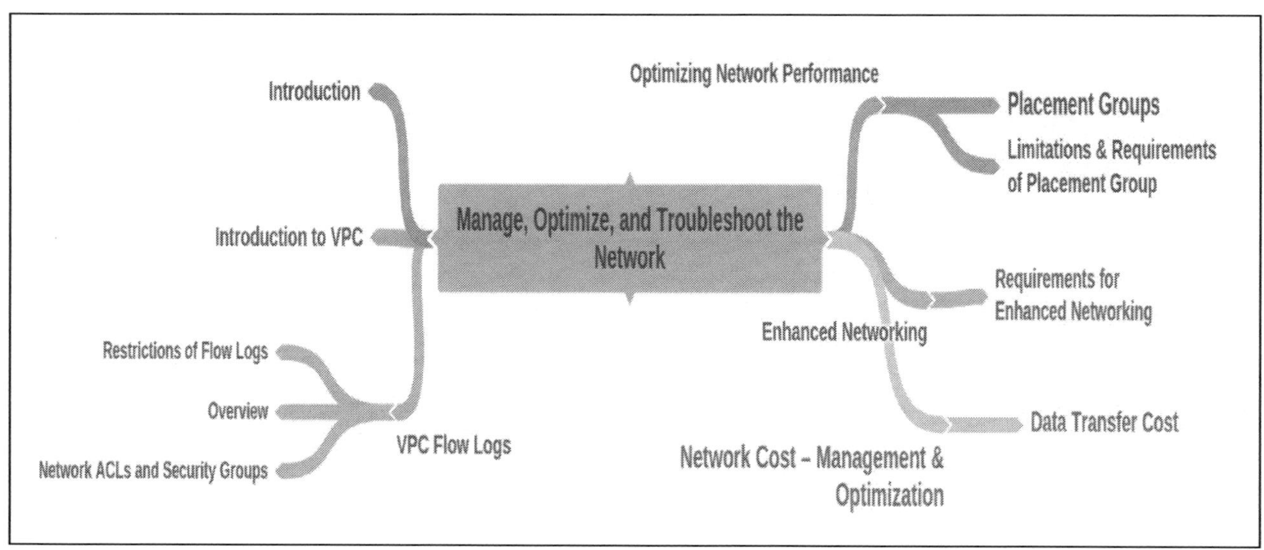

Figure 6-08: Chapter Mind Map

Practice Questions

1. Amazon VPC lets you provision your logically isolated section of the __________ where you can launch AWS resources in a user-defined virtual network.
   a) AWS Cloud
   b) AWS EC2
   c) ENA
   d) ENI

2. A __________________ is a cloud computing model, which offers an on-demand configurable pool of shared computing resources allocated within a public cloud environment.
   a) Virtual Public Cloud
   b) Virtual Private Could
   c) Enhance Network Interface
   d) Elastic Network Adapter

3. Amazon VPC is the networking layer for __________.
   a) Amazon S3
   b) Amazon EC2
   c) ENA
   d) ENI

4. Which application feature allows you to collect the IP traffic information going to and from the network interfaces in your VPC?
   a) Security Groups
   b) Network ACLs
   c) VPC Flow Logs
   d) Placement Groups

5. Flow Logs capture the data related to __________.
   a) IP traffic
   b) Metadata
   c) S3
   d) EC2

6. A Flow Log can be created for ____________.
   a) VPC
   b) Subnet
   c) Network Interface
   d) All of the above

7. VPC Flow Logs monitors which type of traffic for the entities that they are attached to?
   a) Ingress
   b) Egress
   c) Both of the above
   d) None of the above

8. Publishing log data to CloudWatch or S3 requires ________________.
   a) IAM role
   b) AMI
   c) ACL
   d) None of the above

9. A flow log record is a log event, which consists of fields describing the network flow. Each record consists of 5-tuple.
   a) False
   b) True

10. Network ACLs are _________.
    a) Stateless
    b) Stateful
    c) Both A and B
    d) None of the above

11. Why is the Accept Record generated?
    a) Because ACL allows ICMP traffic.
    b) Because Security Groups allow ICMP traffic.
    c) Because ACL and Security Groups allow ICMP traffic.

d) None of the above.

12. What is the name of the application that lets you run multiple OS on one physical server?
    a) Processor
    b) Hypervisor
    c) Virtual Machine
    d) Guest Operating System

13. Which one of the followings does not offer their hypervisor?
    a) Cisco System
    b) Citrix System
    c) Oracle
    d) Parallels

14. Which one of the following types of virtualization is also the characteristic of cloud computing?
    a) Storage
    b) Application
    c) CPU
    d) All of the mentioned above

15. For proper functioning, enhanced networking requires how many things?
    a) One
    b) Two
    c) Three
    d) Four

16. The Elastic Network Adapter (ENA) supports network speed of up to ________ for supported instance types.
    a) 100 Gbps
    b) 1000 Gbps
    c) 50 Gbps
    d) None of the above

17. _____________ are logical groupings or clusters of instances in the selected AWS region.
    a) Network ACLs
    b) Placement Groups
    c) Security Groups
    d) Enhanced Networking

18. While creating a Placement Group, how many strategies can you define?
    a) Three
    b) Two
    c) Six
    d) Four

19. A Cluster Group is the logical grouping of the instances within _________ Availability Zone.
    a) Multiple
    b) Single
    c) Same
    d) Different

20. The availability of Partition Placement Group can be made by using?
    a) API
    b) AWS CLI
    c) API and AWS CLI both
    d) None of the above

Answers:

Chapter 01: Introduction to Cloud Computing
1. **A** (AWS Region) **Explanation:** The region is an entirely independent and separate geographical area. 2. **A** (IaaS) **Explanation:** Infrastructure as a software provide basic building blocks for cloud 3. **B** (SaaS) **Explanation:** Software as a Service provides a complete product as web service provided by service provider that is handled and run by them. 4. **B** (Hybrid) **Explanation:** Hybrid deployment model is mixture of on-premises, private cloud and third part public cloud and it is in between on-premises and cloud. 5. **A** (Encryption) and **D** (Security) **Explanation:** The AWS cloud provides plenty of security and encryption features with governance capabilities that enable continuous monitoring of your IT resources. Your security policy can be embedded in the design of your infrastructure. 6. **C** (Deploy Quickly) and D (Security Increase) **Explanation:** Deploy quickly, even worldwide: Deploy applications across multiple geographic areas. Increase efficiencies: Use automation to reduce or eliminate IT management activities that waste time and resources. Enhance security: Cloud providers have teams of people who focus on security, offering best practices to ensure you are compliant. 7. **C** (AWS Virtuous Cycle) **Explanation:** The AWS pricing philosophy is driven by a virtuous cycle. Lower prices mean more customers are taking advantage of the platform, which in turn results in further driving down costs. 8. **A** (Stateless Application) **Explanation:** Stateless Applications – An application that needs no knowledge of

previous interactions and stores no session. It could be an application that when given the same input, provides the same response to an end user.

9. **C** (Elasticity)

Explanation: Elasticity - Implement Auto Scaling to horizontally scale up and down automatically depending upon your need to reduce cost. Automate turning off non-production workloads when not in use. Use AWS managed services wherever possible that helps in taking capacity decisions as and when needed.

10. **D** (Spot)

Explanation: Spot Instances - Available at discounted pricing compared to On-Demand pricing. Ideal for workloads that have flexible start and end times. Spot instances allow you to bid on spare computing capacity.

Chapter 02: Networking Refresher

1. **C** (Seven)

Explanation:

The OSI model consists of seven layers used to transfer data from one person to others globally.

2. **A** (Transport Layer)

Explanation:

Transport Layer transfers data between the users and provides reliable data transfer services to the upper layers. The transport layer also provides acknowledgment of successful data transmission and sends the next data if no error occurred. TCP and UDP are the protocols, which work for the data transmission at layer 4.

3. **A** (ISO Standards)

Explanation:

OSI stands for Open-System Interconnection originated by International Standards Organization (ISO), which divides the network communication into seven layers.

4. **B** (Presentation)

Explanation:

The presentation layer is also called Syntax Layer because this layer is concerned with the syntax and semantics of the information exchanged between the system.

5. **C** (Network Layer)

Explanation:

The Network Layer is the third layer of the OSI model, and this layer is responsible for providing a data routing path for network communication. Data is transferred in the form of a packet via logical network paths.

6. **A** (DNS server)

Explanation:

At a high level, it is the look-up system responsible for changing hostname (www.ipspecialist.net) into IP address, and it also allows you to open up the hostname in the web browser to obtain an IP address.

7. **D** (255 Characters)

Explanation:

The hostname has the maximum of 255 characters.

8. **B** (By contacting remote DNS server)

Explanation:

The DNS query service asks the server for the additional information of the requested domain; then it sends the request to a business DNS server to ask the record for the requested domain. The local DNS receives this response and reports them back to the client workstation.

9. **A** (Five Steps)

Explanation:

IPSec provides a VPN tunnel connecting two public internet endpoints over which traffic is isolated and encrypted. The IPSEC VPN goes through the five steps to transfer the data over VPN.

10. **B** (At the source VPN endpoint)

Explanation:

The first step in IPSec is introducing the interesting traffic. The interesting traffic is the data generated at the source VPN endpoint. Interesting traffic is the data, which matches with some rule set.

11. **C** (BGP Peering)

Explanation:

Two routers that established a connection to exchange BGP information are referred to as BGP peers. The BGP peers share routing information between them through BGP sessions, which run over TCP.

12. **C** (MED)

Explanation:

MED is BGP supported matrix used to influence or to provide preference directive for the traffic that is entering your network. It is used to redirect and confirm the method of route selection when providing a route to a router which is quite similar to BGP route selection method.

13. **C** (Low MED Value)

Explanation:

In the case where during a route if everything would be same, same weight, same local preference value, same network, and same prefix, the same origination, the same destination, then an AS will pick the lowest MED value to reach to the destination.

14. **A** (Autonomous System)

Explanation:

Autonomous System is a set of routers, which lie under the single technical administration. An Autonomous System is a single network or a set of networks and routers, which lie under the control of one single administrative identity.

15. **A** (Broadcast)
    D (Network)

Explanation:

When calculating the usable host per subnet, the formula 2^bits-2 is used. The subtracted two bits are reserved for network and broadcast addresses.

16. **C** (30)

Explanation:

Number of Bits = 32-27 = 5

Number of Host = 2^5 - 2 =32 = 30

17. **B** (Frames)

Explanation:

On the Datalink Layer, we have frames, which contain different sets of information and this layer also handles sequencing and flow control.

18. **C** (Two)

Explanation:

All IP addresses are divided into portions. One part identifies the network (the network number), and the other part identifies the specific machine or host within the network (the host number).

19. **A** (Subnetting)

Explanation:

IP Subnetting is a process of breaking a large IP network in smaller ones. By Subnetting, we create multiple small networks from a single large IP network. A subnet is a small network that is created from the large IP address. In subnetting, we break a large network into multiple smaller networks, and these networks are known as subnets.

20. **B** (Static NAT)

Explanation:

In Static NAT, a single Private IP address is mapped with the legally registered public address. It is a one-to-one mapping between local and global address.

21. **C** (VLAN)

Explanation:

A VLAN is a group of devices connected through one or more LANs that are configured to communicate attached to the same wire. They are located in many different LAN segments. Because VLANs are based on logical instead of physical connections, they are extremely flexible.

22. **A** (Access Port)

Explanation:

An access port is used to transport the traffic through the specified VLAN allocated to it. It will not deliver exclusive identifying tags.

23. **B** (Trunk)

Explanation:

Trunk Port is a port which holds multiple VLAN across it. When the traffic crosses the trunk, it is tagged on entry, and it is potentially untagged on exit. A trunk port can carry untagged packets simultaneously with the 802.1Q tagged packets.

24. **A** (IKE Phase 1)

Explanation:

The purpose behind using the IKE phase 1 is to authenticate the IPSec peers and to set up a secure channel between the peers to enable IKE exchanges.

25. **D** (65534)

Explanation:

Class B contains 65534 hosts per network.

Chapter 03: Deployment Management

1. **B (AWS OpsWorks)**

Explanation: AWS OpsWork is used to configure and operate the instances of Chef and Puppet because it is a configuration management service. It also helps to provide high-level tools for management of EC2 instances as well. OpsWork can work with other application, which is complex regardless of its architectural plan. In hybrid architecture, it provides single configuration management for deployment of the application. It supports Linux as well as windows server.

2. **C (AWS CloudFormation)**

Explanation: AWS CloudFormation is such a service, which allows you to take a hardware infrastructure and convert it into a code. With the help of CloudFormation, you can manage your resource in less time and target only the application on AWS cloud.

3. **B (2)**

Explanation: Environment tiers are divided into two environments;

Web server environment hosts web application and handles HTTP(S) requests.

Worker environment hosts web application and handles long-running or scheduled background processing tasks.

4. **D (IAM roles)**

Explanation: With CloudFormation, you can create IAM roles and assign them.

5. **C (Free)**

Explanation: CloudFormation, itself is free; you only need to pay for the resources that you have created in CloudFormation.

6. **B (JSON) and D(YAML)**

Explanation: In CloudFormation, when you create a template, the format of template is JSON or YAML.

7. **A (2)**

Explanation: There are two main elements of the template;

- Mandatory Element
- Optional Element

8. **A (False)**

Explanation: CloudFormation will automatically work out the provisioning order based on dependencies for each resource.

9. **C (Elastic Beanstalk)**

Explanation: Elastic Beanstalk will be a helpful service for those who do not know much about cloud and only want their environment up and running.

10. **B (VPC)**

Explanation: With the help of CloudFormation, you can enable VPC peering, or you can build multiple VPCs in a single template.

11. **B (CloudWatch)**

Explanation: In Elastic Beanstalk, you are able to access CloudWatch for monitoring purpose and are notified on specific events or health checks. You can also access log files without logging in the application server. With the help of Elastic Beanstalk, you can modify the setting of the application server.

12. **A** (Single region for multiple AZ)

Explanation: In Elastic Beanstalk, fault tolerance is not configured for multiple regions, but it will be configured in a single region for multiple AZs.

13. **B (OpsWorks)**

Explanation: AWS OpsWorks allow you to build and manage the stack flexibly and simply along with its linked applications and resources. With the help of OpsWorks, the operational task becomes automated like code deployment, configurations of software, database set-ups and server scaling.

14. **D (Layer)**

Explanation: One or more layers in a stack can be used to specify how a group of EC2 instances is configured for a specific task.

15. **C (5)**

Explanation: There is a group of lifecycle events in each layer, which relates to different stages of instance lifecycle.

- the set-up
- deploy
- configure

- undeploy
- shutdown

16. **A (OpsWorks)**

Explanation: OpsWork is generally a GUI to deploy and configure the infrastructure fast.

17. **B (Create deletion policy on those resources)**

Explanation: In CloudFormation, you can also specify deletion policy for resources in the template, or you can define the creation of Snapshots of Volumes and database instances before deletion.

18. **A (Stack)**

Explanation: A stack is a group of resources or is like a container for the resources, which are managed together like ELB, EC2 instances, EBS Volumes, etc.

19. **A (RDS instance)**

Explanation: Elastic Beanstalk has the capability for provision of RDS DB instance. With the help of environment variables, the connectivity to that DB instance is disclosed to the application.

20. **B (Resources along with its configuration)**

Explanation: When you provision resources in CloudFormation, you need to define the list of resources along with configuration value, which you actually provision.

Chapter 04: Design & Implement Hybrid Networks at Scale

1. **B** (Reactive Reasons)
   C (Proactive Reasons)

Explanation:

The reasons for migrating in cloud are grouped into two i.e. Reactive Reasons and Proactive Reasons. Reactive reasons are negative or deadline driven. This type of reason generally occurs due to business pressure or any type of deadline. Proactive reasons are related to any technical improvement or positive change in business.

2. **A** (Indirect Connection)

Explanation:

Hardware connectivity options supported by AWS are Software VPN, Hardware VPN and Direct Connect.

3. **B** (CGW)

Explanation:

CGW i.e. Customer Gateway is the logical representation of your Customer Premises Equipment (CPE). It is placed where you specified the external IP address of the CP device and it defines which type of routing the device is using which i.e. static or dynamic.

4. **B** (Public Virtual Interface)
   D (Private Virtual Interface)

Explanation:

Virtual Interfaces are of two types:

- Public interfaces
- private interfaces

Public interfaces are created to use public services provided by AWS such as DynamoDB and S3 whereas, Private interfaces are created to access VPC.

5. **D** (Consistent Latency)

Explanation:

Consistent latency cannot be achieved by using Software VPN connectivity because it uses the public internet.

6. **C** (Hours)

Explanation:

AWS charged VPN services based on two components:

- Per hour VPN connection charge of the VPN object
- Data transfer charges

7. **B** (Hardware VPN)

Explanation:

Hardware VPN is the preferred way whenever VPN connection is required, consistent latency and high performance is not important. It is also a low cost link. Whenever time to deploy is important, use VPN connection and whenever consistent latency and performance is important, Direct Connect is a better option. If you have low budget, go for VPN and if you can afford expenses then go for DX.

8. **E** (All of the above)

Explanation:

VPN connection configuration is produced when a VPN connection is created, which contains the IP addressing, IKE information, IP stack information, and optionally BGP information. These configurations are download-able and pre-formatted by AWS for common VPN End Points (VPN EPs) so they can be applied on a customer side router

9. **C** (Software VPN)

Explanation:

Software VPN use case is to connect multiple VPCs in same or different regions. It is a cost effective solution but with inconsistent latency and speed.

10. **C** (Dynamic Hardware VPN)

Explanation:

Due to limited budget, select Hardware VPN. If the customer router is BGP capable, then one should select Dynamic Routing otherwise select Static Routing. The Customer Router supports BGP therefore the connectivity should be by using dynamic hardware VPN.

11. **B** (Static Hardware VPN)

Explanation:

Due to limited budget, select Hardware VPN. If the Customer Router is BGP capable, then one should select Dynamic Routing otherwise select Static Routing. The customer router does not support BGP therefore, the connectivity should be by using Static Hardware VPN.

12. **B** (Letter of Authority)

Explanation:

LOA (Letter of Authority) document is also provided, which list the port of DX router. You and your partner can cross connect by using LOA with the facility management team between the physical port of the DX router and the physical port of your or your partner's router.

13. **A** (Physical Connection)

Explanation:

Cross connect can be created between physical port of the DX router and the physical port of your or partner's router. This physical connection (X-Connection) is the physical fiber connection of 802.1 Q Trunk. You can also establish this physical connection between your customer router and customer network.

14. **C** (Hosted VIF)

Explanation:

The Virtual Interfaces can be created by using your own AWS account by using external account. The VIF created in external account are known as hosted VIF.

15. **C** (Public VIF)

Explanation:

When you created the VLAN of public interface, the direct connect non-internet path to the public services is available. AWS advertises the public IP ranges use for public services to the Customer Router and you as a customer is advertising public IP addresses your router uses to the network of AWS public service.

16. **D** (Public VIF)

Explanation:

For minimizing the risks for traffic transit over a DX link:

1. Remove the private VIF
2. Create a public VIC across DX

3. Utilize the two public IP endpoints that are provided by VGW, which is attached to VPC and is able to use IPSec VPNs. Set IPSec VPN between the Customer router and VGW public endpoints via public VIF.

Using this strategy, the data packets will move from the customer router to the VGW public endpoint in a secured protocol (encrypted) and at the endpoints they are decrypted and moved into the VPC via VGW to the required destination.

17. **B** (Transfer IN)

Explanation:

Internet Transfer IN charges are the charges for accessing the internet for the utilization of resource in AWS account. It is the free facility.

18. **C** (Cloud Hub)

Explanation:

AWS provides a service known as Cloud Hub, which combines the benefits of a mesh network with resiliency provided by an Enterprise grade system.

Chapter 5: Configure Network Integration with Application Services

1. **A** (Route53)

Explanation:

Route 53 is a service of Amazon, which provides highly available and scalable cloud DNS web service that implicitly connects user requests to IT infrastructure running in AWS.

2. **D** (Latency based)

Explanation:

You can use latency-based policy when you have multiple resources in different regions, and you want to direct the traffic to the region that provides the best latency.

3. **C** (Geo-location)

Explanation:

Geo-location policy will send your traffic based on the geographic locations of your users.

4. **A** (Hybrid DNS)

Explanation:

The use of hybrid DNS came that uses Route53 with the conjunction of an on-premises platform like AD.

5. **C** (Load balancing)

Explanation:

Amazon Route 53 performs the main three services:

- DNS services
- Domain registration
- Health checks

6. **D** (The DNS port number is 53)

Explanation:

Route 53 is a DNS service and the port for DNS is port 53.

7. **C** (X-Forwarded for the header)

Explanation: If you require a public IPv4 address of your end users, then you can use X-forwarded for header because, when we use ELB, its private IP is only shown to EC2

instance, so the instance does not know from where the specific request came from. To know the end user, we can use X-Forwarded for Header.

8. **D** (All of the above)

Explanation: Elastic Load Balancing supports routing and load balancing of Hypertext Transfer Protocol (HTTP), Hypertext Transfer Protocol Secure (HTTPS), Transmission Control Protocol (TCP), and Secure Sockets Layer (SSL) traffic to Amazon EC2 instances. Elastic Load Balancing provides a stable, single Canonical Name record (CNAME) entry point for Domain Name System (DNS) configuration and it supports both Internet-Facing and Internal Application-Facing load balancer.

9. **B** (External Load Balancer)

Explanation:

It is a public or internet facing Load Balancer. It is used by clients to communicate to the public subnets of VPC.

10. **D** (/27)

Explanation:

Size of the subnet is at most /27 or less in the external subnet.

11. **B** (A record)

Explanation:

When ELB is created, it is allocated with a domain name, which is an A record.

"name.region.elb.amazonaws.com"

By using this domain, the name client reaches the front end ELB.

12. **B** (Cross Zone Load balancing)

Explanation:

Cross Zone Load Balancing is a feature through which you can distribute the content across all instances inside subnets of VPC equally.

13. **C** (Sticky session)

Explanation:

A sticky session feature, which is also known as session affinity that enables the Load Balancer to bind the user's session to the specific instance. If the instance is unhealthy, then the session is re-assigned again to another instance.

14. **A** (30)

Explanation:

The valid value for the interval in health check of ELB is 5-300 sec with default 30.

15. **B** (Amazon S3)

Explanation: Simple Storage Service S3 helps to easily store and fetch data from anywhere on the web with web service.

16. **A** (Object Storage)

Explanation: Amazon S3 is a cloud object storage.

17. **A** (Optimizing of Archiving data)

Explanation: Amazon Glacier is also a cloud storage service, but this storage is used for optimizing data archiving and cheap cost long-term backup.

18. **D** (1024 bytes)

Explanation: A key can be up to 1024 bytes of Unicode including embedded slashes, backslashes, dots, and dashes.

19. **B** (Data transfer out) and **C** (storage)

Explanation:

In S3, you need to pay for storage, request, data transfer out, transfer acceleration and storage management.

20. **C** (Requester Pays)

Explanation:

You can allow Requester Pays on a bucket when you need to share the data or files, but do not want to be charged for the requests received for operation uploads and data downloads.

21. **B** (Cross Region Replication)

Explanation:

You can replicate the contents of one bucket to another bucket automatically by using cross-region replication. Through this replication, you can replicate new objects simply into any other AWS Region for reduced latency, compliance, security, disaster recovery, and few other use cases.

22. **A** (Pre-signed URL)

Explanation:

Pre-signed URL is used for sharing your object with others. By using a Pre-signed URL, you can make bucket privately accessible to the authenticated user.

23. **A** (Geo-restriction)

Explanation:

Geo-restriction is assigned to distribution and distribution can only have one Geo-restriction. By default Geo-restriction is disabled, but when you enable it, you need to define the Geo-restriction type. There are two types of restriction:

- Whitelist is where by default all countries are blocked, and you need to define which country needs to be whitelisted, meaning allowed for access distribution.
- Blacklist is where by default all countries are allowed, and you need to define blacklisted country, which you need to block for distribution.

24. **D** (A and B)

Explanation:

The custom SSL certificate may be obtained from Trusted CA, ACM and Self-signed. When the origin is ELB, then you can use ACM and Trusted CA because ELB does not support self-signed. While for Non-ELB origin, you can use Trusted CA.

25. **B** (100)

Explanation:

The price class needs to be selected at the creation of distribution. It has three options:

- 100- the US, CA, and EU (Edge Locations)
- 200- include all 100 class Edge Location + Asia (Edge Locations)
- All- include all 200 class Edge Location + SA and AU (Edge Locations)

Chapter 6: Manage, Optimize, and Troubleshoot the Network

1. **A** (AWS Cloud)

Explanation:

Amazon VPC lets you provision your logically isolated section of the AWS cloud where you can launch AWS resources in a user-defined virtual network. You have full control over your virtual networking environment, including a selection of your IP address ranges, the generation of subnets, and configuration of route tables and network gateways.

2. **B** (Virtual Private Cloud)

Explanation:

A Virtual Private Cloud is a cloud computing model, which offers an on-demand configurable pool of shared computing resources allocated within a public cloud environment while providing a certain level of isolation from other users of the public cloud.

3. **B** (Amazon EC2)

Explanation:

Amazon VPC is the networking layer for Amazon EC2. It was released after the EC2 service. EC2-classic and EC2-VPC are two different networking platforms that are available within AWS because of VPC. (EC2 classic is only available for those accounts, which were created before the launching of VPC).

4. **C** (VPC Flow Logs)

Explanation:

VPC flow log feature allows you to collect the IP traffic information going to and from the network interfaces in your VPC. You can publish the data collected by the flow logs to either Amazon CloudWatch or Amazon S3. These logs are helpful in several tasks; such as, you can troubleshoot if specific traffic is not reaching an instance.

5. **A** (IP traffic)

Explanation:

Remember that flow logs capture the data related to IP traffic; this does not mean that you can get the IP data, but it provides you the ***metadata*** of the traffic under monitoring.

6. **D** (All of the above)

Explanation:

A flow log can be created for a VPC, subnet, or network interface. If you create a flow log for VPC, all network interfaces within that VPC will be monitored; same is the case with subnets but, creating flow log for a specific interface will only provide information about the attached interface.

7. **C** (Both of the above)

Explanation:

VPC flow logs monitor Ingress and Egress traffic for the entity (VPC, subnet, ENI) that they are attached to. Flow logs can monitor traffic for all traffic or can be restricted to accepted or rejected traffic only. This configuration is done when you are creating a flow log.

8. **A** (IAM role)

Explanation:

Publishing log data to CloudWatch or S3 requires an IAM role. By default, flow logs do not have permission to write data to CloudWatch or S3. There must be an IAM role with proper permissions so that the flow logs can assume that role in publishing data to the storage that you have chosen.

9. **B** (True)

Explanation:

A flow log record is a log event, which consists of fields describing the network flow. Each record is a 5-tuple and for a specific capture window. 5-tuple is a set of values specifying the source, destination, and protocol for an IP flow.

10. **A** (Stateless)

Explanation:

Network ACLs are stateless, meaning that the responses to allowed traffic are subject to the network ACL rules. This information recap is necessary if you are using flow logs to monitor an overly restrictive or permissive Security Group or network ACL rules.

11. **C** (Because ACL and Security Groups allow ICMP traffic)

Explanation:

The Accept Record is generated because your ACL and Security Groups allow ICMP

traffic, therefore, it is accepted in the flow logs. The network ACL does not allow ICMP outbound, therefore, the reply to ping is blocked and that is the reason for the Reject Record.

12. **B** (Hypervisor)

Explanation:

Using virtualization, we create multiple environments from a single, physical hardware system. A software called Hypervisor is attached to the physical server. The hypervisor lets you split one machine into multiple separate, distinct, and secured environments that are known as VMs (Virtual Machines).

13. **A** (Cisco System)

Explanation:

Cisco System does not offer their hypervisor.

14. **D** (All of the mentioned above)

Explanation:

To enable all these characteristics, the resources must be highly configurable and flexible.

15. **C** (Three)

Explanation:

For proper functioning, enhanced networking requires three things. First, as mentioned earlier, enhanced networking cannot be enabled on any instance, there must be an instance that supports enhanced networking. Second, the instance should have an Intel or ENA drive, and finally, the AMI that you are using should be tagged as the AMI prepared for enhanced networking.

16. **A** (100 Gbps.)

Explanation:

ENA supports at maximum, 25 Gbps of network speed. C5, C5d, F1, G3, H1, I3, m4.16xlarge, M5, M5a, M5d, P2, P3, R4, R5, R5a, R5d, T3, u-6tb1.metal, u-9tb1.metal, u-12tb1.metal, X1, X1e, and z1d instances use the ENA for enhanced networking. The Elastic Network Adapter (ENA) supports network speed of up to 100 Gbps for supported instance types.

17. **B** (Placement Groups)

Explanation:

Placement Groups are logical groupings or clusters of instances in the selected AWS region. Placement Groups are specifically used for launching cluster compute instance types. (e.g. cc2.8xlarge. You can launch or start instances in a Placement Group, which determines how instances are placed on the underlying hardware.

18. **A** (Three)

Explanation:

While you create a placement group, you specify one of the following strategies for the institution:

Cluster – clusters instances into a low-latency group in a single Availability Zone.

Partition – spreads instances throughout logical partitions, making sure that instances in a single partition do now not share underlying hardware with instances in different walls.

Spread – spreads times throughout underlying hardware.

19. **B** (Single)

Explanation:

A Cluster Group is the logical grouping of the instances inside a single AZ. A Placement Group can span peered VPCs within the identical location.

20. **C** (API and AWS CLI)

Explanation:

A Partition Placement Group is a set of instances spread across partitions. Partitions are logical groupings of instances, wherein contained times do not percentage the identical underlying hardware throughout special partitions. Partition Placement Groups are presently handiest to be had via the API or AWS CLI.

Acronyms:

ACL	Access Control List
AD	Active Directory
AMI	Amazon Machine Images
API	Application Programmable Interface
AS	Autonomous System
ASN	Autonomous System Number
AWS	Amazon Web Services
AZ	Availability Zone
BGP	Border Gate Way Protocol
CDN	Cloud Distribution Network
CGW	Customer Gateway
CIDR	Classless Inter-Domain Routing
CLI	Command Line Interface
CPE	Customer Premises Equipment
DHCP	Dynamic Host Configuration Protocol
DNS	Domain Name System
DX	Direct Connection
EBGP	Exterior Border Gateway Protocol
EC2	Elastic Compute Cloud
ELB	Elastic Load Balancer
ENA	Elastic Network Adapter
ENI	Elastic Network Interface
HA	High Availability
HDFS	Hadoop Distributed File System
HTTP	Hyper Text Transfer Protocol
IAM	Identity Access Management
IBGP	Interior Border Gateway Protocol
ICMP	Internet Control Message Protocol
IGW	Internet Gateway
IKE	Internet Key Exchange
IP	Internet Protocol
IPV4	Internet Protocol Version 4
ISP	Internet Service Provider

LAN	Local Area Network
LOA	Letter of Authority
MED	Multi-Exit Discriminator
NACL	Network Access Control List
NAT	Network Address Translation
NTP	Network Time Protocol
OAI	Object Access Identity
OSI	Open-System Interconnect
PAT	Port Address Translation
PCoIP	PC over IP
PPS	Packets Per Seconds
RDS	Relational Database Service
S3	Simple Storage Service
SA	Security Association
SG	Security Group
SR-IOV	Single Root I/O Virtualization
SSH	Secure Shell
SSL	Secure Socket Layer
TCP	Transmission Control Protocol
UDP	User Datagram Protocol
VF	Virtual Function
VGW	Virtual Gateway
VIF	Virtual Interface
VLAN	Virtu
VM	

References:

Networking Refresher

https://www.techopedia.com/definition/6006/application-layer

https://en.wikipedia.org/wiki/Virtual_LAN

https://www.cisco.com/c/en/us/td/docs/switches/lan/catalyst4500/12-2/25ew/configuration/guide/conf/vlans.html

https://searchnetworking.techtarget.com/definition/virtual-LAN

https://www.cisco.com/c/en/us/td/docs/switches/datacenter/nexus5000/sw/configuration/guide/cli/CLIConfigurationGuide/AccessTrunk.html#33020

https://www.techopedia.com/definition/27009/access-port

http://www.ciscopress.com/articles/article.asp?p=29803&seqNum=3

https://techterms.com/definition/ipv4

https://www.juniper.net/documentation/en_US/junos/topics/topic-map/security-ipsec-vpn-overview.html

https://blog.cdemi.io/beginners-guide-to-understanding-bgp/

https://www.noction.com/blog/bgp_bestpath_selection_algorithm

https://www.ibm.com/support/knowledgecenter/en/STQRQ9/com.ibm.storage.ts4500.doc/ts4500_opg_3584_IPv4_IPv6_prefix_subnet_mask.html

https://www.cloudflare.com/learning/dns/what-is-dns/

https://networklessons.com/bgp/how-to-configure-bgp-local-preference-attribute

https://www.computernetworkingnotes.com/ccna-study-guide/subnetting-tutorial-subnetting-explained-with-examples.html

Design and Implement AWS Networks

https://aws.amazon.com/answers/networking/aws-single-vpc-design/

https://docs.aws.amazon.com/vpc/latest/userguide/vpc-ip-addressing.html

https://aws.amazon.com/quickstart/architecture/vpc/

https://docs.aws.amazon.com/aws-technical-content/latest/aws-vpc-connectivity-options/aws-vpc-connectivity-options.pdf

https://docs.aws.amazon.com/vpc/latest/peering/what-is-vpc-peering.html

https://docs.aws.amazon.com/vpc/latest/peering/vpc-peering-basics.html

https://www.coresite.com/solutions/cloud-services/public-cloud-providers/amazon-web-services-direct-connect

https://aws.amazon.com/directconnect/getting-started/

https://docs.aws.amazon.com/AWSEC2/latest/UserGuide/enhanced-networking.html

https://aws.amazon.com/blogs/devops/introducing-application-load-balancer-unlocking-and-optimizing-architectures/

https://docs.aws.amazon.com/elasticloadbalancing/latest/classic/introduction.html

https://docs.aws.amazon.com/vpc/latest/userguide/VPC_Subnets.html

https://docs.aws.amazon.com/AWSEC2/latest/UserGuide/using-eni.html

https://docs.aws.amazon.com/vpc/latest/userguide/vpc-nat-gateway.html

Design & Implement Hybrid Networks at Scale

https://docs.aws.amazon.com/vpc/latest/userguide/what-is-amazon-vpc.html

https://aws.amazon.com/directconnect/faqs/

https://aws.amazon.com/premiumsupport/knowledge-center/public-private-interface-dx/

https://docs.aws.amazon.com/directconnect/latest/UserGuide/Welcome.html

https://docs.aws.amazon.com/directconnect/latest/UserGuide/WorkingWithVirtualInterfaces.html

https://docs.aws.amazon.com/directconnect/latest/UserGuide/WorkingWithVirtualInterfaces.html#vif-prerequisites

Configure Network Integration with AWS Services

https://docs.aws.amazon.com/Route53/latest/DeveloperGuide/routing-policy.html

https://medium.com/tensult/amazon-route-53-routing-policies-cbe356b851d3

https://spanougakis.wordpress.com/2011/05/01/edns-what-is-all-about-2/

https://tools.keycdn.com/dig

https://help.dyn.com/edns-client-subnet-faq-info/

https://docs.aws.amazon.com/Route53/latest/DeveloperGuide/route53-dg.pdf

https://aws.amazon.com/route53/

https://www.networkcomputing.com/network-security/amazon-route-53-concepts-and-configurations

https://aws.amazon.com/route53/faqs/

https://www.dnsknowledge.com/whatis/round-robin-dns/

https://aws.amazon.com/premiumsupport/knowledge-center/internal-version-website/

https://d1.awsstatic.com/whitepapers/hybrid-cloud-dns-options-for-vpc.pdf

https://docs.aws.amazon.com/Route53/latest/DeveloperGuide/hosted-zones-private.html

https://docs.aws.amazon.com/vpc/latest/userguide/VPC_DHCP_Options.html

https://docs.aws.amazon.com/directoryservice/latest/admin-guide/dhcp_options_set.html

https://docs.aws.amazon.com/AmazonS3/latest/dev/S3Torrent.html

https://docs.aws.amazon.com/elasticloadbalancing/latest/classic/elb-https-load-balancers.html

https://docs.aws.amazon.com/elasticloadbalancing/latest/classic/using-elb-listenerconfig-quickref.html

https://coderwall.com/p/mtcskq/signing-amazon-s3-urls

https://docs.aws.amazon.com/AmazonS3/latest/dev/PresignedUrlUploadObject.html

https://docs.aws.amazon.com/AmazonS3/latest/dev/UsingBucket.html

https://docs.aws.amazon.com/AmazonS3/latest/dev/S3_Authentication2.html

https://aws.amazon.com/s3/pricing/

Manage, Optimize, and Troubleshoot the Network

https://docs.aws.amazon.com/AWSEC2/latest/UserGuide/placement-groups.html#concepts-placement-groups

https://acloud.guru

https://docs.rightscale.com/cm/dashboard/clouds/aws/ec2_placement_groups.html

https://www.sumologic.com/aws/vpc/use-aws-vpc-flow-logs/

https://docs.aws.amazon.com/vpc/latest/userguide/flow-logs.html

https://github.com/open-guides/og-aws#billing-and-cost-management

About Our Products

Other products from IPSpecialist LTD regarding AWS technology are:

 AWS Certified Cloud Practitioner Technology Workbook

 AWS Certified SysOps Admin - Associate Workbook

 AWS Certified Solution Architect - Associate Technology Workbook

 AWS Certified Developer Associate Technology Workbook

 AWS Certified DevOps Engineer – Professional Technology Workbook

 AWS Certified Advanced Networking – Specialty Technology Workbook

Upcoming products from IPSpecialist LTD regarding AWS technology are:

 AWS Certified Big Data – Specialty Technology Workbook

 AWS Certified Security – Specialty Technology Workbook

Note from the Author:

Reviews are gold to authors! If you have enjoyed this book and helped you along certification, would you consider rating it and reviewing it?

Link to Product Page:

Made in the USA
San Bernardino, CA
11 April 2019